Praise for *The Political Outsider*

In this bold, creative, and beautifully written book, Roy challenges the notion that populism represents an aberration of democracy and traces its lineage to authoritarian strains in what she terms curative democracy in India since the 1970s. *The Political Outsider* is a brilliant addition to the literature on populism in India and in many other parts of the world.
Amrita Basu, Amherst College

This excellent book presents an interesting and original interpretation of the rise of populism through the historical course of Indian democracy. It is written with clarity and verve and adds significantly to our understanding of Indian democracy as well as the theoretical discussion of the rise of populism.
Sudipta Kaviraj, Columbia University

The Political Outsider is about India's 'long Emergency' that commenced in 1975 … this period in Indian political history needs to be understood as formative for the subsequent evolution of Indian democracy right up to the present moment, casting a lasting shadow over the political life of the Republic. Two key terms run through the book: curative democracy, and outsider politics. Unlike classical autocrats, even the most authoritarian contemporary populist will not openly claim to work to subdue or dismantle democracy. They will rather claim to be out to 'cure, revive, renew, or restore a presently flawed or diseased democracy'. Trump, Modi, Milei, Kejriwal… all fit the bill as embodiments of such outsider politics that aims to 'clean the house' or 'drain the swamp'.
Kenneth Bo Nielsen, *Journal of Contemporary Asia*

Srirupa Roy is Professor and Chair of State and Democracy at the Centre for Modern Indian Studies at the University of Göttingen. Her books include *Saffron Republic: Hindu Nationalism and State Power in India* (with Thomas Blom Hansen); *Visualizing Secularism and Religion: Egypt, Lebanon, Turkey, India* (with Alev Çinar and Maha Yahya), and *Beyond Belief: India and the Politics of Postcolonial Nationalism.*

THE POLITICAL OUTSIDER

Indian Democracy and the Lineages of Populism

SRIRUPA ROY

navayana

The Political Outsider : Indian Democracy and the Lineages of Populism

ISBN 9788198067036

First published in India, 26 January 2025
Under license from Stanford University Press, Stanford, California
For sale only in South Asia

Navayana Publishing Pvt Ltd
155 2nd Floor
Shahpur Jat, New Delhi 110049
navayana.org

Printed by Saksham Enterprises, Delhi
Distributed in South Asia by HarperCollins India
Subscribe to updates at navayana.org/subscribe

CONTENTS

ACKNOWLEDGMENTS

THE OXFORD ENGLISH DICTIONARY says that to acknowledge is to admit, to recognize, to confess. Yes! to all of this, and so much more. I admit, recognize, confess, and celebrate the glorious company and comfort of people and places that the long journey of book writing has gifted me. In no particular order, thank you!

To my wonderfully responsive and supportive editors at Stanford University Press, Dylan Kyung-lim White and Thomas Blom Hansen, and to the anonymous reviewers of the manuscript who pushed for clarity in such constructive and sharp ways.

To the institutions, colleagues, students, and friends who gave me such abundant intellectual and material room and resources to think, to write, to doubt, to move: the political science department at the University of Massachusetts-Amherst and the Five College South Asia studies community; the University of Göttingen's Centre for Modern Indian Studies (CeMIS); the Merian-Tagore International Centre of Advanced Studies (ICAS:MP); the Social Science Research Council's InterAsia Program. Thank you, Nick Xenos, Barbara Cruikshank, John Hird, Paula Chakravartty, Gianpaolo Baiocchi, Amrita Basu, Lynn Peterfreund, Sangeeta Kamat, Buju Dasgupta, Banu Subramaniam, Karin Klenke, Rupa Viswanath, Nate Roberts, Ravi Ahuja, Sebastian Vollmer, Patrick Eisenlohr, Birgit Priemer, Gabriele Räbiger, Ulrike Beisiegel, Dominic Sachsenmaier, Ritajyoti Bandyopadhyay, Devika Bordia, Sebastian Schwecke, Michaela Dimmers, Saeed Ahmad, Aastha Tyagi, Malini Ghose, Ashwin Subramanian, Laila Abu-er-Rub, Ravi Vasudevan, Ravi Sundaram, Debjani Mazumder, Dwaipayan Bhattacharyya, Seteney Shami, Holly Danzeisen.

Thank you for sharing the richness of intellectual community with your invitations, encouragement, and your generative engagement with my work: Thomas Blom Hansen, Amrita Basu, Ravinder Kaur, Sankaran Krishna, Prasenjit Duara, Partha Chatterjee, Sudipta Kaviraj, Ayesha Kidwai, Nayanika Mathur, Karuna Mantena, Rohit De, Mrinalini Sinha, Manu Goswami, Radhika Mongia, William Mazzarella, Shivi Sivaramakrishnan, Anu Sharma, Carola Lentz, Joya Chatterji, Faisal Devji, Peter van der Veer, Heike Liebau, Margrit Pernau, Subir Sinha, Rashmi Varma, Gyan Prakash, Jeremy Adelman, Anandita Bajpai, Niraja Jayal, Zoya Hasan, Ajay Gudavarthy, Pralay Kanungo, Sanjay Srivastava, Tanika Sarkar, Mary John, Anuj Bhuwania, Stéphanie Tawa Lama-Rewal, Pratiksha Baxi, Nandini Sundar, Amita Baviskar, Nivedita Menon, Sumathi Ramaswamy, Kajri Jain, Lisa Björkman.

Vital research support and insights from Radha Kapuria, Farah Yameen, Aheli Chowdhury, Devanjan Khuntia, Devilina Bose, and Ashwin Subramanian at many different stages of the book made all the difference. So did the patience of those who responded to all the endless questions I kept asking and gave me generous access to their work: Ashutosh, Shazia Ilmi, Somnath Bharti, Pawan Kumar, Prashant Bhushan, Upendra Baxi, Sopan Joshi, Sagarika Ghose, Abhay Mohan Jha, Monideepa Banerjie, Aakaash Kumar, Q. M. Naqvi, Rahul Pandita, Aditya Raj Kaul, Narendra Nag, Neha Dixit, Nakul Sawhney, Aniruddha Bahal, Siddharth Varadarajan, Aman, Shweta, and Priya Hingorani, Rebecca John, Pamela Philipose, Vipul Mudgal, Sachin Jain, Sevanti Ninan, Paranjoy Guha Thakurta, and others I cannot name, thank you.

Friends-who-are-family, you know you made this book. I hereby bestow all its flaws on you: Paula Chakravartty, Gianpaolo Baiocchi, Rupa Viswanath, Nate Roberts, Kai Friese, Malini Ghose, Brinda Dutt, Rashmi Varma, Subir Sinha, Bani Abidi.

Kavita Datla, Usha Zacharias, and Annie Mathews, I so wish I had finished this before we ran out of time. I miss you.

To my families who make the world possible: Rahoul Roy, Liz Clay Roy, Radhika Roy, Prannoy Roy, Brinda Karat, Prakash Karat, Mira Vachani, Nand Vachani, Shonali Bose, Atiya Bose, Rohini Kandhari, Nilita

Vachani, Riyaaz Ray, Zayira Ray, Ameya Imani Roy, Indu Ramchandani, Sangita Maya Baa. And for all and always, Mamma, Indrani Roy.

To Lalit Vachani and Laila Roy Vachani, alpha and omega of this book and everything else in between and after. I admit, recognize, confess, and celebrate that you are mine.

INTRODUCTION

CURATIVE DEMOCRACY AND THE POLITICAL OUTSIDER

POPULISM IS IN THE crosshairs of global public attention today. Scenes of mass public outrage where ordinary people rise up against the rule of corrupt elites take center stage around the world. From the resounding victories of populist parties and their strongmen leaders in electoral democracies, to the "public assemblies"[1] of insurgent occupations in streets and squares, and the virtual but no less visceral outbursts of populist anger in social media worlds, the present marks the decisive arrival of a new kind of politics in the global history of democracy.

Populism has several distinctive features. Foremost among them is the attack on established systems, institutions, and practices of representative and electoral democracy. The moralizing rhetoric of populist discourses cleaves political and social space into two antagonistic halves and pits the virtuous people against a degraded and corrupt political elite. Populists argue that popular sovereignty, democracy's core commitment, requires bypassing and dismantling existing institutions and practices of political representation such as elections and parliaments. Populism's specific affect also stands out. Political legitimacy is linked to public displays of spontaneous mass outrage that veer away from the cool deliberations of individual reason endorsed by liberal democratic theory. Finally, from the Philippines to the United States, Brazil to Turkey, India to Spain, populism celebrates and venerates the redemptive agency of political outsiders. Only those who are not a part of the establishment or "the system" will be able to restore the lost promise of democracy and bring power back to the people and the people back to power, it is argued.

What explains the salience and attraction of such a politics? When, why, and how did an angry politics that hails political outsiders and rails against establishment institutions and elected representatives become so influential in modern democracies? What does it mean for democracy, and what for that matter do we mean by democracy, when diagnoses of democracy's disappointments, failures, and sicknesses become the grounds for exercising political agency and authority? When political action and intervention in a democratic political system is enabled by cynicism and disenchantment toward that very system?

These are the questions that this book addresses through an examination of contemporary India, where one-third of the world's democratic citizens live. Defying the many dire predictions at the time of its establishment as an independent republic in 1947, when the constitutional guarantee of universal franchise to a predominantly nonliterate and impoverished citizenry seemed like a foolish gamble that was guaranteed to end in quick disaster, the world's most populous democracy is now more than seventy-five years old. But it is equally a place where the critique of democracy is intense and strident, and where the politics of populist outrage dominates contemporary public culture.

Political life in millennial India has witnessed spectacular eruptions of civic anger. Spanning real and virtual worlds, in the early decades of the twenty-first century numerous *Justice for* campaigns were launched by commercial media to demand justice for ordinary citizen-victims of crimes committed by powerful, politically connected individuals. Massive street protests of citizen movements against corruption took over urban public spaces across the country in 2011.

In recent years, this trope of victimized people suffering at the hands of a predatory elite and a dysfunctional political system has also reaped large electoral rewards. Since 2012, the populist language of redemptive outsiders who will combat the system and bring the people back to power has been harnessed by political parties such as the Aam Aadmi Party (Common Man's Party, AAP for short) and the Bharatiya Janata Party (Indian People's Party, BJP for short) in successful electoral campaigns. The strongman populist regime of Narendra Modi and the BJP, in power since 2014, projects him as the ultimate outsider to the elite establishment that has wrested power from the Indian people for far too long. Modi's carefully crafted public image is that of a celibate self-made man of humble origins; a former tea seller from the vernacular worlds of Gujarat, at far remove from the cosmopolitan English-speaking power elites of the capital city. If the size of electoral mandates and the vigor of media acclamation are the indicators to go by, he has very successfully fashioned himself as the consummate outsider, a heroic messiah figure tasked with the urgent work of curing democracy and redeeming the people.

In a paradox that is not unique to India and might well be a generalized and global democratic condition, the continued existence of electoral democracy is powered by the intense criticism of, and loud expressions of public distaste and disenchantment toward, electoral politics. This conjunction of democratic endurance and condemnation in India is fertile ground for an inquiry into the populism-democracy relation. It departs from the prevailing scholarly consensus on the subject to chart an alternative genealogy and trajectory for populism, as we will soon see.

BEYOND EXCEPTIONALISM: LINEAGES OF POPULISM[2]

There is a large and vigorous body of scholarly work on populism.[3] The subject is approached from many different academic disciplines, but there are several shared presumptions. The first and most prominent is the presumption of electoralism. For the most part, when we talk about the rise of global populism, it is about the electoral victories of organized political parties in a formal democratic system. The contemporary public and scholarly imagination of populism is mostly preoccupied with the growing electoral popularity of particular political parties and leaders, and explaining the populist vote is usually the main analytical task. Second, the electoral preoccupation of contemporary discussions means that they are usually presentist in their focus, and are concerned with explaining a current and exceptional outcome, namely the most recent populist vote. "The populist problem" is approached as some kind of deviant occurrence that stands outside the terrain of democratic politics-as-usual. It is an aberration or puzzle that needs to be explained because it is so different, so sudden, and so abnormal.

Psychologism is a third presumption. Contemporary discussions of populism frequently place populism on the couch, as it were, and identify some kind of internal psychic drive or emotion on the part of the individual voter as the prime explanatory mechanism. Variously described as anger, resentment, and *ressentiment*, these individual emotions are seen to scale up to reproduce a collective version of the same psychodynamic, which enables the political act of voting for a populist figure or party.[4] Finally, most discussions of global populism advance a thesis of media mystification and reference the powers of media (particularly digital and social media) to persuade and ultimately distract or delude the voter from her real concerns. With this narrative of the largely passive voter-as-viewer who is misled and duped by fake news and media spin to support populist parties, populism is put on the couch in a second sense, we might say.[5]

All these presumptions rest on rather fragile empirical ground. For one, as even a cursory glance at the large corpus of work on "the age of anger" will show, the theses of psychologism and media manipulation often rely on anecdotes rather than sustained empirical evidence for how particular media-driven or psychological and emotional dynamics actually induce individuals to undertake the specific political act of voting for a populist political party. And where empirical data are provided, they tend to present a correlative rather than explanatory or causal picture. We get aggregate maps that associate particular kinds of voter emotions and "states of mind" with particular kinds of voter behavior and voting outcomes. But even if supporters of populist parties can be located in places where we can also locate particular knowledge deficits ("low information") and social emotions such as anger and resentment, the explanatory mechanism for emotionally motivated or media-motivated political action is usually missing. Why would resentful and angry voters bother to cast a vote; why not opt out of politics altogether? Beyond correlation, what are the actual pathways that connect fake-news consumption to the decision and act of voting for a populist?[6]

Existing explanations are also hampered by the selective empirical evidence that they draw upon, of cases where contemporary populism casts its deviant shadow across the well-tempered landscape of Euro-American liberal democracy. These are the mainstay of contemporary populism scholarship, which, despite a few forays into comparative terrain, is mostly theorized as an Atlantic rim phenomenon. The view that results, of populism as some kind of monstrous interruption of normal democratic politics, cannot so easily accommodate the many cases of populist politics from other parts of the world where the preexisting political dispensation, though democratic, was never entirely liberal to begin with.

Finally, the presentist and electoralist understanding of populism fails to engage a very simple empirical fact. Populism does not fall from the sky. Populist electoral victories have antecedents as well as afterlives. The lineages of populist politics stretch well before and beyond the contemporary moment of voter choice. It is located not just in the moment of the electoral exception but in the unremarkable rhythms of everyday, normal democracy. In the words of anthropologist Matt Wilde, "in order to understand populism, we need to think about a lot more than populism."[7]

This book is about the "lot more." I zoom out from the exceptional figure of the angry populist voter to the historical lineages and the political-institutional contexts that have fueled the rise of populist politics. If populism is a "thin-centered ideology"[8] or worldview of political and social life as a Manichean moral combat between a unitary and pure people and a dissolute and corrupt elite/system, then we need to understand how it both converges and conflicts with other, existing and older, ideas of the people: the central subject of modern political thought and practice.

If we take such an approach, two things quickly become evident. First, an investigation of populism's backstory that goes beyond the immediate moment of electoral victories by distinctive new campaigns of angry politics in the name of a newly assertive political subject, "the people," leads us to plenty of banal, bureaucratic-institutional processes and influences as well that have also fueled populism's rise. In other words, it is not just an overtly emotional and exceptional politics of anger that produces the people/elite binary, and foments the idea of anti-establishment insurgency that is the distinctive hallmark of populism. Historically patterned rhythms and routines of democratic politics; institutions that are crucial to democratic governance; events that have been widely hailed as advancing the cause of democracy; and things considered to be crucial for democratic well-being have all had a role to play in populism's rise and salience.

Second, a closer examination of the broader historical and political context of populism reveals that a particular idea about democratic change fuels such a politics. If, instead of proceeding from the assumption that populism is sui generis, we ask where it comes from or what it comes out of, then we see that populism is a project of democratic reform fueled by an imagination of democracy's "repairable lapses."[9] The core of populist political appeal is the call to cure, revive, renew, or restore a presently flawed or diseased democracy. I term this broader political context and project *curative democracy*, and it is the main subject of this book. I contend that contemporary populism both in India, the specific geographical location of my study, and in several other parts of the world is the latest manifestation of an older and ongoing politics of curative democracy that took root in the 1970s through the first half of the 1980s (the "Long 1970s").

Moving between twenty-first-century populist politics and its late-twentieth-century predecessor, curative democracy, this book intervenes in discussions about populism by offering a "consequent" rather than a causal explanation of its rise.[10] I show that the present moment of populist outrage politics in India is a legacy of an older project of curative democracy that has enjoyed political and cultural legitimacy and institutional heft for more than four decades. The specific political lineage that I trace in order to make this argument is that of *outsider politics*, the distinctive institutional and normative formation that was central to the idea of the democratic cure first articulated in the 1970s in India, and which is at the core of the twenty-first-century populist project as well.

Other features of populism, most notably the people/elite binary, have commanded a great deal of scholarly and media attention in recent times. But the idea of the political outsider as the agent of populist redemption; the normative justification of populist movements and leaders in terms of their distinctive outsider status; and the location of representational authority in some putative pure space outside politics are the beating heart of the populist imagination. In the remaining sections of this introduction, I flesh out these arguments and the concepts of "curative democracy" and "outsider politics" that drive the book.

CURATIVE DEMOCRACY AND OUTSIDER POLITICS

In the first two decades after independence from British colonial rule in 1947, the projects of democratic founding and "nation-building" dominated the national political agenda of the new Indian republic. Post-independence public culture was saturated with images and promises of newness. The end of two hundred years of colonial rule in India was marked by the partition of colonial territory into the sovereign nation-states of India and Pakistan—an act that led to human displacements and deaths on an unprecedented scale. The violent contexts of Indian independence and the daily precariousness of national existence very literally confronted the nation-builders. Thousands of refugees arrived in the capital city of Delhi each day. Refugee camps sprang up within walking distance of the majestic colonial buildings where delegates wrote a new constitution for India. Shadowed by these experiences, the Nehruvian vision of newness was more cautious than triumphalist, more hopeful than assertive, although the theme of new births and new beginnings, of politics as an uncertain but also exciting experiment, always remained at the forefront.

The broad umbrella of nation-building covered ideas of social, economic, as well as political change. The term was associated with a wide range of initiatives. These included the building of monumental dams; the adoption of educational curricula that aimed to foster "scientific temper" and "youth discipline"; the creation of cultural displays for annual Republic Day parades that showcased the official nationalist theme of unity-in-diversity; and the establishment of new model townships and urban settlements that, through their rehabilitation of partition refugees, very literally enacted the promise of sovereign national beginnings that was so integral to the mythology of decolonization. This was not unique to India. In the middle of the twentieth century, similar nation-building projects were launched by newly sovereign nation-states across wide swaths of Asia and Africa.[11] Within two decades, there was a gradual but perceptible shift. Starting in the late 1960s, the norm of newness was reconfigured as renewal and recovery. A quite differently inflected project of curative democracy took hold in India. From now on, the main goal of political action was not so much the establishment of democracy, but rather its recovery, reform, and cure.

This journey *from nation-building to democracy-rebuilding* was signposted in India by two significant political developments. The first was the dramatic proclamation of a national emergency in June 1975 by Prime Minister Indira Gandhi that suspended the normal operations of electoral democracy and rights protections, citing grave and imminent dangers to the stability and security of the country. The second was the equally dramatic and surprising decision to annul the emergency and restore the electoral process nineteen months later, in January 1977 (elections took place in March 1977). Both these inimical events—the end of democracy and the end of authoritarianism, respectively—were legitimized and publicly justified in the same way, as urgent and necessary acts of democratic salvation or remedy. The distinctive logic of curative democracy came into its own with these twin acts of democratic annulment and restoration. Outlasting the specific circumstances of its birth at moments of exceptional crisis, it would bend the arc of Indian politics well after the 1970s came to an end.

Turning Points: The Long 1970s

The idea of curative democracy emerged in the context of a gradual but definitive shift in the norms and practices of political mobilization and legitimization in post-independence India. India's democracy at the time of its birth was unique both for the sheer ambition of the universal suffrage that it granted all of its citizens all at once—never before had so many millions of individuals been given an unqualified right to vote regardless of property, education, or gender considerations—and for the deep and complex social inequalities along the fault lines of caste, religion, class, and region that fissured the country.[12] As he completed his work of drafting the constitution, Bhimrao Ambedkar, the chair of the Draft Committee, would declare to the Constituent Assembly in November 1949:

> On the 26th of January 1950, we are going to enter into a life of contradictions. In politics we will have equality and in social and economic life we will have

> inequality. In politics we will be recognizing the principle of one man one vote and one vote one value. In our social and economic life, we shall, by reason of our social and economic structure, continue to deny the principle of one man one value. How long shall we continue to live this life of contradictions? How long shall we continue to deny equality in our social and economic life? If we continue to deny it for long, we will do so only by putting our political democracy in peril. We must remove this contradiction at the earliest possible moment or else those who suffer from inequality will blow up the structure of political democracy which this Assembly has so laboriously built up.[13]

The contradictions that Ambedkar noted between the political promise and the actual social conditions of democracy were managed in the first couple of decades after independence by the distinctive architecture of the "Congress system" of party organization and political mobilization instituted by the ruling Congress party, the organizational legatee of the anticolonial nationalist movement. Combining the co-optation of local notables into party structures with a flexible ideological orientation that allowed both right-wing and socialist factions to coexist with a single political party, the Congress party was able both to ensure its own electoral dominance and reproduce political order in the new republic. The Congress system secured political consent to a centralized authority by continually negotiating and compromising with multiple and contending local social forces, deferring to entrenched traditions of hierarchical social patronage to allocate party tickets, and tempering legislative and policy proposals if they were resisted by powerful local social interests.[14]

By the late 1960s, the steady "massification" or social expansion of electoral democracy strained political institutions with the mounting pressure of social claims, and placed the Congress system of managed negotiation in crisis. The leadership struggles that seized the Congress party after the death of Prime Minister Jawaharlal Nehru in 1964 also played their part. Shortly after Indira Gandhi, Nehru's daughter, became the party leader and the third prime minister of India, the Congress party split into two rival partisan formations in 1969, the Congress (Organisation) and the Congress (Requisitionists), the latter headed by Indira Gandhi. As the sixties came to a close, the flexible big-tent system of managing differences within a single capacious party organization that had multiple power centers gave way to narrow and centralized party formations dominated by a single leader, and heightened levels of interpartisan conflict.

The People as Political Subject

As political contestation moved from intraparty to interparty arenas, the modes of political mobilization and legitimization shifted as well.[15] Indira Gandhi as leader of the breakaway Congress (R) bypassed existing Congress institutions and practices of locally mediated voter mobilization to address a new political subject, the people. Indira Gandhi presented herself as a decisive leader executing bold and swift actions to save an imperiled political system that had failed to deliver the fruits of democracy to its citizens. This gained public traction in the context of the 1971 Bangladesh liberation war. Evoking the myth of Hindu goddess Durga's battle against the forces of evil, Indira Gandhi's authorization of military intervention by the Indian Army in support of the East Pakistan/Bangladesh independence fighters was widely hailed across the country.

The narrative of the victorious goddess of avenging justice sharpened its populist edge in the early 1970s. Gandhi's dramatic election campaign slogan from this period was *garibi hatao*, or remove poverty. With its emphatic flourish, it conveyed the decisive immediacy of the Great Leader's actions, which set her apart from the sclerotic indifference of the existing political system. At the same time, the grand flourish of the promise meant that the benchmarks and measure of its fulfilment remained open-ended.

The economy was a key site of populist political address in this period. This involved the reorientation of a central theme of the official nationalist imagination. The post-independence "Nehruvian" nation-building project was tethered to a specific developmentalist vision of India as a homogeneous economic space planned and guided to progress along a linear trajectory by a centralized state.[16] This idea of development as a progressive process of "becoming" was now supplanted by a new emphasis on immediate achievement and "doing," and on the importance of visibly decisive action. Through measures such as the abolition of state payments and privileges for pre-independence-era aristocrats, and the nationalization of private banks, Gandhi signaled her commitment to fight the system of entrenched economic privilege with swift and immediate effect.

An oppositional, zero-sum understanding of the relationship between economic and political rights also became commonplace. Through her policies as well as a series of constitutional battles between the executive and the judiciary over the principles of judicial review, Gandhi increasingly recast the economy as the domain of authentic popular sovereignty, and hence the main priority of her government. The urgent economic needs of the people were, in this reckoning, more important than so-called second-order constitutional protections of individual political and civil liberties.

The idea of economic needs was specified mostly in relation to values like efficiency, speed, and order rather than to structural inequality as such. The specter of "economic offenders" who engaged in hoarding, smuggling, tax evasion, and the amassment of "black money"; the adulteration of food supplies meant for the public distribution system by corrupt state agents; and the ominous shadow of the "foreign hand" and "CIA involvement" that hovered around the edges of just about every statist pronouncement in the early 1970s animated the languages of political mobilization and legitimization in this period and brought an increasingly "paranoid style" to bear on public discourse.[17]

In sum, the end of the 1960s and early 1970s in India saw a new language of political mobilization emerge. Breaking from the prevailing Congress system's logic of locally mediated and socially segmented appeals, the incumbent political regime of Indira Gandhi addressed an amorphous constituency of the people. In the new economic populist imaginary, individual and civil rights were cast as an obstacle to the realization of popular sovereignty. By the mid-1970s, the devaluation of individual rights and freedoms took the very material form of the emergency declaration that suspended fundamental rights of individual citizens in the name of realizing order, security, and economic progress.

Cleansing Politics and Curing Democracy

Alongside the turn to economic populism, the early 1970s in India also saw an intensified engagement with the theme of political corruption and the indictment of so-called "dirty politics."[18] The discourse of antipolitics, of political aversion and skepticism toward power and rule, has a deep historical presence in the South Asian subcontinent. Through the twentieth century, antipolitical thought and practice had a strong influence on the colonial and postcolonial polity. The Gandhian strand of anticolonial politics, with its emphasis on moral "truth force" and the cultivation of sacrificial and renunciatory modes of political address, made a virtue of giving up political power.[19] The Nehruvian nation-building project worked to insulate "sublime" statist reason from the sordid squabbles of "petty politics." The rise of interpartisan competition in the 1970s led to frequent and highly publicized episodes of "politicking," "horse-trading," frequent partisan defections, and the visible presence of money as a force in electoral politics.[20] The long-standing theme of distaste for the pursuit of political power was reworked into a repudiation of the corrupt worlds of electoral politics in particular.

From the late 1960s onward, the corruptions of electoral politics and the malign workings of the money-politics nexus were targeted by both government and opposition with increasing stridency. The call to rescue democracy from the scourge of politics became the central refrain of the Indira Gandhi regime's efforts to delegitimize social protests against its authority, as well as of the protest movements themselves. The student-led Navnirman (reconstruction) movement in the state of Gujarat started as a protest against an increase in hostel food prices and culminated in a demand for the ouster of the state government. The call for "total revolution" (*sampoorna kranti*) issued by the Gandhian socialist leader Jayaprakash "JP" Narayan saw millions of people take to the streets in the early 1970s to demand a thorough cleansing of the political order. All of these actions upheld a curative vision of democracy, a term that I will explain below. The festering sore of money-infested, power-hungry politics had to be excised from the corrupted body politic to restore Indian democracy to perfect constitutional health, they agitated.[21] In an ironic twist, the Congress government under Indira Gandhi that these movements targeted would reproduce a similar discourse about remedial actions to cure the diseased democracy. Its emergency declaration of June 1975 suspended the normal procedures and constitutional protections of democratic politics in the name of saving democracy.

For the next twenty-odd months, governance for the protection and benefit of democracy entailed its abeyance. Between June 1975 and

March 1977, India was ruled under constitutional emergency provisions that strengthened the hand of the central executive and hollowed out deliberative as well as countermajoritarian institutions like the parliament and the judiciary. The suspension of civil liberties and fundamental rights protections enabled the mass imprisonment of perceived opponents of the Indira Gandhi regime. These included leaders and members of opposition political parties and of Hindu right-wing movements and organizations such as the RSS and the Ananda Marg; communist and socialist activists; journalists; and media owners critical of the ruling establishment. Controversial policies of media censorship, slum demolition, and the compulsory sterilization of male, disproportionately poor and minority citizens were implemented. All these acts were justified in remedial or curative terms, as bitter but needed medicine to restore India's democratic health.[22]

The restoration of democracy in the aftermath of the emergency continued this pattern of repetition and relay between power and counterpower, of a common call to salvage and cure democracy. Surprise elections that were called by Indira Gandhi, ostensibly to demonstrate public consent and revalidation of the emergency regime, led to her ouster by an opposition coalition in March 1977. As we will see in the chapters that follow, the post-emergency project of democratic restoration in the late 1970s and beyond advanced many emergency-era curative idioms and practices. They reproduced many of the ideas that had previously anchored the project of emergency rule, the very object of their "never again" efforts. Departing from prevailing views of the emergency as a temporary aberration in Indian politics, this book shows how these post-emergency efforts to restore democracy in fact carried forward ideas and practices of curative democracy and populist logics of extra-electoral representation that were consolidated during the emergency itself.

The Curative Democracy Complex

I use the term *curative democracy* to refer to the complex of ideas, institutional interventions, and policy decisions that have the explicit aim of fixing and curing—hence *curative*—an existing system of political democracy. Together, these entrench new legitimization vocabularies in political and public cultural arenas where actions in the name of curing democracy garner sanction and approval. But this is not only about normative innovations. There are material effects as well, for instance when laws on electoral reform and freedom of information that aim to end and prevent political corruption impact the ability to get a ration card that will grant access to subsidized food.[23]

The curative democratic complex has several distinguishing features. First, it offers a *diagnosis of disease and cure* in which the democratic political system is approached as a discrete entity that can both be stricken by disease and targeted by specific kinds of remedial interventions. There is, moreover, a critical urgency to the diagnosis. This is the second distinguishing feature of curative democracy. The call to cure democracy is generally framed as a *call to immediate action*, and the health of democracy is invariably diagnosed as critically impaired, democracy on life support, as it were.

Immediacy is all about the visibility and suddenness of actions. Curative democracy projects involve sudden, public, and dramatic acts and decisions, such as the drama of Indira Gandhi's emergency proclamation in June 1975, and the parallel drama of the equally sudden suspension of emergency in January 1977. The political theater of the India Against Corruption movement's *bijli pani satyagraha* (electricity water campaign) from 2012 is a more recent example. The spectacle of activists scrambling up electricity poles to rejoin wires and provide electricity to people unable to pay the inflated electricity bills in Delhi very literally enacted the movement's resolve of immediately acting against political corruption and curing the ills of the system right away, here and now.[24]

In recent years, the mobilization repertoires of the Hindu nationalist BJP party have included such performative displays of immediate remedial action as well. The incumbent Indian prime minister Narendra Modi's main public identity is that of a decisive, larger-than-life action hero who undertakes swift, sudden, and big actions. His demonetization policy of 2016 is an iconic example. Late on a November evening that year, Prime Minister Modi interrupted the regular television broadcast schedule to announce that, in order to immediately excise the festering sore of black money and political corruption that infected the body politic, two of the most widely used Indian currency notes would cease to be legal tender that very night. In the immediate aftermath of the ironically nicknamed "demon" policy, its adverse effects on individual lives and livelihoods were widely reported in the media. Although demonetization was widely predicted to weaken the BJP's electoral chances, the party in fact gained in electoral popularity during crucial state-level elections the following year. The BJP's campaign emphasis on demonetization as the ultimate act of immediate, daring, and risky decision-making—an act that signals Modi's disregard for political power and his willingness to make electorally unpopular decisions in order to achieve a higher public purpose—may indeed have found some kind of public traction. We will revisit the "eventocratic"[25] reign of Modi in the final chapter of the book and see how the concepts of curative democracy and outsider politics clarify the puzzle of Modi's continued electoral success despite the havoc and misery caused by demonetization.

Political Outsiders

The third notable feature of the curative democratic complex has to do with the nature of the just-in-time remedial actions that it proposes, and the identity of the curative agent who is authorized to undertake them. Only the interventions of a *political outsider* who has nothing to do with the messy intrigues of electoral politics and the hunger for power that it breeds can cure democracy, it is held. Democracy's external doctors can be of several different kinds. As the following chapters show, curative democracy projects in India have involved interventions by non-state institutions such as the media, state agencies such as the judiciary, and parastatal or quasi-governmental autonomous ombuds institutions. On other occasions, curative agency has been invested in individuals invested with superior intellectual-technical, entrepreneurial, moral, religious, or even magical/superhuman powers. Common to all of these varied expressions of institutional and individual curative agency is the assumption of political exteriority that places democratic sovereignty and the true power and authentic interests of the people outside the domain of electoral politics.

Elections are commonly regarded as the sign and measure of democracy, and the formal distinction between authoritarian and democratic systems is based on the occurrence of free and fair elections in the latter. Assessments of Indian democracy are strongly influenced by such an electoralist understanding. Both (official and popular cultural) self-presentations and external commentary about the "world's largest democracy" regularly highlight the conduct of elections as a sign of India's democratic vibrancy.[26] But the curative democracy paradigm adds another wrinkle. As much as they are celebrated, elections are also condemned as the vectors of democratic disease. They are seen to elicit and enable "dirty" political machinations and manipulations, to corrupt and corrode the public interest and the common good.

Extra-electoral Representation

Unlike the ideals of political transcendence and renunciation that have long informed the "saintly idioms" of South Asian political cultures,[27] the outsider norm of curative democracy projects in fact demands a renewed and intensified engagement with politics. Curative democracy is about going outside electoral politics in order to cure it. Political transformation is a central aim: the mission is to repair and restore rather than overturn or escape the existing political system. It is in relation to this restorative and politically engaged impulse of curative democracy that its fourth significant feature gains meaning, namely the emphasis on *extra-electoral forms and practices of representation*.

Questions of representation and mediation remain front and center in discourses of curative democracy. The democratic cure aims to produce better and truer mediators and representatives of the people, not to get rid of representation as such. Curative democracy is essentially a project and process of representative claims-making that locates the agency and responsibility of "authentic representation" of the people outside the domain of electoral politics.

We will encounter several different kinds of extra-electoral representative claims in the chapters that follow, all advanced in the name of the people, in the name of repairing a broken democracy. In the Long 1970s, when the idea of curative democracy first took shape in India, extra-electoral representational authority was mainly vested in non-state organizations such as the media, civil society, and social movements, and in non-electoral state agencies like the judiciary. In many cases, this took the conjoined form of "concern networks" that brought media, civil society, social movements, legal actors, and judicial institutions together to advance a common claim about being the true representatives of the wounded and suffering people. The unfettered agency of executive decisions was also included in the field of extra-electoral representation, beginning with Indira Gandhi's justification of the emergency as an effort to save Indian democracy.

In later decades, the space of extra-electoral representation was increasingly filled by community and culture-based discourses and formations, which claimed the moral mantle of truly representing the people in the name of religion, caste, or regional identity. In the early decades of the twenty-first century, still another set of claimants to representational authority emerged, this time from the field of corporate and entrepreneurial capital. New formations of "inclusive capitalism" and "pro-poor capitalism," and the decisive agency and leadership skills of CEOs and "captains of industry," gained media and public attention in the new millennium, as figures who would set things right for India.[28]

In each of these cases, the goal of democratic health was defined as the realization of new and better ways of mediating the will of the people. From the curative democracy projects that coalesced around normative notions of cultural community, to those that advocated for the interventions of capital, the authority of the change agent invested with the power of curing the sick system was imagined in representational terms, as a type of intermediary authority. The emphasis on mediation and representation yielded policy choices that took curative democrats away from participatory or direct democratic agendas and goals. The book will explore these divergences in further detail, building on the insights of recent scholarship on "monitory democracy" to document how curative democracy encourages power scrutiny more than power sharing or active political participation by citizens.[29]

Modulating Nationalism

The final feature of note in curative democracy projects is their relationship to prevailing norms of nationalism. The main political subject that curative democracy discourses addressed when they first emerged in India during the 1970s and 1980s was the people: *janata*, *lok*, *makkal*. At first, these ideas evolved on separate tracks. The evolution of curative democracy projects in the post-emergency period that legitimized the exercise of political agency by non-electoral representatives such as the media, judiciary, civil society, and social action groups unfolded in tandem with another kind of political-cultural mobilization in the domain of electoral politics: the rise of Hindu nationalism. The ideas of the nation that were taken forward by Hindu nationalist movements and parties in the 1980s were linked to cultural and ethno-religious idioms. Hindu nationalist or Hindutva ideology configured the nation as an ethno-religiously homogeneous and territorially bounded "imagined community," and mobilized supporters using "blood and soil" discourses of belonging, inclusion, and exclusion. The people in whose name democracy was being saved and repaired was by contrast an "open signifier" that lacked the ethno-religious and territorial distinctions and the solidary frameworks or community-building emphases of nationhood discourses.

Over time, especially as Hindu nationalism moved from the space of social movement insurgency to that of government,[30] the clear lines between the two normative orders of people/democracy and nation/community were muddled. Communal nationalist discourses were modulated into a national populism that did not stay limited to ethno-religious modes of imagining community. Moving beyond the parameters of collective identity formation, Hindu nationalism in present-day India seeks to reconstitute democracy and political order along majoritarian lines in the name of the people, often deploying the very languages and practices of curative democracy that many of its avowed left-liberal adversaries have used over the years. Promoting a politically lethal blend of majoritarian assertions of Hindu political power and discourses of democratic reform and people power, the Hindu-first transformation of the Indian republic is undertaken in the name of salvaging and redeeming democracy and popular sovereignty. And as the curative inflections of Hindu nationalism open up a political space for strongmen leaders and their decisive actions, what also changes is Indian democracy itself. The concluding chapter will consider the dynamics and implications of this change.

CONCEPTUAL CONTEXTS

Antipolitics as Depoliticization

At first glance, the concept of "antipolitics" seems to resonate with the idea of curative democracy that I have outlined above. There is by now a considerable body of work on the origins, character, and normative significance of the phenomenon named as antipolitics in different world regions. Postcolonial contexts feature prominently in the scholarship. Both the high developmentalism of mid-twentieth-century nation-states across Asia and Africa, and their "structural adjustment" into liberalized market economies at century's end, are cited as examples of antipolitical formations or "anti-politics machines," to use the evocative terminology of anthropologist James Ferguson.[31]

In these discussions, the term *antipolitics* refers to the ensemble of institutions, norms, and practices that work to insulate governance and policy decisions from the allegedly negative and harmful effects of politics, defined as the actions of electoral representatives and institutions, or more broadly, as debates and contestations between different viewpoints and values. Antipolitics is seen as a depoliticizing "instrument effect," that is, a particular instrument or technology of state and capitalist power that works through depoliticization.[32]

For instance, in Ferguson's much-cited account of World Bank–aided development projects in Lesotho, he documents how the antipolitical developmental regime shifts matters concerning public goods, resource allocation, and redistribution away from the thrust and parry of political debate and contest in legislatures and other public forums. Instead, these are decided by technocratic experts whose actions and rationale remain inscrutable to citizens. Like a fantastical antigravity machine from science fiction that suspends gravity at the flick of a switch, the antipolitics machine of development hands down enormous life-changing decisions without public warning, reason, or debate. Moreover, depoliticization does not only ensure that controversial decisions are shielded from public scrutiny and dissent. With the conversion of every issue into a technocratic problem to be addressed by the developmental apparatus, the reach of bureaucratic state power is extended over social surfaces. The antipolitics machine thus strengthens the hand of the state, and the nexus of state and capital that governs late modernity.

Democratic theorists also advance a similar view of antipolitics *qua* depoliticization. Although it purports to offer general and even universal perspectives on democracy as such, most democratic theory is in fact regionally circumscribed. Political systems in Europe and the United States are their primary, although unacknowledged, referent. In these social and political contexts that share little in common with the postcolonial and liberalizing states in Asia and Africa that informed discussions of the antipolitics machine, a similar dynamic of antipolitics as a "powerful depoliticization" is also seen to unfold.

Thus, for scholars like Colin Crouch, Erik Swyngedouw, and Wendy Brown, antipolitical depoliticization in Atlantic rim countries—what Crouch glosses as "post-democracy" and Swyngedouw as "postpolitics"—is essentially an instrument and vocabulary for elite control of democratic political systems or the reproduction of oligarchy.[33] For these authors, the defining feature of antipolitics is not so much the elaboration of bureaucratic power that the "machine theorists" of postcolonial developmentalism identified. Rather, it is about the "rule of consensus" that reduces and evacuates political conflict and difference, and the relentless privatization and individualization of social and collective concerns and issues. This has been a pervasive theme in scholarship on Britain's New Labour governance in the early decades of the twenty-first century, where the Labour Party under Tony Blair is seen to have practiced a depoliticizing "mode of statecraft."[34]

As the very term *post-democracy* implies, these developments are seen to harm democracy in different ways. For Crouch, the rule of consensus leads to widespread political apathy and cynicism. When political parties across Europe and America abandon their ideological commitments and distinctions to converge around a single neoliberal agenda, citizens are denied meaningful political choice and they disengage from politics. For Corey Robin, the link between antipolitical depoliticization and elite power is the main concern. The distinctive psychopathologizing discourse of fear in American politics that constitutes fear as a subject and object beyond politics is quite directly related to elite bids to gain and maintain power, he argues.[35]

Jacques Rancière's critique of antipolitics proceeds along somewhat different lines. For him, more than consensus formation and the expansion of insulated technocratic power, depoliticization involves attempts to "harmonize" the "structural heteronomy" of government and society that he holds to be intrinsic to democracy. Rancière defines democracy as the contingent "rule of nobody" where the entitlement to govern is based on chance or lot rather than divine sanction or social determination: "the power of the people is not that of a people gathered together, of the majority, or of the working class. It is simply the power peculiar to those who have no more entitlements to govern than to submit."[36] This means that there is always and necessarily a gap or "structural heteronomy" between social and governmental configurations, and governing arrangements are constantly open to challenge or change because anyone can claim the title to govern. Attempts to tame such volatility and streamline the relationship between government and society—the socialization of rule, in other words—can only diminish democracy in this account. This is precisely what Rancière sees as the main danger of antipolitics.

Another line of democratic critique of antipolitics has to do with the intensification of enmity, or what in Carl Schmitt's terms might be called the "ultrapolitical" dimensions of antipolitics.[37] The erasure of conflict, contingency, and difference in and by an antipolitical order requires that another, fundamental or constitutive antagonism be cast in stone. Erik Swyngedouw and Slavoj Žižek have pointed out that depoliticized consensus formation creates an absolute divide or a radical enmity between the consensual "order of police" and the unstable zone of political dissensus, "the political," which must be kept at bay at all costs, rendered unsayable and invisible. Depoliticized antipolitics produces a "direct militarization" that troubles democracy, setting up an irreconcilable opposition between absolute good and evil, friend and enemy, that denies any possibility of encounter and engagement across difference.[38]

Finally, the democratic critique of antipolitics is usually framed as a critique of a fallen present that is contrasted with a "truly political" past. In a curious reversal of the teleologies of progress that present democracy as an onward march toward ever more democratized futures, many of these discussions offer up a retrospective nostalgia about a rich and meaningful political past that we have left behind. A wide range of authors of different ideological persuasions have advanced this narrative, drawing upon both liberal accounts of the atrophy of civil associational life and the hollowing out of the public sphere by the techno-consumerist colonization of life-worlds, and critical Marxian perspectives on the alienating drive of capital, particularly in its neoliberal financial manifestations. A politically vibrant golden age shines through these accounts like a lost talisman, calling readers to gaze wistfully toward a lost era of animated citizens who once "bowled together," engaged in meaningful debate over shared goals, and rose up together to try to win the world.[39] This moment of political plenitude is invariably located in a specific time and place. As Jonathan Dean has pointed out, "Europe 68" usually serves as the unstated benchmark of political radicalism in these laments about the depoliticized present.[40] This is a place-time that is doubly distanced, by history as well as geography, for the twenty-first-century non-European democracies where the vast majority of the world's democratic population actually lives.

Antipolitics as Extrapolitics

Although the view of antipolitics as a depoliticizing technology of (state and capitalist) power dominates scholarly discussion today, there are other conceptual and intellectual genealogies that we must consider as well. A second and quite different body of work on antipolitics gained considerable public and scholarly traction in the 1970s. Here, instead of emphasizing the depoliticizing effects of technologies of power and showing how the disavowal of politics strengthened ruling regimes and led to a substantial de-democratization, the focus was on quite the opposite, that is, how actions and spaces outside politics could confront and maybe even change and overturn dominant power.

The idea of antipolitics as a mode of countering rather than extending state-systemic power came out of a politically engaged world of intellectual "dissidence" in Cold War Eastern Europe, at a time that we can retrospectively identify as the last decade of the Soviet bloc's existence in the 1970s and 1980s. Figures like Václav Havel, Adam Michnik, and György Konrád made influential contributions to this philosophy, each advancing a vision of an antipolitics as a space and act of hope and a necessary counterpoint to the alienating effects of systemic power. In their understanding, the turn away from politics did not lead to disempowerment and alienation as the depoliticization school had predicted. Rather, by avoiding the fields of power and politics, the individual could experience a meaningful and authentic, "truly human" life lived in joyous concert with others.

The writings of Hungarian intellectual György Konrád are exemplary in this regard. In his manifesto on antipolitics from the late 1970s, Konrád called for the cultivation of the very stance of political indifference and citizens' apathy toward formal political institutions that several decades later would be a cause of concern for democratic theorists worrying about the rise of public cynicism and distrust. "Let the government stay on top . . . we will live our own lives underneath it"[41] is the antipolitical injunction for Konrád: a "method of politics that functions in the negative, [in which] resistance is fomented through deconstructive efforts."[42]

Like Konrád and other Eastern European dissidents whose writings and artistic works grappled with the everyday realities of life under socialist rule in the aftermath of the failed Prague Spring uprising of 1968, the Czech writer (and future president) Václav Havel also elaborated a vision of an authentic space and mode of engagement that lay outside the alienating structures of "post-totalitarian" politics and power. In his famous text *Power of the Powerless* from 1978, Havel describes how dissidence in a post-totalitarian system can only grow out of the "living humus" of "pre-political" space. The distinctive feature of post-totalitarian polities is their absolute commandment to "live within a lie," Havel memorably argued. Unlike the structures of totalitarian power, where authority is localized and identified in discrete formations "out there," post-totalitarian systems are enmeshed with the interior rhythms of everyday, individual lives. Ordinary individuals are the agents as well as the objects or victims of post-totalitarian power; in the course of living their everyday lives, they actively participate in and reproduce the myriad falsehoods and ideologies that sustain and consolidate rule.[43]

Accordingly, for Havel, post-totalitarian power can only be challenged by individual efforts to live differently or to practice what he called "living within the truth." Purposive political strategies and organized plans of opposition and resistance do not make any difference. The power of the powerless does not lie in grand revolutionary plans of utopian transformation. Instead, it lies in individuals responding to their existential needs and desires for a meaningful, authentic, and dignified life by doing things differently, things that have nothing to do with politics at all. Sometimes, as they grow into larger and more organized "parallel structures" and institutions governed by authentic human emotions of belonging, trust, and care, these prepolitical actions can seed a "parallel polis" that challenges the established order. But this is a contingent outcome. Macro-level impacts at the formal or institutional level are contingent and cannot be planned for or predicted. For Havel, the substance and horizon of meaningful change is the individual, intimate, and the everyday. Change requires the cultivation of what Gil Eyal calls a "technology of the self," and attention to issues and concerns such as individual moral responsibility that are usually dismissed as nonpolitical, unpolitical, or prepolitical.[44]

It seems that for antipolitics to be imagined as a form of "counterpower" laden with transformative potential rather than a technology of power that legitimizes existing structures of state/capitalist rule, the idea of transformation itself had to be rescaled and recast from macro-social and abstract to micro, personalized, practice-oriented or experiential registers. Antipolitical dissidence, as conceptualized by thinkers like Konrád and Havel, is not about creating an organized resistance that consciously aims to achieve social transformation and to build oppositional structures that combat the existing system of rule on its own terrain and terms. Instead, any kind of macro-level, social and political change is a contingent and even accidental by-product of transformations at the level of the individual. Her quest for living an authentic, dignified, and truly human life is the main focus of antipolitics in the Eastern European dissident imaginary.

A variant of the "antipolitics as counterpower" thesis was also advanced in Western European intellectual-political contexts in the same decade of the 1970s. The particular "post-'68" social and political context of Western Europe that, in the aftermath of the militant mobilizations of the previous decade, combined a sense of both intense politicization and awareness on the part of citizens with resigned pragmatism and disillusionment about the effectiveness of citizens' actions to actually bring about tangible change seeded the new political-philosophical understanding of antipolitics. At one level, this closely resonated with Eastern European dissident ideas that we have already encountered, about withdrawing from organized political contest and resistance to focus on the development and articulation of alternate spaces and practices of living beneath politics and thus "within the truth," as Konrád and Havel put it. But there were also important differences between the conceptions of antipolitics that animated the geopolitical worlds of divided Europe in the 1970s, which had to do with the relative weight given to spontaneity versus organization, individualized versus communal-social action on either side of the Iron Curtain.

For the most part, Western European variants of antipolitics emphasized the importance of associational forms and activities in bringing a "new politics" into being and the continued relevance of organized and purposive forms of collective action. Although these were staged outside the precincts of formal institutional politics, they were centrally engaged and occupied with questions of institutional change and intervention. Unlike the political-exit option that Eastern European dissident ideas of the antipolitical advocated particularly during the early years of dissident intellectual production, Western European ideas were focused on the articulation of political voice in new ways. The latter version of antipolitics was not so much a call to "live beneath," as to live "athwart" and against power. Confronting and engaging establishment forces and institutions and intervening to change the existing dispensation of power was a key priority for Western European antipolitical advocates. They emphasized the importance of organized associational activities and various kinds of public, collective action aimed at influencing formal modes and channels of power from "outside."

The idea of a political outside/elsewhere featured prominently in Western European discourses about antipolitics. The coordinates of exteriority were mapped around electoral and party politics. To qualify as antipolitical, the spaces of intervention had to be completely distanced from the intrigues of party politics and their preoccupations with power. Western European variants of antipolitics also stressed its organizational dimension, and called for action by civil society groups, social movements, non-governmental organizations, and other "non-party" and "extra-electoral" organizations. Suzanne Berger describes Western Europe at the end of the 1970s as a classic instance of a Gramscian "interregnum." In this situation of transition between forms of political and social order, Berger identifies a new "antistate and antiparty" orientation of politics across Western European countries. "The disjunction between the growing politicization of everyday life and the decay of the political parties that in the past articulated and aggregated demands . . . the principal manifestation of these shifts can be found in the antiparty and antistate values of virtually all new political movements of both the Right and Left in Europe today."[45]

In India, the idea found intellectual expression as the "non-party political process" or "non-party political formation," in approximately the same period as the Western and Eastern European discourses of antipolitics that we have reviewed. The concept was developed by scholars and public intellectuals such as D. L. Sheth, Rajni Kothari, and their colleagues at the Centre for the Study of Developing Societies (CSDS) in Delhi and popularized in the 1970s and '80s. The non-party political formation was defined in spatial as well as scalar terms. As the negative term indicated, it was imagined as a normative space explicitly disconnected from the political party and its world of electoral hustle. It was also about a more intimate and small-scale practice of a grassroots democracy that was closer to the people. Discussions emphasized the indigeneity of the concept as well, and contrasted the Indian roots of the idea of the non-political with Western models of parliamentary democracy. In terms of political ideology, most proponents of the non-party political process aligned themselves with Gandhian ideals, and several were influenced by indigenous variants of non-Marxist socialism as practiced by figures like JP Narayan, Rammanohar Lohia, and others.[46]

Antipolitics as Negative Sovereignty

The discussion so far has reviewed some prominent variants of the antipolitics-as-counterpower thesis. As we have seen, all of these advocate for extra-electorally constituted spaces and mode of action, whether "non-political" and "pre-political" forms of spontaneous individual action, or purposive collective action undertaken by non-party organizations such as civil society, social movements, NGOs, and action groups. A final version of the antipolitical thesis we must consider moves beyond these individual and group coordinates of agency to locate antipolitical counterpower within the domain of formal institutional politics. Pierre Rosanvallon's proposal for a "counter-democracy" of institutions that can exercise "negative sovereignty" powers of oversight, veto, and judgment over representative government is an influential example of this approach.[47]

According to Rosanvallon and other scholars like John Keane who have critically engaged with the concept of political representation, levels of public distrust and apathy are steadily rising in representative democratic systems around the world today, and the artifice and impossibility of representative democracy as a conjoined political form is laid bare.[48] Representation and democracy, after all, involve two distinct and even opposed political logics. There is nothing inherently democratic about the system of political and electoral representation. Citizens today feel increasingly distant and disconnected from the very people and institutions who are supposed to represent them. Narrow, partisan political agendas pursued by self-interested politicians and power-seeking political parties dominate the public arena. This problem of representative government's "democratic deficit" can be addressed by new kinds of institutions and mechanisms that effectively scrutinize or monitor power, theorists of "post-representative democracy" argue. Keane uses the neologism *monitory democracy* to directly reference this idea.

Similar to the extrapolitical imaginaries of counterpower that drove the projects of Eastern European dissidence, Western European antipolitics, and Indian non-party politics, theories of post-representative democracy understand the political outside to be the locus of re-democratization. They hold that only practices, actors, and institutions that are manifestly disconnected from the messy worlds of partisan politics can effectively supervise, evaluate, and block the politicized actions and decisions that these worlds produce. This is the only way to restore to democracy its two elemental properties: accountable government and impartial judgment.

However, there is a significant divergence over the normative goals of self-actualization, participation, and voice that animate the different ideas of how to get outside politics. The arguments about dissidence, antipolitics, and non-party politics all emphasized some form of engaged action on the part of the ordinary individual citizen. Even if these were acts of avoidance, recusal, or renunciation of formal-institutional politics, they involved *active* decisions and activities, and the exercise of judgment and reason. The monitory democracy/counter-democracy paradigm by contrast assigns a generally passive role for the individual citizen. The agents of negative sovereignty are various kinds of (individual or organizational) representative bodies, such as ombuds organizations, expert committees, tribunals, media, whistleblowers, and other entities that primarily take on mediating roles between citizens and their elected representatives. In sum, for negative sovereignty theorists, the space outside politics is imagined as a representational and largely institutional space that enables accountability and judgment, quite distinct from the authentic and vital "lifeworld" that animated the dreams of nonpolitical counterpower in the 1970s and 1980s.

Curative Politics and Democratic Modulation

As the above discussion makes clear, the concept of antipolitics has multiple and often conflicting interpretations. For some, it is a technology of power, a ruse or sleight of hand perpetrated by state and capitalist forces on an unknowing citizenry. For others, antipolitics represents quite the opposite. It is a normative proposal for how citizens and polities can in fact regain democratic sovereignty. There is very little shared ground between these perspectives, and to endorse one means a wholesale denial of the other. In the binary terms of the prevailing conceptual paradigm, antipolitics either subverts or advances democracy; it is either an instrument of establishment power or its very opposite, a mode of citizen empowerment against the establishment. It cannot be both.

It is precisely these false choices imposed by dichotomous thinking that my discussion of curative democracy sets aside. Taking on board the diversity of institutional actors and the uneven power relations that structure projects of democratic reform, curative democracy takes shape in this book as an historically contingent field of multiple and competing practices, ideas, and institutions, which is saturated by many different political energies. The idea of the political outside as a cure for democratic disease and debilitation is an open signifier that has been deployed for varied purposes by state and non-state, establishment as well as insurgent actors, I will argue. The sociopolitical content and import of curative democracy is necessarily varied. It cannot be assigned a singular and stable normative value as either good or bad for democracy. It yields a "diversification of political practices" rather than a "retreat from politics" as such.[49]

All of this means that the study of curative democracy requires historically and empirically embedded modes of analysis that, unmoored from the usual prescriptive and typological frameworks, ask about the various institutions, actors, historical contexts, and shifting social relationships that have shaped variants of such a politics. For each lamentation about democracy's sicknesses and each invocation of the redemptive powers of the political outside, we must ask about the kinds of representational authority and claims-making that are involved, instead of assuming that they are either democratizing or authoritarian. Questions of context and timing also become important. Can we explain why curative democracy projects become publicly salient at certain moments in time, and not in others? Can we explain why certain imaginaries of the political outside gain visibility and public legitimacy and are materialized in tangible policy and institutional forms, whereas others are dismissed as fanciful utopias?

I have followed these lines of inquiry in this book to make an argument about curative democracy's Indian career: how proposals and actions to cure or mend a democratic political system held to be diseased and broken in some fashion became increasingly visible in the national public arena from the late 1960s onward. These projects and ideas were propelled forward by a motley crew of individuals, groups, and institutions that included both state and social actors arrayed against governmental power in a political-economic context that could not be neatly classified as liberal-democratic, authoritarian, or neoliberal. Curative democracy projects were neither straightforward technologies of power nor weapons of counter-power. They had specific but lasting political effects. They legitimized the political authority of outsider figures, prioritized non-electoral representation, and made "impassioned morality" rather than detached reason the main currency of democratic public life.

The question of democratic consequence, or how curative projects impact democracy, calls for a context-specific response as well. Here, too, the task is not to evaluate whether democracy as such is strengthened or weakened by the curative impulse, but to map the different kinds of democratic modulations that curative projects produce. As I will argue in the chapters that follow, the call for a democratic cure and the accompanying rise of outsider politics, non-electoral representation, and impassioned morality together recast Indian democracy as a specifically *proprietorial formation* in which citizenship and normative political agency were defined around notions of owning rather than belonging to the national polity.

These political logics of "ownership democracy" play a significant and enabling role in contemporary populism. Both in India and other parts of the world today, populists mobilize around ideas of political reclamation; of regaining, reclaiming, and restoring an intimate possession of one's own. The populist claim is all about fixing and curing *one's own* broken democracy. The fire of indignation fueling the populist imagination is stoked by undeserving usurpers wrongfully taking over "our" place. As we will soon see, these proprietorial claims about democratic restoration and repair are advanced from a fissured and uneven social landscape. There is a definite sociological dimension to this form of politics. Curative democracy, outsider politics, and ownership claims on democracy are all socially modulated articulations that reveal and confirm the inequalities that structure Indian social worlds.

OUTLINE OF THE BOOK

The argument is developed over five chapters. The first part of the book, *Elements*, documents the influential presence of norms and practices of curative democracy and outsider politics in contemporary India. I look at cases from the formal domain of electoral politics and the worlds of commercial news media, where curative democratic norms and practices have gained visibility and prominence in recent decades. Chapter 1 examines the spectacular rise of a new Indian political party, the Aam Aadmi Party or Common Man's Party, whose campaign to clean up Indian politics and establish a new, noncorrupt, and transparent political order that will serve the interests of the "common man" has reaped rich electoral dividends since 2012, the year of its founding. This is an exemplary instance of the politics of curative democracy. The first aim of this chapter is to document this phenomenon and establish its salience in contemporary Indian political life. The second aim is to understand the political consequences of curative democracy. How do imaginaries of curing democracy, of clean politics and new politics, shape the terrain and stakes of political contestation and power? Drawing upon ethnographic research and extensive interviews with party workers, and visual and textual documentary records of the party's organizational and mobilizing practices, the chapter maps the everyday micro-practices of curative democracy and the distinctive forms of outsider political agency that are enabled and extended by this political vision. Exactly who gets to cure democracy? Who gets to be a political outsider?

Chapter 2 examines media imaginaries of curative democracy. Through a close look at the social worlds and distinctive work practices of commercial television news media in the early decades of the twenty-first century, I show how a distinctive vision of media's "change agency" took hold, which saw media professionals position themselves as curative democrats. Departing markedly from the liberal-democratic expectations of media as a neutral fourth estate, the role of India's newly liberalized television news media was not so much to provide objective and neutral information as it was to shake up the system and make a difference.

In the second part of the book, *Lineages*, I investigate the historical roots of curative democracy in India. When and how did these ideas about democratic redemption by political outsiders, and the associated complex of institutions and practices that sought to cure the existing democratic system in the name of the people, gain public traction and legitimacy? Chapters 3 and 4 answer this question by turning to a surprisingly underexplored time in Indian political history. This is the "post-emergency" period from the late 1970s to the early 1980s, which followed the period of emergency rule (June 1975–March 1977).

The post-emergency years are widely regarded as a time of democratic restoration, when democracy-as-usual returned to India following Indira Gandhi's sudden and surprising decision to call elections in early 1977. Following the dramatic electoral defeat of Gandhi's Congress party, a new government was formed by the Janata or people's front, a coalition of opposition parties. The newly elected Janata government immediately set about the task of reversing the harmful effects of the emergency regime and putting democracy back on track. In the familiar telling of this tale, things soon settled down and the emergency experience was remembered as an unfortunate but temporary blip in the normal course of Indian democracy.

These chapters tell a different story. Documenting the ambivalent historical origins of curative democracy and outsider politics, I offer a revised political history of India that moves away from "emergency exceptionalism" arguments, to track the long shadow that the emergency cast upon the future course of Indian democracy. Moreover, I argue that the post-emergency period saw the modulation and not the return of Indian democracy. Although the rejection and reversal of the emergency regime was the main task at hand, many emergency-era norms and practices were in fact carried forward, in surprising and unintended ways. It is in this ambivalent context that projects of curative democracy and outsider politics took hold. The promises of democratic reform initiated and led by non-electoral forces such as the media, the judiciary, civil society, and social movements; the calls for "eminent" political outsiders to provide moral leadership and counsel to the people: all grew out of the peculiar admixture of authoritarian and democratic politics that contoured the post-emergency political field.

These chapters also address the more general question of political democracy's relationship to authoritarian political forms. Moving beyond the stark opposition of authoritarianism and democracy, I consider instead their intimacy and complicity or mutual reinforcement. India's experience of democratic reformation in the shadows of an authoritarian past, when democracy's return took forward ideas and practices of people-making, sovereignty, political agency, and representation that a non-democratic old regime had put in place, is not a uniquely Indian outcome. It invites us to consider how democracies might die as they live—through everyday granular complicities and compromises of power; through banal bureaucratic continuities with formally disavowed pasts as much as dramatic regime breakdowns and frontal authoritarian assaults.

The chapters in this section examine various democratic restoration initiatives of the late 1970s and early 1980s that contributed to the rise and hold of outsider politics and curative democracy. Chapter 3 follows the Shah Commission of Inquiry, the official body that was set up by the Janata government to inquire into the "excesses of the emergency." I document how the deliberations of the Shah Commission, and the wider public contexts in which these were communicated and received, produced a new normative imagination of political exteriority. State sovereignty and popular sovereignty, the former associated with law and procedure and the latter with morality and justice, were placed on separate tracks. The chapter discusses the consequences of this separation, and shows how it gave rise to the idea of the political outside as the place of democracy's renewal.

Shifting focus from the political outside as a desired normative space, chapter 4 considers the distinctive forms of political agency that outsiders have exercised in Indian democracy. Through a discussion of two iconic post-emergency innovations, the judicial instrument of public interest litigation and the media practices of "new journalism" and investigative journalism, the chapter documents the authoritative emergence of political outsiders and the making of an intermediated democracy. It shows how new kinds of non-electoral agents and institutions, new techniques of extra-political agency, and new representational claims beyond the ballot box, gained visibility and legitimacy as the intermediaries of democracy's sovereign people.

The Conclusion returns to the contemporary moment once again, to ask how the temporal detour to the Long 1970s makes a difference in our understandings of the present and futures of democracy in India and other parts of the world. Without making causal claims, I end the book by tracing the long and crooked arc that connects the political outsider of the 1970s to the strongman politics of the present.

Slow Research: Notes on Structure, Process, Method

Moving from the present to the 1970s and back to the new millennium's second decade, this book is structured to reflect its process of circuitous and slow research. I initially set out to explain the changing relationship of millennial politics and economy, or how the pro-market restructuring of the Indian economy in the 1990s and beyond had transformed democratic politics in the country. The new politics of new India was my main concern. How had economic liberalization substantially altered the fundamental equation of democratic politics—who gets what, when, and how—and altered as well the public evaluations of these outcomes? How was the new cui bono of Indian democracy judged by its citizens: as right, unfair, intolerable, or a matter of indifference?

I started by investigating two exemplary cases of new politics that were squarely located in our twenty-first-century present, the phenomenon of mediatized democracy or the increasing political clout wielded by television news media, and the successful electoral career of a new political party that was explicitly committed to a political program of transformational politics. The research trail soon strayed from the millennial horizon. It led back several decades and took me to the 1970s and the 1980s as a turning point for democratic politics, when ideas of political innovation and of *democratic* change or reform, not just economic reform, had gained definitive ground. In a manner that was quite different from the usual forward momentum of narrative discovery, individual pieces of the research puzzle that I wrestled with for more than a decade joined up in a reversed and rather haphazard pattern to tell a bigger story. I moved from my original interest in the politics of the present to an earlier time that I had not expected to go to at all.

The process of zooming out or backing up into the Long 1970s was the outcome of my efforts to trace the political genealogies of the present. For instance, when researching the origins of the Aam Aadmi Party, I followed several founder-members to their (self-described) political initiation in the fields of post-emergency activism in the late 1970s and 1980s. Researching the everyday worlds of Indian television news opened out a similar trail of discovery. I found that many of the signature media practices associated with the commercial news media "revolution" of the twenty-first century, such as the hidden camera "sting operations" and the so-called crusades of media activism in the name of justice for ordinary citizens, were originally invented in the late 1970s and early 1980s. The repeated genealogical forays to the post-emergency years did not only temper claims about millennial innovation and the newness of new India. They redirected attention from the idea of economic reform to that of reform itself as a specific political imagination, and pushed me to think about what it means to call for democracy's cleansing and cure as opposed to, say, its expansion or deepening. They drew me to the idea of the political outside/political outsider that loomed large in the post-emergency political field, and to the paradoxical and troubling continuities between emergency and post-emergency visions of curative democracy and outsider politics that I write about here.

The arguments of the book also reflect the long and winding research and writing journey that has produced it. I have been wrestling with different versions of these ideas for over a decade. Over this period, I have moved across three continents and have been located in three different academic worlds of the United States, India, and Germany. My formal job profile and research specialization as a comparative political scientist working on India remained unchanged, but each relocation in a new academic milieu brought me to the study of politics and India with a new set of questions. Moreover, my earlier books were written over a single concentrated period of complete focus on their subject matter. This one, however, was interrupted by several personal and intellectual detours where I found myself thinking and writing about a range of topics that were quite different from the one I had set out with. The subject of this book became a moving target, and the questions I was asking had to be constantly revised and refined. The conceptual and political grounds of my project would shift with each revisit, and yet another facet of the democracy question would come to light. The ideas that I have eventually settled on, about curative democracy, outsider politics, and the Long 1970s, have been churned out of these shifting grounds. They are located at the intersections of these rather untidy, back-and-forth lines of inquiry.

We are familiar with the methodological virtues of multidisciplinary and multi-sited research. The experience of researching and writing this book has underlined an additional, and different, methodological imperative, that of *multi-theme* (or *multiplex*) *research*, where research questions are necessarily plural and lead off into multiple and unexpected empirical and theoretical directions. Whether this should be called an eclectic or a scattershot method I leave up to the individual preference of the reader. Following the trail of curative democracy and the political outsider has meant engaging with a wide range of specialized themes and topics that are embedded in different disciplinary constellations, fields of scholarship, comparative referents, and temporal frames. Media, political parties, public interest litigation, civil society, and social movement activism: each of the themes addressed in the pages that follow has opened up new and different knowledge worlds for me, and pushed forward unexpected and challenging but exciting lines and angles of inquiry.

I

ELEMENTS

THIS SECTION OF THE book maps the core elements of curative democracy—the foundational and constitutive "norms and forms" that structure contemporary political interventions undertaken in the name of healing and fixing democracy. Repeated and widely recognized across diverse public contexts, three elements make up the curative democratic projects that hold sway in India and in many other parts of the world today. First is the diagnosis that democracy is diseased and broken, that it is in urgent need of a cure. It is important to note the specifically *curative* or restorative element here. Democratic despair can be expressed in different ways. It can be a lament for an irreversible decline or fall, perhaps accompanied by nostalgic recollections of a never-to-return golden age of democratic plenitude. It can be a somber catalog of democracy's present inadequacies, which fosters radical dreams of different new worlds. A curative diagnosis of democracy plots yet another arc. Neither irreversible nor disjunctive, it is a stock-taking of democracy's *solvable* problems. It is all about returning to a former condition of democratic health. Return, repair, restoration, reform. Neither rejection nor revolution.

Following from this is the second elemental form of curative democracy: the redemptive agency of the political outsider. Curative democratic projects look to the political outside. They authorize and celebrate particular non-electoral modes of political representation. Democracy's cure is invariably linked to the timely interventions of individuals and institutions that stand outside and apart from the system. Third, all curative democratic projects draw on distinctive affective registers of public outrage and anger. Quite different from the rational "well-tempered self" of liberal democracy, here the citizen is an angry, distrustful, and thoroughly fed-up political subject who calls for immediate change. Enough!

Sick democracy, energetic political outsiders, and angry citizens fill the pages that follow. They are tracked through the everyday worlds and political interventions of two prime agents of curative democracy in millennial India: a new anti-corruption political party and commercial television news media organizations. In different but related ways, these self-described "crusaders" for the *aam aadmi*, the ordinary people, positioned themselves in the first decades of the twenty-first century as political outsiders who would heal and restore Indian democracy back to its original constitutional health. We will see that the social identities of these crusaders are quite complex and varied. In contrast to the broad-brushstroke depictions of the elite or middle-class provenance of such politics that dominate so many of our discussions today, exploring the worlds of Aam Aadmi Party workers and commercial television news workers confronted me with fragmented and heterogeneous social milieus that defied any easy classification as elite or subaltern. The chapters that follow take up this finding of social heterogeneity and try to make sense of this mixed and mixed-up world of curative democracy outside the paradigm of celebratory cosmopolitanism.

ONE

NEW POLITICS[1]

IN DECEMBER 2013, A new Indian political party called the Aam Aadmi Party (the Party of the Ordinary Citizen/Common Man, popularly known as AAP)[2] won the state assembly elections and formed the government in the northern Indian state of Delhi.[3] The victory was notable not just because of the electoral novelty of a brand-new party defeating well-established rivals to decisively win an election. The AAP's electoral triumph also signaled the arrival of a distinctive anti-establishment outsider discourse in Delhi's political culture. Promises to clean up the corrupt and inefficient politics of electoral democracy, bring new and politically untainted representatives into public office, and enable ordinary and politically uninvolved individuals to be effective citizens dominated the AAP electoral campaign, and the strong electoral mandate that the party received showed that a great number of Delhi's voters believed in these promises.

In the aftermath of the elections, it seemed that these campaign promises were being realized. A new "anti-establishment establishment"[4] was taking shape. Almost all the new AAP legislators sworn into office were political novices from a range of different career backgrounds. For instance, the chief minister and party leader Arvind Kejriwal was an engineer and ex-bureaucrat who had resigned from the Indian civil services in 2001 to set up a nongovernmental organization that fought political corruption and advocated for transparency and the freedom of information.[5] Somnath Bharti, the newly appointed law minister, was another political outsider. A thirty-nine-year-old lawyer who had also been trained as an engineer at the same elite institute of engineering education as chief minister Kejriwal, the Indian Institute of Technology in Delhi, Bharti had a flourishing legal practice that allowed him to lead a comfortable upper-middle-class life in South Delhi.

Bharti's election campaign was centrally focused on the party's agenda of new and transformative politics. At small neighborhood meetings and large public rallies in his South Delhi constituency of Malviya Nagar, he promised to usher in a new era of efficient, transparent, and noncorrupt government, and urged party workers and voters to join him in his efforts to clean up the system. One such exercise took place on the night of January 14, 2014, just about two weeks after he assumed office as Delhi's law minister.

Close to midnight, Bharti and a group of male AAP supporters stormed into the South Delhi neighborhood of Khirki, armed with smartphones and video cameras, to conduct a surprise raid on an alleged drugs and prostitution ring run by African residents. Witness statements after the event described how the AAP team tried to force their way into a house where several African migrants lived. Claiming that it was a brothel, they demanded that the women in the house come outside and show their identification documents to the law minister and his men. Local police constables were called to enforce the demand. But the police refused to follow Bharti's instructions to enter the premises without a valid warrant or a female police officer on the team, and the minister called for "higher-ups" in the police hierarchy to intervene.

The AAP men continued with their self-appointed task of law enforcement while they waited for a new police team to arrive. Some of the AAP workers gave chase to several African women who were out on the street at the time and had run away, frightened by the commotion. Bharti and a few others turned their attention to a car parked on the side of the road in which some women were seated, also of African origin. The men entered the car and filmed their discovery of a "suspicious" white powder inside, heckling and taunting the passengers all the while and insisting that they go for medical tests. A new police team eventually arrived on the scene, and another angry altercation ensued when they too refused to follow the law minister's directive. Several hours later, the crowd dispersed without a resolution.

Unsurprisingly the midnight raid attracted a lot of media attention, and journalists demanded explanations from the AAP leadership. Bharti argued that his actions were both morally and legally valid; he had responded to the legitimate concerns and fears of Khirki's ordinary citizens. A video prepared by AAP supporters circulated widely on social media, claiming that the raid was an exemplary democratic act. Titled *Khirki ka sach* (Khirki's truth), it presented testimonies from residents about their difficult existence amid the menace of sex and drugs peddled by African "foreigners" in the neighborhood, and the failure of the police to act on their many complaints. The video concluded with several Khirki residents praising the law minister's timely intervention and his commitment to their needs and interests.[6]

This video presentation of Bharti's raid as an exemplary democratic act of responsive intervention, something that had taken place only because the good citizens of Khirki had called for such an action, was echoed and amplified by the AAP leadership. At a press conference convened shortly afterward, chief minister Kejriwal presented the Khirki raid as proof of the new party's commitment to the common man, contrasting the decisive interventions of Bharti and his men with the studied indifference and failure to act on the part of the Delhi police. The intransigence of the Delhi police who were controlled by the central government, and their refusal to accept the authority of a popularly elected law minister, Kejriwal argued, was yet another example of how establishment forces beholden to selfish concerns of power and pelf routinely let the people down.

Amplifying this populist plotline of the battle of representation, of how the true representatives of the people were challenging those who had wrongfully usurped the mantle of popular representation all these years, the AAP government announced an indefinite public strike, highlighting the unequal distribution of powers in Indian federalism to present itself as the brave little state fighting against the autocratic central establishment. Party leaders demanded that the home ministry of the central government, under whose authority the Delhi police functioned, should immediately fire the police chief and other senior police officers. The demand was framed in terms of popular sovereignty and its restoration: how, by changing the peculiar federal arrangement that placed Delhi police under the exclusive control of the central government, the sovereign will of the people of Delhi could be realized.[7]

In the AAP's official narrative, the democratic value of the Khirki raid was not just about the immediate relief that party workers had delivered to the residents of Khirki that night. Rather, the raid and the subsequent activism that it sparked had wider and far-reaching significance as acts of curative democracy that would clean up and fix the broken political system. For the AAP and its many advocates, Bharti's dramatic and decisive interventions brought the party's promise of delivering accountable and truly representative government to the *aam aadmi* one step closer to fulfilment.

Outside party circles, however, a rather different account of the raids prevailed. In marked contrast to the positive media attention that the AAP attracted in this initial phase of its existence, media coverage of the Khirki raid was strongly critical. Several commentators described Bharti's initiative as an illegal form of vigilante action.[8] It was also condemned as an act of racially motivated discrimination and violence. The accounts of the raid, when groups of Indian men had dragged terrified Nigerian and Ugandan women into their vehicles and forcibly insisted on urine and blood tests, were startling and disturbing to many who thought that Bharti had gone too far. Individuals had been targeted for engaging in illegal "sex and drugs" activity purely on hearsay, just because they "looked African." From this perspective, far from being democracy's salve, the Khirki action expressed and further sharpened the violent inequalities and the discriminatory ethos of Indian democracy.

Delhi's large migrant population includes migrants from several African countries. Although they come to the city for many different reasons, most live precarious and vulnerable lives on the margins of legal and social legibility in urban areas such as Khirki, a densely populated neighborhood with a variety of semi-legal tenancy arrangements. Despite the diversity of their individual circumstances and migration contexts, African migrants in India are commonly subjected to a historically entrenched and socially sanctioned regime of racial distinction, hierarchy, and anti-blackness that reflects the complex legacies of colonialism and caste stratification in the South Asian subcontinent. Racial tensions have heightened over the recent decades of accelerated economic growth, deepening economic inequality, and a visible increase in African migrant presence in Indian cities. Alongside the micro-injuries of casual racial slurs and the slow boil of everyday discrimination manifested in extortionate rents, the absence of even basic tenancy rights of privacy and security, the inability to register businesses and open bank accounts, and the denial of visa extensions and regularizations, there have also been several incidents of overt violence against Africans in Delhi and other major Indian cities in recent years.[9] For critics of the AAP's interventions in Khirki, the raids had to be understood against this racially charged backdrop of urban life in Delhi. From this perspective, Bharti's actions emerged out of and furthered racist and counterdemocratic political imaginaries. They were violent assertions of hierarchical power.

The difference between these two sharply opposed views on the Khirki raids, the one that celebrates a bold intervention to repair and fulfill the promises of democracy, the other that condemns an expression of racialized hierarchy, drives this chapter. How do we understand the Khirki raid and the broader political project of political cleansing and curative democracy that it is a part of? What exactly are calls to cure democracy calls to *do*—what forms of individual, collective, and institutional agency do curative democracy projects enable? What are the social roots and contexts of curative democracy—who gets to be a curative democrat and a political outsider acting in the name of the common man? And what exactly is this common, this ordinary, that legitimizes all of these efforts of democratic reform and remedy?

I answer these questions by taking a close look at the political praxis of India's Aam Aadmi Party in the initial years of its existence as it went about the task of party-building and mobilizing individuals to work for its mission of a new and clean politics. I draw on two distinct types and periods of field research: (1) in-depth and ethnographic participant-observation research on the everyday practices of party-building, volunteer mobilization, organizational routines, and voter outreach by AAP full-time party workers, part-time volunteers, and electoral candidates during the party's first electoral campaign (2013) when it was struggling to establish itself as a viable political force;[10] and (2) shorter and interview-centered return visits to previous fieldwork subjects and sites at a time when the AAP formed the government in Delhi (2015, 2018, 2019).

Through this ethnographically grounded examination of both the insurgent/anti-establishment and governance/establishment phases of the AAP, this chapter maps the details of the democratic reform imaginary of curative democracy that gained public salience in early twenty-first-century India. These include the distinctive notions of "terminal democracy" or the diagnosis of a diseased and moribund democratic system that urgently requires restorative intervention; the *aam aadmi* (ordinary citizen or common man) as the main political and moral subject of democracy (and also the main victim of democracy's present dysfunction); and the political outsider as the authentic representative of the people and the agent of democracy's redemption and cure.

The chapter also documents the socially situated character of AAP politics. I show that the AAP's distinctive projects of democratic reform and new politics have socially uneven effects. They are connected to and resonate within particular socioeconomic milieus, and they empower certain kinds of individuals to act and represent more than others. I suggest that more than political equality and popular participation, AAP's imagination of a new and clean politics is concerned with the restoration of social authority. It is a form of *ownership* or *proprietorial democracy*, a term that I explain in further detail below. The two accounts of the Khirki raids may be less inimical than it would appear at first glance.

ESTABLISHING THE ANTI-ESTABLISHMENT

Anti-corruption

The AAP was established as a new political party in November 2012. Its political origins lay in a series of anti-corruption street protests that erupted in Delhi in the spring and summer of 2011 and were widely covered by national and international media. This was the Anna revolution, so named after the elderly rural activist Babu Kisanrao "Anna"[11] Hazare, whose hunger strike[12] drew thousands of citizens to Delhi's Ramlila Maidan to protest the endemic corruption of the political classes.[13] Although the media presented the protests as spontaneous uprisings of angry citizens, a considerable degree of organizational support and preparation from India Against Corruption (IAC), a loosely allied group of civil society activists that had formed in the early months of 2011, had laid the groundwork.[14] Arvind Kejriwal, a former civil servant and well-known right-to-information[15] activist, was a leading member of this group. Fierce disagreements within the IAC in the aftermath of the summer protests created strained relations between Kejriwal and Hazare in the fall of 2011.

A major source of tension was the question of political entry, that is, whether the cause of anti-corruption and democratic reform should be addressed from within or outside the arena of party politics. Against this backdrop of contention, the formation of a new political party marked a definitive parting of ways with the Hazare movement's commitment to political renunciation, although Kejriwal and other AAP members stressed the reluctance of their political decision, and repeatedly described their political entry as an act of *majboori*, or compulsion. Nevertheless, the very fact of existing as a political party, and of approaching the goal of political reform through the "dirty" electoral politics that it accused of tarnishing and corrupting the political system, set the AAP apart from the various movements of political transcendence that have regularly surfaced in India, the Gandhian variant of the Indian nationalist movement being the most well-known of these.[16]

As a direct legatee of the anti-corruption agitations of 2011, the AAP's primary identity was that of an anti-corruption party. The IAC movement's demand for a Jan Lokpal bill, that is, legislation to create a national ombuds institution that would hold political representatives accountable, anchored the AAP's electoral campaign as well. The party vowed that it would quit office if it failed to enact the legislation within fifteen days of forming the government. Vivid accounts of the recent multibillion-rupee corruption "scams" implicating incumbent national and state governments were campaign staples. The theme of corruption was offered up as the master narrative for all the problems faced by ordinary citizens in the course of their daily lives, no matter how banal or small.

Take, for instance, the six main points highlighted in the manifesto that the AAP released ahead of the 2013 elections. If elected to power the party promised to (1) pass a Lokpal [ombudsperson] bill establishing independent oversight and prosecutorial/punitive authority over public servants within fifteen days of entering office; (2) enable *swaraj* or self-rule by devolving decision-making power on developmental issues to local *mohalla sabhas* [neighborhood assemblies]; (3) reduce electricity bills by 50 percent after a mandatory audit of private electricity suppliers was carried out by the controller and auditor general's office; (4) provide all residents of Delhi with seven hundred liters of free water daily and ensure that the city's apex water supply agency, the Delhi Jal Board, placed all information about the supply and distribution of water in the public domain; (5) build sanitation and waste management infrastructure; and (6) establish civilian "Citizens Security Forces" to provide security to women, children, and senior citizens.

The first five of these points were directly connected to the anti-corruption theme, either in diagnostic terms (for example, corruption was explicitly identified as the reason why electricity and water bills are high, or why sanitation infrastructure is so inadequate), or as iterations of demands that were raised during the anti-corruption movement of 2011 (such as the passage of a Lokpal bill). Even the sixth point on women's security was linked to the same theme. To address public concern over the increasing incidence of gender and sexual violence in the capital city, the AAP chose to highlight the lapses of the political system, and focused on the willful neglect of police and the judiciary as the main source of the problems. Crumbling hospitals, racing electricity meters, unqualified schoolteachers, empty water taps, and violence against women all stemmed from the same root cause of the political system's failure, party activists averred.

Once elected to power, the AAP pledged to bring all of this to a swift and decisive end by installing an elaborate architecture of monitoring and regulation involving material apparatuses like surveillance cameras, and legal and institutional structures like independent ombuds agencies to hold authorities accountable. In the new era of good governance that it would usher in, water taps would run fast and free, lights would shine bright and cheap, streets would be wide and clean, students would graduate from high-tech neighborhood schools, women would be safe, and excellent health care would be readily available for all, the party promised.

Several critics argued that this rather vague and negative idea of ending political corruption was the party's sole cause, and speculated that the lack of a constructive agenda was a serious limitation on the party's ability to attract voters.[17] But party leaders explicitly challenged such accounts of the AAP as a party with a single and negative agenda of anti-corruption. As Yogendra Yadav, a political scientist and founding member of the party, argued in an interview, "while on the face of it, the AAP looks like an anti-corruption movement, the most powerful strand in it is about the radical restructuring of political power."[18] In a similar vein, Yadav's colleague and prominent public interest lawyer Prashant Bhushan defined the party's aim as that of "chang[ing] the very system and functioning of democracy" so that "local people" have "control."[19]

Bhushan and Yadav's rather anodyne phrases capture two key elements of the AAP's positive political vision: *ownership democracy* and *transformational politics*. Along with the *aam aadmi* or the ordinary citizen from which the party's name derives, these were the main normative anchors of the AAP's political project at the time of its electoral debut. Let us take a closer look.

Aam aadmi

The idea of the ordinary was the party's foundational and defining idea, its master concept. The 2013 election campaign addressed the ordinary citizen or the common man as the main political subject of democracy, and hence the main constituency that the AAP represented. Two distinct but related projects unfolded in parallel: establishing that the AAP was indeed the authentic representative of the ordinary citizen, and specifying what ordinariness meant in the first place.

The party's claims of ordinary representation were advanced with the help of several different kinds of symbolic and communicative practices and choices. These included the selection of a mundane household object, the *jharu* or broom, as the party's official electoral symbol;[20] the "bush shirt-*chappal*-muffler"[21] sartorial garb of Arvind Kejriwal, which connoted urban middle-class respectability and nondescript humbleness to Indian audiences; and the circulation of images of party leaders crowded into a Maruti Suzuki Wagon R car driven by Arvind Kejriwal that figured within a single image of a car both the AAP's distance from other political parties and its intimate familiarity with the ordinary lifeworlds of the urban middle classes.[22]

But what, who, and where was this ordinary? The AAP's inaugural election campaign offered varied answers to this question. The *aam aadmi* was an empty and shifting signifier that did not have a singular or stable referent. Multiple meanings of the ordinary surfaced in the course of the 2013 campaign, and different themes and social identities were emphasized in different social settings. In the double entendre–filled speech of popular Hindi poet and public speaker Kumar Vishwas as he enthused a large crowd that had gathered in an empty lot in Chhattarpur constituency late on a September evening in 2013, the *aam aadmi* was caste Hindu, male, north Indian. Ordinary citizens in this urban village were *mitti ke beton*, sons of the soil, Vishwas reminded the crowd:

> Why aren't you clapping and cheering louder? Why do you sound like those rich ladies in the 7 crore [million-dollar] houses of New Friends Colony who are worried about smudging their lipstick? Go ahead and shout *Bharat Mata Ki Jai*, Victory to Mother India, in a *mitti ke beton* way![23]

The manicured public parks of Vasant Vihar, a "posh" residential area in the RK Puram constituency, configured the ordinary citizen differently, more lipstick lady than earthy son, to quote Vishwas' imagery. Speaking to a group of elderly citizens resting on Vasant Vihar's park benches after their morning walk, the AAP candidate Shazia Ilmi described "our" *aam* concerns in a mix of fluent English and Hindi. She related these not to the poor quality of government schools that the speakers at the Chhattarpur rally had lamented, but to the crumbling park benches that "those people," the "uneducated types" in power, had refused to repair.[24]

A short distance but entire world away, the narrow snaking alleys of the Bhanwar Singh Camp campaign site yielded yet another version. In this semi-legal settlement lacking basic civic infrastructure, the *aam aadmi* addressed by the AAP campaign belonged to the urban precariat. Like the walkers in the Vasant Vihar park and the urban villagers of Chhattarpur, he was described as a victim of callous politicians. But in this slum location he bore other burdens as well. He was a victim of his own ignorance, fear, and *gandagi ki aadat* (dirty habits), party worker Omendra Bharat ruefully observed.[25]

As these varied constructions of ordinary identity make clear, the political demands of the ordinary were very different across different social settings. In the name of the *aam aadmi,* the AAP campaign called for different kinds of redemptive and remedial actions. In some instances, ordinariness was the staging ground for moral righteousness. The AAP campaign called the *aam aadmi* to action as a redemptive agent of politics, the true subject of democracy who had been mistreated and neglected for too long, and to whom the party was giving a space and a voice to realize herself as an effective citizen. At other times, the injunction of the ordinary was pedagogical and protective. Activating older meanings of the *aam aadmi* as a member of the marginalized socioeconomic classes whose well-being and betterment guided the project of national development, ordinariness connoted deprivation and vulnerability. Here the AAP campaign called the ordinary citizen to action as a subject of instruction and improvement, as someone who was ready to be guided and instructed by the party to be a proper citizen (such as by learning to vote for the right reasons).

There was a clear sociological pattern to these variations of political demand. The call to morally righteous action and the call to instructional citizenship were addressed to different social constituencies: the former to middle-class and elite residents, and the latter to the urban poor. As the AAP sought to bring together the disparate social classes that inhabited the city, the capaciousness of the *aam aadmi* as a term that could be filled with very different meanings, and the open-ended cause of anti-corruption that could be linked to a wide range of societal problems, from the insecurities faced by women on the streets of Delhi to the lack of civic infrastructure, served this aim.

Ownership Democracy

The AAP campaign also drew on and furthered a distinctive politics of *ownership democracy*, summed up in Bhushan's description of democracy as a system where local people have control. The association here of democratic politics and political agency with the specific act of control is instructive. For the AAP, the ideal citizen speaks from the position of an owner or proprietor of a (national) political system, an agent whose main intention is to control the object that she or he possesses. Moving beyond the usual vocabularies of belonging, community, and solidarity that are associated with the idea and practice of citizenship, AAP discourse emphasizes the ownership or proprietorial ties that bind citizen and state, and invest the owner-citizen with the right to demand answers, accounts, and accountability from his government.[26] It is from this position of ownership that projects of democratic repair and remedy are proposed: the citizen acts to fix something that already belongs to her or him. The claim of citizenship is constituted as a reminder, an activation of existent rights and entitlements, rather than a demand for something different and new.

This is a distinctive formulation. Drawing attention to the historically contextualized "grounds of citizenship," the anthropologist Julia Eckert has shown how different countries reveal "different grounds of legitimation [of citizenship] at play and different ways of reasoning as to why one is owed rights by the state."[27] For instance, marginalized urban citizens make claims on the state by harnessing ideas of "contributor rights" in Brazil, logics of international comparison in Turkey, and professions of loyalty and appeals to reciprocal obligation in Georgia. Even though the formal act of claiming a citizenship right is identical, the mode of claims-making, the meaning of the right, and the imagination of citizenship and of the state are quite different in each of these cases, she shows. The AAP's vision of democratic citizenship presents yet another variation, of citizens making claims on the state through the assertion and activation of ownership rights.

In public discussions and campaign rallies leading up to the December 2013 elections, a common refrain of AAP leaders and volunteers was the *malik-naukar*, or master-servant, relationship. Repeating almost verbatim the phrases that had popularized by right-to-information activists in the previous decade, party leaders and workers promised to restore power to its rightful place and orientation: the people as master, the government as "paid servant." The association of government with the idea of service of some kind is hardly new, and phrases like "public service" or "public servant" are familiar descriptors for the role of government in society both in India and elsewhere. Nevertheless, there were two aspects of the AAP's *malik-naukar* discourse of proprietary citizenship that set it apart from prevailing linguistic conventions: first, the specific sense of servitude and its attendant power hierarchies that are conveyed in contemporary uses of the Hindi word *naukar*, and second, the idea of the paid servant and of the wage relation as the means by which people-as-master can legitimately call the government-as-servant to account. These in turn point to another key dimension of proprietary citizenship discourses, namely the normative centrality of the taxpayer-citizen in their imagination of democracy.

The discourses of the AAP campaign in 2013, like those of the right-to-information and anti-corruption activist movements from which the party had emerged, presented the taxpaying citizen as the main protagonist of democratic politics and the act of taxpaying as a fundamental and even a constitutive democratic act. Take for example the 2006 promotional video on the "Drive Against Bribes" campaign led by Parivartan [Change], a nongovernmental organization founded by the AAP's main leader Arvind Kejriwal[28] to promote the awareness and use of right to information legislation by residents of Delhi's slum settlements. In the opening scenes of the video we see Kejriwal surrounded by a large crowd. Gesturing animatedly to his audience, he asks forcefully, "Those who pay taxes please raise your hand!" The camera pans over the obviously working-class gathering, capturing the hesitation and incomprehension of onlookers. Kejriwal counts the meager handful of raised hands and launches into a passionate speech in a scene that is worth reproducing in full as a textbook example of the taxpayer-citizen theme and the political imagination of ownership democracy.

[Kejriwal]: Out of so many people just eight people pay taxes? Lies, all lies! All of you pay taxes. You don't even know that you pay taxes. Even the poorest of the poor has to pay taxes. Even a beggar has to pay taxes.

[Voice-over]: Every citizen pays a lot of taxes, sometimes without one's knowledge.

[Another activist expands on Kejriwal's point]: When a baby is born, tax is charged on the first injection administered to it. When a person is dying, tax is charged on the last medicine given to him. A person keeps paying taxes to the government right from his birth to his death.

[Kejriwal]: Who is the owner of all this money collected as taxes? Is it the government officials or the public? We are the owners of these taxes. The government officials are our servants because they get their salaries out of our money. So, government officials are our . . . ?

[Crowd shouts back]: SERVANTS!

[Kejriwal]: All the ministers are our . . . ?

[Crowd shouts back]: SERVANTS!

[Kejriwal]: We are the masters and they are the servants! Who is the master of this country? We are the master of our country. The public is the master of this country. . . .

[Voice-over]: But in this relation of master and servant in the last fifty years the master never demanded accountability from his servant. He had no idea how his hard-earned money, paid as taxes, has been spent all these years. He doesn't even know how to ask for accounts. . . .[29]

The three main ideas of ownership democracy are captured in this brief scene. First, the video presents taxes as the defining or constitutive element of democratic citizenship. Paid by the rich as well as the "poorest of the poor," they create common ground between otherwise disconnected social constituencies. Taxes are also the means and ground of democratic accountability. The payment of taxes turns citizens into masters and government officials into paid servants who can be held to account. Second, democratic empowerment is envisioned in terms that are more proprietorial than participatory. The demand is not so much to join and participate in decision-making, but to claim oversight and "monitory power" over governing practices and arrangements.[30] It is not so much to share power, but to exercise control over the powerful and remind government officials and elected representatives of their subordinate position in the hierarchy of state-citizen relations.

Third, the master-servant analogy used by Parivartan volunteers, as well as by the AAP in subsequent years, shows that discourses of ownership democracy activate a hierarchical political imagination. The master-servant rhetoric was particularly resonant in the urban milieu of the "JJ colony"[31] or the paralegal urban settlement in which the Parivartan video was shot, where many inhabitants earned their living as domestic workers in the houses of the city's rich and middle classes, commonly referred to as *naukars* or servants by their employers. Holding out the promise of a radical reversal of roles—the last shall be first—it left the hierarchies of servitude undisturbed. The dream was to become the master, rather than the leveling or even the questioning of master-servant inequalities as such.

Transformational Politics

The final set of political themes that anchored the AAP's political vision was about distinction and innovation, or what we might term transformational politics. Marking its difference from the 2011 anti-corruption movement's well-publicized call to exit the corrupt and dirty mess of electoral politics,[32] the AAP urged political entry, but in ways that would fundamentally transform the practice of politics itself. Like anti-party parties or outsider parties in other parts of the world, the theme of bringing about a radically new or transformational politics, of enabling Indians to say "no to politics of substitution, yes to politics of alternatives,"[33] was foregrounded by the AAP in its founding phase.

Moreover, transformational politics was presented as a systemic enterprise that went well beyond the usual canvas of legal and policy changes that feature in electoral campaigns, to a promised overhaul of the cultures and conditions of politics as such. Casting itself as the agent and enabler of a *doosri azadi*, a second freedom movement, and likening party work to the regime-overturning actions of militant anticolonial nationalists in the early decades of the twentieth century like Bhagat Singh and Chandrashekhar Azad, the AAP offered a grand redemptive vision for Indian democracy that connected mundane acts like voting and campaigning for a party to the revolutionary actions of larger-than-life historical heroes.

Here the specific choice of Singh and Azad as historical exemplars is significant. By calling upon supporters and voters to emulate individuals who had contradicted the prevailing reformist anticolonial common sense of the time in order to carry out assassinations, bomb attacks, and other daring acts of revolutionary resistance against the British Empire, the AAP underscored the ambitious scope of its transformational politics. To support the party, the 2013 campaign repeatedly emphasized, was to inhabit history and be worthy of remembrance and recall by future generations. In interviews, many AAP workers emphasized these themes of historical agency and meaning when describing their motivations for party work. When their future grandchildren asked them one day what they had done during the struggle for India's *doosri azadi*, the actions and choices that they were making today would furnish them with a fitting reply, they told us. As they explained it, their work for the AAP allowed the quotidian and banal present to be remade as the glorious past of an anticipated future, the transformational moment when true democracy would finally be established in India.

The new politics of "Democracy 2.0" that the AAP spoke of, to quote a phrase coined by party intellectuals Yogendra Yadav and Anand Kumar,[34] did not exist only as an exhortation or a future promise. Rather, it was configured as a visible and material set of activities that took place in the present. Embodying, and visibly demonstrating its distinctive brand of transformational politics, was of vital importance to the party's mobilizing practices, as I explore in further detail below. New politics was about manifestly *being* the change. It was about the public presentation of particular acts that were visibly different from politics-as-usual. These included practices of fundraising, candidate selection, and public communication, in other words, all the classic components of party politics. In each of these domains of party practice, the AAP strove to visibly demonstrate its embrace of a new way of *sachai* and *imandari*, truthfulness and honesty, that marked a radical departure from the corrupt and mendacious ways of establishment political parties.

Displaying Distinctions

Campaign finance was the first arena of differentiation. The AAP's commitment to financially transparent modes of fundraising was prominently foregrounded in its official discourse. Campaign events highlighted the party's unique policy of accepting only "white" or legal donations, and drew attention to the publicly accessible political donations database that featured prominently on the AAP website. Practices of candidate selection and the distribution of tickets were also singled out. For the Delhi assembly elections of 2013, the AAP created and publicized a system of candidate selection that combined "public input" and "character vetting," borrowing from models of participatory democracy as well as from corporate financial practices such as credit checks. Indeed, the very fact that there was such a publicly acknowledged system was itself a considerable departure from the usual opaque backroom deals of Indian party politics.[35]

Communication and publicity comprised a third arena of differentiation. The party's innovations in the use of new and social media technologies, and the involvement of people not usually associated with party political campaigns in India, such as information technology (IT) professionals, self-described "internet geeks," and nonresident Indians from across the world, attracted considerable media attention and yielded a fortuitous cascade of publicity.[36] The AAP's high-visibility reliance on new and social media and digital interventions was described by the party as well as by outside observers as an ingenious means of direct public address that bypassed mainstream media (commercial television channels and newspapers).[37]

Finally, the AAP established its distinctive identity as the agent of a decidedly new politics through its careful cultivation and demonstration of a specific model of political leadership. This was quite literally embodied in the figure of party leader Arvind Kejriwal, whose personal biography and sartorial style set him apart from the familiar and derided figure of the Indian politician or *neta*. Illustrating the party's reliance on a visible or materially manifest politics of newness, Kejriwal's physical appearance and demeanor came up for special emphasis in the party's discourse. Party narratives dwelled on the ordinariness of Kejriwal's biography: his small-town, humble origins as "no one's son" that was a reference not to unknown paternity of course, but to the Kejriwal family's distance from established circuits of political power. Campaign speeches spoke of how the diminutive "*saade paanch foot Kejriwal*" [five-and-a-half-foot-tall Kejriwal] was battling and defeating the bloated political establishment. The media also picked up on this theme. The *New Yorker*'s description of Kejriwal's visual appearance as akin to that of an "industrious schoolteacher" is only one example of how his presentation as a new kind of political leader was linked in public discussions to an appraisal of his personal look and style, whether his middle-class attire or his soft-spoken, conversational oratory.[38]

The theme of a different leadership was also presented in several other ways. Official party statements repeatedly emphasized how the bulk of AAP's leadership comprised successful professionals with nonpolitical careers, whose comfortable lives and social statuses meant that they did not regard politics as an arena for personal enrichment. In what would soon become a defining theme of party rhetoric, the AAP's leadership cohort was also singled out for its commitment to a politics that was above identity. The political outsiders at the helm of the AAP signaled in various ways their distance from and distaste toward the matrix of caste and communal calculations in which India's partisan political culture is steeped.

An example often cited by the party leadership was that of Shazia Ilmi, a member of the AAP's national executive, whose electoral campaign from the South Delhi constituency of RK Puram was showcased as an exemplary instance of post-identity politics. Ilmi's example was cited as an instance of how, defying the usual calculations about ethno-religious vote-banks that drive electoral strategies in Indian party politics, a party had chosen a Muslim woman candidate from a constituency where Muslims were a negligible presence. Ilmi herself would repeatedly make a similar point when discussing with us her reasons for joining the party. The AAP, she argued, was the only political party that did not treat her as a particular type, a secular Muslim or a Muslim woman. "Here I am just Shazia." I will examine the particular normative implications and the empirical viability of this idea of general or unmarked identity[39] later on in the chapter. For now let me note its signaling function in the AAP's political project of newness.

The discussion thus far has focused on the official political agenda of the AAP. Differing from the widely held view that the AAP's initial appearance on the Indian political scene was linked to the negative and single-issue agenda of anti-corruption, I have pointed to the party's broader and positive political and ideological vision of ownership democracy and transformational politics. However, formal pronouncements and vision statements can only provide a partial answer to the question that this chapter addresses, about the societal foundations and engagements of new, anti-establishment parties such as the AAP. How did these ideas circulate beyond leadership circles, in the wider social spaces that sustained the party? How and why did they motivate individuals to join the party? How were these formal commitments interpreted and put to work by party workers and volunteers? In the next section, I address these questions by looking at the everyday practices of party-building. Drawing upon research conducted in party offices in three Delhi constituencies, I document how the official precepts of the party, and the broad intention of curing the existing disease of democracy, were given life by party workers in the course of their daily party activities.

An Ordinary Volunteer

Chhattarpur is one of the seventy legislative assembly constituencies of the state of Delhi, located on the southwestern border between Delhi and the neighboring state of Haryana. Electoral politics in this constituency is widely seen to be dominated by the "old politics" of identitarian voting that AAP explicitly rejects. For instance, in previous assembly elections all political parties have fielded candidates belonging to the Gujjar caste, since it is widely believed that a non-Gujjar candidate would not be electorally viable in a constituency where Gujjars comprise a sizable percentage of the population.

Hrishipal "Pehelwan" (Hrishipal the Wrestler) had defeated three other short-listed applicants to be nominated as the AAP candidate from Chhattarpur for the 2013 assembly elections. Hrishipal was a literal big man of the area. A former wrestler from the locality of Ayanagar in the Chhattarpur constituency, he owned a thriving local *akhara* or wrestling academy, and also ran a flourishing real estate business. Like the other politicians from Chhattarpur, including the incumbent member of the legislative assembly (MLA) from the Congress, Balram Tanwar, and his BJP rival Brahm Singh Tanwar, Hrishipal belonged to the Tanwar (Tomar) subcaste of Gujjars. Living in the agrarian hinterlands of Haryana outside the city limits of Delhi, numerous individuals from these rural farming communities had reaped windfall profits from the commercial land markets generated by Delhi's urban expansion in recent decades.

Hrishipal was clearly a man of significant means. In our research team's conversations with local residents we were repeatedly given details of the numerous expensive sport utility vehicles and farmhouses that he owned.[40] Most of these accounts of Hrishipal's wealth ended with affirmations of his personal modesty, and how he had remained amazingly "simple." Stories about his single pair of trousers made of "old-fashioned terrycot" were legion. We heard anecdotes about how Hrishipal rejected air-conditioning during Delhi's blistering summers and slept outdoors on a basic rural-style *charpai* (string cot). We heard about how he had defied social and family expectations to insist on the receipt of a mere one-rupee token dowry for his son's wedding.

We met Rajdeep Pathak,[41] a volunteer working on Hrishipal's campaign, during our first visit to the Chhattarpur campaign office on a hot and sticky Sunday afternoon in September 2013.[42] Located opposite the Gujjar Football Heroes Playing Field in the Ayanagar locality of Chhattarpur, the office was located in a single-floor building owned by Hrishipal. A sparsely furnished room with a few scattered red and white plastic chairs, a small desk tucked away in one corner, and a wooden bench heaped with AAP banners and posters served as the main office area. Pathak spent most of his time in a small computer room that led off from the main office, working with a team of four other men on a bank of desktop computers. Several people in the main office directed us to Pathak as someone who could tell you everything about the local affairs of the AAP in Chhattarpur.

Pathak was thirty-two, married with two children, he told us. He lived in the Jaunapur locality of Chhattarpur. He worked as an assistant manager with an automobile retail company, where he managed their sales of commercial vehicles. Film stars like Amitabh Bachchan used to be the only icons and heroes who mattered to him, he recounted. But then he read about Anna Hazare—*Time magazine ka hero, world ka hero* (*Time* magazine's hero, world hero)—and was inspired to visit the anti-corruption protests at Delhi's Ramlila Grounds in the summer of 2011. He encountered Arvind Kejriwal there, and everything changed. Now everybody else is "below Arvind," Pathak said, even nationalist icons like Jawaharlal Nehru and Mahatma Gandhi. "Arvind comes forward by keeping people alive, Gandhi got people killed," he declared cryptically.

Kejriwal's decision to form a political party toward the end of 2012 provided Pathak's self-described hero worship with a concrete outlet. In the summer of 2013, after six months of careful financial preparations, he went to his boss and submitted his resignation letter, informing him of his plans to work for the AAP. Overcome with tears at his own inability to follow Pathak's lead, the boss tried to convince him to stay, but to no avail. Pathak remained resolute, and left to work for the AAP.

This encounter assumed special significance in Pathak's narrative. With evident pride, he repeated multiple times the contrast at the heart of the story. Despite being the sole breadwinner of his family, he could easily walk away from his job to join AAP, but his wealthy boss remained trapped in the web of social and familial obligations and failed to exercise his free will. Each new iteration of this narrative drew approving murmurs from his colleagues in the party office who had gathered around us as we conversed. In emphasizing the considerable costs of his decision, Pathak's account of joining the AAP resonates with a broader and enduring discourse about political sacrifice that has considerable traction in Indian political history.[43] Pathak's motivational narrative also extended beyond these familiar sacrificial parameters to foreground the risks that he had taken. He told us about the subterfuge that his daily political work involved. He put on his work clothes and walked out his front door carrying his office lunchbox each day, fooling his unsuspecting family into believing that all was business as usual. Working with the AAP was not just a noble act of self-sacrifice but a heady adventure, he told us.

More than the emphasis on individual sacrifice and daring, however, the theme of effective citizenship dominated Pathak's account of his party activities—how individual citizens could engage in concrete actions that set things right in immediate and palpable ways, at both the individual and the wider social level. Pathak was not the only one to offer such accounts. Like the "success stories" circulated by right-to-information movement activists that anthropologist Martin Webb has documented,[44] numerous "intervention stories" of effective citizenship proliferated within the everyday spaces of the AAP's social worlds and served as key instruments of party building.

Intervention Stories

Intervention stories are narratives about seemingly intractable problems encountered by the archetypal ordinary citizen that are solved by timely and simple acts of intervention by an AAP volunteer. The intervention stories that we encountered in AAP campaign officers covered a wide range of problems. Some addressed issues of infrastructural breakdown and inaccessibility: potholed roads, blocked sewage drains, soaring electricity bills, no electricity, extortionate water bills, empty taps. Others targeted the nondelivery of other kinds of government services, from unfulfilled passport applications to "ration problems" or the failure to receive one's due share of subsidized food supplies from the state-owned public distribution outlets despite being legally entitled to such provisions. Still others focused on access to the law and the basic constitutional entitlements of citizenship, for instance, the inordinate legal delays and the difficulties that ordinary citizens faced when trying to register criminal complaints at police stations.

Although they addressed very different problems, all the stories shared some common features. First, regardless of the level of difficulty or the longevity of the problem, all intervention stories presented solutions as simple, ready-to-hand, and fundamentally easy. Moreover, all of the solutions were about acting "as per rule," a phrase that we repeatedly encountered during discussions with party workers and which referenced extant constitutional and legal architectures in the country. For many of our informants, problem-solving entailed acts of constitutional-legal reactivation and reminder rather than legislative innovation. We already have everything we need to fix the problem, they told us. Most intervention stories underscored the importance of legal and procedural knowledge, and described how individuals who were familiar with the fine print of legislative detail could solve all kinds of intractable problems.

For example, for Sandeep Bisht, an AAP volunteer who had recently returned from the United Kingdom to work for the party during the election campaign, problems of voter registration could be solved merely by activating provisions on page 4 of the voter registration form itself. Bisht was speaking about the AAP's voter registration drive and his own work with an independent but allied initiative, Vote Ki Shakti (Power of the Vote), that helped citizens in Delhi navigate the complex and indifferent bureaucracy of voter registration in Delhi. Ordinary citizens, particularly those from among the urban poor, were routinely denied their voter identification cards because they could not produce the required documentary proof of identification and residence. However, some "legally knowledgeable" people had carefully studied all the written regulations and procedures governing voter registration, Bisht told us. And it turned out that salvation lay in the details. The law itself already provides the solution to our problems, he announced excitedly. It's as easy as that![45]

The second notable feature of intervention stories was their use of evidentiary practices and the reliance on visual forms of evidence in particular to establish governmental wrongdoing.[46] AAP workers punctuated their telling of intervention stories with multiple such "show-and-tell" moments, turning to the photo library on their smartphones for visual images of the problem under discussion: a potholed road, a pile of garbage accumulating in the hallways of Delhi's Safdarjung Hospital. The reliance on visual evidence also encouraged individual AAP volunteers to undertake their independent investigations.[47] Rajdeep Pathak exemplified the citizen-sleuth. He spent a large part of his days taking photographs of "wrong things," as he termed his large collection of smartphone photos. For Pathak, each photograph captured both a vexing problem and an act of effective citizenship. For instance, a photograph of an open garbage pile outside a hospital elicited both a discussion of the enormity and pervasiveness of this problem, and a detailed account of how Pathak had kept confronting the hospital superintendent about the situation until he eventually gave in and organized the correct disposal of garbage, "as per rule." He expressed both indignation and pride as we scrolled through the photo library together.

The third significant feature of the AAP's intervention stories was their distinctive affect as emotional narratives of heroic achievement. Visibly choking up with emotion, Sandeep Bisht recounted to us the story of a tearful elderly slum dweller who showered him with blessings when she finally received her voter identification card. This was his main motivation, he said. The memory of this encounter pushed him to keep working for the AAP under difficult and uncertain circumstances.

In most instances, the interventions that AAP workers described were simple and prosaic acts that involved the application of practical know-how rather than extraordinary expertise. Bisht had helped the woman by informing her about the technical procedures and rules of voter registration. Nevertheless, the impact of these solutions was invariably described as momentous and life-changing. Most intervention tales ended with melodramatic scenes of public gratitude: the tearful old woman blessing her new son, the cheering crowds gathering around Malviya Nagar candidate Somnath Bharti as he successfully mediated a long-standing dispute between neighbors.

The popularity of intervention stories among AAP workers sheds light on a significant mechanism of party-building, namely, the party's provision of "action-spaces" for individuals to enact particular fantasies of effectiveness and achievement. As the many anecdotes about effective interventions made clear, their work for the AAP allowed individuals to realize themselves as decisive agents who had the manifest capacity to get things done, people who were able to take command and change things. By joining the party, individuals could enact preferred, expanded, or aggrandized visions of themselves.

These were diverse visions. For instance, evoking a familiar trope of long-distance or diaspora nationalism that has also been deployed by other political parties in recent decades, most notably the Hindu nationalist BJP,[48] many of the non-resident Indian (NRI) volunteers that we interviewed spoke of how their work for the party enabled them to give back to and reconnect with India.[49] For others, the enactment of a preferred self took a different route. For IIT Kanpur graduate and former software engineer Omendra Bharat, the campaign manager of the RK Puram constituency between August and November 2013, party work provided an opportunity to express his poetic skills. He used public rallies as occasions to recite some of his own poetry, and whiled away idle time in the office assiduously searching YouTube to see if new videos of his poetry performances had been uploaded.

For another former engineer who held a senior leadership position in the influential alumni association of the IITs and was working as an advisor to the Malviya Nagar campaign, party work brought forth a managerial or "CEO self." At meetings that he ran, party workers were exhorted with business management maxims and lessons, interspersed with stern commands to brush up their spreadsheet analysis and PowerPoint presentation skills. As many of the party workers did not own a computer or have an email account, these commands were often lost in translation, we noted.

In the course of our research we frequently encountered such simulations of managerial authority and the use of languages of "management-speak" by AAP workers. Significantly, many of those bustling around with slides and spreadsheets did not actually work in managerial or executive positions. The command-and-control dynamics that we observed in AAP offices seemed to reflect particular fantasies of preferred selfhood and projects of aspirational self-making more than lived experience and expertise.

Newness Projects

The AAP also relied quite heavily upon public performances of "newness" during its first election campaign, that is, actions and practices that sought to convey in visible and public ways that the AAP was a new and altogether different kind of political party. Newness projects[50] took several different forms. One prominent category involved anti-*neta* (anti-leader) performances, or the self-presentation of AAP candidates as the diametrical opposite of establishment politicians. AAP candidates conspicuously avoided the white *khadi* homespun cotton garb of the stereotypical Indian politician, and signed a pledge to reject the conventional trappings of political power if they were elected to office. During their daily door-to-door efforts to canvass votes, party workers made much of this pledge, of how *lalbatti gari* (official cars with flashing red light beacons), large official residences, and excessive security detail for elected representatives would be prohibited in the new political future.

The radical difference of the AAP's political culture was also staged and enacted in the course of routine and functional campaign activities such as fundraising. Take for instance the *chande ka chaadar* (donation sheet) routine that concluded campaign rallies and public meetings.[51] At the end of every public event organized by the party, AAP workers walked around the venue carrying a white sheet (a *chaadar*), collecting "alms" from the gathered crowds while loudly declaring that this humble, intimate, and fully transparent practice of fundraising was completely different from the murky financial transactions of other political parties.[52] AAP workers repeatedly emphasized the voluntary and spontaneous nature of AAP audiences at these events, how people showed up "for free," and even spent their own limited resources in order to attend an AAP event.[53]

Rajdeep Pathak spoke proudly of the time when Chhattarpur party workers had organized a motorcycle rally in September and each participant had to spend at least five hundred rupees on fuel. In Pathak's recounting of the event, this expenditure was the true measure of the rally's success: it showed that AAP was supported by *aaye huey log*, people who have come on their own. All other political parties have to rely on *laaye huey log*, "brought people" who are paid to attend the party's events, he told us. As workers described how the receipt of two rupees from "the rickshaw puller who had nothing" was worth more than the largest check that any corporation could ever give them, it seemed that performances of newness called for an emphasis on the meagerness rather than the plenitude of the party's wealth. The AAP was new and different *because* it was small and poor, completely unlike the rich and strong establishment parties that contested Indian elections.

A second category of newness projects involved public performances and declarations of renunciation. Claiming political legitimacy through dramatic gestures of giving up political office is a familiar act in Indian democracy.[54] For the AAP workers, however, the renunciation drama came with a twist: the object of renunciation was social and economic rather than political power. The narrative of giving up considerable material comforts and security for the sake of the party was central to the self-presentation of party workers, especially senior leaders and electoral candidates.

This was a story that implied a priori possession. How can we give up what was never ours? What resulted was a curious practice of emphasizing the considerable wealth and success of AAP candidates vis-à-vis the *aam aadmi* they were trying to mobilize and persuade. Instead of identity and proximity, the AAP campaign of 2013 highlighted the extraordinariness of the AAP activist and the social distance between the party and those it aimed to represent.[55] This made for some discordant and unsettling scenes, for instance when, during a campaign visit to the Bhanwar Singh Camp, an unauthorized settlement comprising a ramshackle assortment of makeshift dwellings without running water, sewage lines, or paved roads, the RK Puram candidate Shazia Ilmi used her stump speech to describe in great detail the three lakhs of rupees ($4,000) monthly salary, "foreign car," and air-conditioned house that she had given up. Trust me, Ilmi effectively said, *because* I am rich.

The final way that AAP workers presented themselves as agents of newness was by showcasing counterexamples of the old politics that the party was challenging. The specter of the slum voter loomed particularly large in the AAP worker's imagination: the desired and reviled subject whose votes held the key and also constituted the main obstacle to the party's success. Just about every party worker I spoke to would invoke the problem of the slum voter at some point in our conversation. For AAP workers, the slum voter was both the object and the agent of old politics. Thus at one level the miserable civic conditions of Delhi slums attested to the political and moral bankruptcy of the existing government and its cultures of indifference and cruelty vis-à-vis these marginalized citizens. At another level, by willingly participating in the corrupt practices of vote-buying, slum voters were held to be responsible for their own misery. Five hundred rupees was the mythical figure that, along with free *daaru-murgi* (alcohol and chicken), apparently convinced Delhi's slum residents to "sell their daughter's future" by selling their vote.

While there is considerable anecdotal evidence of political party workers offering various kinds of material inducements to voters, there is no evidence that this has any influence on the act of voting, that is, that votes are actually bought.[56] Indeed, as Lisa Björkman has observed in her ethnography of the role of money in a Mumbai municipal election, all too often there is a negative relationship between levels of monetary expenditure and electoral success. In Björkman's ethnography, the party and candidate that spent the most on vote-buying was the one that lost the election. But such insights were missing from the AAP workers' depictions of political praxis in Delhi's slums. Dispensing with their usual insistence on evidentiary politics and documented proof, party workers offered up confident narratives about the politically dirty slum that were based on surmises and generalizations about things that "everybody knew."

Their stories were politically consequential. The idea of the known slum that the AAP party-building drew on in its founding phases shaped the party's subsequent strategies of political outreach. For instance, I observed a marked contrast between the *jan sunwais*, or public hearings, that candidates and party workers held in middle-class and elite residential areas of their constituencies, and those that took place in the camps and *jhuggis*.[57] That the AAP was the only political party that even ventured to these latter locations was an indisputable fact, and many residents in the camps that I visited remarked on this. However, it seemed that for party workers the public visibility of their physical presence in these locations was prioritized more than interactions with residents about their actual concerns and demands. In contrast, outreach efforts in middle-class and elite residential colonies (gated communities) quite frequently involved in-depth discussions and meetings with prospective voters.

For AAP workers in the three constituencies that we focused on, the colony[58] and the camp constituted discrete and disparate political spaces where newness projects were realized in different ways. An open-ended politics largely without certitudes and prejudgments unfolded in the elite and middle-class colonies. Party workers and candidates were open to criticism, solicited opinions, and admitted mistakes, and the AAP's promise of newness was linked to its manifest practice of a "modest and evolving politics," as party leader Yogendra Yadav described it. In contrast, party work in camp settlements was informed by a rather different political approach based upon prejudgments about the old politics that necessarily dominated these places. The needs and interests of slum residents were held to be self-evident and already known, and campaign interactions did not require sustained discussions and consultations with residents. In contrast to the "evolving politics" that marked the AAP's newness projects in the housing colonies, newness projects in camps and *jhuggis* called for the political reeducation of recalcitrant citizens trapped in the known mires of old politics.

MODULATIONS, 2014–20

As we know, the 2013 campaign yielded rich dividends and culminated in a dramatic electoral success story for the AAP, giving it 23 out of 70 seats in its inaugural elections. However, it fell short of a majority and the AAP could stake its claim to forming the government only after it secured the requisite support and commitment to legislative cooperation from the Congress, the very establishment force against which the AAP had launched its anti-establishment challenge.

If the AAP's electoral victory and the decision to solicit Congress support in 2013 were dramatic and largely unexpected events, so too were subsequent developments in the political life of the party. Shortly after the surprise of the electoral victory and the formation of the Delhi state government with Congress support in January 2014 came the grand theater of political renunciation. After just forty-nine days in office, a period that saw many dramatic scenes unfold, from the midnight raid of Somnath Bharti to the spectacle of the chief minister and his cabinet staging a hunger strike and sit-in on the streets of Delhi, the AAP government abruptly resigned. Its failure to deliver on the election promise of enacting the Jan Lokpal legislation was cited as the reason. Delhi was placed under the exceptional authority of centrally administered President's Rule in March 2014.

Political surprises continued to pile up. On the electoral front, the AAP's fortunes oscillated wildly. In the summer of 2014, the party contested more than four hundred seats all across the country in the general parliamentary elections but won just four of these. Most AAP candidates lost by margins large enough to forfeit their electoral deposit. Along with several other prominent AAP leaders, the former chief minister Arvind Kejriwal was among the ranks of the soundly defeated. Only a few months after his electoral triumph in Delhi, he lost decisively to BJP party leader and prime ministerial candidate Narendra Modi in an electoral contest in the constituency of Varanasi that the AAP had built up as an epic David-versus-Goliath battle.

The electoral arc reversed again the following year, from loss back to victory. In early 2015, the ignominy of the parliamentary debacle was wiped out by an overwhelming electoral victory for the AAP in the state assembly elections. Arvind Kejriwal and his men[59] returned to office after winning 67 out of 70 seats. The oscillations continued with every successive election that the party fought. The victory in the Delhi state elections of 2015 was followed by electoral defeats at the municipal and national levels in 2017 and 2019 respectively, and then a decisive victory in the state assembly elections of 2020. After winning 62 seats and almost 54 percent of the popular vote,[60] chief minister Kejriwal and his cabinet were sworn into state office for a third time in February 2020.

Brand Kejriwal

Along with the seesaw of electoral surprises, there have also been a series of high-visibility organizational disruptions within the party over the years. Several prominent party leaders, including founding members like Yogendra Yadav and Prashant Bhushan, were expelled, and went on to join political rivals or to form their own political party.[61] These internal changes in party organization and leadership unfolded against a broader backdrop of multiple and overlapping national crises.

The AAP's political career has coincided with the national rise of a Hindu majoritarian political party, the BJP, that actively seeks to remake the fundamentals of political and social order to reflect its vision of India as a "Hindu first" nation. The BJP's efforts at majoritarian transformation intensified after May 2019 when it won the parliamentary elections for a second time. A series of major policy, legal, and constitutional changes were swiftly enacted that led to considerable social and political churning. Examples include a constitutional amendment in August 2019 that ended the political autonomy of the Muslim majority state of Jammu and Kashmir, and the passage of a Citizenship Amendment Act in November 2019 that linked Indian citizenship to religious identity in a manner that explicitly discriminated against Muslims, sparking public protests across the country. Numerous incidents of media censorship and police violence, arrests of students, activists, and dissenters charged with "anti-national" sedition, and a protracted episode of institutionally enabled mass violence against Muslims in Delhi in February 2020 also roiled the country.

As these varied crises buffet and transform the material field of politics in which the AAP functions,[62] the party's vision and practice of new politics and its mission of curative democracy have been modified in several ways. First, there have been noticeable changes in the organizational cultures and structures of the AAP. In 2013, I had encountered a party that many described as a political start-up, an organization whose horizontal structures, minimal entry (and exit) barriers, encouragement of individual initiative, and largely informal style of everyday work culture enabled the individual enactments of effective citizenship that were central to the party's identity and to its mobilizing successes. However, once the AAP transitioned from an oppositional to a governmental formation, this flexible mode gave way to a centralized and hierarchical organizational structure that vested effective authority in Arvind Kejriwal and a small group of trusted advisors, and placed a high premium on displays of personal loyalty to Kejriwal.

The idea of representing the *aam aadmi* remained important to the party's self-presentation. After 2014, however, this was linked to the representational authority and leadership of Kejriwal, the singular individual who was simultaneously extraordinary and ordinary, *khas* and *aam*, the uncommon common man. Describing the AAP's second state assembly campaign in 2015, Sanjeev Kumar, the former campaign manager of the Chhattarpur constituency, explained:

> People say that the *sangathan* [organization] is crucial, but what we really need is a strong leader, the brand has to be liked by the people and only then can it be marketed. . . . Arvind is a good product, that is what matters.[63]

Kumar's endorsement of a Brand Kejriwal points both to the personalization of the party's appeal around the figure of Kejriwal, and the imprint of political marketing and commodification on the 2015 election campaign. In marked contrast to its inaugural campaign, later campaigns of the AAP have relied quite heavily on paid consultancy and political marketing services.[64] This conforms to the general trend of digital publicity and marketing that has dominated the field of Indian elections in recent years, with political parties increasingly relying upon paid campaign consultants and publicists for national and state campaigns. Campaign work has expanded to include data-gathering as a key task. The abstractions of number, code, and category, and the "micro-target" of the digitally constituted voter profile, as much as the material work of voter persuasion through direct encounters and dialogues with actual individuals, drive workers of the present-day AAP.[65]

Winnability, Pragmatic Politics, Service Delivery

The new consensus that the AAP was a product or brand that had to be marketed to citizen-consumers also reflected and advanced a new strategic calculus and a new set of criteria for the selection of electoral candidates. As I have discussed in earlier sections of this chapter, a distinctive political outsider norm had guided candidate selection during the first AAP campaign of 2013. The party pledged to field politically inexperienced first-time candidates. The AAP promised to choose candidates on the basis of their individual ethical conduct and proven track records of professional accomplishment, rather than their political connections, patronage obligations, or their caste and religious identities. However, later campaigns of the AAP relied on a different set of candidacy criteria. In the state assembly elections of 2015, for instance, party tickets were given to defectors from other political parties, the very kinds of individuals whom the inaugural campaign had shunned as being politically tainted. Contrasting the political naïveté that had clouded the past with the clear-eyed calculus of political experience that guided the present, AAP workers explained to me in 2015 that a new calculus of "winnability" was now the driving compulsion. Here is Sanjeev Kumar again:

> I told Arvind, this time just drop all the talk about principles; first we need to have the keys to the government, we need to win. Let's get a candidate with around a 15,000 votebank. This was Kartar Singh Tanwar, a former BJP councilor with political experience and also a votebank of 15–20,000.[66]

Kumar's observations reflect a new approach to the project of political change. At the start of its political career, the AAP had called for people to undertake immediate and publicly visible acts that effected change in the here and now. But in the 2015 campaign, being the change also meant the cultivation of political patience and caution. Political transformation was now configured as a stagist process that unfolded gradually, and that required many necessary compromises, suspensions, and even reversals of foundational first principles. First, "the keys to the government."

With the temporal reorientation from immediate to more gradual visions of change came a discursive and policy emphasis on "pragmatic politics" and "service delivery." Civic infrastructure and public services such as water, electricity, schools, health care, roads, internet connectivity, and urban security have always been central concerns for the AAP, and much of the party's diagnosis of the defective and diseased political system has related to the failures and inadequacies of these essential public services. The 2013 campaign had linked these service and infrastructural failures to the problem of political corruption (and the system of crony-capitalist private monopolies that it had fostered). This diagnostic frame of anti-corruption, and the angry politics of outrage that it summoned, was reworked in subsequent elections. As the AAP moved from oppositional to governmental terrain following its victory in the state assembly elections of 2015, the focus of its public discourse shifted from rage against the corrupt system to the efficiency, simplicity, and nifty ingenuity of the technocratic solutions that the party could offer, thanks to the unique wealth of expert knowledge and the specialized cosmopolitan experience in its ranks.

Like the flexible and polysemous idea of anti-corruption that addressed very different social classes, the AAP's promise of service delivery was also targeted to diverse social constituencies. At one level, the pledge to provide accessible government schools and health care clinics was specifically addressed to the constituencies of the urban poor and working classes whose lives would be materially affected by the availability of such services. At another level, the AAP's service delivery agenda was a promise about world-class techno-modernity made to the party's middle-class supporters: the infrastructural fix and the ingenious and cutting-edge technologies that would propel India into the ranks of the civilized nations at last.

Post-ideology, Post-identity

Along with the growing prominence of service delivery and pragmatic politics as campaign themes, the characterization of the AAP as a post-ideological and post-identity party formation has also intensified over the years. The distinction between the old politics of caste and religious votebanks practiced by establishment parties, and the new politics of effective citizenship offered by the AAP, is a familiar staple of party discourse. As the candidate Shazia Ilmi had pointed out during the 2013 campaign, explaining the allegedly unusual choice of her candidacy in a constituency where Muslims were a negligible proportion of the electorate:

> "I wanted to break away from identity politics. You have Hindu politics, Muslim politics, Jat politics. . . . So I said, why not gender politics, why not fight for gender justice? I want to be in politics as a citizen of this country, not as a Muslim." Ilmi laughed and added, "All my affluent friends, though, tell me I should have chosen a Muslim constituency."[67]

Subsequent election campaigns amplified and expanded Ilmi's account of the civic freedom that the AAP had afforded her. Campaigns in recent years have prominently showcased the AAP's supposedly "post-ideological" politics, presenting this as one of the main distinctions and advantages of new politics in the AAP era. For instance, during the campaign for the state assembly elections in 2020, AAP candidates repeatedly drew attention to their transformed engagement with the Muslim question. They emphasized how the party had rejected the usual religious-cultural template to take up the "real developmental needs" of Muslim citizens, engaging Muslims not as special minorities to be protected but as equal citizens to be served.

But what is a real need? The AAP's post-ideological and post-identity project mandates a narrowing of the political agenda to issues of service delivery and pragmatic politics alone. For instance, in 2020 the AAP leadership maintained a studied silence on the anti-citizenship amendment protests that were raging across the country and had led to popular protests and occupations of public space in the predominantly Muslim neighborhood of Shaheen Bagh in Delhi through the months of December and January. Even though concerns about citizenship and constitutional rights were at the heart of the protests, for the AAP the Shaheen Bagh protests were matters of "religious controversy," and eruptions of particularist identity politics that had to be avoided.

The avoidance was selective and partial. The red line of religious identity that it had vowed not to cross did not prevent the AAP from liberally interweaving Hindu scriptural and mythological references in the 2020 campaign,[68] nor from launching a pilgrimage subsidy scheme for senior citizens in 2018. Hailing the initiative as a sign of its responsiveness to citizens' needs, the AAP government provided financial and logistical support for citizens to undertake religious pilgrimages to government-approved sites. Of the fifteen listed sites, nine were Hindu pilgrimage destinations, and only one was associated with Islam.[69]

In sum, the AAP's post-identity project and the call to transcend the trappings of religious identity do not leave all identities behind in the same way. As the Muslim question is recast from a special concern about minority protection to a general matter of developmental needs that affects all citizens, the Hindu question is reframed as well. But the reframing of the Hindu question works in a different way, as an unmarking rather than a substitution. The 2020 campaign and the pilgrimage policy of the AAP government presumes and constitutes a default Hinduness that transposes a partial and particular interest to a register of general concern.[70] In this conflation of India and Hindu, it seems that the AAP's dream of a new politics may not stray that far from establishment majoritarianism after all. The place beyond identity and ideology that AAP gestures toward remains located within the fractured and uneven field of social power in contemporary India.

It is to this matter of social location and power, and the co-constitution of the social and the political, that I now turn in the final section of this chapter.

CURATIVE DEMOCRACY AND THE SOCIAL QUESTION

This chapter has examined how the project of curative democracy—the call to clean up politics, and fix and cure the diseased and broken system of democracy—gained political and social legitimacy in India and brought a new political party to power in 2013. To explain the seeming paradox of how the denigration of electoral politics became an instrument of political legitimation and electoral success, I moved away from the usual voter-centric approaches to the study of political parties. I looked instead at the work of party-building and the motivation and mobilization of party workers and volunteers to join and work for the AAP in the absence of any instrumentalist expectation of reward or profit. The promise and the opportunity to undertake extraordinary action and exercise change-agency, to stand up and stand out and actively "be the change," was the party's main attraction. The AAP's curative democracy project did not just present a new discourse or idea. It created a set of political and social action-spaces and opportunities for individuals to express and enact their preferred selves as effective citizens and agents of change.

These were also spaces where a distinctive form of proprietorial politics or what I have termed an "ownership democracy" flourished. The call to cure and change democracy was about acting to cure and change *one's own* system—it was premised upon, and in turn shored up, a specific claim of possession and ownership. While ownership claims can be linked to different kinds of sociopolitical affects, for example, belonging, solidarity, loyalty, and love, AAP party-building cultivated and prioritized proprietorial investments in sentiments and structures of political and social control. Being a change-agent with and for the AAP was about exercising authority over people and situations, and multiple "small sovereigns" or "little big men" flourished within the spaces of the party in its founding period.

Hierarchies of Authority

Belying the open-ended terms of the call to action, AAP's action-spaces were in fact differentially constituted. Some performances of effective citizenship were foregrounded and valued more than others. For instance, in the Malviya Nagar constituency during the campaign of 2013, the greater effectiveness of *parey likhey log* (educated people) within the party was singled out on multiple occasions. The fact that the candidate Somnath Bharti was an IIT graduate as well as a lawyer was the main highlight of his introduction at public meetings. At a planning meeting called to review the lackluster performance of the campaign, party workers were reminded (by another IIT alumnus) that AAP's main distinction from other political parties was the large cohort of "educated people" in the party, especially in the leadership.[71] The "civilized politics" that they practiced would enable democratic reform and recovery; this should be the "main selling point" of the campaign, he argued.[72]

A different leadership hierarchy structured the Chhattarpur constituency in the course of the 2013 campaign. Unlike the managerial leadership of the AAP campaign in Malviya Nagar, and the value that it placed on the professional qualifications and experience of party workers, particularly those from professions such as law, engineering, medicine, and corporate management, Chhattarpur's leaders were hailed for their prowess in *taakat dikhana*—the "shows of strength" or the public displays of force and amassed energy that characterized AAP mobilizations in this constituency. These performances of muscular leadership were restricted to specific kinds of gendered and caste subjects. All those who occupied positions of authority within the Chhattarpur branch of the party were men, and almost all from the Tanwar caste.[73]

Rajdeep Pathak, whom we encountered earlier in the chapter, belonged to this cohort of AAP leaders in Chhattarpur. His agency as an effective citizen and an authority figure in the local campaign office drew both on his individual investigative skills and on his social networks, which allowed him to gather other young men in public displays of collective action such as motorcycle rallies through the streets of Chhattarpur and angry street protests outside police stations. Both these divergent sets of leadership resources were valued, the one constituted around professional skills, and the other around masculinist assertions of public muscle power. But as the AAP moved beyond the 2013 campaign, the incompatibility between these two legitimating principles of action, *taakat* and *parai-likhai*, heightened internal party tensions. Many prominent members have exited the AAP over the years, citing irreconcilable differences in values.

The fractures within the Chhattarpur campaign in 2013, and in the wider party organization in subsequent years, reflect strong disagreements over how the immediate strategic goals of party-building and electoral victory were to be achieved. What kinds of leaders and authority figures did the party need to grow and to win—those with professional experience or those with social and political *taakat*, "English types" or "Hindi types," moral exemplars or seasoned politicians? There have been different answers to these questions over the years. For instance, and as we have noted already, a new priority of "winnability" and a differentiation between pragmatic means and idealistic ends came to structure the strategic thinking of the AAP after its first election campaign in 2013, and the profile of AAP candidates shifted substantially from political outsiders to insiders. But what these disagreements over the appropriate constitution of party leadership and representation have mostly left unchallenged is the societal terrain and terms of political agency. The question of who gets to be a curative democrat and undertake extraordinary actions in the name of the ordinary citizen has met with a consistent answer over the years.

The action-politics of the AAP are largely authorized by a sense of democratic entitlement and ownership that is rooted in the highly stratified social worlds of contemporary India. The claims of political ownership; the proprietorial calls to regain control over one's own system and the elected representatives who are supposed to serve us; and the language of *malik* and *naukar*, master and servant, that pervaded the action-spaces of the party were authored by specific kinds of classed and gendered bodies. The vast majority of party workers that I encountered during the initial phase of party-building in 2013 were male, Hindu, and came from a range of different middle-class and dominant-caste backgrounds. Each campaign team also included several volunteers from among the city's poor and working classes who lived precarious lives in semi-legal slum tenements. However, these individuals were not given supervisory authority or decision-making responsibilities.

In the course of my research, I encountered numerous AAP volunteers who had previously participated in the Youth For Equality (YFE) movement of the mid-2000s, a protest movement led by upper-caste students in north India against a proposed expansion of the Indian government's affirmative action program of reservations for students from historically discriminated and oppressed caste groups to gain admission in public institutions of professional education.[74] Accounts of YFE activism featured frequently in our conversations with party workers about their trajectories of politicization, second only to the anti-corruption movement of 2011 that figured as the original moment and main source of political awakening in their narratives. The YFE movement had harnessed sentiments of righteous outrage and indignation at the normative reversals effected by caste reservations. In 2006, thousands of student protesters had come out onto the streets of Delhi to angrily oppose the matter-out-of-place dystopia of marginalized caste groups allegedly privileged and advantaged by reservations policy. A few years later, this outrage against upended caste hierarchy was transposed to the domain of governance and political representation where an upside-down chaos was seen to prevail as well—*malik* as *naukar*, *naukar* as *malik*. The former YFE activists within the AAP called for a restoration of political order, for things to be put back in place and for the right people to regain control. A decade after the anti-reservation movement that sought to restore power to the right people, a similar quest for order would frame and found the AAP's curative democracy project. Its vision of real democracy would be linked to notions of mastery and control, rather than to the democratic norms of freedom and equality.

The influence of the command-and-control imagination of democracy was reflected in the AAP's pedagogical approach to the so-called slum vote. As I have observed in earlier sections, a "camp versus colony" spatial and sociopolitical distinction has structured the AAP's party-building and voter mobilization efforts since the time of its first electoral campaign. In contrast to the more consultative and at times even supplicatory practices of voter mobilization in middle- and upper-class residential colonies, AAP volunteers addressed slum voters with a pedagogical and disciplinary discourse about their "uplift." When the campaign moved to the camps and tenements of Delhi, the demand and promise of political agency and effective citizenship were linked to an explicitly vertical relation of authority: the volunteer who instructed and improved the sorry conditions of the slum on the one side, and the slum resident who followed and learned to be an active citizen on the other. References to the filthy slum, a term used to describe both the physical spaces and the way of life of residents, abounded in the AAP's campaign discourse in 2013. On a campaign visit to Kanak Durga camp, the RK Puram campaign manager and former YFE activist Omendra Bharat described the *cockroach ki zindagi*, the cockroach lives of the slum, and urged "us," we the "educated people," to intervene. Even something as simple as "telling them" to vote for their own interests could be the change that was needed, he urged.

After winning the elections and coming to power in 2015 with a large and stable majority, the hierarchical contours of instruction and command became more pronounced in the AAP's political discourse. As I have already noted, the organizational structure of the party grew more centralized, and vested most decision-making authority in Kejriwal and a small group of male advisors. Unsurprisingly, as the AAP moved from opposition to government, its everyday practices and work cultures began to reflect and stage governmental authority. The party was constituted as an establishment formation. From spaces of insurgent action, AAP's action-spaces transformed into sites for power displays, where state authority was materialized and affirmed. The intervention stories that I had encountered on the campaign trail, when volunteers animatedly described their individual initiatives of being the change, the exciting times when they had jumped into the fray and single-handedly saved the day, were modulated into narratives about official authority and proximity to state power, and the possession of insider authority and influence. Governmental connections were now treated as valuable currency within party circles, and the norm of political distance and innocence was supplanted by new priorities of political knowledge and expertise.

My research visits with informants in 2015 involved both a spatial reorientation—from cramped constituency offices in South Delhi to the sparsely populated top floors of the Delhi Secretariat in the northern end of the city, the seat of the state government—and the revision of some of my earlier research findings about the acts of ordinary agency that drove the party. For instance, I found that the strong cultures of voluntary work for the party had continued. However, a sizable group of volunteers were now in advisory and consultancy roles, working on technocratic projects of policymaking rather than the voter mobilization activities that had been the sole focus of AAP volunteers in 2013. There was also a discernible status hierarchy between the professionals and experts who had access to the party leadership in the Delhi Secretariat, and the foot soldiers who remained at the local constituency offices and interacted with their local elected representative (the MLA, member of the legislative assembly).

The hierarchy was replicated in the local constituency offices that I revisited after the AAP came to power. It now reflected political knowledge and insider influence, rather than technocracy and professional expertise. More than his crowd-getting powers, the value of a local party worker was now indexed by his governmental connections and ability to work the phone to solve problems. Replicating the scenes of pedagogical intermediation that Martin Webb observed in his ethnography of right-to-information activists in Delhi's colonies,[75] the AAP's local offices were configured as spaces of brokerage and mediation between uninformed citizens and the mysterious workings of state power. Party publicity from this period emphasized the dialogic and participatory arenas of the AAP's signature events, the *mohalla sabhas* and the Delhi Dialogue series.[76] However, conversations with party workers stressed their pedagogical and instructional functions, as occasions for teaching the skills of civic agency to ordinary citizens.[77]

The governmental phase of the AAP has also deepened the social fault lines within the party, and widened the gap between the social constituency of the ordinary that the party claims to represent, and the extraordinary forms of political representation that it actually provides. Since its formation in 2012, the gender and caste base of AAP membership has shifted further in the direction of male, dominant (and intermediate) caste representation, and this is especially pronounced in leadership circles. In 2019, a journalistic report on the AAP found that Dalit and Muslims were a negligible presence in the party leadership, and that men dominated the party.[78] Three successive AAP governments in Delhi have yielded a meager total of two female cabinet ministers.

Yet even as the social bases of party leadership have narrowed, its political power has expanded. Over this same time period, the AAP has grown from an incipient anti-establishment mobilization to an established governmental formation. Social exclusion and political agency can coexist; the former might even be an enabling condition of the latter. It is to this relationship between the social and the political that I now turn, by way of a research vignette that illustrates how social power grounds and enables political agency. As this extract from my field notes from April 2019 shows, the curative mission of AAP volunteers and sympathizers is embedded within and expresses a specific social class location.

AAP Dekho, See for Yourselves

Field Notes, April 19, 2019

In the summer of 2019, AAP volunteers organized a series of "AAP Dekho" tours to visit health clinics, schools, and waste management plants run by the AAP government in Delhi. Advertised via social media (WhatsApp groups, Facebook, and Twitter), these events were billed as opportunities for "well-wishers" of the party and "curious citizens" to directly view the AAP government's initiatives and service delivery achievements. *AAP dekho*: see for yourselves, see AAP!

After signing up on the Facebook page of the AAP, I follow WhatsApp instructions to the neighborhood of Dwarka in west Delhi on an April morning in 2019. Eleven of us gather outside a *mohalla* (neighborhood) health clinic, all visibly upper-middle-class, English-speaking professionals in their fifties and older. One couple lived in Pennsylvania for many years before retiring and relocating to India, and all the others have traveled abroad or seem to have direct knowledge about life in advanced industrial countries. Over the course of the morning, this will emerge as the main comparative benchmark for measuring the AAP's performance in Delhi. Whether and how the sights on our tour match up to America (or Germany, or Singapore, or Dubai) will be a frequent topic of conversation.

Paul Thomas,[79] the volunteer who is leading the AAP Dekho tour, is a pleasant and chatty man in his late thirties. He works as a consultant in Delhi[80] and volunteers for the AAP on weekends. He is very enthusiastic about the AAP Dekho initiative. It exemplifies the AAP's mission of political innovation, of always coming up with original and meaningful initiatives, he tells us. AAP Dekho is a way for citizens to directly see things for themselves and hold government accountable. The tour is up front and honest, and will show us what the mainstream media does not. "We will see how actual citizens are actually benefiting from this government," Thomas explains.

The Dwarka health clinic, a portable cabin parked inside the compound of a government school, is our first stop. A long line of patients has already formed inside even though the clinic has just opened. All the waiting patients that morning are women, several with young children. The tour group turns into inspectors as Thomas encourages us to look around and "inspect" the clinic, to go into the toilet and evaluate its state of cleanliness for ourselves. I demur, but one of the group members insists that I must go anyway. "It's not really clean you know," she whispers conspiratorially. "You should take a photo."

We troop inside the doctor's office and stand there, watching and listening while the patients discuss their medical problems. In the brief pause between patients, tour group members quiz the doctor. What is the difference between working here and working in a private hospital? they ask. Why are "tabs" (tablet computers) not being used to record patient data? Why is the air-conditioning switched off? The sudden drop in temperature would not be good for our patients who come in from the extreme heat and have to go back out there again, the doctor replies patiently. Our group does not seem terribly convinced by her answers, and as we leave the room, several people point out quite disapprovingly that the doctor does not wear a white coat or carry a stethoscope.

Before we leave, we talk to some of the patients waiting outside the examination room and listen to their complaints about long lines and cursory consultations. Sanjay Sharma,[81] a tour group member in his sixties, wearing an IIT Alumni T-shirt, asks for the clinic's "complaint box" to be brought out and placed in a prominent location. "You must write your complaints and place them in the box and call the mobile number listed here if you are not satisfied by the service. The child that cries gets the milk, *jo baccha rota hai usko dudh milta hai*. If you raise your voice, you will get your issues heard," he tells the waiting women. "We must motivate," he explains to me.

Sharma's motivational call is taken up by other group members on the next stop of our tour, a larger "polyclinic" where *mohalla* clinic doctors refer patients for specialized medical consultations and diagnostic tests. A couple of elderly men from our group walk among the waiting patients, distributing stickers that say "Keep Smiling!" We are here at your service. Tell us your complaints and concerns and we'll report it straight to Kejriwal *sahib*, they announce. But we leave before anyone takes up their offer, and move to the next site: the new government School of Excellence in Dwarka, one of five such schools of excellence in the city.

Inside the sparkling new school building there are no students since it is a Saturday afternoon, but the principal gives us a gracious hearing and explains the educational structure and mission. Everyone is delighted to hear about the generous resources that the government has provided, and the state-of-the-art facilities available for students in government schools that have been institutionally neglected for decades. The principal describes the school's efforts to bring about an "attitude shift" among parents. The mandatory parent-teacher meeting each month teaches parents about the importance of school attendance. They have learned that they cannot go away to the village for long holidays with their children anymore, she tells us. The initiative is well received by our group.

The tour group is visibly impressed by the school with its articulate and enthusiastic teachers, shining tablet computers, cheerful wall murals, and spotless cafeteria benches. "No one can tell the difference between low and high society here," one elderly gentleman says approvingly. "Instead of becoming criminals they will get opportunities." "Yes, low society should also get a chance," his neighbor replies. They describe the school to me as a material glimpse of the "equal society" that will exist in India one day ("by 2040," says one of the tour group members), an equality that is repeatedly described as the experience of not knowing and specifically of not being able to *see* the difference between "high" and "low."

We drive to our final location, the Rajokri sewage treatment plant, near a stone quarry surrounded by small makeshift housing structures and open drains. The contrast with its immediate environment is striking. We enter the plant gates to find a serene and verdant open space with a pond in the middle, surrounded by elegant rushes and carefully tended flower beds. The pleasing aesthetics of the space are complemented by the innovative and sustainable engineering design of the plant. The engineers in our tour group are clearly impressed by the technical details.

As we stand around, I notice a security guard walk up to a small group of men sitting on the grassy banks of the pond, in a small patch of shade that they have found on this blazing April morning. He brusquely asks them to leave right away. Two young boys walk through the park, clutching schoolbooks. They are ninth graders going to their math tuition classes, they reply to my questions. The guard breaks up our conversation and shoos them out, like chickens. "They will destroy the plants and flowers; they don't know how to treat the place properly," says the guard. He explains that the park stays locked. It is only opened when "people like you" come to visit. "The public" can come here when we organize a public event.[82]

The man from our tour group hands out one of his Keep Smiling stickers to the contractor who has supervised the construction of the plant. "Can you tell me what's written here, can you say it out loud?" he says with an encouraging smile, clearly implying that the contractor is nonliterate.

He moves on to another topic without waiting for a response. "You must work a lot in the sun, look at how dark you've become," he says jocularly. "That's my natural color," the contractor replies, and the conversation shifts again.

The tour ends soon after. As I drive home, the AAP Dekho WhatsApp group bursts into excited life with photographs and glowing commentaries about all the great "achievements" that we have just witnessed, and the era of new and clean democracy that is surely on its way.

CONCLUSION: WHY MRS. GIDUZ ACTS

Although it was not pointed out and named in this way, a key revelation on the AAP Dekho tour was about the practice of ownership democracy. We saw that day how the AAP's political mission to change and cure the (broken, diseased, corrupted) system advanced a distinctive proprietorial political claim. Political demands for inclusion and empowerment in contemporary democracies are usually issued from subject positions of marginalization and exclusion, as those outside established circuits of power strive to make new and different worlds. In contrast, curative agents advance political claims on the basis of an a priori sense of belonging or entitlement: it is *their* system and *their* democracy that requires repair and remedy. Moreover, curative political demands are almost always about a restoration or a reclamation. In the curative democratic project, the transformational future is modeled as a return to a past state of good order, when everything will be again as it once was.

These proprietorial and restorative projects are linked to particular social locations and subjectivities. Some people are empowered and authorized to act publicly as curative democrats; others do not because they cannot. My research with AAP party workers since the party's founding in 2012 suggests that there was a definite social pattern to the exercise of political agency within the party. The AAP's vision of a new politics did not include a new sociality. The verdant spaces of the Rajokri plant that remained out of bounds to local schoolchildren is an example of how the AAP's efforts to clean up Indian democracy have mostly left the existing, and highly unequal, matrix of Indian social relations undisturbed. The intersecting hierarchies of caste, gender, class, and religion that order social life in the country structure the action-spaces of new politics and curative democracy as well.

This finding about the social lineaments and contours of curative political agency is relevant beyond the immediate discussion of the AAP. Against Hannah Arendt's famous definition of the political act as an original act of inauguration that, freed from the constraints of meeting the prosaic and immediate needs of survival and social reproduction, brings something non-utilitarian and altogether new into the world, the political and the social are shown instead to be tightly enmeshed, to constitute and enable each other.[83] These intimate entanglements of the political and the social solve a paradox of political action that one of its most prominent theorists had puzzled over. In Arendt's otherwise exhaustive discussion of action, the question of the social identity of the actor is markedly absent. Indeed, for Arendt, the separation or bracketing of the social is the political's condition of possibility. The attack of the (social) blob, to use Hanna Pitkin's evocative phrase, spells the end of politics.[84] But this very ability to bracket is selectively invested in particular socialities. We are able to transcend the dull compulsions of necessity and labor and the antinomies of politics from some social locations and not others. It is because Arendt discounts this selective who of action that she is ultimately unable to find a satisfactory answer to her question of why—what explains why action occurs at some points and not others; why does action occur at all?

Shortly after her arrival in the United States in 1941, Arendt spent two months with the Giduz family in Winchester, Massachusetts, in order to learn the language and customs of her new country. She was intrigued by her landlady, and her thoughts on Mrs. Giduz, communicated in letters to her family and her mentor Karl Jaspers in the early 1940s, germinated an intellectual trajectory that would eventually culminate in *The Human Condition* and its theory of action, seventeen years later.[85] Mrs. Giduz is annoying, Arendt writes. For one, she is quite bossy. As Elisabeth Young-Bruehl describes it in her political biography, "Arendt was irritated by

Mrs. Giduz's efforts to supervise, to protect, to make her guest into the child she herself never had."[86] Mrs. Giduz's disapproval of smoking, her vegetarianism, and her "outdoorsiness" are other things that annoyed Arendt. For Arendt, Mrs. Giduz's love of hiking was uncomfortably similar to the *Wandervogel* of the early-twentieth-century German youth movement that was heavily invested in German nationalism.

But the lasting vexation of Mrs. Giduz lay in how she exemplified what was for Arendt the peculiar American combination of social conformity and political freedom. On the one hand, Mrs. Giduz represented petit-bourgeois, small-town conformity. Arendt described her as holding deep racist prejudices and expressing a condescending attitude to new immigrants like herself. But on the other hand, Mrs. Giduz was an exemplar of political activism. She engaged in furious letter-writing campaigns to congressmen to protest the internment of Japanese-Americans, a cause that she should not have identified with since she had no connections to the community, Arendt noted.

Writing to Jaspers in 1946, Arendt puzzled over Mrs. Giduz's peculiar assertion of political agency. This was equally for Arendt a puzzle of American politics. Although there was a high degree of "social conformism," racism, and what she described as a fundamental *Ungeistigkeit* or mindlessness in America, "people feel that they share in responsibility for public life here to a degree unknown to me in any European country . . . [there is here] this great political-practical urging and passion to straighten things out."[87]

Arendt's puzzle of how political assertion springs out of "social slavery," as she termed it, is connected to her reading of Mrs. Giduz as a subject interpellated by social conformity. Another perspective might find the key to the puzzle of Mrs. Giduz's passion to "straighten things out" not in social conformity but instead in social *hierarchy*, that is, her relative class privilege as petit-bourgeois landlady, and her racial privilege that Arendt herself remarked upon but then overlooked when she discussed Giduz's political activism. From this perspective, Mrs. Giduz's exercise of political freedom is authorized by her specific social location and sense of social identity. Recognizing *who* Mrs. Giduz is would explain Arendt's puzzle of *why* she acts politically.

We can apply this insight to the AAP's political project as well. Called to curative action as outsiders to the political establishment, most of the party workers and the senior leadership in particular have been social *insiders* of some kind (along caste, gender, or class lines) from the time of its founding in 2012 until the present. Their efforts to clean up and fix the political system seek not so much to redistribute privilege, but rather to align political and social power. The normative goals of order and control, more than other normative values associated with democracy like individual liberty or social equality, guide the curative democratic interventions of the party.

Somnath Bharti's midnight raid of 2014, the opening story of this chapter, played out in these worlds of socially formed political agency. Our task is not to decipher the real motivation and meaning of the raid by choosing between democratic responsiveness and racialized hierarchy, the respective conclusions that were reached by AAP's supporters and its critics. Rather, it is to recognize that these contradictory and inimical actions—the leap to bold and decisive actions in the name of the ordinary people, and the violent assertion of social hierarchy and control—are intertwined, and they reinforce each other.[88]

TWO

TRANSFORMATIONAL MEDIA

THIS CHAPTER EXPLORES THE mediatized politics of curative democracy: how the call to cure the diseased political system—and the urgent and angry cadences of this call in particular—has been shaped and amplified by media actors.[1] Starting in the early 1990s, a series of policy and regulatory changes "liberalized" or opened up India's state-protected economy to private and international capital and competitive market forces. The television news media industry also underwent substantial changes at the time, and evolved from a state monopoly to a fiercely competitive commercial media system oriented around economic profits. Since the turn of the present century, Indian television news has been competitively traded as a monetized commodity. Liberal-democratic "fourth estate" commitments of a public interest media that provides free and fair information to citizens appear to have conspicuously been abandoned in the "tabloidized" field of sensational television news that proliferates across the country today, with scarce heed to either objectivity or fact.

However, in the course of conducting field research with broadcast journalists and television news organizations in the first decade of the new millennium, a time of intense and rapid media commercialization, I frequently fell into conversations that highlighted the responsibility and mission of journalistic work and stressed that newsmaking was all about making a difference to ordinary people. It would be easy to explain this as empty rhetorical flourish or deluded self-understanding. But this still begs the question of why *this* particular justification (or delusion) is at work. Why does media's democratic importance continue to be the main message, why does the fierce competitive scramble for advertising revenue in news media worlds continue to call up the normative ideal of the ordinary people and journalistic responsibility toward them?

By way of addressing these questions, this chapter explores the idea and practices of media responsibility and mission that suffused the frenetic worlds of Indian commercial news television in the first decades of the twenty-first century. I argue that, contrary to the trajectory of normative decline that conventional discussions of media commercialization emplot, a new normative vision of media's role in democracy, what we could also term a new news value or media ideology, animates contemporary news worlds and the broader cultures of Indian politics. We often overlook how commercial news media worlds are distinguished not so much by the absence of news values but rather by practices of normative reinvention.[2] As we will see, contemporary for-profit news media organizations and professionals invest in new norms of democracy and publicness in the process of marking out a distinctive professional and political identity for themselves as democratic political actors.[3]

My focus is on the distinctive idea of "transformational media" that animates contemporary news worlds. In contrast to liberal ideals of objective media, here the media's role as democracy's fourth estate is not about informing the public by objectively or neutrally reflecting facts and conveying balanced opinions.[4] Rather, it is to bring about social-political change; to actively intervene and make a difference. In the age of the television news revolution, liberalized media are constituted—and constitute themselves—as active change-agents and not as neutral mirrors of society.[5]

In what follows, I examine the transformational media norm and the media practices that have accompanied the shift from "observer to participant media" in India.[6] The first section of the chapter maps the contours of liberalized media worlds. Drawing upon ethnographic field research that I conducted between 2006 and 2008 during the peak years[7] of television news media expansion in Delhi and other cities in the Hindi heartland of northern India, I show how media liberalization along with the broader socioeconomic project of economic liberalization constituted new relations between state, society, market, and media, and reoriented the existing conditions of newsmaking. Through ethnographic vignettes of the everyday work cultures of television news, I offer a socially located account that links the emergence of new media norms and practices to the social and political changes effected by media and economic liberalization, namely regulatory ambiguity, intensified competition, social mobilities, and the fragmentation and dispersal of political authority.

A set of distinctive newsmaking practices and work cultures evolved out of these liberalization contexts, and the next sections of the chapter examine these in closer detail. Through a discussion of media "sting operations" and media activism campaigns, I establish how a new normative ideal and professional imperative of news as a transformational narrative, a story told to make a difference, gained ground. For journalists in liberalizing news worlds, the main professional mandate was not so much to provide objective information to a citizenry. Instead, it was to stand out from the competition by telling a different and new kind of story that shook up "the system." The narrative demand was to convey "emotional truths"[8] that elicited angry recognition and confirmation, and mobilized and assembled the people in visible scenes of public protest. The transformational power of news journalism was also linked to a set of concrete actions undertaken by journalists and media organizations, who worked with civil society organizations and the judiciary to restore democratic power to the people. Media took on a representational role that went beyond discursive storytelling, to actual engagements and interventions in democratic politics, as self-described "crusaders" and representatives of the people committed to the cause of democratic change.

The chapter concludes by considering the broader political and social effects of the transformational media norm. The role of media as a change-agent that confronts unrepresentative political elites in the name of the people reflects this book's central theme: the power and legitimacy that putative political outsiders or non-electoral actors enjoy in India's democracy.[9] The practices of sting journalism and media crusades documented in this chapter complement the effective citizenship projects of the Aam Aadmi Party that the previous chapter explored. Both are examples of how representative claims-making in Indian democracy, as in many other democracies around the world today, is increasingly linked to assertions of distrust and distaste for electoral politics.

Journalistic practices of revelation and exposure, like the AAP party worker's public performances of immediate and decisive remedial action explored in the previous chapter, pit the corrupt, indifferent, and cruel establishment against a victimized people. They create the diagnosis of a democracy in terminal crisis and decline on which the politics of populist redemption thrives. But what are the terms and modes of such redemption? And what for that matter is the system that oppresses and denies the people their sovereign rights and freedoms? In the concluding section of the chapter, I address these questions by examining the social relations and contexts that drive and shape assertions of change-agency by media actors.

The previous chapter documented the ownership politics practiced by the Aam Aadmi Party (AAP) and concluded that the call to cure democracy and fix the system was linked to and possibly even constituted by hierarchical social relations. My field research with AAP party workers showed that in many instances, the efforts to create a new politics mapped onto older hierarchies of caste, class, and gender. I found that specific kinds of social subjects—dominant caste, male, Hindu, middle-class individuals—mostly exercised curative political agency and held leadership and decision-making positions within the AAP. It is not a coincidence that the anger against electoral politics has erupted at a time of "representative plebeianization"—when the demographic character of electoral representation is changing, and elected representatives come from social backgrounds that are quite different from those of their rather patrician predecessors.[10] This chapter shows that similar kinds of hierarchically informed ownership politics also pervade contemporary Indian news worlds. The idea of democratic reform promoted by many TV journalists is also connected to a logic of social restoration. It is invested in hierarchical imaginaries of social and political order that call for the restoration of the *right* people to power.

The final point that the chapter addresses is about the object of media transformation, or the much-maligned political system that sting journalism and media activism campaigns set out to expose and oppose in the name of the people. Through the discussion of a spectacular and prolonged episode of media activism around a double homicide that saw several narrative shifts and contestations over the identity of the real victim and the real perpetrator, I draw attention to the constitutive ambiguity and instability of the populist fault line.

According to Ernesto Laclau and many other theorists of populism, the binary antagonism between the people and the system/establishment/elites is the main premise of populist politics.[11] Establishing an "equivalential chain" between the diverse social demands that cleave a body politic, and subsuming these differences within an overarching narrative of opposition between "the system" and the unitary people, is essential to the populist project. For Laclau, it is the enabling condition of politics itself.[12] However, these equivalences are neither permanent nor complete. The singular populist fault line and the unities that it opposes—the people on the one side, the system on the other—are contingent political fictions, and they frequently run up against the fissured landscape of social fractures and inequalities. The system and the establishment, like the people, are empty signifiers that mean different and often contradictory things to differently located social groups and subjects. The chapter ends by exploring some of these contradictions in the project of transformational media, and suggests that the redemptive claims of media change-agency, and outsider political agency more broadly speaking, are partial and contested. Angry politics, or the distinctive political form of public outrage that marks our contemporary global era of mediatized democracy, has an uneven and unstable political effect, as we will see.

LIBERALIZED MEDIA WORLDS[13]

Up until the early 1990s, there was only one news channel in India, the state-owned Doordarshan. Over the next two decades, a staggering total of 268 news and current affairs channels were licensed by India's Ministry of Information and Broadcasting.[14] As the first decade of the twenty-first century drew to a close, India had more news channels than anywhere else in the world. In 2010, Indian television was estimated to reach 134 million households or 500 million individuals (that is, approximately 60 percent of the country's population). Generating annual revenues of 265.5 billion rupees (approximately $6 billion) in 2009, the television industry comprised almost half of the "Indian entertainment and media market," which at the time was the fourth largest in the world.[15]

Indian media liberalization unfolded in the larger context of economic liberalization in the country, which began in the 1980s with little public debate or knowledge and a "narrow support base."[16] In India as in many other countries at the time, the policy consensus for market-friendly "structural adjustments" of state-protected economies emerged across World Bank consultants, ministries of finance, and the private sector, with little public support outside of a small urban elite. This is significant given that at the time some 70 percent of India's citizens lived and worked in rural areas and that some 40 percent, by conservative estimates, lived below the poverty line. As political scientist Rob Jenkins describes it, the process was largely one of economic "reform by stealth." Key decisions were taken by executive fiat, outside the frameworks of parliamentary deliberation.[17]

The process of media liberalization unfolded in similarly gradual and ad hoc terms, shaped by lobbying efforts by media owners and individualized concessions made by state officials. It was more a process of nonregulation rather than deregulation. The transformation of a state-monopolized news television arena into one comprised of multiple privately owned news media organizations involved a series of small and incremental innovations. Rather than a single policy decision to liberalize the media, the discretionary authority of the state to grant specialized, one-off deals to individual media owners fueled the remarkable expansion of Indian television news.[18] As several of my informants have noted, the Hindi term *jugaad* or improvisation[19] is an apt description of this process. It yielded a commercial television news sector that remained in many ways a statist project, embedded within and sustained by the tangled proximities of state and market forces that distinguished the new economic order in the 1990s and beyond.[20]

This had an effect on two important dimensions of the television news media industry: its ownership structures, and the social composition of the journalistic workforce. A wide range of new media proprietors entered the industry, many of whom were not motivated by considerations of economic profit alone. The patchwork and *jugaad* trajectory of Indian media reform created a minimally regulated investment terrain where different social actors realized diverse aspirations. These ranged from profit-seeking on the part of established capitalist enterprises to power-seeking, that is, attempts by various actors to garner and consolidate political and social influence. For instance, as media scholar Padmaja Shaw has observed in her study of Telugu news television in the southern Indian state of Andhra Pradesh, the dramatic expansion of Telugu news media channels was fueled in large part by the availability of "speculative capital" within "grey" or illicit economies, coupled with the growth of what she described as a "lumpen political class" that saw in the establishment of a news channel a path to social and political legitimacy and influence.[21] Shaw's account resonates with my own observations about the social composition of media owners in states such as Madhya Pradesh and Bihar, where I found that the majority of regional and local television news channels were owned by entrepreneurs engaged in real estate, construction, cable distribution, finance, transportation, and other businesses where semi-legal economic transactions were commonplace.[22]

The *jugaad* quality of Indian media reform also changed the social composition of the media workforce. The relative ease with which television news channels could be established—until 2010 a net worth of 30 million rupees (approximately $650,000) was the threshold for official recognition by the Ministry of Information and Broadcasting—led to a dramatic proliferation of news channels. The resulting demand for personnel effectively widened the pool of media labor to include subjects from social backgrounds that would have excluded them from employment in the print media industry, where the minimum requirements of higher education were met historically by a narrow group of national and regional elites. The commercial television news industry had a very different operational understanding of qualifications and expertise than its print journalism counterpart from an earlier era, although an analogous "newspaper revolution" has also transformed the social composition of print journalism over the previous decades.[23]

The social expansion of the television news media workforce also coincided with broader sets of political changes in the country. Along with media liberalization, the last decades of the twentieth century saw a series of multi-party coalitions form the national government. Regional parties emerged as powerful forces in national politics, fragmenting political authority and changing the social character of political representation.[24] The news media industry's foundational requirement of access to high politics in Delhi now required engaging with multiple sources of political power, and animated a search for new networks and connections.

As political authority was "plebeianized" and regionalized with the entry of new social actors into electoral politics,[25] journalists' access to power was routed along pathways that were quite different from those that connected journalists and politicians of an earlier era. New media ideologies gained legibility and prominence, reconfiguring existing cultures and practices of newsmaking and advancing a new institutional role for media (and journalists) in political and social life. The following vignette of everyday life in Indian news worlds illustrate some of these changes.[26]

Crime Beat

Field Notes, August 21, 2008. Delhi and Noida (suburb of Delhi). The news editor had assigned me to follow Ravi Arora[27] for the day, a crime reporter with IBN-7, a leading Hindi news channel in Delhi. As I waited for him in the newsroom, I copied down the words on a sign tacked to the wall that seemed to be particularly appropriate for the day that awaited me with all its exciting potential: *Har har shikar par / Ab hamari nazar / Payenge har manzil par / Har keemat par.* Fixed is our gaze now on every single prey, gain it we shall at every stage, whatever be the cost.[28]

Ravi didn't look particularly happy about having a follower, and my eager questions about the agenda of the day's crime beat were met with a terse and cryptic response. "Call girls." A few additional details followed on the long car journey between Film City, in the suburb of Noida, where the majority of news channels were located, and South Delhi, where we were headed. As the SUV negotiated the snarl of traffic on the Noida-Delhi highway, cameraman Amandeep More[29] and I learned that we were going to attend a press conference (a "PC") scheduled for noon at the

Sarita Vihar police station, where five or six call girls, two "pimps," and some clients had been brought in the previous night.

How were they apprehended? I asked. We'd find out at the PC, Ravi and Amandeep replied. Where were the women from? They'd tell us at the PC. How did we know they were call girls? The PC would reveal all. Ravi and Amandeep did not seem to be curious at all about their assignment. Demolishing all my preconceptions about how resourceful journalists hunted down elusive bits of information and pieced them together to solve a crime mystery, the crime-reporting routine thus far seemed like that of any other news beat I had encountered during my research on television newsrooms in Delhi: structured around a press briefing by state officials.

Stuck in traffic, our car with its IBN-7 logo and red-lettered press sticker attracted repeated glances from drivers and passengers in neighboring vehicles. *TV wale hain na?* You're TV folks, right? someone eventually shouted out, and Ravi grew more expansive in the glow of all this public recognition. He was one of three crime reporters at IBN-7, he told me, and he'd been working there for a year and a half after a stint at BAG films, a television production house that was also based in the Delhi-Noida region. He hadn't really thought about journalism as a career option when he was growing up in the eastern state of Bihar. But television work was a good way to get to and stay in Delhi, the national capital and the main hub of power and recognition as Ravi saw it. Most Hindi journalists were from the northern states of Uttar Pradesh and Bihar, though Amandeep was from Maharashtra, in the west.

We soon fell into a familiar conversation about the *majboori*, or compulsions, that drove television news coverage in India. This had to do with the "TRP system" of television rating points that measured viewership numbers for individual channels, programs, and time slots. TRPs determined advertisement placement decisions, and this in turn affected the revenue streams of television channels, in a business that was heavily dependent on advertising rather than subscription revenues. Intense competition over TRPs had driven down the standards of news, Ravi and Amandeep explained.

This was a familiar story. During my fieldwork with news organizations and journalists in India during the news boom period of the early twenty-first century, I kept encountering similar journalistic narratives about declining news values under conditions of extreme commercial competition. Media professionals routinely bemoaned the commercially driven ratings system and held the competitive environment that it promoted to be responsible for all that was wrong with Indian news television. TRPs were responsible for the obsession with "breaking news" or the rush to be first with the news story that dominated the daily work of journalism. TRPs were also responsible for the long working hours of journalists. "Competition drives everything and everybody today," Amandeep sighed. Much like the reflexive self-understandings of commercial Hindi filmmakers in Mumbai that the anthropologist Tejaswini Ganti has described in her ethnography of the social worlds of Hindi commercial cinema,[30] news workers in Indian television news channels drew on a language of compulsions and constraints to distance themselves both from the commercial/profit-making aspects of their work and from the inexplicable tastes and preferences of the "ordinary viewers" whose viewing habits had generated high TRPs for mediocre news programs.

A phone call interrupted our conversation. Could we roll up the windows, please? That was the office calling. Ravi needed to take a "phono," a live phone interview with the studio-based anchor. Amandeep and I were enlightened about the story along with the TV audience as Ravi in a booming baritone proceeded to summarize the details of the crime with an impressive authority, providing details he hadn't shared with us. Eleven people had been caught by the Sarita Vihar police in a raid on a housing complex in South Delhi the previous night, and an IBN-7 team was now rushing to the spot to follow up on two lines of inquiry, he informed viewers. Was this a sex racket? And did the call girl story link up to something bigger, deeper, and darker? For more information, keep tuning in, this is Ravi Arora from the crime team at IBN-7. Although in his conversations with us, Ravi did not seem to have a clear idea or much of an interest in our assignment, he had a firm and definite story for the television audience, delivered in crisp and compelling prose.

Our rush to the spot encountered a snag. The driver couldn't locate the Sarita Vihar police station and we had to stop several times to ask for directions. Ravi, like many other young journalists, was a relative newcomer to Delhi and he was unfamiliar with many parts of the city. The residential area of South Delhi, located at a considerable distance from the Noida media enclave where most news channels were located, was uncharted terrain, and *they*—the people at the assignment desk, in the office—had not given us any specific instructions. The many failings of *they* and *them* were recurrent themes in my fieldwork, and repeatedly surfaced in my conversations with journalists from Hindi as well as English news channels. The division between "desk" and "field," producers and reporters, those who anchor and those who gather the news—a division that only thinly masked social and economic divides of caste, class, cultural-linguistic capital—was reproduced in my field notes from that day as a sharp fault line traversed by sentiments of contempt, resentment, and plain irritation.

Inside the police station, Ravi bantered with the police constable at the reception desk, asking for news. Yes, the station officers said, there were call girls, maybe three or four. Were the pimps caught as well, and what about the customers? Ravi asked. Wait for the PC, you'll find out all you need to know there, we were told, and Ravi waited without further questions, fiddling with his phone. We were eventually ushered into the station head's office, where reporters from several other national and city channels were waiting. The conversations ground to an abrupt halt when some police constables entered the room and told us to go to the hallway for a "photo parade." Three teenage boys in handcuffs were brought before us. They are members of the Mittoo gang, a constable told us, and the cameras were turned on. Who's your chief? a reporter called out. Rahul, one of the boys replied. There were no further questions from any of the assembled journalists.

Five young women with *chunnis* (scarves) covering their faces were brought out and made to stand with the Mittoo gang, a female police officer on either side. A table was set up at one end of the hallway, and police officers placed several mobile phones and cardboard boxes filled with liquor bottles on it. The cameramen crowded around. After filming a quick pan shot of the women, they turned to film the police officers who were standing at the table, pointing to the objects there. The police are expanding their publicity efforts, Ravi explained. They've put on three shows for us today: women, phones, and *sharaab* (alcohol). Press folk are coming so let's give them all we have, they must have thought, he sniggered to me conspiratorially.

Despite the impressive police publicity show on offer, Ravi was visibly disappointed with what he saw. Low-profile call girls and low-profile customers, he grumbled. It's a bailable offense, it's nothing big at all. Nithari, a recent sensational and highly publicized crime that had dominated the headlines for the alleged involvement of a serial killer and accusations of cannibalism, had a Bangladesh angle, but I don't think this one does. Why did you shoot? The tape is wasted, he reproached Amandeep. How are these people going to be treated by the police? I asked, not willing to write off my much-anticipated day on the crime beat. Maybe there's a story there? Ravi dismissed my suggestion. The human rights people are around these days so there's no more *marpit*, roughing up; there's nothing there. We need a proper story.

Maybe the press conference, now relocated to the Hauz Khas police station in South Delhi, would give us the story we were looking for. The other journalists at the Sarita Vihar police station clearly thought the same way, and we all reassembled in Hauz Khas a short while later. Several other TV crews from big national channels joined us there, attesting to the important status of Hauz Khas in the police administrative hierarchy. District Police Commissioner (DCP) Shukla began the press conference, speaking into a thick silence that blanketed the room in anticipation. The police had busted a flesh trade last night, he announced. The team had caught four girls, one madam, two pimps, and a few customers, locals from Sarita Vihar and Khanpur. How long had this been going on? Where else do they operate? Is it a big gang? Is there alcohol smuggling as well? The questions came at Shukla, but soon the topic changed abruptly, and we shifted to the other elements of the Sarita Vihar photo parade. There were two successful police raids the previous day, Shukla told us. Two hundred boxes of alcohol were found in a black Santro car going toward Haryana. It's for the upcoming elections, but we don't know for which party, he said. What about the mobile phones that we were shown, shouted a reporter. That's the Amit Mittoo gang story. They are known and wanted criminals in the South Delhi district. Their names are Kamal, Balbir, Latif, and Sushil *urf* (alias) Sonu and they rob buses and snatch necklaces, the DCP narrated. Why are they called the Amit Mittoo gang, I wondered, but no one asked that question. Are they an *antarrajya* interstate gang? Ravi shouted out, still in search of his story. Well, they work in border areas like Faridabad, so maybe you can say that, Shukla offered.

The press conference was over in less than ten minutes, and the reporters seemed satisfied that they had all the information they needed. Names, type of crime, and a possible angle of an interstate operation had all been noted.[31] There might be a story here. As we began saying our goodbyes, Ravi's phone rang with the news that the day wasn't over. We were told to rush to the Delhi Cantonment area because "a colonel has done something to his daughter." Other phones were ringing in the room; it seemed that everyone was being sent to "Delhi Cantt." Further and wildly divergent details emerged as we swapped notes with each other. It wasn't a colonel and his daughter, some reporters said. A foreigner had been arrested, it's probably because his passport has expired, it's a nonstory and we are wasting our time, they concluded. But the Aaj Tak and Times Now channels were covering it as a story, so we all had to cover it too.

The afternoon traffic was much slower and it took us almost an hour to get to the Delhi Cantonment, where the headquarters of the Indian Army and various institutions for the military (including military housing) are located. When we reached the location, there were at least four outdoor broadcast (OB) vans from major English and Hindi news channels already in place. Ravi pushed his way into the crush of reporters standing outside an unmarked building. Newer details emerged: the story had changed again. Two Ethiopians (gender unspecified) had been arrested in Pegs N Pints, a bar in Chanakyapuri, Delhi's diplomatic enclave, and that's why we were all here. It's a story about army prostitution, Ravi told me; it's big. I puzzled over the connection between Delhi Cantonment, Chanakyapuri, Ethiopia, and the Indian Army, but didn't gain any clarity.

Some English-language journalists arrived and the reporters sifted themselves into two separate language clusters, each sharing stories and jokes that highlighted the incompetence of desk, the ignorance of anchors, and the corruption and greed of stringers. The *Angrezi* (English language) journalists also traded stories about important political figures and tried to impress each other with juicy nuggets of political insider information.

Ravi shared a new narrative angle: the story could be a plant to falsely implicate Ethiopians. It could be a case of drugs that is being passed off as a prostitution story. We all know that it's the Nigerians and South Africans who do drugs in India, he said. Gautam[32] the English language journalist went along with the fake story theory, but took it in a different direction. This could be a big story, not about Ethiopians at all, but about Pakistan's "honeytrap," he confidently pronounced. A thoughtful silence descended as we considered the various angles and possibilities before us. Anything could be unfolding here. We waited until 6 p.m. but no one came to give us a briefing, and there were no other people around to interview for a sound bite.

Eventually a small group of elderly women going for their evening walk stopped to ask why so many reporters and OB vans had gathered there. Which channel would it come on that evening? What do you feel about what has happened? an enterprising journalist asked, milking every encounter for a newsworthy bite even though none of us knew what exactly had happened. *Sabki beti hain*, they're everyone's daughters, said the women mysteriously, smiling beatifically as they walked on. The cameras remained shuttered, and we packed up to go home. We'll find a stock shot of the Ethiopian embassy and that should be enough, Amandeep and Ravi agreed. Too bad we couldn't get a single live shot.

Later that night I watched the prime-time news on IBN-7. Toward the end of the bulletin, there was a brief mention of Delhi Cantonment, where a "major and a *jawaan* [ordinary soldier]" may have allegedly been taken hostage for a brief while. Further details are awaited, the anchor said, and moved on to another story. When and how did the Ethiopian angle and the "Pakistan honeytrap" turn into a military hostage situation, I puzzled, but my field notes didn't provide me with any answers.

Beat Story

The fieldwork vignette illuminates two key features of liberalized news worlds in India. First, a lot of news work involved banal, repetitive, and quite tedious activity. Every evening, lurid fast-moving graphics crowded television screens as excited anchors broadcast urgent "breaking news" to Indian audiences in rushed, fever-pitch voices. But to go behind the frenetic pace of these television news broadcasts was to experience news work as a prolonged wait for technology to function, traffic to unsnarl, and state officials to make an appearance. The beat described above was about crime: momentous, one-of-a-kind events. However, my experiences were structured around the unremarkable and unexceptional rhythms of days when nothing much happened. Moreover, although my field research encounters focused on distinct news beats—crime in Delhi arguably had little in common with the regional politics beat in Bihar that I also followed—I found that they all shared a common assembly-line approach, with individual media professionals (journalists, camerapeople, producers, anchors, editors, and so on) focusing on small, discrete, and highly specialized tasks that were assembled together as news only at the moment of live broadcast.

Television news work seemed a version of piecework.[33] This was not about the mode of wage payment—the media professionals I accompanied on each of the shoots were paid monthly salaries that were based on full-time work-hour specifications—but the labor process and form, and the value and recognition that accrued to media labor. All the journalists I encountered had a very specific and fragmented task to complete that conformed to a standardized set of news production conventions. Their main job as they saw it was to deliver according to this fixed format, and to do so as quickly as possible. Speed and timeliness was of the essence, measured according to how fast or slow they were compared to other channels broadcasting the same news item.

Amandeep, the cameraman on the crime shoot, had to film a certain number and type of images (cutaways; exterior shots; "crowd pans" for any story that referenced mass gatherings, etc.). Ravi the crime reporter had to get bites from certain categories of individuals that fit a pre-given formula (an authoritative statement from a police officer; a *vox pop*[34] from an "ordinary passerby"). The journalists I followed in Patna, Bihar, had to chase down "reaction bites" from politicians. Back in the main offices, at output desks and broadcast studios, the work process was similarly fragmented. Its rapid temporal flow and acceleration—the value of television news was, above all, measured in terms of speed, who was "breaking first"—was even more keenly felt.[35]

At one level, all these were highly formulaic, widget-making tasks where little to no innovation or independent thought was required, and news work was about conforming to a set of fixed conventions. At another level, however, the foundational expectation of providing a "good story" gave media workers a considerable amount of narrative autonomy and responsibility. Indeed, the quest for an impactful narrative that stood out from the competition was the main task at hand in all the media spaces that I visited. I found that informational tasks such as the gathering and verification of facts and evidentiary truths that are conventionally associated with news work were overshadowed by the drive to craft a distinctive narrative frame. The beat reporters that I shadowed were in search of a good story,[36] but their quests did not prioritize the collection and verification of empirical details and facts.[37] I was also struck by the fact that independent validation and the cross-checking of empirical details did not seem terribly important to the daily beat routine. On the contrary, most journalists tended uncritically to reproduce the information handed out by state officials, particularly those associated with the law and order and security agencies of the state, for example, the police and the military.[38] There was a clear imprint of state-centrism on the commercial news media field,[39] although this was vehemently disavowed by contemporary journalists as a hallmark of "old journalism" of the *dirigiste* Nehru era.

Second, news work was structured around a fiercely competitive dynamic of mimetic comparison. The everyday work cultures of news worlds were pervaded by an acute anxiety about what "the others" were doing and airing, and whether and how one's own work surpassed these comparative benchmarks. Comparative evaluations of the news produced by competitors was an integral feature of everyday news work. In every newsroom, a bank of TV monitors occupied a prominent location, keenly watched by media professionals of all stripes, from senior editors to novice video cutters on the output desk. A continuous hum of chatter about what X or Y rival channel was leading with, and the likely displeasure of the bosses when they failed to see the same news lineup on their own channel, was the ambient soundtrack of the workplace. A foundational piece of folk wisdom offered by all the journalists I spoke to was the importance of covering the same news at the same time as other channels. The replication of news bulletins by multiple news channels so that near-identical images, banner headlines, and voice-overs streamed across multiple news bank monitors with only minor tweaks and adaptations was a common feature of India's commercial news media space. Media workers were driven by the imperative of comparison and emulation/mimesis.

But alongside the quest to reproduce the news items and "rundowns" that rival channels aired, mimetic competition also drove Indian news journalists to stand out in some fashion. Newsmaking meant both replicating and distinguishing themselves from their peers. There was widespread consensus among media professionals that having a good story or a "good angle" was the primary way to achieve this distinction,[40] and conversations frequently centered on the relative worth of competitor stories. During each of my forays into the media field, I encountered rueful, envy-tinged speculations about how other journalists had managed to land a big story. What were the criteria or measures of narrative worth? In most of my conversations, the import of a news story was related to how it stirred or shook people up. The narrative quest that shaped TV newsmaking practices in early-twenty-first century India committed journalists and media organizations to a specific idea of media's transformational agency: how news media had the power to *do something to* society and the people/public/*janata*; how news media were not so much neutral and passive observers but rather were active participants and makers of social change.

I inquired about how this was to be achieved. What were the sources of media's transformational power? I received conflicting responses that mirrored the multiple social divisions and distinctions that proliferated in Indian television news worlds. Like other new economic industries associated with the liberalization regime in India, the workspaces of television news media organizations were riven and agitated by a "clash of capitals" as newer entrants into the profession came from social, economic, and linguistic-regional backgrounds that were quite different from earlier generations of media professionals. In these contexts of social flux, the making and marking of distinctions was a central feature of everyday social relations. News work was structured around a keen awareness of various kinds of differences and hierarchies: field versus desk; Hindi versus English; "metro" versus small town. Competing claims about the media's ability to produce good and big stories that made a difference animated these distinctions, opening up more questions than they settled.

My day on the crime beat with Ravi Arora had concluded with such a moment. Standing around in the Delhi Cantonment waiting for a news story, social distinctions and clashes took on a materially tangible form. Hindi and English language journalists from different television channels (sometimes from the same media house) formed separate clusters. Each argued that the other had failed to grasp the correct narrative. Was the media's narrative power and change-agency a matter of authentic and embodied representation? Did social-demographic proximity to the ordinary or the popular make a difference—were Hindi journalists, particularly those from nonmetropolitan backgrounds, able to innately and intuitively get the story? Or, was the big picture clarified and finessed by the access to networks of state power that the English journalists from metropolitan and elite social backgrounds enjoyed? Hindi and English-language journalists who gathered outside the Delhi Cantonment office that day had different and opposed answers to these questions. Claims about extraordinary insider access countered claims to ordinary heartland origins and roots, without any final resolution.

Drawing upon fieldwork within the Indian television news industry during the boom years of the early twenty-first century, this section of the chapter has traced the effects of India's gradual and *jugaad* processes of media liberalization and the distinctive conditions of mimetic competition to which they gave rise, on the everyday cultures of newsmaking. I have suggested that transformational news narratives—news stories that had specific kinds of transformational effects in and on society/the people—came to be idealized and privileged over the conventional informational functions of news media. The question of how such transformational agency could best be exercised by the media remained open. Reflecting the fractured contexts of Indian media worlds, media professionals from different social backgrounds advanced contending claims about who could best produce transformational news stories. All agreed, however, that the transformational power or change-agency of news narratives was their main purpose.

What was the measure and sign of a transformational media narrative? What exactly did the exercise of change agency entail? To answer these questions, the next sections examine media stings and media activism campaigns, two types of change-making media practices that were deployed by TV news journalists and media organizations in the early years of the new millennium.

Stings

Satyashree Gandham, a senior editor at Cobrapost, an independent media organization in Delhi, crisply summarized the meaning of her work. "These are big, fat stories. They give the bigger picture, they throw open the system. The idea is to understand more than right and wrong as shades of gray. These stories are about absolute wrong."[41]

When our conversation took place in the autumn of 2014, Cobrapost was a niche content-producing operation that employed a few reporters and was staffed mostly by interns and students. Their main job was to produce "sting packages" in multiple media formats and market them to media organizations for publication or broadcast. Sitting in their sparsely furnished office in an apartment building in Delhi, it was evident that Cobrapost's economic outlook was rather tenuous, and that the company, along with its unique product, the media sting—the covertly obtained media recording, and subsequent public dissemination via media technologies, of a "person committing a crime"[42]—was struggling for public relevance. It was getting increasingly difficult to find a media organization that was willing to purchase and publish a Cobrapost sting, and the company had been forced to change its business model the previous year. Since 2013, Cobrapost was registered under a nonprofit society that qualified for tax exemptions and solicited donations from private entities.

Things were different just a few years ago. In the early years of the twenty-first century, media stings were at the epicenter of public and political attention both within and beyond India. Investigative journalists like Aniruddha Bahal, the founder of Cobrapost, were the much-hailed and admired vanguards of the media revolution that this distinctive and audacious media practice had inaugurated. Sting operations, as they were called, had unseated leading politicians from office and garnered major national and international professional laurels for journalists. Stings had contributed to the popularity of demands for accountable government that were subsequently taken up on a national scale by the national anti-corruption movement, India Against Corruption, and the Aam Aadmi Party, as we've discussed in chapter 1.

Sting journalism came to public attention in 2001[43] with Operation West End, an undercover hidden-camera investigation carried out by journalists Mathew Samuel and Aniruddha Bahal for the newsmagazine and website *Tehelka*.[44] The journalists posed as arms dealers from a fictitious company called West End International and networked with officials in the defense and military establishments over a seven-month period with the ostensible aim of securing a government contract for a "handheld thermal camera," a piece of defense equipment that didn't actually exist. Filming these interactions with a hidden camera, the journalists documented their journey "up the ladder of graft," as the editor of *Tehelka*, Tarun Tejpal, has described it.[45] Political leaders such as the president of the BJP and senior military personnel were captured on camera while ostensibly engaged in various acts of impropriety that ranged from the acceptance of cash bribes to demands for foreign-branded liquor and trysts with sex workers.

The public revelations of the West End tapes predictably created a national political scandal and eventually led to the resignations of several of the chief accused, although as William Mazzarella and Anirban Gupta-Nigam have observed, the flurry of scandal and sensation soon died down and "business as usual" prevailed in Indian politics. Operation West End was in the end a non-event. Its only lasting political outcome was to end the career of BJP president Bangaru Laxman, the sole Dalit political leader of a national political party.[46]

In its immediate aftermath, however, Operation West End had a significant impact on the Indian media. The public attention and buzz that it generated encouraged many others to emulate the *Tehelka* journalists and carry out their own hidden-camera investigations on different topics. By the late 2000s, the phrases *sting karna* or *sting karwa do*—literally, to do a sting or to have a sting carried out—had become commonplace in Indian television newsrooms. In media circles during the first decade of the twenty-first century, there was widespread agreement that programs featuring stings garnered high viewership numbers and drove up the ratings points that were the main measure of competition and profitability in the news media industry. Several commercial news channels established in-house "sting units" or specialized teams of journalists working on various undercover projects that were broadcast in a weekly sting bulletin. Some journalists such as Aniruddha Bahal set up companies like Cobrapost to undertake freelance sting operations that would be sold as ready-made audiovisual packages to television news organizations.[47]

Stings comprise a distinctive subgenre of investigative journalism and have several unique features. First, as the term *operation* conveys with its connotations of secretive military actions, stings are always covert ventures. Journalists use hidden cameras to record activities and subjects who are not aware that they are being filmed. This state of unawareness and ignorance on the part of powerful individuals—the subjects of stings are usually state officials, politicians, or individuals entrusted with some kind of public representative function—is central to the media practice. It contrasts with the knowledge possessed by the journalist and the viewer, to constitute the sting as a practice of democratic empowerment that inverts prevailing hierarchies of power. In marked contrast to the murk and muddle of everyday life, where knowledge (and hence power) is monopolized by political representatives, the ordinary citizen as the viewer of the sting is positioned as a subject who enjoys the privilege of exclusive information and deep knowledge. In the distinctive time-space of the sting she is the wielder of optic power.

The second distinctive feature of stings is their reliance upon visual and spectacular forms of public communication. The practice of sting journalism as it evolved in twentieth-century and early millennial India involves the audiovisual recording of material that is intended for eventual public dissemination, mostly through the internet or television channels. Moreover, although the material for a sting is covertly gathered through surreptitious means, its public presentation takes place with considerable fanfare. Stings are usually announced with a set of "grand reveal" events such as launch press conferences, promotional trailers, and the publication of specially commissioned companion op-ed pieces in newspapers and magazines. Edited and packaged into exposés that erupt spectacularly within the public domain, stings prime viewers that they are about to see something of great democratic consequence. The main innovation of the sting is presented as the ability to make visible a key aspect of reality that is usually hidden, unacknowledged, or too abstract to grasp.[48] Drawing on Jeffrey Green's work on contemporary democracy's optical turn, we could say that the main public address of the sting is to the "eyes of the people." Eschewing conventional ideas of how rational-critical deliberation and the cultivation of "voice" ground and strengthen democracy,[49] the promotional discourse around stings[50] emphasizes the importance of practices of witnessing and direct observation for the exercise of empowered democratic citizenship.

Third, stings offer narratives of revelation and exposure; they are about telling as much as showing.[51] The secrecy, risk, and adventure of the covert operation are integral to the sting's allure, but there is more to the media practice than the act of hidden-camera documentation. Along with the body of exclusive visual evidence gathered by the investigative journalists, the anchor's introduction, the explanatory voice-over, editing techniques, and special effects that make sense of the grainy, shaky, and otherwise "poor images" are essential elements.[52] The narrative explanation invariably takes an expositional or revelatory form. From the "promos" or promotional excerpts that are aired on television channels to entice viewers into watching a future broadcast, to the opening scenes of a sting bulletin, stings are narrated as exposés of shocking misdeeds that, regardless of what the actual incident is about, are held up as symptoms of the widespread corruption and rot that fester in the institutions and politics of Indian democracy.

The narrative element that is introduced at the stage of postproduction packaging (involving editing, the insertion of special effects, the recording of voice-overs and anchor segments) is central to its meaning as a specific kind of revelatory intervention. The poor and raw quality of the images recorded by the hidden cameras indexes reality as such.[53] To decipher and understand their significance, another level of (didactic) explanation is required. As much as the drive to visibility, the existence of the sting as a *khulasa* or revelation/exposé turns on the intermediary interventions of explanatory voice-overs, editing techniques, and various kinds of graphics and special effects that enable viewers to discern the bigger picture from the grainy swirl of pixels.

But what exactly is being revealed or exposed? A list of stings conducted in the aftermath of Operation West End (from 2001 onward) brings a wide range of issues into focus, from consumer fraud to terrorism and religious corruption. Although at first glance these appear to be very diverse concerns,[54] they are in fact narrated as variants of a single theme: the failure of representative politics and parliamentary democracy. Corruption in private schools and hospitals; consumer fraud committed by business enterprises; "scams" undertaken by NGOs, are all re-presented as outcomes of regulatory oversight failures—instances of a governmental and political lapse. Sting journalism in India has almost exclusively focused on moments where representatives of the people (government officials, politicians) and institutions and practices of parliamentary democracy are seen to have flagrantly violated their assigned responsibilities and contributed to the crisis and breakdown of democracy. Regardless of the specific problem at hand and the cast of characters involved, each sting emplots a similar narrative arc that ends in a denouement of system breakdown and crisis. Moreover, this conclusion is presented as a validation of a known and accepted fact rather than the discovery of something new.

Stings, then, do not confront the viewer with the unknown and unimaginable. Instead, they confirm her worst suspicions and fears, and convert tacit presumptions into explicit and visible facts. As the journalist Mathew Samuel described the practice of sting journalism during Operation West End, "all we had to do was to put an image on what was a commonly known thing."[55] The visual evidence of BJP leader Bangaru Laxman's antics added ballast to the existing public perception that "they"—the political representatives supposed to serve and further the interests of the people—were up to no good. This is the fourth distinctive feature of a sting: it is a media practice that enlists and amplifies already-existing public discourses and sentiments about systemic dysfunction and corruption to make the case for a pervasive, widespread, and endemic crisis.[56] Framing corruption and wrongdoing in iterative and cumulative terms—this *too* is corrupt and broken!—sting narratives offer grim diagnoses of terminal decline.

Fifth, stings are distinguished by their affective discourse of public outrage and anger, and their emotional appeal to ideas of victimhood and heroic action. Regardless of their specific subject matter, the public presentation of stings strikes a common note of anger and exasperation. This is really the last straw, enough is enough! At far remove from liberal media norms of objectivity and neutrality, sting exposés of egregious wrongdoing by the political classes and the system draw on emotional registers of high moral outrage and indignation. They marshal archetypes of the politician as villain, the people as duped victim, and the sting journalist as brave hero.

This brings me to the final signature feature of sting journalism: its reflexivity, or the fact that it is a media form and practice in which the role and agency of the media takes center stage. Alongside their dark portrayal of democratic disease and decay, stings present visions of democratic redemption and change effected by the media. Contrasting media practitioners and institutions to the corrupt officials and politicians caught on camera, sting narratives hail them as the new and true agents of popular representation, as the change-makers who dare to make a difference. Indeed, media professionals and media technologies are the main protagonists of these stories. The journalists who outwit the authorities with their hidden-camera investigations, the producers and editors who package the exposé and enable its public dissemination, and the anchors in the studio who introduce the story are all part of a righteous "crusade."[57] In the narrative of the sting, they are the ones undertaking a risky media practice in the name of the people, fulfilling the democratic duty that elected representatives have so flagrantly abandoned.

The discussion so far has focused on the formal and discursive attributes of the sting as a specific kind of media text or object. This aligns with much of the existing scholarly writing on stings, where a hermeneutic or interpretive approach offering speculative readings of the cultural-social meaning of particular stings like Operation West End is most common.[58] However, we also need to approach the sting as a distinctive media practice that has tangible material and social effects, and to supplement the hermeneutic readings of stings with sociological and ethnographic inquiries into the conditions and contexts of their production. From this perspective, we see that the innovation of sting journalism did not only put new kinds of discursive tropes into public circulation. It also impacted social and work relations. For instance, the sting journalist emerged as a new kind of professional and social authority figure. The prospect of undertaking a sting motivated many aspiring entrants into the news media profession, as a quick and certain way of attracting recognition and professional traction in a fiercely competitive sector. In the frenzied competitive fray of Indian media worlds, the pursuit of a sting story was one way to achieve the coveted goal of standing out.[59]

During my fieldwork in news media organizations, sting journalists and their feats were invariably discussed in admiring tones. The actual practitioners of this craft would claim their work as a badge of professional distinction and honor, and reminisce about individual stings that had "made a difference."[60] In my interviews with Cobrapost team members, for instance, the sense of democratic responsibility and their self-understanding as the true representatives of the people/the public who had long been abandoned by politicians and state officials was a prominent theme. In the reflexive accounts of journalists like Bahal, what set them apart from the rest of the journalistic fray was this sensibility of representative obligation and commitment to democratic remedy and transformation, along with healthy doses of daring, courage, and persistence. In their accounts, these were qualities that only the sting journalist possessed.

This had implications for journalistic practice. The insistence on the uniqueness and singularity of sting journalism also meant that its craft diverged from that of regular journalism. In their role as change-agents, sting journalists set themselves up as unconstrained agents who were unmoored from the tacit and explicit procedures and codes that governed the work of ordinary journalists.[61] In the name of the people and the cause of democratic representation, sting journalists invented their own set of professional and ethical codes and conventions.[62] Media organizations that encouraged and promoted sting journalism on the grounds of audience appeal (and hence the prospects of greater advertising revenue) also gave sting journalists more autonomy and more resources to pursue their journalism.[63]

The recursive or self-referential authority of the sting journalist became evident to me in the course of interviews when, in response to questions about how particular topics were chosen, how tip-offs and leaks were verified and information validated, the answers I received described the journalist's exercise of independent judgment, the unique decisions, individual "senses" or intuitions, and strange coincidences[64] that made particular sting operations possible.[65] Shaunak Sen's discussions with sting journalists like Mathew Samuel documented a similar assertion of the sting journalist's singularity or uniqueness, and a similar setting aside of established journalistic conventions such as avoiding or else minimizing the use of unnamed sources; cross-checking information; and seeking out responses, reactions, and rebuttals from parties named in a news story prior to its publication. All of this was justified in the name of the urgency and the democratic importance of the sting operation. This led to a curious paradox. Even though transparency and accountability were the much-cited normative touchstones of sting journalism, the actual media practices involved unaccountable individual decisions and considerable secrecy and obfuscation. As William Mazzarella has noted, "the politics of immediation" and transparency—the fantasy that the citizen-subject can directly see, know, and join in the churns and flows of power—relies centrally upon mediation.[66] While his observation specifically relates to the discursive registers and cultural political imagination of sting journalism, we see here that it applies to its practical or material dimensions as well.

Another distinctive effect of stings that also related to the paradox of the "mediated politics of immediation" was the growing salience of informal sets of intermediary actors and networks for the news media. Stings are produced by what some have called "access journalism" and "leak journalism," a journalistic practice that is heavily dependent on intermediary figures such as "fixers" or brokers, and the cultivation of informal networks.[67] The cultivation of contacts, and jockeying for privileged political access, is standard journalistic practice. However, sting journalists have to go about these tasks in quasi-legal ways, without disclosing details about the sources and modalities of the sting.[68] Only a handful of stings have publicly presented their backstories, and as a result we know little about the actual interests that drive revelations of wrongdoing.[69] They are motivated by concern for democracy and the public interest, journalists and media houses tell us.[70] The role that state and political actors have played in enabling the exposure of governmental lapses remains out of sight in the celebration of media's nonpolitical change-agency through its sting operations.

MEDIA ACTIVISM

Along with sting journalism, a second type of newsmaking practice also gained traction in India's liberalized news worlds. Glossed as "media activism," this involved publicly visible demonstrations of the media's distinctive capacities for social mobilization and legal and policy change. If stings drew attention to the media's powers of exposure and revelation, media activism campaigns showed how media professionals and organizations could tangibly mobilize people and get political institutions to do things differently.

The most common form of media activism that gained popularity in the mid-2000s was the *Justice for* retrial campaign, in which journalists and media outlets took up specific cases of alleged judicial mistrials and delays—each campaign was launched in the name of a specific person, for example *Justice for Jessica*, or *Justice for Priyadarshini*—and demanded prompt institutional remedy and compensatory action by the state. To understand how these activities affected the media-democracy relation and strengthened new norms of responsible media and civic virtue, let us take a look at the three most iconic *Justice for* campaigns from this period.

Justice for Jessica

In April 1999, Jessica Lall, a twenty-nine-year-old model working as a bartender at a South Delhi nightclub, was shot and killed by an angry customer when she refused him a drink. The killer, Siddharth Vashisht (known as Manu Sharma), the son of a Congress party politician from the northern Indian state of Haryana, was apprehended by the police and prosecuted in a lower trial court in Delhi. Several key witnesses to the shooting soon turned hostile, prompting public speculation about political pressure and the use of political connections by the Sharma family. The court acquitted Sharma in early 2006, and the verdict sparked off a flurry of reports in the print and television news media about the "miscarriage of justice." Two English-language news channels, NDTV and CNN-IBN, launched campaigns titled *Justice for Jessica* with Jessica's sister Sabrina Lall as the spokesperson for her sister's cause, demanding a reinvestigation and retrial of the case.

Prominent news anchors like Barkha Dutt (NDTV) and Sagarika Ghose (CNN-IBN) foregrounded the story in their news bulletins and shows, and their channels hosted several talk-show-style discussions on different aspects of the case. News channels also organized an interactive public campaign, inviting viewers to send text messages in support of a petition addressed to the Indian president, requesting reinvestigation and retrial. NDTV received more than 200,000 text messages.

Through February and March 2006, news channels publicized numerous public protest events such as marches, rallies, and candlelight vigils held in the India Gate area in the heart of Delhi's political zone (close to the houses of parliament, ministry offices, and the official residence of the president), all demanding justice for Jessica. News anchors nudged citizens to attend by providing detailed information about the time and location of the protests, and reporters and camera crews broadcast live from the protest scenes. Young people featured prominently in the protest imagery. An iconic image of the *Justice* protests was that of a candlelight vigil at India Gate, where hundreds of young people stood together, silently, the quiet resolve on their faces illuminated by the glow of lit candles in a direct citation of a popular movie scene from a recent blockbuster Bollywood film *Rang de Basanti*.[71] Protest commodities like T-shirts and temporary tattoos with *Justice for Jessica* slogans became quite popular as media pressure for the "system" to "do something" continued to build up in studio discussions, op-eds, and blogs.

The media mobilization achieved its purpose, and the Jessica Lall case was reopened for scrutiny. Within a month of the trial court's acquittal verdict, the police commissioner petitioned the Delhi High Court to review the case, and the court issued fresh warrants against the accused. Working on an unusual "fast-track" timeline, the High Court reached a new conclusion on the case in seven months, reversing the sessions court's decision and sentencing Sharma to life imprisonment in December 2006. Sharma's appeal against the verdict was struck down by the Supreme Court a few years later, and he remained in prison until 2020, when he received parole on account of his "good behavior."[72]

Justice for Priyadarshini

The case of Priyadarshini Mattoo was older than Jessica Lall's murder, but it was taken up by the media only in 2006, in the immediate aftermath of the *Justice for Jessica* campaign. Like Jessica, Priyadarshini Mattoo was a young, middle-class woman living in Delhi. In 1996, the twenty-five-year-old law student was raped and killed by a classmate, Santosh Singh, the son of a high-ranking police officer.

The case went to trial and the sessions court judge acquitted Singh in 1999. Judge G. P. Thareja concluded that although he believed that Singh was the culprit, the presentation of evidence by the prosecution was inadequate and so he had to give Singh "the benefit of the doubt" and acquit him. Thareja also noted the biased actions of the police, such as manufacturing evidence and giving false depositions under oath. "The rule of law doesn't seem to apply to the children of those who enforce it," he observed, and the then Indian president, K. R. Narayanan, concurred with a similar albeit cryptic remark sometime later: "the cathedrals of justice have become like casinos."[73]

In 2002 the Central Bureau of Investigation, the lead investigative agency of the Indian state, appealed to the Delhi High Court against the acquittal. The case then entered the Indian judicial labyrinth of delayed hearings, with no resolution in sight. Seven years later, Priyadarshini's story was caught up within the media attention economy created by the *Justice for Jessica* campaign, and was similarly framed as a miscarriage of justice that called for an urgent remedy. In the summer of 2006, immediately after the public mobilizations seeking justice for Jessica, news channels launched a new campaign, *Justice for Priyadarshini*.

Similar to the media prominence that was given to Jessica's sister, the Priyadarshini campaign foregrounded a family member, Priyadarshini's father, Chaman Lal Mattoo, as the empathetic human subject demanding justice. Along with Mattoo, several students, in particular the Delhi college student Aditya Raj Kaul, who shared a common Kashmiri Pandit ethnic identity with Priyadarshini Mattoo, and a new group, United Students, emerged as the visible faces of the media campaign.

The *Justice for Priyadarshini* campaign saw intensive media coverage about the case and its subsequent mistrial. There were many television studio discussions and the broadcast of stories about Priyadarshini's life that, through their portrayal of a sparkling and happy young woman, emphasized the cruelty and tragedy of her violent death. Priyadarshini, like Jessica, came across in these media portraits as the quintessential regular or ordinary young person, the girl next door who could be "anyone's" daughter or sister. Like the Jessica campaign, the Priyadarshini campaign sparked numerous public demonstrations (mostly in Delhi, but there were some in other Indian cities as well), candlelight vigils, and a lot of debate and discussion on the matter in print, broadcast, and internet media. TV channels issued public appeals for citizens to sign a petition addressed to the Indian president that Aditya Raj Kaul and the United Students group had initiated, asking for a retrial of the case. The journey of Kaul and other students to personally hand over the petition to the president at his residence in Rashtrapati Bhavan was telecast live. Visual special effects such as slow motion and repeat frames intensified the drama of the meeting and heightened the resemblance to the near-identical scene from the popular film *Rang de Basanti*, where the film's youthful protagonists had also made a similar journey to the apex of constitutional authority on behalf of the ordinary citizen-victim.

A few months after the Jessica campaign yielded an official response and action, the Priyadarshini campaign enjoyed a similar success. In the context of increasing media pressure and visibility, the Delhi High Court speeded up its review of the case in July 2006 and began to hold daily hearings. In October 2006, in a dramatic reversal of the trial court judgment, Santosh Singh was pronounced guilty and sentenced to death. The death sentence was eventually commuted to life imprisonment by the Supreme Court the following year. Singh has received parole several times since then, on various grounds ranging from attending his daughter's birthday party to appearing for his law exams.

Justice for Nitish

A third media campaign for justice that resembled the other two in its diagnosis of a "miscarriage of justice," in another case that pitted an ordinary victim against a politically connected perpetrator (and against the "system" more generally speaking), focused on the death of a young man, also from Delhi. In February 2002, Nitish Katara, a twenty-four-year-old management graduate, was set on fire and beaten to death in the outskirts of Delhi. The police apprehended two male relatives of Katara's girlfriend Bharti Yadav and charged them with a motivated "honor killing." Just like the Jessica and Priyadarshini murders, Katara's alleged killers were from a political family. Bharti and her brother, Vikash Yadav (one of the chief accused), were the children of D. P. Yadav, an influential politician[74] in the state of Uttar Pradesh, which had jurisdiction over the case. The trial continued with sporadic hearings over the next four years. The proceedings were hampered by the absence of Bharti Yadav, a crucial witness who had since moved to London, and had been dropped from the case as a prosecution witness as a result of what many alleged to be political pressure from the Yadav family.

In the spring and summer of 2006, Indian news media picked up on the case and aligned it to the ongoing media campaigns around the cases of Jessica Lall and Priyadarshini Mattoo. The specific demand was not for a retrial, but for Bharti Yadav to return and be impleaded as a material witness and for the trial to be completed. More than four years had passed since Katara's murder, and the case still remained open. Katara's mother was the visible face of the *Justice for Nitish* campaign. Like Sabrina Lall and Chaman Lall Mattoo, the charismatic family members who respectively fronted the *Justice for Jessica* and *Justice for Priyadarshini* media campaigns, Nilam Katara was an articulate figure who persuasively and passionately advocated for justice for her son. She was portrayed by the media as another "everywoman," a universal figure who could be "anyone's" mother.

Responding to a much-publicized judicial appeal by Nilam Katara, the Supreme Court shifted the trial from Uttar Pradesh to a Delhi court, away from D. P. Yadav's influence. Under the media glare, the pace of the trial picked up in a fast-track court. There were several twists and turns that intensified media discourse about the impunity enjoyed by the powerful and the denial of justice to ordinary citizens. Several prosecution witnesses turned hostile and withdrew crucial eyewitness testimonies. Upon her return and eventual testimony, Bharti Yadav formally denied ever having a romantic relationship with Katara, casting doubt on the honor killing theory. Nilam Katara's public appeals for justice took on a new urgency.

The media campaign yielded positive results. The Delhi trial court reached a guilty verdict two years later, in 2008, sentencing the Yadavs to life imprisonment. The verdict was upheld against appeal in the Delhi High Court, and subsequently in the Supreme Court as well. However, the apex judiciary turned down the Katara family's petition to convert the life sentence to a death sentence, and also reduced the life term from thirty to twenty-five years.

The Yadavs remain in prison at the time of writing in 2023, and their parole appeals continue to attract media attention, emplotted within the familiar media narrative about the influence and impunity that the powerful and "politically connected" enjoy at the expense of ordinary citizen-victims-like-us.

THE ARCS OF MEDIA JUSTICE

All three media campaigns had a common narrative arc that went beyond individual named victims and specific acts of violence, to emplot a more general and more enduring story. Stock characters and plot points staked out a triangle of redemption between ordinary citizens, the system, and the media, in which angry citizens, activated and enabled by the responsive media, won justice from an indifferent system dominated by unaccountable elites.

Along with this populist story line, the cascade of *Justice for* campaigns also introduced into the public domain a distinctive set of media ideologies that we might call, following Luc Boltanski and Eve Chiapello, a new spirit of media capitalism.[75] The legitimation vocabularies of the campaigns reflected the distinctive contexts of private media and market economy in "new India."[76] Chief among these was the theme of newness itself, which came up repeatedly in my conversations with journalists about the meaning and importance of media activism. The *Justice for* campaigns were heralded as creatures of a new media moment of "communicative abundance";[77] they were unknown and indeed unthinkable at earlier moments of Indian media history. Explaining why campaigns were launched on specific issues and why they attracted so much public attention and involvement, the conversation invariably turned to the distinctive sensibilities of liberalized media and its marked difference from what passed as news in the earlier era of state-run television.

My interlocutors drew on a series of value-laden contrasts between old and new news practices, which referenced a bigger distinction between the political cultures of old and new India. Unlike the top-down, high-politics-and-dignitary-centered news produced by statist "old media," the new private television news channels that came up after the 1990s were seen to focus on human interest and "people-centric" issues. They covered what Sagarika Ghose described as stories about "other" and "regular" people. Ashutosh, the editor of IBN-7, a Hindi news channel, concurred with this claim about how the new media's content choices reflected a different and democratic sensibility that prioritized individual agency over statist control: "[n]ow with economic openness, society has gone through a complete change and there is a new group of people with different aspirations, it's no longer about government and state."

Others made a similar case for new media's democratic ethos and proximity to the people in terms of the distinctive choices of form, style, and, above all, the language that was on offer in 24/7 news cycles. As Q. M. Naqvi, the senior editor of Aaj Tak, saw it, his channel's popularity stemmed from the fact that wide swaths of society recognized and identified with the version of everyday "lived Hindi" used in its news programs. Diverging sharply from the linguistic conventions of formal "high Hindi" that had dominated the bombastic and plain boring broadcasts of the state news channel Doordarshan over the past decades, Aaj Tak news reached and "touched" the people in intimate ways, Naqvi explained:

> Aaj Tak's language is one that everyone understands . . . the trick is to ask who is our audience, what is the language they use? Our audience isn't metropolitan, they come from small towns and villages, they are migrants. We want to bring back their idiom, give them back what they heard in their childhood. The idioms of Hindustan's small towns, we will simplify those and give it to them so that they can get back their roots. So that they will say this is my very own program, this is my very own speech.[78]

The fact that media professionals and participant-organizers of media activist campaigns would stress the inherent democratic value of their work and celebrate the contemporary cultures of commercial newsmaking set off against the "bad old days" of state television is not surprising. Of note instead is the democratic imagination itself, that is, the distinctive conceptions of democracy that underlie the claim that new media are democratic.[79] In the first instance, responsiveness is taken as the measure of democracy. Instead of conventional liberal understandings of the importance of democratic voice and participation, media activism focuses on practices of listening, and the establishment of a responsive political order. The indifference of the existing political establishment and the unheard voices of ordinary citizens[80] were dominant themes in all three *Justice for* campaigns. The campaigns promised to remedy this ill, and the issue of responsiveness emerged as one of the main justifications for media activism. The media were hailed for fulfilling the essential duty of democratic listening that the elected representatives of the people had abandoned.[81]

Second, urgent and visible action took center stage in the democratic imagination of the *Justice for* campaigns. The celebratory rhetoric around the campaigns highlighted the visible, decisive, and immediate forms of action that media activism had enabled: masses of people taking to the streets, petitions gathering millions of signatures as they circulate in cyberspace, announcements that a new investigation will start immediately, a fast-track court handing down a guilty verdict.[82] Unconstrained by electoral interests, political outsiders like the media and the judiciary were deemed as particularly well suited to take such immediate and unconstrained action. Third, the emotional people emerged as democracy's primary subject. While liberal and social democracy privileged reason, deliberation, and the expression of material interests, media activism was concerned more with the "real feelings" and unspoken aspirations of the people: how to gauge them, how to express and protect them. The wider cultures of newsmaking also reflected this priority. Media professionals frequently claimed that the "dumbing-down" of television news reflected a trade-off between democracy and news quality—commercial television news shows us what the people really want, they averred. From this perspective, the production of sensational, tabloid-style news offended established conventions of news quality. However, it was perceived as more democratic than the objective journalism of the old media era. The association of commercial media with greater democracy aligned the market to democracy's side as well. The rhetoric of market freedom, of how the freeing up of economic forces from state control in the late 1980s and beyond had ushered in new possibilities for democracy in India, pervaded liberalized media circles. The positive news coverage of the new economy, the lack of critical media scrutiny of corporations, the inattention to topics like agrarian distress and growing economic inequality that puncture triumphalist accounts of market capitalism's advance in India: all these attested to the role of liberalized media as cheerleaders and vanguards of the "market revolution."[83]

Finally, media activist campaigns advanced a unitary understanding of democracy as the representation of "the people as a whole." The ordinary citizen at the heart of the *Justice for* campaigns was presented as an unmarked subject who could be "anyone's" parent, sibling, or child. In a similar vein, the campaigns appealed to a general and undifferentiated people who, like the audiences that journalists claimed their news had touched, were called up as an amorphous mass of subconscious emotional drives and feelings. Like the many other performative moments of "public assembly" that would erupt across the globe from Tahrir to Wall Street a few years later, India's early-twenty-first century moment of media activism was described in terms of spontaneity and surprise.[84] In much of the commentary, *Justice for* campaigns were presented as unplanned happenings, spontaneously ignited by feelings of outrage that surged through the social ether as media drew attention to an incident of impunity/ordinary victimhood. Moreover, instead of a purposive and self-aware community sharing a distinctive sense of identity and belonging, the people themselves were called up as a contingent formation, animated and activated to public presence and action by the force of emotional drives. In this understanding, ordinary citizens did not make a reasoned choice to join an elective community or take a particular premeditated course of action. Instead they were "swept up" by the passions ignited by media crusades to become the people.

However, the empirical footprints of the campaigns complicated and contradicted these narratives of spontaneous and general popular assembly.[85] The media worlds out of which these campaigns emerged approached audiences through the segmented grid of an audience-research system (itself modeled on market research methods) based on demographic and socioeconomic data on income, education, residential location. Despite the stated emphasis on media activism's universal appeal to everyone, the niche categories that drove the everyday calculus of news programming structured the *Justice for* campaigns as well. Here the leading role of English language news channels in the three media campaigns that featured middle-class urban, English-speaking figures is significant. The demographic/socioeconomic profile of the ordinary citizens in whose names the campaigns mobilized largely matched the profiles of the channels' target audiences, suggesting that the general address of Indian media activism belied its socially partial, and class and caste-selective operations.[86]

In this regard, a closer look at the actual mobilization processes during each of the campaigns shows that organized and socially embedded networks were centrally involved. The pathways of emotional and empathetic identification with particular stories followed socially determined grooves. For instance, in his recollections about the *Justice for Priyadarshini* campaign, the youth activist Aditya Raj Kaul's coming-of-age story about how he got drawn to campaign action focused on the common ethno-religious identity that he shared with Priyadarshini as a Kashmiri Pandit. From this came a sense of common suffering and victimization, Kaul explained. Kaul's anger against the system was expressed in relation to an older and wider set of grievances about the relationship between the Indian state, Kashmiri Pandits, and the Indian state's perceived "appeasement" of Muslim "militants" and "terrorists" in Kashmir that was responsible for the continued Pandit plight. Kaul was celebrated in the heady rhetoric of the campaign as the quintessential youth leader who embodied and spoke for the universal new Indian. However, in his own narratives about his motivations and his affiliations, it was his particular sense of being in the world as a displaced second-generation Kashmiri Pandit that seeded and distinguished his activist agency and choices.[87] Unlike the well-defined Kashmiri identity roots of the *Justice for Priyadarshini* campaign, the mobilizations around the other *Justice for* campaigns did not reflect or reinforce such well-defined ethnic affinities. Nevertheless, in all these instances, the categories of ordinary citizens, youth, and students in whose name justice was demanded were associated with a socially particular form of political agency. Simply put, the raging fires of civic anger were lit from specific social fragments. Despite the universal-general terms of its address, media activism was in fact located within and contoured by particular caste-class milieus.

The synergies and connections between the *Justice for* campaigns and the Youth For Equality (YFE) movement that entered the media attention economy at around the same time illustrate this point. We encountered the movement in the previous chapter as well, as the catalyst of political consciousness for many AAP party workers. The YFE movement brought thousands of upper-caste youth onto the streets of Delhi and other major metropolitan centers in the early spring of 2006 to protest the extension of caste-based affirmative action or reservations quotas in elite higher educational institutions. The expansive and egalitarian gestures of its name served as a tactical deflection of public attention from its investments in caste hierarchy. The scenes of metropolitan youth anger mobilized around the YFE captured television news headlines several months before the *Justice for* protests. Several of the narrative frameworks that would structure the media coverage of the latter protests, including the explicit self-positioning of media actors as advocates and allies of the protesters, were developed at this earlier moment of YFE-led activism. For instance, the familiar *Justice for* theme of angry and aspirational youth who were pushed to take a stand against an establishment beholden to "vested interests" was first activated during the Youth For Equality protests. It was associated with the vivid and spectacular images of young medical students clad in white coats protesting caste reservations outside Delhi's All India Institute of Medical Sciences, the country's leading institution for medical education.

Like the later protest vocabularies about justice for ordinary citizens, the Youth For Equality protests advanced general and universal claims: youth for equality, against the death of merit. However, these were undercut by the specific visual imagery of the protests. The only register in which the sight of white-coat-clad medical students holding brooms signified a shocking scandal and incited angry demands for change was that of caste hierarchy, which held that all youth were not in fact the same. Some pursued merit through medical education and others engaged in degrading forms of manual labor such as cleaning or sanitation work. There was danger and scandal when these mutually exclusive categories of birth-assigned work and fortune were muddied, when affirmative action for lower-caste students in elite medical institutions "killed" the order of educational merit. As the visual codes and tacit languages of the Youth For Equality protests clarified, the open and ecumenical categories of youth, student, and merit were in fact partial and limited to a particular caste-class milieu.[88] When the *Justice for* protests erupted a few months later, several Delhi-based Youth For Equality chapters joined in, embedding the ordinary citizen's cause of justice in a specific social location without explicitly naming it as such.

The practice of coded nudges and "dog whistles" that transposed hierarchical assertions of caste identity and difference into tacit registers of communication also prevailed within the worlds of liberalized Indian media. As the next and concluding section of this chapter shows, these were fractured social contexts whose divisions were acknowledged in nudge-and-wink innuendos. The exercise of transformative agency by the media, where media were seen to align with the people to redeem and restore democracy, was oriented around a singular fault line of people versus the establishment. Cutting across the myriad cracks and tears in the social fabric, the great divide posited by populism "chained" diverse social demands into a single common assertion made by the people as a whole, to use Laclau's terms. But as we will sec, this would remain a contingent and unstable assertion. In the divided media and social worlds of liberalizing India, the system and the establishment, like the people themselves, meant many different things.

SOCIAL FRACTURES

Caste Stories

Field Notes, January 13, 2008. Patna, Bihar.

Over lunch, Virendra told me the story of how he became a television news journalist. After completing his undergraduate degree in history at an elite educational institution in Delhi, Virendra came back to his family's ancestral land in Bihar and took up farming, growing cash crops of sugarcane and mustard. He had a lot of spare time on his hands and started growing winter annuals, engaging in some kitchen gardening, and reading a lot. He got involved in a court case as a litigant and the experience spurred him on to study law and become a lawyer.

With independent resources and property income, Virendra did not have to depend on a legal professional career for his livelihood, and pursued several other interests. He started writing for an English-language national daily, and also worked as a freelance stringer for various newspapers and news channels. He joined the television news industry in 2006, as the Patna correspondent of a prominent Indian national news channel. The channel management had been impressed with his fluency in English and Hindi and his familiarity with both metropolitan and regional political worlds, he told me. He had benefited from his social connections in Bihar, as a member of an upper-caste landowning family, and by the educational capital that his elite Delhi education had provided him, most notably his English-language fluency.[89]

Our conversation soon turned to the topic of caste and journalism, and we discussed the recent publication of a study that had highlighted the predominantly upper-caste composition of Indian newsrooms. In 2006, a study published by academics and journalists had attracted public attention for its empirical findings about the caste composition of Indian journalism. After collecting and categorizing information about the caste identities of senior journalists and media professionals, the Media Study Group report's authors, Anil Chamaria, Jitendra Kumar, and Yogendra Yadav, concluded that there was a massive overrepresentation of individuals from upper-caste backgrounds in the media, particularly when it came to leadership and authority positions in media organizations (for example, owners, editors, senior management, senior journalists).[90]

The report attracted a great deal of media and public attention. Opinions were strongly divided on the empirical accuracy of the findings and the objectivity and robustness of the data on which they were based. Although Virendra did not challenge the empirical details of the report, he was skeptical about its larger significance. Even if the sociological findings were true and Indian media were dominated by journalists from upper-caste backgrounds, this did not tell us anything about quality and practice of journalism, he argued. "Just because journalists are from one caste doesn't mean they are biased." To prove his point, he said he would tell me a story about his experience with a "Dalit bureaucracy" in a district in Bihar.

All the officials in the district were anti-Brahmin, Virendra said. In recent years, they had activated the Prevention of Atrocities Act on multiple occasions, accusing upper-caste residents of the area of various kinds of criminal and illegal discriminatory acts against Dalits. It is in this context of widespread and ongoing intercaste antagonism that the district magistrate called Virendra one day and asked him to attend an official function on Ambedkar Jayanti, the birth anniversary of Bhimrao Ambedkar, Indian's chief constitutional architect and a major political icon of Dalit communities.

When Virendra reached the venue, the superintendent of police was onstage delivering a fiery speech against upper castes. Looking around during the superintendent's speech, Virendra noted that all the officers and politicians seated on the stage were Dalit. He suddenly became aware that except for the row reserved for the media, where everyone was upper caste, mostly Brahmin like himself, all those seated in the audience were Dalit as well. Along with caste difference, Virendra noticed another distinction. The dignitaries seated on the podium had chilled bottles of Bisleri (a brand of bottled water) and Coca-Cola placed in front of them. The audience members, however, had to quench their thirst from a battered, repurposed oil barrel filled with tepid Rooh Afza (a local soft drink concentrate) that was undoubtedly mixed with *ganda pani*, unfiltered dirty water, he told me. Another hierarchy cut through the caste divide that day, as Dalit political elites enjoyed drinking privileges denied to all the ordinary citizens, Dalit audience members as well as Brahmin journalists.

Shocked and annoyed, Virendra decided to intervene. In a tone that was loud enough to be overheard, he announced to one of the event organizers, "We're Brahmins, we want the Bisleri." The district magistrate was shamed into action. The unequal relationship between the people and their political representatives had been made public in an embarrassing manner by linking it to the disavowed hierarchies of caste. Hastily abandoning his podium and his special bottled water, the magistrate made a show of "coming down" to the level of the audience and drinking their Rooh Afza.

The story ended. At one level, it confirmed the findings of the study that we had been discussing. It portrayed the caste-divided worlds of politics and media in India, a country where a "Brahmin row" of journalists could encounter a "Dalit podium" of state officials. At another level, however, Virendra's story was not about caste divisions as such. Rather, it drew attention to the intersections and transactions between different orders of difference and inequality, and to the coded dog whistles that transposed disavowed assertions of hierarchy into normatively acceptable registers. It is in this tacit and coded register of communication that Virendra's story fulfilled its main purpose, as a story that challenged the thesis of upper-caste bias in the media (recall that he had offered the story to refute the Media Study Group study). By showing me how Dalit officials benefited themselves at the expense of ordinary citizens, Virendra suggested that the lower-caste capture of political institutions rather than upper-caste domination of the media was the real problem at hand.

Coded communication was central to Virendra's story line. He told me how he had dwelled on the difference between Bisleri water and Rooh Afza in order to communicate a vital political and social point to the district magistrate. But coded communication about caste was also integral to the narrative form itself, to the way in which the "caste story" was always communicated indirectly through imputations, metaphors, and elisions, and this is what remained with me well after I left Bihar. Virendra spoke in code throughout that afternoon, drawing me into a presumptive solidary circle of insiders on the basis of the academic and social connections and networks that had brought me to the interview, and the class-caste readings of my individual presence. Virendra's exasperation was not only about the imperious indifference of Bisleri-drinking officials. The story was about the scandal of Dalit officials acting in a high-handed way. A double reversal of power relations was at stake. Political representatives were "out of line" and caste subjects did not know their place. How dare *they* act like this, was the unspoken comment that hovered uneasily over our conversation that day. The point was never explicitly expressed, but the message was communicated, and received, through oblique and tacit references.

Virendra was not alone in his coded references to caste distinctions. Through the course of my research, Indian media worlds were suffused with social divides and hierarchies that went unnamed. The sociological fact of upper-caste preponderance in the news media was mostly expressed in indirect ways, evident in the kinds of jokes and the casual manner in which casteist slurs were tossed around in newsrooms, in the mocking and insulting ways in which journalists spoke about Dalit politician Mayawati, and in the strong support for the Youth For Equality movement and their anti-reservations campaign that I encountered in newsrooms large and small, national as well as local. Caste hierarchies also revealed their traces in the everyday practices of news work, including that of professional recruitment. Surveying a section of local stringers newly recruited by the Patna office of a national news channel, I found that the thesis of upper-caste domination was borne out at the lowest levels of the media profession as well. Of the 57 stringers who had been recruited by the channel, over 90 percent (52) were from upper-caste backgrounds. Focus group interviews with students enrolled in media institutes in Delhi, Patna, and Bhopal revealed a similar sociological composition. An overwhelming majority of students and aspiring media professionals were upper-caste.[91]

Of significance here is not just the numerical preponderance of individuals from a particular caste group in media organizations, but *how* caste as a specific, hierarchical kind of social and political relationship was articulated and experienced in the everyday life and work contexts of Indian media. A fact that was often missed out by the single-issue focus of discussions about upper-caste dominance in the media was that caste coexisted with other kinds of social differences and inequalities. It was one among multiple fault lines that fissured media worlds.[92] Distinctions of class, gender, regional origin, religion, and linguistic capital textured social relations in the Indian media, which were patterned but not singularly determined by caste hierarchies. Moreover, as we have already seen, caste relations and identities were invariably expressed in indirect and tacit ways. Caste elicited coded communications. It was a whispered and translated presence in newsrooms. The disavowal and deferral of caste into other, normatively acceptable registers of public expression produced insider communities that were brought together and fortified by a shared understanding of implicit codes. Indian media worlds were riven by multiple and unspoken social divisions, and the exercise of transformational agency by the media in the name of the people would be refracted through these unevenly textured and fractured social contexts.

In the fractured social worlds of Indian television news, the redemption narrative of media taking on the establishment in the name of restoring democratic power to the people did not stabilize around a single and shared meaning. The establishment and the people-as-victim were defined in contested and conflicting ways, and journalists offered competing narratives of democratic decay and competing accounts of responsibility and causality. As the following example of a media crusade that created a storm of public attention and got political and judicial institutions to take action will show, what counted as the redemptive solution for some was, for others, the very problem itself. The system that was blamed for the death of democracy, and the accompanying call to go outside politics for democracy's cure, meant very different and sharply opposed things.

Two Bodies

On the morning of May 16, 2008, the blood-soaked body of a fourteen-year-old girl, Aarushi Talwar, was found in her suburban Delhi bedroom by her parents, Rajesh and Nupur Talwar, an upper-middle-class professional couple in their mid-forties. Both were dentists who ran a successful practice.[93] The local police from the Noida police station[94] immediately announced that the chief suspect was the family's Nepali migrant "domestic help," Hemraj Banjade, who was missing from the house since that morning. They offered a reward of 20,000 rupees for any information leading to his capture. The murder soon became national news, and featured as the lead on all prime-time news bulletins on national English news channels. Hindi channels departed from the standard convention of ninety-second news stories to feature the *Aarushi hathyakand* (Aarushi murder story) for almost an hour at a time, with other news confined to the ticker tape at the bottom of the screen.

In the initial days after the murder, the photographs splashed across the front pages of the daily papers were of Aarushi, of the police holding up Hemraj's passport identification page before the cameras, and of grieving relatives and friends of the Talwars. These visuals accompanied a familiar narrative that has become a staple of crime news in urban India:

the "domestic help did it!" narrative about domestic workers such as cooks, cleaning women, chauffeurs, gardeners, and guards committing violent crimes against their employers within the apparently safe and secure confines of middle-class homes. The specter of crime at home haunts the metropolitan imagination in contemporary India. In media representations, life in Delhi and other major cities is a fearful experience of law-abiding middle-class citizens being robbed, drugged, and killed in their sleep by domestic workers who have cleverly hoodwinked their unsuspecting employers and gained their trust and free access to their homes. The media narrative about crime at home is simple, almost Manichean in its analysis and depiction. The object of sympathy is invariably the middle-class employer-victim, and the villain is the domestic worker who has committed the crime. Other structures and practices of violence, such as the employer's violence toward the "servant,"[95] rarely figure in these accounts.

The initial media coverage of Aarushi's murder confirmed this existing narrative of crime at home. The Talwar home was impeccably middle-class, in fact upper-middle-class in terms of the professional and educational qualifications of the family and their English-speaking habitus. Rajesh Talwar had a professional degree from the United Kingdom and ran a successful dental practice along with his wife, Nupur, also a qualified dentist. Aarushi was a vibrant young girl, whom teachers and friends remembered as a bright and vivacious student. Hemraj, the initial culprit, was also an all-too-familiar archetype. He was a forty-something Nepali migrant who had recently been hired by the Talwars. Like many other employers, they didn't know his exact age, nor did they know much about where he came from beyond the fact that it was a village in Nepal close to the residence of another former employee of theirs. Like many other "liberal-minded" employers, they had neglected to verify his identification documents with the police, and had trusted him to work in their house as a full-time domestic worker, live in the "servant's quarter" attached to their apartment, and be alone in the house with Aarushi when they were at work.

When Hemraj was found missing on May 16, the police appeared to have a solved case before them. Clearly, Hemraj had killed Aarushi and then "absconded," a story that was duly reported in all the papers and on television the following day. The Noida police detained several of Hemraj's relatives and friends for questioning, and offered a 20,000-rupees reward for information on his whereabouts. Media attention quickly shifted to the fugitive hunt, and television channels fulfilled their public service obligations by flashing "wanted" bulletins about Hemraj and publicizing details of the bounty.

Three days later the "domestic help did it" narrative was dramatically transformed and images of Rajesh Talwar replaced Hemraj in the headlines as the prime suspect in what was now renamed as a double murder. The reason for this abrupt narrative shift was the astonishing discovery of a second homicide.[96] One day after Aarushi's murder, Hemraj's body, with similar wounds and injury marks, was found on the terrace of the Talwar's apartment, and the postmortem report confirmed that he had died at around the same time as Aarushi. There were *two* bodies. The alleged perpetrator was a victim as well.

Not surprisingly, the media uproar that followed the discovery of Hemraj's murder[97] highlighted the ineptitude of the local police, who had neglected to visit the terrace in the course of their investigations even though there were visible bloodstains on the staircase that led to it. An embarrassed police force hurriedly tried to compensate with a flurry of new measures that included the transfer of the existing police officers and their replacement with more qualified and senior officers from the regional police headquarters.[98] Hourly assurances were given to reporters that the "case would be cracked" soon. Numerous speculations and conspiracy theories proliferated in the media, many of which were attributed to unnamed but official sources.

On the afternoon of May 23, television channels started flashing the breaking news of Rajesh Talwar's arrest. Shortly after, the inspector general of police (Lucknow) addressed a packed press conference that was telecast live on all national news channels. Inspector General Gurdarshan Singh announced that Rajesh Talwar was being arrested and charged with the murders of his daughter Aarushi and "*naukar* Hemraj" or "servant Hemraj." He described this as an "honor killing," a South Asian stereotype of patriarchal violence against women that is enacted to preserve and protect female chastity and the family/kin honor that this symbolizes.

Singh explained, without offering any evidence to support his rather astonishing claims, that Rajesh Talwar's discovery of Aarushi and Hemraj in a "compromising position" that night had led him to kill them and then cover up his actions.[99] Adding to the sensational narrative that had made an already violent set of homicides a scenario of considerable moral turpitude as well—the middle-class minor girl involved in a relationship with a much older "servant"—Inspector General Singh announced that Rajesh Talwar's effort to suppress information about his own affair with a colleague, which Aarushi and Hemraj knew about, was an additional motive for the murder.[100]

The media storm intensified after Talwar's arrest. Public conversations swirled around the shock of a father killing his own daughter. The fact that Talwar was a successful professional from an upper-middle-class background, at far remove from the rural-feudal contexts in which honor killings were said to take place, fueled frenzied and polarized debate. For some media commentators, the police revelations shone a light on the dark and twisted worlds of elite Indians. Others cast doubt on the police narrative itself and drew attention to the lack of evidence to back up Singh's allegations. Reflecting the divided terrain of Indian media worlds, English- and Hindi-language news media journalists offered sharply opposed perspectives on Talwar's guilt (and hence on the veracity of the police allegations). This divergence continued over time. For instance, an interview given by Aarushi's mother, Nupur Talwar, to an English-language news channel was heralded as proof of her innocence by English-language news channels and of her guilt by Hindi channels.[101]

Just about all the media discussions about the murders drew upon a narrative of class distinctions to make their point. Hindi news channels ran with the police story, and several channels featured lurid reenactments of what allegedly happened on the night of May 15–16. Much was made of the supposedly elite and dissolute lifestyle of the Talwars, and fingers were pointed to Rajesh Talwar's alleged affair as well as to other examples of inappropriate family dynamics that established the Talwars' distance from the mainstream of ordinary Indian life.[102] In marked contrast, journalists from English-language media organizations condemned the honor killing theory as a preposterous tale that showed up the vast distance between the social class-caste milieu of the Noida/Uttar Pradesh police force and the urbane middle class worlds of the Talwars. A combination of ignorance and class antagonism was held to be driving the police "witch hunt" against the Talwars, and their "character assassination" of a dead teenager. As an English-language television anchor on a prominent national channel explained to me in an interview, "The cops are behaving as if an affair is this huge big deal, for god's sake."[103]

Soon political leaders entered the fray, taking positions on the case and the police investigation that once again attested to the myriad fissures of caste, class, language, gender, and political partisanship that split India's social worlds. The Uttar Pradesh chief minister and Dalit political leader Mayawati defended her police force from media criticism and announced that there was indeed "strong evidence" against Rajesh Talwar. Opposition politician and union minister Renuka Chowdhury angrily countered that unlike the childless Mayawati she was "speaking as a mother," and demanded strong punitive action against the police officers who had maligned Aarushi with their unsubstantiated allegations.[104]

By early June 2008, in the face of mounting political criticism, chief minister Mayawati transferred the case to the Central Bureau of Investigation (CBI), a central governmental agency that investigates major crimes of national significance (terrorist attacks, espionage-related offenses, or the orchestration of riots). Media commentaries hailed this as a positive development. Reputed as a nonpolitical institution that specialized in "world-class" investigative skills and technologies, the CBI was expected to deliver justice in ways that eluded the bumbling and "politically compromised" Uttar Pradesh police force. Indeed, the CBI team appeared to deliver on this promise with impressive speed. Just a few weeks into its investigation, the target shifted from Rajesh Talwar to a group of Nepali-origin domestic workers (and a dental assistant) from the neighborhood who were acquaintances of Hemraj. However, even after a prolonged period of detention and the conduct of several controversial "scientific tests" such as narco-analysis, brain mapping, and polygraphy in the effort to establish the truth about the murders, the CBI failed to gather legally admissible evidentiary proof against the three men, and had to release them.[105]

Media criticism grew increasingly strident. This time the charge led by Hindi news media was that the Talwars had managed to influence the investigation and pin the charges on "lower-class" servants. The CBI responded to the public pressure and transferred the investigation to an entirely new team in the autumn of 2009. The pendulum of accusation swung wildly one more time. The new investigative team returned to the theory of the Talwars as the main suspects, now including Nupur Talwar as well in their narrative about parents who jointly committed the honor killing and its subsequent cover-up.

The swirl of accusations, investigative efforts, and legal appeals by the Talwars continued over the ensuing years. The case careened from one dramatic conclusion to another, for close to a decade. The CBI filed a "closure report" in late 2010 announcing that it was unable to solve the case but hypothesizing that the Talwars were the likely suspects. The report predictably raised a media storm that in turn triggered a judicial process. In early 2011 a trial court converted the closure report into a criminal charge against the Talwars and initiated a fresh judicial inquiry. In November 2013, Judge Shyam Lal handed down a guilty verdict sentencing the couple to a life term and Talwars were sent to prison. Four years later, in October 2017, the Allahabad High Court reversed the trial court verdict and acquitted the couple. The twists and turns in the case are ongoing. In 2018 the CBI, joined by Hemraj's widow, appealed to country's apex judiciary, the Supreme Court, against the High Court verdict. The legal process continues and the murders remain unsolved to date.

CONCLUSION: WHICH SYSTEM?

Two aspects of this long investigative-juridical journey stand out. First, although it ended in a nonconclusive manner and the demand for justice for Aarushi and Hemraj remains unmet even today, more than a decade later, the case saw an unusual amount of institutional action and the close involvement of multiple state agencies. Local police from two states, the CBI, state forensic laboratories and hospitals, central prosecutorial agencies, and multiple layers of the judiciary, from trial courts to the apex Supreme Court, all played important roles at key junctures of the case.

The alacrity of institutional response was in large part a response to the close media attention that the murders and their subsequent investigation and trials attracted. The intense mediatization of the case was its second notable feature. The Noida double murders were in many senses the ultimate mediatized event of twenty-first-century India. Although there have been several other spectacles of crime and justice in the country that made headline news, the manner in which media pervaded all dimensions of the Aarushi/Hemraj case for the course of almost a decade, from the earliest police investigations that followed the discovery of Aarushi's body in May 2008, to the judicial acquittal of the Talwar couple in October 2017, was quite unique.

By mediatization, I do not only mean the media's representational and publicity work that converted the double murders into a national issue taken up in formal institutional contexts such as cabinet meetings and parliamentary sessions and in candlelight vigils and street marches demanding justice for Aarushi. Media organizations and actors were central participants and players in the case. They influenced and drove its checkered course and eventual outcome. Without the involvement of the media, many critical investigative and judicial developments would not have taken place. At the very inception of the case, the crush of journalists at the scene of the crime destroyed crucial forensic evidence. Subsequently, the relentless media demand to "crack the case" pushed the Noida police to publicly name a culprit without adequate supporting evidence.[106] Media spectacles such as the televised broadcast of Gurdarshan Singh's press conference announcing the initial police theory of a honor killing, and Nupur Talwar's television interview where her refusal/inability to break down and cry on camera set off a cascade of public discussions about her likely guilt—wouldn't an innocent mother cry over her daughter's brutal murder?— yielded decisive institutional actions and changed the course of the investigation in lasting ways.[107] Police and CBI investigations as well as judicial trials were driven by a constant relay of speculations, rumors, and leaks of information and documents between the media and state agencies (the police, forensic agencies, the CBI, state prosecutors). The various investigative and judicial shifts and the final inconclusive outcome—the Talwars are acquitted but we still don't know who committed the murders—are effects of this porous and interconnected field. Defying the autonomy mandate of liberal democracy, media and state in fact share a common "action-space," and media are a part of the very system that they condemn.[108]

The media trial staged around the Noida double murders was a full-blown expression of this chapter's chief concern, namely media's transformational power or change-agency. The terms of the transformational mandate, of media as an agent that makes things happen, were fulfilled here in a tangible way. The media storm around the Noida double murders had lasting effects, converging with other media practices like sting exposés and *Justice for* campaigns to bring public recognition to a specifically populist imaginary of democracy that has continued to gain social influence in the intervening years. In this, democracy is cast as the project of ordinary people rising up in anger to reclaim their sovereign power from an indifferent and corrupt establishment dominated by vested interests. This binary opposition of ordinary people against the distant and corrupt system fuels the contemporary political imagination in India today, and similar Manichean dramas of angry politics echo across many other parts of the world as well. The lengthy duration of this media event established the narrative as a familiar common sense of Indian media and public worlds.

What got consolidated as well was a distinctive idiom and performance of virtuous anger. Public expressions of anger and outrage were read, unproblematically and readily, as signs of civic virtue. Defying the long-standing liberal democratic emphasis on norms of cool reason and thoughtful deliberation, the Aarushi-Hemraj media trial amplified the language of righteous anger that had been popularized by other contemporaneous media practices like the sting and the *Justice for* campaigns. Media condemnations of the Talwars as well as media criticisms of the CBI-police-judiciary "nexus" were expressed through similar registers of "enough is enough" outrage. They were vocalized in nightly television debates and talk shows as a fearsome cacophony of high-decibel noise. Emotions, and angry emotions in particular, were claimed as a ground of citizenship and political agency. The rush of emotions rather than the preplanned calculations of rational interest drove us to assert our agency as active citizens. The importance given to behavioral science measures of subconscious and subliminal drives and motivations during the investigation and trial of the murders, and the media's willingness to accept truth claims based on scientifically questionable, legally inadmissible, and ethically controversial tests and procedures such as brain mapping, narco-analysis, and polygraphy, added to the legitimacy of "emotional truths."

The Aarushi-Hemraj media trial also shone a spotlight on the knots and the frays in the populist narrative. As English and Hindi media drew on divergent ideas about the victimized ordinary people and the nature of the system that was to blame, the fractures in the populist fault line stood exposed. As we have seen, strong disagreements about the Talwars' guilt were voiced in the media, which mapped onto the language and class divisions of Indian media worlds. Both supporters and critics of the Talwars drew on similar arguments about the wrongdoings of the system in order to make their point. For those who believed that the Talwars were innocent, the system comprised the police, the trial courts, and the investigative officers in the CBI. This "nexus" was held to have violated existing conventions of law and morality in order to frame two ordinary citizens for the most heinous of crimes.[109] For those who believed the opposite, that the Talwars were guilty, the system was also to blame. Only now, it was about the Talwars' ability to swing media narratives in their favor and manipulate the judicial system into granting an acquittal.

If from one perspective, the Talwars were the ordinary victims of a cruel system, from the other they were its privileged beneficiaries. All agreed that the murders and their aftermath exemplified the impunity that India's powerful routinely enjoyed. However, the contours and determinants of power—who was powerful, at whose expense—and the identity of the system/the establishment were fiercely contested. Although they shared affective idioms of outrage, anti-establishment discourses did not settle on a common locus and target. The Aarushi-Hemraj media trial showed us, quite literally, that the people have two bodies.

11

LINEAGES

A CONTEMPORARY HORIZON HAS oriented this book thus far. The preceding chapters located the interventions of curative democracy and outsider politics in the specific time-space of the twenty-first-century Indian present, with economic liberalization (and media liberalization) as a proximate context and influence. We have seen that the project of democratic reform and cure in India is connected to a project of economic reform that began toward the end of the twentieth century. By the early years of the twenty-first century, it modified and eventually replaced the planned developmentalist model of Nehruvian economy with a global capital- and market-friendly "open" economic order. The effects of economic liberalization were not limited to the policy domains of trade, taxation, and capital investment. Instead, as Ravinder Kaur and others have shown, the normative and institutional contours of citizenship, social relations, and cultural identities were transformed substantially as well.[1]

An era of "new politics" has been inaugurated in post-reform India, in which the call to cleanse, cure, and fundamentally overhaul the democratic system—to right-size and align the polity with the newly dynamic, open, and free economy—holds sway. A new political subject, the ordinary citizen, has replaced the collective figure of "the masses" that tethered postcolonial democracy and nationalism. From the energetic action-spaces of the Aam Aadmi Party mapped in chapter 1 to the transformational agendas of commercial news media that chapter 2 explores, a distinctive project of curative democracy and outsider politics has taken hold that makes the contempt and distaste for electoral politics the paradoxical precondition for political action and engagement.

However, economic reforms and the political shifts associated with the "new spirit of (market) capitalism" cannot be the only grounds of our concern. Curative democracy has an older backstory that takes us to a time *before* the churning of economic liberalization. This is the period of the late 1970s and early 1980s, when a concerted project of democratic restoration was carried out in the immediate aftermath of the Indian emergency by state institutions like the Shah Commission of Inquiry and the Supreme Court, and by a range of non-state actors such as media, civil society, and social movements, often acting together in networked formations. Amplified and elaborated in a post-liberalization context in the 1990s–2000s, the normative vision of curative democracy and outsider politics had an earlier, post-emergency provenance. Moreover, in what amounts to a significant historical irony, the post-emergency project of democratic restoration carried forward many of the ideas and practices that were consolidated during the emergency itself, the very regime that it aimed to counter and reverse.

This section of the book explores these antecedents and ironies in closer detail. By locating curative democracy, outsider politics, and the populist project in this earlier historical moment, I do not aim to provide a definitive origin story nor to claim a causal connection between post-emergency and post-liberalization contexts. Instead, I draw attention to an ambivalent moment of political transition from four decades ago, when democratic and authoritarian forms mutated into each other in both intended and unintended ways. The inquiry into the "descent and emergence" of curative democracy and outsider politics pushes us to rework received understandings of democratic antinomies and exceptions, and consider instead democracy's intimacies and entanglements with its authoritarian shadows. "The search for descent is not the erecting of foundations: on the contrary, it disturbs what was previously thought immobile; it fragments what was thought unified; it shows the heterogeneity of what was imagined consistent with itself."[2]

THREE

THE LONG EMERGENCY

ON APRIL 15, 1978, an Indian parliamentarian named Keshavrao Dhondge raised a "Short Notice Question" in the Lok Sabha, the lower house of parliament, concerning a suicide in central Delhi's Patiala House court complex. Patiala House at the time was the seat of the Shah Commission, the government-appointed commission of inquiry that was investigating the recently lifted Indian emergency. From June 1975 until March 1977, the incumbent Congress government under the leadership of Prime Minister Indira Gandhi had suspended parliamentary democracy and ruled the country under the terms of emergency law. Elections were postponed, press censorship was imposed, thousands of political prisoners were detained and tortured, and constitutionally guaranteed fundamental rights were set aside by a political regime that concentrated decision-making authority in Gandhi and a small group of individuals who owed her personal loyalty.

India's emergency experiment with authoritarian rule was short-lived. A surprise election called in March 1977 produced an equally surprising result: the decisive national defeat of the Congress party for the first time since independence. The national government was formed by a new political coalition, the Janata [people's] Party, which fought the election on a single-issue campaign of "defeating dictatorship" and "restoring democracy." These promises were at the top of the Janata government's policy agenda in the first flush of its electoral triumph. Emergency rule was swiftly revoked. As further proof of governmental commitments to the goals of democratic restoration and authoritarian overcoming, a series of commissions were appointed to inquire into the various misdeeds of the recent past. A commission led by a retired chief justice of the Indian Supreme Court, Jayantilal Shah, was the most prominent of these, charged with the sweeping mandate of inquiring into the entirety of emergency-era "excesses," as they were officially termed.

The Shah Commission's proceedings attracted an enormous amount of public and media attention. Its open call to Indian citizens to come forward with complaints and accounts of the troubles that they had suffered during the twenty-one months of the emergency yielded over 50,000 responses. Sizable audiences filled up the rooms in Patiala House during the Commission's hearings. Daily newspaper reports and radio bulletins carried news about the sessions to distant publics. Excited speculations swirled about the heady air of post-emergency India. Who would admit to what regarding their role and responsibility for the various misdemeanors, lapses, and excesses of the emergency? How would Indira Gandhi respond to the Commission's summons? Would this larger-than-life figure who had swept aside existing structures of democratic constraint now meekly agree to be bound by the procedures and judgments of a commission set up by her political rivals? What of Sanjay Gandhi, the prime minister's son who had authored the notorious emergency policies of slum demolition and forced sterilization although he did not hold any official position? How would this "extra-constitutional authority," to use the euphemism of the time, respond to the inquiries of a legally sanctioned commission?

It is in this context of daily drama and spectacle, where socialites in chiffon saris were said to throng Patiala House in order to catch a glimpse of fallen political heroes,[3] that a dramatic event of an altogether different order took place. On the April 13, 1978, Kundlik Raghumane and his wife, Rukmani, arrived in Delhi from Rahuri village in the western state of Maharashtra.[4] They reached Patiala House at about 8:30 a.m. and sought out a Mr. Degwekar, a deputy superintendent of police from Maharashtra currently deputed to the Shah Commission. The couple wanted information on the status of the complaint they had submitted to the Commission in the summer of 1977 regarding the "great excesses that were committed on this Rahuri family during [the] emergency," when Raghumane and his wife were forcibly sterilized by two local constables. Degwekar informed them that the Shah Commission had not selected their case for an independent inquiry, and had instead referred it to the Maharashtra state government in September 1977. There was no further information.

Raghumane was very disturbed by this news. Before their trip to Delhi, the constables allegedly responsible for their sterilization had met the couple and taunted them about the Shah Commission's ineffectiveness. And so, the police report concludes, Degwekar's information

> seems to have caused great mental disturbance to the deceased. It is learnt that the deceased had brought with him some liquid in two bottles which he was very zealously guarding and even went to the extent of slapping his wife on her being inquisitive about it. The deceased drank the liquid contained in these bottles in the office of the Deputy Superintendent soon after knowing the position of his complaint. The deceased is reported to have told his wife that he would not go back to his native place and rather die if no action is taken on his complaint.

The liquid was insecticide, and Raghumane died in the hospital later that night. He was cremated on May 15 following a postmortem inquest. His widow stayed on in the Shah Commission's premises for another two days, looked after by a "lady constable," and then left Delhi with her brother. The parliamentary question in the Lok Sabha, raised on the day of Raghumane's cremation, was answered on the basis of the case summary that we have reviewed above.

The minister of state for Home, the Shah Commission's parent ministry, explained to members of parliament that Raghumane's suicide was not the Commission's fault. In fact, the Shah Commission had done exactly what it was supposed to do. In keeping with established procedures, it had transferred the complaint to the Maharashtra state government "for suitable remedial action and inquiry" by a specially constituted investigating authority. But Maharashtra did not take any action, and did not appoint any such authority. And so the chain of blame and responsibility stood clarified. "If the Maharashtra Government had initiated some kind of inquiry, this would have given satisfaction to the complainant and this tragedy would not have occurred," concluded the official report on the suicide. The matter was deemed to have "lost its urgency," the file notation observed, and the file was closed on May 6, 1978.

Why reopen it today? At one level, the suicide of Kundlik Raghumane, like all suicides, is an exceptional event, a sudden interruption in the flow of normal life. The event did not seem to matter much even at the time of its occurrence, when it failed to attract any public attention barring a fleeting parliamentary mention. Its only material trace is in a skimpy four-page file in the National Archives of India that I found by mistake, because of a wrongly transposed digit on a file reference number. But at another level, the "suicide in the premises of the Shah Commission," as the file is drily labeled, is an exemplary and illustrative event. Raghumane's act and the manner of its subsequent parliamentary justification highlight the conflicting imperatives of democratization that prevailed in post-emergency India, of redressing governmental misdeeds and building governmental credibility at the same time.

The Raghumane case showed that these were irreconcilable goals. The Raghumanes had approached the state seeking redress for the injustices that they had suffered during the emergency. The Shah Commission had acted to secure the credibility of the state. Establishing that state action was rule-bound and lawful and thus completely different from the arbitrary and personalized power that was wielded during the emergency was the main task at hand. And so the Commission responded to the request for timely justice by scrupulously following its established procedure of categorizing cases, selecting some for a full commission-level investigation, and referring others to individual states for further action. These procedural acts of categorization and federal buck-passing were the effective context of the suicide. They catalyzed Raghumane's desperate act, and also served as the official explanation for what had happened: how Raghumane's failure to get justice, although unfortunate, remained within the bounds of procedure and reason.

The gap between procedure and justice that Raghumane's death opened up is the subject of this chapter. In what follows, I examine how state sovereignty and popular sovereignty, the former associated with law and procedure and the latter with morality and justice, were placed on separate tracks in the late 1970s after the end of the Indian emergency. I discuss the consequences of this separation, and show how it shaped the normatively influential idea of the political outside as the source and site for democratic renewal.

THE GENERATIVE EMERGENCY

In 2015, a flurry of publications marked the fortieth anniversary of the proclamation of the Indian emergency. Authors of different political persuasions urged Indians to remember a moment that has received cursory mention in existing narratives of Indian democracy, whether triumphalist or critical. Ironically, the call to remember echoed the very terms that had allowed the emergency's forgetting. Although they came from quite different ideological perspectives, most of the efforts to counter emergency amnesia offered up accounts of an extraordinary moment of political deviance when democracy in India was derailed or interrupted. The exceptionalism of the emergency was the main focus. It was remembered and forgotten on the same terms, as a temporary and aberrant episode at considerable remove from the normal politics of Indian democracy.

But this thesis of emergency as aberration is difficult to substantiate in empirical terms. India's emergency did not end with a dramatic rupture of "regime change." There were no substantial punitive sanctions against the ruling elites of the emergency regime. Indira Gandhi, the leading architect of the emergency, returned as prime minister in a massive electoral victory less than three years after emergency's end. Alongside this dramatic example of continuities between the emergency and its aftermath at the level of the highest political leadership are the examples of numerous individuals who, notorious for their roles in the project of authoritarian rule between 1975 and 1977, continued to enjoy power and privilege, some up until today.[5]

Moreover, the continuities and connections between the emergency and subsequent political periods do not just exist at the level of personnel and institutions. Many emergency-era policy formations and normative orders were also carried forward into the time of democracy. Many emergency policies, including notorious ones that were directly identified with the various undemocratic "excesses" of the time, such as the policy of slum demolition in the name of urban beautification, and the curtailment of civil liberties in the name of an unspecified threat to national security, were revived in the post-emergency years. They continue as familiar features of the Indian political landscape more than four decades later. The available empirical evidence refutes the deviance hypothesis about the emergency: there are ample institutional, normative, and policy links between the emergency regime and its successors. And so it is not that the emergency has been forgotten or shadowed. Rather, it has cast a decisive shadow over all that has come after.

Setting aside the thesis of emergency deviance, this chapter takes another approach to the emergency, viewing it as a "historical event." I use the term *historical event*, following William Sewell, to mean a sequence of occurrences that is recognized as notable by contemporaries, and that transforms political and social structures and the "landscape of contention."[6] To view the emergency as a historical event is to move from the analytical project of recuperation and memorialization of a time past, to one of tracing the active presences and living lineages of the emergency in our times. The emergency is seen here not in terms of its political-historical death or irrelevance, but its generative properties of world-making: how it produced new political and social orders that continue to imprint Indian democracy many years later.

I approach the generative dimension of the emergency quite literally, through a focus on the immediate aftermath of the emergency, that is, the post-emergency period of 1977 to the early 1980s when several new political innovations on the part of state and non-state actors gained public visibility. These were undertaken to address twinned goals that informed political and public cultural actions in this period: the learning of "emergency lessons" and the "restoration of democracy." As I will show below, the latter was intimately linked to the former. Contrary to what the term restoration connotes, it was not a simple return to a given status quo ante of democracy, but rather its active remaking and reimagination in light of the emergency experience. What we have in this period, then, is a very direct authorization of political change *by* the emergency—the emergency as generative of new sociopolitical worlds.

Surprisingly, this period of the immediate aftermath of the emergency has received short shrift in most accounts of Indian political history. In the narrative arc of emergency accounts, the high point is the electoral defeat of Indira Gandhi in the March 1977 elections. What happened after is largely seen as unproblematic and uninteresting: a self-evident epilogue or coda where democracy was simply restored or returned. But does this view of how the status quo ante returned after 1977—the emergency experience brushed away like a pesky fly on history's skin—bear out historical and empirical scrutiny? What exactly was it a return to or of? To raise these questions is to move away from the predetermined narrative of democratic restoration and look at the post-emergency as a historical moment and dynamic political formation in its own right, when democracy was not so much restored or returned as reshaped and modulated, imprinted by the enduring traces of its authoritarian past.[7] The varied compulsions of change-amid-continuity that prevailed after emergency's end shaped democratic practices and norms in distinctive ways.

More specifically, the aftermath of the emergency saw the normative and institutional consolidation of "outsider politics" in Indian democracy. Various initiatives of political innovation unfolded in the late 1970s and early 1980s in India, when a range of state and non-state institutions and actors took upon themselves the task of inaugurating a new post-emergency order. The remainder of this chapter focuses on one of these initiatives: the Shah Commission of Inquiry, which we caught a brief glimpse of in the opening sections. Through a discussion of the Commission's proceedings, I show how the political outside came to be seen as the definitive source and site of democratic salvation. The exercise of extraconstitutional authority by individuals who were political outsiders and did not hold any formal position in government was central to the project of emergency rule. Ironically, the restoration of democracy in the aftermath of the emergency would legitimize the rise of an outsider politics as well.

The Emergence of the People

As the introductory chapter has noted, the emergency consolidated the hold of a particular populist logic of politics in India. A new idea of the unitary, "ordinary people" as the sovereign subject of democracy, which departed from prevailing political imaginaries of collective sovereignty and subjectivity such as the "cultural nation" or the "downtrodden masses," served as the emergency's normative foundation. The genesis of this goes back to the late 1960s, and the entry of Indira Gandhi into institutional politics as the leader of the Congress party, and subsequently as the prime minister of the country.

Indira Gandhi's swift rise within the Congress was the product of a hardnosed calculation by senior party bosses, the so-called Congress Syndicate, that a politically inexperienced woman disconnected from local patronage networks—a *gungi gudiya* or "dumb doll," as she was contemptuously described by senior congressmen—would be easy to manipulate. But what transpired within a few short years was quite the opposite: the political decimation of the syndicate, the deinstitutionalization of existing party structures and parliamentary constraints on political authority, and the resulting elevation of a singular leader claiming a direct and unmediated access to the people.[8]

These outcomes were shaped by historical circumstance as well as by deliberate political maneuvers. For instance, the outbreak of war in 1971, where the Indian military intervention on the side of the East Pakistan/Bangladesh liberation fighters against Pakistan culminated in a military victory, aided Indira Gandhi's iconization as the divine warrior-mother of the nation. Along with such contingent events, carefully crafted initiatives by Indira Gandhi's Congress such as the *garibi hatao* or "banish poverty" campaign theme of the 1971 elections, and a deliberate embrace of high socialism in the late 1960s and early 1970s,[9] enabled Gandhi to present herself as the true and authentic champion of the people, an outsider battling the corrupt world of establishment politics and entrenched elite power.

The language of populist antagonism, pitting Indira Gandhi as the embodiment of the unified will of the people against the machinations of (increasingly unspecified) malign political and economic interests, grew stronger in the early 1970s. This was a period marked by increasingly assertive protest mobilizations and strikes across the country. Any act deemed to thwart or check her authority was presented in this framework, as proof of a conspiracy against the people-nation. "India is Indira, Indira is India," in the infamous phrase of Congress leader D. K. Barooah.

Soon all forms of opposition, from student protests, trade union activism, internal Congress party factionalism, and interparty political contestation in parliament, to the exercise of constitutionally sanctioned check-and-balance authority by bureaucratic and judicial agencies of the state, were read into the singular master narrative of the people under siege. In mid-June 1975, the Congress response to the adverse judgment of the Allahabad High Court in an electoral malpractice suit against Indira Gandhi unfolded in this register of populist indignation, and indicted the judiciary for its anti-people stance. Defending the prime minister in parliament, parliamentarian H. R. Gokhale passionately declared,

> It is truly laughable that an individual who has been elected by millions of people and the entire nation regards unarguably as its leader should be pronounced to be unfit for being elected by one single individual, no matter how high a position he may be occupying.[10]

A few days later, the judicial decision was effectively overridden and the people's "unarguable" leadership choice secured by the declaration of an official state of emergency.

From its earliest enunciation in Indira Gandhi's public radio broadcast on the morning of June 26, 1975, the emergency was presented as an action undertaken in the name of democracy and the people. Emergency governance, it was argued, would cure democracy by stemming and reversing the prevailing social chaos and fear caused by militant agitations, spiraling inflation, corruption, bureaucratic inefficiency, infrastructural breakdown, bitter factional feuds within and between political parties—in short, by politics itself.

Political Modulations

The populist orientation of the emergency, along with the discourse of saving democracy as its main justification, yielded a distinctive style of governance and transformed existing political discourses in at least three distinctive ways. First, the period between June 1975 and January 1977 saw the increasing clout of new kinds of political actors who had neither been elected nor constitutionally appointed to office of any kind. Decision-making authority shifted to these "extra-constitutional" agents—the close circle of unelected advisors, loyalists, and friends gathered around Indira Gandhi's younger son, Sanjay Gandhi,[11] who played a key role in policymaking and the everyday business of civic governance, particularly in Delhi.[12]

There were efforts to reorient existing constitutional priorities as well. The omnibus forty-second amendment to the constitution effectively elevated the nonjusticiable directive principles of the Indian constitution over its fundamental rights provisions, and asserted parliamentary sovereignty in all matters related to the realization of these directives.[13] Fundamental rights frameworks called upon the state to protect the existing bundle of rights possessed by citizens as individuals or groups. In contrast, constitutional directive principles committed the state to a future horizon of emancipatory possibilities for the people en masse, and to the realization of particular socioeconomic goals—an eclectic mix that ranged from cottage industry and cow protection, to the abolition of bonded labor.

By prioritizing directive principles, the emergency regime gave the normative imaginary of citizenship an explicitly aspirational meaning. The relation of state and citizen was recast in terms of promised futures rather than existing rights. This in turn meant the reimagination of political representation in pedagogical terms, as the act of giving voice to the "true interests" of a silent and unaware people. As Indira Gandhi put it in her Independence Day address of 1976:

> Complete independence does not mean merely electing your own representatives. Nor does it consist of permitting newspapers, representing the views of a mere handful, to publish whatever they wanted. Freedom means that its gains should reach every Indian home; that they reach the people who are not able to voice their demands, those who are not even fully aware of what they wanted and those who have hitherto remained the deprived ones.[14]

A second notable feature of emergency-era governance in the name of the people had to do with the social contours of the popular imaginary.

The earlier Nehruvian idea of the national masses had primarily referenced rural spaces and various forms of social and economic backwardness. Emergency-era policies modified this social imaginary of the "humble peasants and hungry masses" to address a distinctive, mixed-class configuration of urban middle-class consumers and the rural poor. The keystone of the emergency was the Twenty-Point economic program that was announced by Indira Gandhi on July 1, 1975. Committing the government to a series of measures that would immediately and tangibly transform the adverse economic situation that prevailed in the country, it exemplified this logic of heterogeneous popular assembly.[15] The program called up the commons as a serial equivalence of material deprivations. In the Twenty-Point charter, housewives confronting price sticker shock were on par with bonded labor. Low-income tax-exemption ceilings for the urban middle classes were deemed equivalent to the problem of rural indebtedness.

Third, the emergency inaugurated a new political value system structured around the normative ideals of enthusiastic discipline,[16] efficiency, speed,[17] and the immediacy and decisiveness of governmental action.[18] The inaugural issue of *India Today*, the iconic magazine of Indian "new journalism" that was launched in December 1975, gives us an insight into dominant ideas of political virtue in the emergency era. In a section titled "What People Say," which went on to become a standard section in the magazine, a sample of individuals were asked for their opinions on the emergency, and what had changed in the six months since its imposition. Had the emergency lived up to its promise of fixing the problems of democracy and giving the people relief? Here were the responses that the magazine chose to present as representative of public opinion—a selection that clearly reveals the urban, middle-class character of the emergency-era imagination of the people:[19]

> *Taxi driver Trilochan Singh*: "The emergency has been a bad thing for our trade . . . but as an individual I am all for it." . . . Trilochan reflected that perhaps it was because people who engaged in unlawful activities could alone afford taxis, which cost a rupee for a kilometre ride. . . . Regular checks on the road since the emergency have also made things a bit tough.
>
> *Paul Stass, Belgian visitor*: "The last time I was in Calcutta, two years ago, I was surprised and shocked at the indiscipline." . . . But in the two

months Paul has been in India so far, he has seen no signs of violence. "Not even a procession," he said surprisedly. He felt efficiency had improved, especially in the transport systems.

Kuldip Singh, liquor store and restaurant owner in Delhi: The emergency had made him realize that there was more to business than making money and that businessmen too had some other obligations to society. He said he supported the emergency but understandably would not support total prohibition.

Om Prakash Narain, senior clerk in the postal department: "The change in government offices after the emergency has to be seen to be believed . . . [E]veryone, from the head of department down to the peon, comes to work dead on time, regular surprise checks have discouraged truant playing, efficiency has increased tremendously and all pending work has been disposed off."

Dr. Rajesh Malhotra, executive director of firm manufacturing electrical components for air conditioners and refrigerators: There are few takers for luxury items, Dr. Malhotra says, since the emergency has hit the affluent and those with black money where it hurt—in their pockets. . . . "We are now faced with a different set of customers—the middle income group, which wants full value for its money." The emergency has also brought in its wake better industrial relations between the management and workers and this has pushed up the production.

Dipankar Gupta, second-year economics student: The emergency had transformed the university campus, which once used to be the spawning ground of revolutionaries, drug addicts, and the like. The all-powerful student unions had disappeared, attendance in class had improved tremendously on pain of expulsion, and police around women's colleges had put an end to "eve teasing." Transport used to be the biggest hassle, he said. It was virtually impossible to get a bus during the peak hours, but now the system has improved tremendously.

Mrs. Vimla Kapoor, a middle-class Indian housewife: Is glad the emergency came when it did. She said, "Things were going from bad to worse. I couldn't even get baby foods unless I paid an exorbitant price." Mother of two children, Mrs. Kapoor also welcomed the move for display of price lists in every shop and called it, "The best thing that could have happened."

Mr. Kapur, owner of Delhi jewellery store: Sales have dropped tremendously . . . [O]ne reason for the drop in sales is because people are wary

> of investing in jewellery after recent raids by the income tax authorities who have uncovered huge amounts of undeclared jewellery.[20]

As the excerpt shows, conceptions of political virtue linked emergency populism to an urban middle-class constituency that valued fair prices, good transport, easy shopping, and disciplined, drug-free campuses.[21] Conceptions of political vice were more socially expansive. As many have noted, the emergency heightened a paranoid style of Indian politics. Public discourse of the time was suffused with specters of mysterious forces, "foreign hands," and "fissiparous tendencies" conspiring to bring down the leader and her people en masse, as a whole. The archvillains identified by the emergency state were hoarders, smugglers, and black-market racketeers, and the "economic offenses" that they committed were seen to harm all social groups and rural as well as urban constituencies.[22] Dystopian countervisions of wrongdoing were essential to the performance of popular unity during the emergency, we might say—a finding that also explains the dark streak and paranoid style of emergency populism.[23]

A New Beginning?

On January 18 1977, Indira Gandhi suddenly announced on All India Radio that national elections would be held in six weeks. Following this surprise announcement, several emergency law and ordinances were relaxed in order to enable election campaigning to take place. Press censorship became far less restrictive, and many political leaders were released from prison to join the opposition campaign.

The election was presented to the citizenry by both government and opposition as a grand and momentous choice: a decision that would determine the future of India. The Congress party's election campaign urged voters to choose between "chaos and stability," contrasting the order and discipline of the emergency with the anarchy sure to result if the ragtag Janata coalition, whose leadership had been instrumental in the pre-emergency surge of social protests and militancy, came to power.

On a parallel track, the Janata campaign presented the upcoming elections as a decisive choice between dictatorship and democracy. The official Janata campaign slogan was "freedom or slavery."[24] A contemporary news report conveys some of the rhetorical drama of this election campaign:

> A massive rally at the Ramlila Grounds heard Mr. Desai warn the nation, "This election will determine the future of India. Democracy has been sufficiently weakened in India in the last 19 months. It has been sterilized. This election will decide whether we will remain an independent people or turn into a nation of slaves." . . . Mr. Vajpayee said the issues for the coming elections were crystal clear and never before had they been so evident as now. It was a choice between democracy and dictatorship, between law and lawlessness, between progress and false claims of progress.[25]

On March 21, 1977, the choice was revealed. The symbolism of the event was captured in the visual drama that unfolded on the streets of Delhi through the day, as crowds gathered in front of giant scoreboards outside newspaper offices and watched the vote numbers click over. Voters had ensured a sweeping victory for the Janata coalition, the first non-Congress government in independent India. The emergency regime suffered a massive and decisive defeat. The Congress party's parliamentary strength was halved, going from 350 seats to 153 seats. Even Prime Minister Gandhi could not hold on to her own parliamentary seat. In a historical irony, her constituency of Rai Bareli was won by Raj Narain, the politician whose electoral malpractice lawsuit against Indira Gandhi had set in motion the chain of events that culminated in the June 1975 decision to declare the emergency.[26]

After an intense interval of behind-the-scenes maneuvers and bitter bickering over the prime ministerial post, the Janata government was sworn into office with an ex-congressman, the eighty-one-year-old Morarji Desai, at the helm. At one of the final campaign rallies in Bombay, journalists had queried a Janata party member, the former Bombay High Court justice M. C. Chagla, about the Janata's program once it came to power. "What greater programme can a party have than the restoration of democracy!" he said.[27]

The Janata party was voted into office with a massive electoral mandate. The time to deliver on the program had now arrived. But as we will see, the task of democratic restoration would have different, and conflicting, political meanings.

THE DILEMMAS OF DEMOCRATIC RESTORATION

The first task confronting the new Janata government was the formal restoration of Indian democracy, that is, returning to the formal and procedural status quo that had prevailed prior to the imposition of the emergency in June 1975. As political scientist Jyotirindra DasGupta observed in a contemporaneous analysis of the post-emergency project,

> since the major issue of the 1977 elections was concerned with how to reverse the authoritarian usurpation of democratic power, the mandate of restoration of the constitutional regime served as the strongest foundation of support for the Janata coalition.[28]

The new government took up the task of constitutional restoration with considerable alacrity. Under law minister Shanti Bhushan, it devoted considerable time to reversing or annulling the many laws and constitutional amendments enacted by the previous government.[29]

Second, credibility demonstrations were in order. The post-emergency government had to establish its capacity and capability with regard to governance, and prove that this new and unknown political formation could effectively replace a party that had been in power for the entire life span of the Indian republic. Several tough and pressing challenges confronted the Janata government in this regard. The challenge of establishing coalitional unity and coherence was chief among these. The "grand old party," the Congress, had been in existence for almost a century at the time of its defeat in the 1977 elections. In contrast, the Janata party was a new and unstable coalition that was bowed down by its own internal contradictions and partisan tensions even at the very moment of its great electoral triumph.

Instead of a shared ideological core, the party was united by a provisional—and some would argue, instrumental—opposition to the emergency regime. The emergency had been a formative experience for the Janata party, as several of its key figures forged political and strategic solidarities in the course of their common experience as political prisoners in the country's jails. Once these bonding conditions of "informal fellowship" changed[30] and the threat from a common enemy dissipated, the ideological fissures in this unwieldy alliance became all too apparent, and undercut the government's claims to have a coherent plan of governance.

Securing the credibility of the new government's transformational claims was another key challenge. In Lee Schlesinger's ethnographic account of the daily experiences of the emergency in a western Indian village, residents were unable to distinguish between emergency and normal governance. From their perspective, there was no perceptible increase in either coercion or efficiency during the emergency. In such a context of perceptual ambiguity, the post-emergency claims of delivering "government with a difference" rang hollow. How could a transformative identity be secured for the post-emergency government when the emergency itself was not seen to constitute much of a rupture?[31] How to establish the novelty of the Janata government when there were manifest legal, institutional, policy, and personnel continuities with the emergency past?

For contemporary observers of the post-emergency period, continuity dilemmas surfaced in multiple arenas of social and political life. For instance, both the Janata government and its predecessor drew upon similar class bases of support. The five political blocs that comprised the Janata front—the economically right-wing Swatantra party; the Hindu nationalist Jan Sangh; the Socialists;[32] the landed peasant party of the Bharatiya Lok Dal; and the various defector groups from the Congress such as the Congress S and U, and the Congress for Democracy—did not bring any new social groups into the ruling coalition. The policy orientations of the new government were consequently very similar to those of its predecessor.

The convergence in economic policy was particularly notable. As Georges Lieten has observed, the post-emergency years extended the strategic choice of political-economic policy ambivalence that had been pursued during the emergency years.[33] Indira Gandhi's practice of "looking right and talking left" during the emergency, to use the pithy phrase of Lloyd and Susanne Rudolph, had resulted in the "stealthy political accommodation" of big business houses even as the regime continued to make rhetorical commitments to Nehruvian socialism, backing these up with several big-ticket policy and legislative measures.[34] This continued in the post-emergency period, when the Janata's explicit embrace of Gandhian socialism[35] was accompanied by a publicly imperceptible but nevertheless institutionally substantive turn to market capitalism.[36] Moreover, while at the rhetorical level the Janata government's endorsement of Gandhian socialist principles of decentralization and small government marked a sharp contrast with Indira Gandhi's centralization of state power, both governments took forward a shared corporatist project of state-society relations. The conciliation and consensus models of industrial relations that were put in place by the Congress prior to and during the emergency (for example, bipartite councils and special tribunals outside the purview of the regular courts for the settlement of industrial disputes) were continued in the post-emergency era.[37]

Political continuities that belied the thesis of post-emergency rupture also included several of the controversial antidemocratic laws and regulations that had earned the emergency regime its authoritarian label. National security legislation authorizing arbitrary detentions under the provisions of the emergency-era Maintenance of Internal Security Act was extended by the Janata government in states such as Madhya Pradesh and Kashmir. Press censorship regimes remained in place in Kashmir well beyond the emergency years. The centralization of executive power in institutions such as the prime minister's office, the cabinet secretariat, and RAW, the intelligence agency (acronym for Research and Analysis Wing), went unchallenged.[38] Moreover, this was not just a matter of institutional inertia, but of active political choice. The dissolution of nine popularly elected state legislative assemblies in April–May 1977 was a notable example of how at least some of the decisions taken by the Janata government emulated those of its predecessor. The "textbook controversy" that broke out during its tenure to reveal the continued vigor of state censorship despite the formal dismantling of censorial regimes was another.[39]

Arguably the biggest credibility dilemma that the new government confronted was related to the continuity of personnel and how this shaped daily public perceptions about the Janata party as an agent of political change. This had a tangible impact on the various official inquiries and investigations into emergency misrule. Media coverage routinely highlighted how bureaucrats who had served under the previous government remained in their positions and actively interfered with ongoing investigations:

> The continuance of the same officials with the present Ministers has made the other officials wary. In one case, a senior official who is attached to a Minister is reported to have torn representations from some officials regarding the alleged misdeeds of his earlier "boss." The people who made the representations are unable to approach the Minister directly since the channel of communication is the same. Another official alleged that some people attached to the Minister in the department he worked, were passing information to his earlier Congress "boss."[40]

Against this backdrop of significant institutional, policy, and personnel continuities between the emergency and post-emergency periods, the new government's claims of transformation and rupture—the claim of newness itself—would require concerted, and repeated, efforts of public persuasion.

Along with the challenges of substantiating its transformational claims, the governance capacities of the new government had also to be effectively communicated to public constituencies. As DasGupta puts it, "even the logic of restoration of constitutionality needs an assurance that a democratically conducted government can either perform better or at least performs no worse than its adversaries."[41] Although the Janata party's campaign promise was freedom, the emergency-era ideals of order and stability were key terms in the existing vocabulary of political legitimation in the post-emergency period as well. Would and could the new government deliver on both freedom and order—goals that had until only recently been framed in terms of their mutual exclusion and constitutive opposition?

The 1977 electoral victory of the Janata over the Congress appeared to have settled the case in favor of freedom. But the question of order and stability continued to exert a strong hold on the public imagination and political discourse in the post-emergency period. A cartoon published in *India Today* in one of its first post-emergency issues, March 31, 1977, conveys the continuing normative attraction of order and stability. It is a simple black-and-white artist's rendition of Jayaprakash Narayan, the iconic leader of the anti-emergency opposition. His arm is raised, pointing to a caption whose message is in the ellipses: "We march to a better . . . yesterday . . . gheraos . . . strikes . . . corruptions . . . riots." The accompanying article cleared up any interpretive ambiguity with its quote from the Congress party general secretary V. B. Raju:

> Stability to an Indian is the most important thing. Even in getting a job, the Indian checks first whether it is "pucca." That is why a Government job is his first preference.[42]

Raju's insistence on stability as a key Indian desire can be explained by his partisanship, as a representative of the Congress party, which had recently fought the elections on a campaign promise of "order over chaos." But the normative importance of order was not restricted to the electoral campaign. Past the symbolic hundred-day milestone of the Janata government, editorials in *India Today* continued to raise the issue:

> In the question of law, order and justice, the Janata government must resolve its basic dilemma—how to ensure liberty without giving the licence to the criminals and how to administer effectively and yet bow before the people. The 100 days of Janata rule shows promise—it is up to them to ensure that it is not a promise unfulfilled.[43]

A final set of credibility challenges confronted by the new post-emergency regime had to do with the peculiar reflexive problem of a state disaffected with itself. Several of the emergency's most controversial political actions had required the participation and cooperation of state actors and ordinary low-level bureaucrats. Their service as "sterilization motivators" had enabled the perpetuation of authoritarian rule. In the post-emergency period, they continued to be pressed into service, now as the public scapegoats blamed for the emergency's excesses.

This had already been set in motion toward the end of the emergency. After the declaration of elections in January 1977, Indira Gandhi began increasingly to acknowledge in her public speeches that there had been several unfortunate governmental "lapses" and "excesses" over the past years.[44] All these were attributed to the overzealous or wayward agency of individual government officers and bureaucrats, rather than to the state and structures of political power. Not surprisingly, these individuals did not appreciate the calculus of blame. In the run-up to the emergency their resentments became a cause for political concern—after all, government officials were voters as well. Myron Weiner's vibrant eyewitness account of the 1977 elections captures the ambivalence, and the potential political threat, posed by the curious phenomenon of a state disaffected with itself:

> The officials . . . resent being used as a scapegoat for the government's excesses. On March 5th a statement was issued by the All India State Government's Employees Federation rebuking the government's attempts to blame its employees for the excesses in the family planning program. The statement said that the state governments had established quotas for motivating sterilization cases. "When employees could not achieve the quota, it resulted in withholding their increments, recovery of double the house rent due, nondrawal of salaries, and even discharge from service. . . . The terror-stricken employees were literally driven to fall on the hapless people. . . . It was preposterous for those in power to assume an air of injured innocence and pretend ignorance of all that was going on under their very nose. . . . Those who drive a wedge between the employees and the people do not serve the real interests of the nation. They serve only themselves."[45]

We can reasonably surmise that many among these disaffected state employees ended up voting against the Congress in the 1977 elections and contributed to its electoral defeat.

This was not the end of the matter. As we have already noted, in 1977 the transition of power from one political party to another was not accompanied by a change in governmental organization or personnel. The problem of bureaucratic disaffection thus did not go away with the eclipse of Congress rule and the formal withdrawal of the emergency. With much the same cast of characters remaining in office, the Janata government inherited the problem of bureaucratic disgruntlement. Adding to its already heavy burden of credibility demonstrations, the post-emergency state's efforts of public persuasion and conviction had to be directed at itself as well. Throughout its tenure, the imperative of credibility would burden the governmental agenda of the Janata party, eventually emerging as the most important political goal, as we shall soon see.

Along with democratic restoration and credibility demonstrations, the third mission that animated post-emergency politics was that of redressal—that is, confronting the authoritarian past by identifying the perpetrators of emergency wrongdoing and bringing them to swift justice. A contemporary news report summarized the task at hand:

> People responsible for the excesses of the Emergency must be punished: there is to be no talk of "forgive and forget," [the prominent Janata front leader] Mr. George Fernandes said in Delhi on Wednesday. . . .
>
> "Can we forgive them the fact that they tried to distort lies into truth? Can we forget, Indira Gandhi, that 14-year-old boys have been sterilized and that you tried to end a whole generation? Can we forgive what was done to the Press to make sure that they told only lies? Can I forget that I was charged with being the agent of a foreign country being supported by their money?"
>
> The crowd shouted: "Never, never," and Mr. Fernandes shouted back that there would be no injustice, everybody would be given a fair trial and if there were not enough courts, then special tribunals could be set up. . . . He emphasized that he did not believe in kicking a man when he was down and that was not his intention, but injustice must never simply be "forgiven and forgotten."[46]

Redress was a key emphasis in the Janata party's election campaign. The Shah Commission was set up for this purpose on May 28, 1977, within six weeks of Janata assuming office. But the Commission was soon caught up in efforts to stabilize and publicize the "pragmatic" rather than the "redemptive" dimensions of the democratic system.[47] Overriding the foundational aims of redress and justice, the credibility imperative described earlier—the effort to secure public confidence in the new Janata government's institutional capabilities—would shape the Commission's work. The shift from redress to credibility would in turn open up the gap between law and justice that was indexed by Raghumane's death.

To understand this shift, we need to revisit the Shah Commission in the wider and dynamic political context in which it worked, and approach it not as a discrete institution ("the Commission") but as a socially embedded process of public communication ("a hearing") that was connected to and traversed by several different political circuits. The Commission's hearings took place alongside and against the backdrop of other political developments that also attracted public and media attention, and its public impact was refracted and modulated through these contemporaneous events and experiences, as we will see.[48]

"The Shah Commission Begins"[49]

On April 7, 1977, two weeks after being sworn into office, the Janata government announced that it was redeeming its main electoral pledge to "punish the guilty of the emergency."[50] Although many had interpreted this to mean punitive measures and criminal charges against the officials and leaders who had authorized and implemented the authoritarian measures of the emergency, the home minister Charan Singh's parliamentary announcement "dashed these hopes to the ground."[51] Instead of grand public spectacles of instant justice and dramatic revenge scenarios, Singh proposed to establish a legally sanctioned commission of inquiry under the terms of the Commission of Inquiry Act of 1952. Headed by an "eminent judge," the retired chief justice of the Supreme Court Jayantilal Shah,[52] the Commission would "look into all complaints of excesses, malpractices, abuse of authority during the Emergency and all matters related hereto."[53]

The Janata government had constituted several inquiry commissions at approximately the same time, each investigating a different aspect of antidemocratic politics during the emergency.[54] The Shah Commission was the most important of these, responsible for the overall determination of political responsibility for the events of the past years, and an overarching indictment of the emergency regime as such. But its importance did not translate into organizational and financial allocations. The Commission was minimally staffed—the lack of adequate personnel to handle its caseload would be a constant complaint—and had to set up office in crowded rooms in central Delhi's Patiala House court complex. In marked contrast to the organizationally baroque bureaucracy that it would investigate, the Commission itself was a lean and simple organization run by two key people: Justice Shah, the chairman, and P. R. Rajagopal, an inspector general of police deputed from the Border Security Force to serve as the Commission's secretary. Three field officers served under them, supervising a team of six to seven investigators. The total combined strength of the Commission at its most complete was around three hundred staff members.

Beyond the broad terms of reference of inquiring into emergency excesses, the Shah Commission was not given any specific guidelines or even a deadline for producing its findings. It had to define its own object and scope of inquiry, standards and procedures of investigation, timeline, and guidelines for conclusions.[55] Its "evolutionary" character[56] came in for considerable public criticism. As we have seen already, this was interpreted as a marked climb-down from the party's electoral promise of bringing the emergency government to swift and decisive justice—an "anti-climactic" deferral of a politically sensitive decision, to quote John Dayal and Ajoy Bose. In fact, however, the Shah Commission's evolutionary design, procedural autonomy, and divergence from the promised path of justice delivery conformed to existing legal norms. The Commissions of Inquiry Act of 1952, which authorized all governmental commissions in postcolonial India, explicitly specified that these were bodies set up to investigate "the truth" in an impartial and disinterested fashion, in contradistinction to judicial bodies that investigated "accusations" or "charges" brought against specified persons in an adversarial format.

In practice, the numerous commissions of inquiry that had been established since independence had disregarded this legal mandate of inquiring into truth ("fact-finding," to use the parlance of the time), and had worked instead to gather information and evidence for specific accusations of wrongdoing and corruption by particular and named government officials.[57] Departing from these established conventions, the Shah Commission's open-ended mandate returned to the original premises of a governmentally commissioned inquiry as a broad-ranging investigation into an episode of wrongdoing that eluded specification, where guilt and responsibility, wrongdoing and culpability were yet to be determined. And so, if in the eyes of its critics the Commission failed to deliver justice, this failure was in fact a mark of its successful conformity to legal strictures that excluded justice delivery from the purview of a commission. In sum, it was not so much the specific drawbacks of the Shah Commission as an evolutionary, minimally resourced and staffed organization that displaced the cause of redemptive justice from the post-emergency political agenda.

Rather, the Janata government's very decision to constitute a commission of inquiry in April 1977 ensured the primacy of legal procedural maneuvers directed toward the discovery of factual truths.

The nonjudicial tracking of the Shah Commission, and the prioritization of truth and facts over justice delivery, reflected a pressing dilemma that was peculiar to the post-emergency context. In the various cases of governmental misconduct investigated by previous commissions, unlawful acts such as financial corruption and rent-seeking by public officials were on the dock. However, emergency wrongdoings were factually unspecified and amorphous. They were primarily *unconstitutional* acts, a category that did not qualify as either a criminal or a civil wrong. Civil and criminal law dealt with cases of individual harm. To judge, condemn, punish, and redeem a crime against the people and the public interest were tasks of a different order altogether. The Shah Commission's efforts were thus directing toward laying the groundwork for a future framing of charges and accusations: not the determination of guilt and punishment for a known and given crime, but the definition of wrongdoing itself. In the language of the Commission, the task at hand was to assist the future framing of charges and the identification of particular "memorialists" who would subsequently be called in to give evidence. It was a pre-judicial rather than a para- or quasi-judicial forum.

With this definitional goal in mind, the Shah Commission decided to solicit public complaints and use these as the basis of all the subsequent investigative work of the Commission. This logistical detail would be emphasized repeatedly in governmental discussions about the Shah Commission. It was also endorsed in the Commission's self-representation as a democratic demand-driven institution that responded to the wishes and initiatives of the people. In response to the advertisements placed in newspapers around the country, an overwhelming number of 50,000 letters poured into Patiala House within two months. The main task that preoccupied the Shah Commission in its initial months was one of categorization and mapping. How to sift through these 50,000 complaints to come up with a legible story about wrongdoing? What exactly were the excesses of the emergency?

Commission officials took a federally weighted approach to these questions. The complaints were divided into four categories, three of which involved delegation to state governments. The first comprised complaints about which the Commission felt not much could be done. These complaints were sent back to the states from which they originated, to dispose of as they saw fit without further advice or intervention from the Shah Commission. A second category of complaints were also sent back to the state, but with specific albeit nonbinding recommendations from the Commission on how to proceed. A third category of complaints were sent to their originating states for further investigation and eventual return to Patiala House, where the Shah Commission would take them up for final consideration and disposal. This left approximately 2,000 cases for the Commission to take up for direct investigation and disposal by its own staff. These 2,000 cases were subdivided into five groups that were taken to comprise the defined universe of emergency excesses.[58]

As the above description shows, the Shah Commission's deliberations and the findings of its hefty 525-page report were based on just 4 percent of the public complaints it received. In a further winnowing, the Commission then turned to governmental files for official documentation that could substantiate the details of the complaints. A final and much smaller subset of eighty-seven cases was taken up for public hearings, with "invitations" issued to officials and other "involved parties" who had been identified through the government documents. The Commission's final findings and recommendations were based on these eighty-seven cases.

Forty years later, occasional material traces of the other public complaints that did not make it to the hearing room of the Shah Commission can be found in its documentary records. My serendipitous discovery of the Raghumane complaint is among these. One can only speculate about the wide array of complaints that must have been sent to Patiala House at the time. For individual citizens, these were incontrovertible instances of emergency wrongdoing, but in the official post-emergency narrative they did not count as a crime against Indian democracy and its people. For the latter category of offense, an officially documented paper trail involving the central government as a perpetrator and also a witness would be required.

In this manner, the Shah Commission's inquiry into the truth turned into an intra-governmental dialogue—a performance that involved government officials, including the commissioners themselves, as the main players. The people in whose name the inquiry was conducted served as the Commission's origin—the Commission proceeded on the basis of the public complaints that it received—and subsequent audience. But, unlike the voicing functions of truth commissions in other parts of the world, or the *jan sunwais* (public hearings) organized by social movements in India, the Shah Commission did not offer many opportunities for individual citizens to speak and be heard. Instead it was mostly the state itself that commanded center stage—the guilty state officials invited to publicly acknowledge their role in the excesses of the emergency, but equally, the diligent, procedural, and lawful commission officials whose methodical persistence would restore the state as a credible institution in the eyes of its disillusioned citizens.

With time, the latter set of performative imperatives overwhelmed the former. The effort to publicly prove that the Commission was a nonpolitical and lawful institution became more important for commission officials than the public exposures of guilt and responsibility for emergency excesses. The files of the Shah Commission reveal the considerable anxiety around this. They show that the Commission's internal deliberations as well as its public presentations increasingly began to focus on issues of procedural correctness and internal consistency. The goals of redress and redemption that had dominated fiery stump speeches during the election campaigns just a few months previously now faded from view.

The Janata government's controversial decision to arrest Indira Gandhi in early October 1977 prompted Justice Shah to suspend commission hearings for almost three weeks. With Indira Gandhi's subsequent refusal to appear before the Commission on the grounds that it was a politically motivated and biased body seeking revenge, the cause of "credibility displays" became all the more pressing. That the Commission was seen to do its job properly became as important as the fact that it was redeeming the election-time promise to "punish the guilty."

But what exactly did such a credibility display entail? What were the strategies of public persuasion that the Shah Commission employed, and what can these tell us about the post-emergency normative imaginary of democracy? The following section answers these questions through a consideration of the Commission as a "communicative performance"—a distinctive event and governmental practice that publicly represents and communicates authoritative meanings.

The Representational Labors of the Shah Commission

Discussions about the political effects or impact of commissions of inquiry usually ask whether the final recommendations and findings of these governmental bodies have brought about any kind of tangible policy and legislative change. By these criteria, the Shah Commission was pretty much a damp squib or a "dead letter."[59] By the time the Commission published its findings between March and August 1978,[60] the intense public interest that had attended its initial hearings had died down, and the publication of its final report did not make much of a media splash. Moreover, in the face of growing internal dissent within the coalition and mounting political opposition from an energized Indira Gandhi, who had come to enjoy growing public popularity in recent months, a politically constrained Janata government was unable to respond to the Commission report by taking the necessary follow-up action that might have led to a judicial trial and eventual punishment.

The Janata government set up special trial courts a year later, in May 1979. However, these did not get very far. The government collapsed in mid-July 1979, and Indira Gandhi was voted back into power in January 1980. Predictably, she ignored the Commission's recommendations and disbanded the trial courts. Upon assuming office, the Congress government ensured that copies of the Shah Commission report were removed from public libraries and destroyed.[61] The Shah Commission very literally sank without a legislative or policy trace, a far cry from the transformative regime-churning action that had been promised at the start of the post-emergency era.

However, as Rupa Viswanath has recently noted, the political effect of a commission is not limited to the legal and policy salience of its final findings. It includes as well its "representational work" of consolidating and communicating normative meanings to public audiences. Analyzing the Misra Commission of Inquiry, which was constituted in 2007 to inquire into the status of linguistic and religious minorities and recommend "modalities" to improve their social and economic marginalization, Viswanath argues that its main representational function was to enact collective deliberation and to quite literally re-present, in a publicly visible manner, the achievement of democratic consensus among the "people as a whole." At a time in which reasoned deliberation is markedly absent from the everyday political life of parliamentary institutions, the Misra Commission positioned itself as an effective site and agent for the expression and reconciliation of diverse social interests.[62]

We can identify similar kinds of representational functions for the Shah Commission as well, but with a key difference. While the Misra Commission sought to communicate ideas of democracy as a politics of deliberative consensus formation, the Shah Commission's representational labors extended a normative ideal of "democracy as response." Here it was not so much the free expression and interaction of diverse social voices, but rather the reactions and responses of the state that were taken to define and affirm democratic existence. The Commission's main representational work, we might say, was to communicate the active presence of the responsive state as the primary symbol and agent of democracy.

State responsiveness was publicly represented and communicated in different ways. The first was through the idea of the "commission as invitation," that is, the insistent emphasis on the publicly engaged and noncoercive character of the inquiry conducted by the Shah Commission. From the solicitation of public complaints, to the carefully worded call to government officials to assist and join commission officials in their investigations, all aspects of the Shah Commission's work were presented in voluntary and participatory terms. This distinguished the Commission as a responsive state institution that reflected the distinctive spirit of democratic participation and response.

Public explanations of the Commission's work located its origins in popular agency, and presented a classically democratic sequence of public call and state response. It was repeatedly emphasized that the Commission began its work of investigation and information-seeking only after receiving complaints from ordinary citizens; that it was an accessible recipient of the people's grievances and confidences, a collector and sorter of information rather than a proactive initiator or adversarial protagonist.

The distinctive institutional identity of the Commission, as a statutory body located outside prevailing adversarial and punitive frameworks, was repeatedly hailed by the government, the media, and by commission officials themselves.

Second, the presence of the newly responsive state was communicated through a heightened attention to questions of procedure and lawfulness that were prioritized over the redress and redemption goals that had originally animated the Commission and the broader idea of post-emergency justice. That the Commission was methodical and rational, and that the truths that it uncovered and established had a coherent and consistent logic, was of paramount importance for the external publicity efforts of the commission. This was reflected both in the public justifications that officers offered about the nature and scope of their work, and in its internal deliberations and organizational decision-making.

The search for procedural consistency and coherence increased the salience of the Commission's classificatory work. The question of how the various complaints were to be sorted, ordered, and delegated soon began to dominate its daily work. More than four decades later, we can easily spot this categorical predilection in the archive. There are numerous and voluminous files describing in exacting detail how the categorization of complaints is to be undertaken. External and internal presentations of the procedural consistency of the commission process took precedence over the question of the Commission's ability to reach a singular and decisive outcome. The prioritization of procedure also affected case selection. As noted earlier, the cases that were taken up for investigation were not necessarily the most excessive or egregious. Rather, they could be consistently documented in and through governmental records.

This led to some odd choices. For instance, close attention was lavished upon the case involving the Congress party's use of government officials from the Directorate of Advertising and Visual Publicity to translate its election manifestos and prepare its posters. The file on this topic runs to more than three hundred pages of collated government documents and official statements. In contrast, the widely known instances of torture of political prisoners during the emergency received less attention from the Shah Commission because the incidents mostly occurred in local police stations without leaving any kind of documentary paper trail for formal verification.[63]

Third, state responsiveness was communicated through the organizational and professional composition of the Commission. The fact that the overwhelming majority of Commission officers were drawn from the police and income tax bureaucracy, the very agencies of the state that had been used as tools of political intimidation and suppression during the emergency,[64] was significant. Much of the public discussions about the Commission focused on this distinctive aspect, of how the very same cadre of officials who had actively perpetrated the injustices of the emergency were now working hard to serve Indian citizens. The Shah Commission thus contributed to the pressing post-emergency task of restoring citizens' faith in state institutions by presenting the face of the responsive state in and through its everyday work.

Media coverage of the time suggests that this communicative endeavor was quite successful. Even when the Commission's ultimate inability to deliver effective justice and redemption was the main topic of discussion, the methodical work of the many honest and dedicated state officials and policemen who worked at the Commission was singled out for praise. The Commission was hailed, and also self-identified, as the hardworking, committed, and honest state agency that offered a welcome contrast to the many lapses of the emergency-era state.

The efforts at reestablishing the legitimacy of the post-emergency state and restoring public trust in its governmental and democratic capacities put a peculiar calculus of blame in place that continues to exert a powerful hold on the public imagination of political wrongdoing today, more than four decades later. Exemplified by the Shah Commission's mandated focus on the emergency's excesses, this was the view that political wrongdoing was some kind of extreme and exceptional aberration that could be easily identified and eventually eradicated by timely interventions. As we have already seen, sifting through the massive volume of public complaints to identify the subset of extreme excesses eligible for investigation was a key priority for the Shah Commission. The actual investigation and eventual conclusion did not, however, confirm the idea of the monstrous or monumental political wrongdoing that had motivated its formation. The Shah

Commission ultimately settled on low-hanging fruit. This was compelled by various reasons, for instance the desire of Commission officials to be seen as neutral and nonpolitical agents; the strategic constraints faced by the fragile Janata coalition government on account of the Congress party's continued political salience even after its electoral defeat; and the continued refusal of senior Congress leaders such as Indira Gandhi, Sanjay Gandhi, and Pranab Mukherjee to give the Commission the information that it asked for.

When we read the Shah Commission's final report, the indictment of the notorious emergency comes across as rather a whimper. Its named and proven exposures of political wrongdoing were mostly of minor officials rather than the decisive wielders of state power. Prior to its formation, and also in the initial phase of its investigative sessions, the discussion of how extra-constitutional power was wielded during the emergency by democratically unauthorized and hence nonlegitimate actors like Sanjay Gandhi and his "Gang of Four" was a dominant theme. However, this soon fell out of the discussion, and the pursuit and indictment of such regime-level authority remained outside the Commission's final remit.[65]

The determination of political transgression was not the only issue at stake here. As particular identified instances of emergency excesses gained public visibility, a new threshold of tolerance was also put in place. Each political wrong identified by the Commission normalized a range of others that failed to meet its transgressive criteria, effectively condoning them as part of the inevitable business of democratic politics-as-usual. The terms of this new normal were reflected in the Shah Commission's procedural guidelines on how to sift out atrocities from tolerable lapses in the flood of public complaints that it received. There were many annoying problems that we had to learn to live with. They were unfortunate and disillusioning, but not extreme or intolerable in any significant way.

We will return to this point about the prevailing sentiment of post-emergency democratic disappointment in the concluding section of this chapter—of how, with the lowering of public expectation, some amount of systemic dysfunction began increasingly to be seen as an enduring irritant in Indian democracy. In a paradoxical and no doubt unintended outcome, the Commission's very endeavors to restore public faith in the post-emergency state through public displays of responsiveness contributed to the growing culture of public cynicism and distrust. From the late 1970s onward, it was widely held that there would always be something rotten in the state of India.

The final way in which the ideal of a responsive state was communicated by the Shah Commission was by highlighting the specifically non-political quality of its actions and interventions, and its institutional identity as a political outsider disconnected from the messy and corrupt circuits of electoral politics and partisan rivalries. One marker of the Commission's outsider identity was the individual career trajectory of Shah and his team members. To use the popular parlance of the time, the "eminent" and "upright" officers of the Commission, particularly its presiding officer, Jayantilal Shah, were hailed as honest professionals known for their probity, individuals who had risen up the meritorious ranks of the civil service or the legal profession without any connections to or interest in the world of politics.[66]

The rule-bound and constitutionally sanctioned character of the Commission's activities also attested to its primary identity as a political outsider. Although the efficient, methodical, and professional aspects of its work were key points of emphasis, the Shah Commission was also seen to be hemmed in by its punctilious observance of due procedure and constitutional limits. The commission files reveal both self-understandings and public portrayals of its work in terms of this quality of constraint: how, in contrast to the arbitrary powers wielded by the emergency state, it was a restrained institution, tied down by the many procedural and legal strictures of Indian democracy.

In a paradoxical outcome, the image of the ineffective Commission secured its democratic credentials as an institution committed to the non-partisan and politically neutral cause of the people. It was precisely in its inability to take decisive action, to actually name and punish the perpetrators of the emergency, that the Shah Commission sought and realized its claim of democratic responsiveness. The failure to realize any concrete result after a year of hearings, investigation, and deliberations proved to be both the Commission's institutional weakness and its normative strength. The former in fact enabled the latter. The many examples of what the

Commission had failed to accomplish were held out as signs of its non-political constitution and stance, of how it had deliberately rejected the temptations of political revenge.

This theme of institutional ineffectiveness gained salience as accusations of "politicking" were leveled against the Commission with increasing vigor. The Shah Commission was established against the backdrop of the controversial Janata decision to dissolve state assemblies run by Congress governments and call for fresh elections on the ostensible grounds of "natural justice and morality."[67] Although the Janata coalition won most of these elections, it was a checkered victory. The irony of the post-emergency government emulating the antidemocratic actions of its predecessor was not lost on public audiences, and the new government came in for increasing criticism of its politically motivated actions. From its very inception, Indira Gandhi accused the Shah Commission of being a political tool of the Janata government, and repeatedly refused its invitations to appear in Patiala House. Several others from among her close associates and former officials of the emergency government, such as her son Sanjay Gandhi and cabinet minister Pranab Mukherjee, also refused, and accused the Commission of being a politicized and partisan body. These accusations soon gained public traction. In October 1977, the dramatic arrest and equally dramatic release of Indira Gandhi by the Janata government in the wake of its first electoral setback in state assembly elections suggested that partisan political motivations were at play. The arrest played into the hands of Indira Gandhi, who positioned herself as the hapless victim of a vengeful Janata regime.

As one of the most prominent institutions of the post-emergency government, the Shah Commission faced considerable pressure to defend itself from these charges of politicization. As we have noted already, this took the form of an insistence on its own ineffectiveness. After all, if the Shah Commission was unable to punish or prosecute anyone, how could it be accused of political vengeance? To counter the charge of politics, the Commission thus produced its own limits. It presented itself as a constrained institution and repeatedly emphasized the many ways in which it failed to act. Passing the buck to the judiciary and the elected government for the actual delivery of emergency justice, the Shah Commission conspicuously confined its action and remit to the level of a stage-setting inquiry that did not, by design, offer any solution or remedy. The communicative success of the Commission—its ability to publicly represent the new and responsive state that marked the return of democracy in post-emergency India—would rest on public perceptions of its limited abilities and eventual failure.

Moral Transcendence and the People's Love

The discussion so far has focused on the Shah Commission as if it occupied the exclusive center of public attention as the main protagonist of post-emergency politics. But the Commission's activities unfolded alongside several events that also received extensive media coverage at the time, and its representational effects were refracted through these equally visible public spectacles. The Commission's work showcased the ideal of a responsive and lawful state and prioritized proceduralism as the defining feature of the post-emergency political field. Other sets of events brought an altogether different normative formation of moralizing politics to public attention.

As we have already noted, the Commission's self-positioning as a political outsider insulated from the vengeful rivalries of electoral politics rested on a distinction between law/procedure on the one hand and the moral imperatives of redemptive justice on the other. The main work of the Commission, and hence the criteria for the evaluation of its success, expressly steered clear of moral eschatologies of punitive redemption. The correct classification of emergency excesses more than their punishment was the key priority. In this way, the outsider maneuvers of the Shah Commission placed state sovereignty with its associated trappings of law and procedure, and the moral code of the people or what we might term popular-moral sovereignty, on separate tracks. Both of these were contrasted to the domain of "dirty politics."

But popular-moral sovereignty was not a uniform or singular formation. Instead, in the post-emergency period, two different understandings attracted media and public attention. They were expressed through two different kinds of public performances that unfolded alongside the political theater of the Shah Commission. The first was the Janata government's repeated public assertions and demonstrations of the exemplary ethical reputation of its leadership—how each figure at the helm of the party was a shining beacon of individual honesty and selfless national devotion. The Janata's understanding of moral authority as an individual character trait of exemplary leaders was conveyed by their acts of abstinence, sacrifice, frugality, and visible demonstrations of detachment from material desires. It resonated with the saintly idioms of legitimacy that have long pervaded Indian political life. Gandhian politics is the best-known example of this. The Janata's reproduction of these enduring tropes appeared to offer the new political party the security of a tested route to public familiarity and legitimation.

The hope was misplaced. The inordinate emphasis on exemplary individual conduct meant that even minor deviations and lapses on the part of individual leaders attracted considerable public and media attention. A new post-emergency media culture was ascendant at this time. The availability of new media technologies in conjunction with the changing social profile of journalists yielded new "news values" or ideas of what counted as news. In this changed media landscape, stories about corruption allegations and "sex scandals"[68] made national headlines with increasing frequency. In a classic hoist-by-their-own-petard scenario, these fueled the growing public criticism of the Janata government's failure to live up to its own promises, and gave Indira Gandhi and her party a fresh lease of political life. As *India Today* summed it up in its issue of July 15, 1977:

> The Janata party made a fetish out of morality. Advertising everything from Morarji's fruit diet to Raj Narain's self-proclaimed celibacy, they promised civil liberty and bread with freedom. Janata leaders squatted on the floors in the secretariat because they were the people's ministers.
>
> The 100 days of Janata rule however has shown up the contradictions between practice and precept. Floor-squatting ministers fought over the allotment of residences befitting their status as senior ministers. . . . While hoarding and profiteering continued unabated, the government failed to take steps against profiteers because they "respected individual freedom and liberty." Janata leaders admitted that some groups had taken money from industrialists for the state assembly elections. A train was delayed because Health Minister Raj Narain was late getting to the station. . . . The

> Naxalites were branded criminals while Jayaprakash blessed the pledge taken by smugglers and Morarji Desai was photographed shaking hands with Haji Ali Mastan Mirza—the King of the smugglers.[69]

Indira Gandhi's political resuscitation involved another type of public performance that was quite different from the Janata insistence on the "spotless moral character" of its individual leaders. This took the form of a literal journey outside politics. In the early autumn of 1977, several news reports and accompanying editorial commentaries took note of several trips made by Indira Gandhi, now an ordinary citizen. Her first public appearance following the June electoral debacle was a visit to a spiritual leader and social worker, eighty-two-year-old Vinoba Bhave, in his ashram in Paunar. The fact that Bhave had undertaken a vow of silence added to the public speculation around the purpose of the visit. Indira Gandhi's refusal to comment further piqued journalistic curiosity and intensified media discussions on the subject.

In its enactment of a journey to a spiritual domain beyond politics, Indira Gandhi's visit to Bhave harnessed the moralizing vocabularies about spiritual leadership ideals that were a familiar feature of Indian public life. A subsequent visit to her political rival, a now-ailing Jayaprakash Narayan, played up this theme even more, of ideal leadership as an act of transcending narrow political interests and jealousies in the cause of a greater national good. Along with her emulation of existing repertoires of moral legitimation, Indira Gandhi also invented new ones as well.[70] In fact, the visit to Narayan was immediately preceded by quite a different type of public foray, whose media coverage associated ideal leadership with displays of collective ardor rather than with evidence of good individual moral conduct. This was the much-commented-upon Belchhi journey of August 1977, which is widely regarded as a key turning point in Indira Gandhi's post-emergency political career.[71]

Media accounts that month alerted the national public to a gruesome incident of violence that had taken place in the village of Belchhi in Bihar a few months ago. In what appeared to be a clear-cut case of caste-motivated violence, several Dalit laborers in the village ("Harijans" in the parlance of the time) were killed by upper-caste landlords in a horribly brutal way.

They were burned alive in a group, and their charred remains were scattered around the village commons.

The issue eventually reached parliament. Angry opposition parties linked it to their increasingly vocal indictment of the Janata coalition's governance record, as another egregious instance of the breakdown of law and order that allegedly prevailed in the country. The Janata government promised an inquiry into the matter. But it did not send any officials to Belchhi or otherwise show any visible signs of institutional response. Instead the task of response was taken up by Indira Gandhi, who made an emotional public declaration that she would immediately travel to Belchhi.

The ensuing trip was even more dramatic than its announcement. Fierce monsoon rains had washed away most of the roads that led to the village, making it practically inaccessible to outsiders. But, as journalists noted with disbelief and admiration, this did not deter Indira Gandhi's resolve to reach the suffering people of Belchhi. A retrospective account of the Belchhi visit by Congressman Pranab Mukherjee, who would later serve as India's president, repeats this sentiment:

> Indiraji's biggest strength was her connect with the common people, especially the grass-roots Congress worker. People found in her the promise of undaunted struggle and iron will. Her visit to Belchi following the massacre of eleven dalits in Bihar's Nalanda district is well known. Belchi was inaccessible by road but that did not stop her. She said, "We shall go walking and we shall go there even if it takes us all night." The road ended in a muddy track. Indiraji's jeep got stuck in the mud and a tractor was brought to pull it out. She jumped out of the jeep and waded through the mud, her saree raised above ankle. It was getting tougher every minute, but she did not give up. An elephant was found and she quickly clambered on, proceeding to complete the three and a half hours journey to Belchi in a manner no national leader had ever travelled. She was determined to reach Belchi and did so purely because of her grit and commitment to the welfare of dalits. Consequently, Indiraji was hailed as a saviour of the under-privileged and exploited.[72]

Press accounts abound of how Indira Gandhi doggedly pushed forward to Belchhi ignoring the many entreaties by party members to abandon her risky journey. So do descriptions of how enthusiastically "the people" greeted her at every stop. The story reached its climactic conclusion with a dramatic elephant ride narrated in the Mukherjee memoir above, and which features prominently in Indira Gandhi's many biographies as well. Disregarding official counsel and the pleas of many worried supporters, Indira Gandhi is said to have abandoned her vehicle and continued to Belchhi on the back of an elephant, indefatigable in her commitment and zeal to reach the people. And when she eventually did, she was rewarded by their love. The people crowded around her in scenes of ecstatic adoration, it was said.[73]

The Belchhi story resonates with media practices today, when intermediated relays of anecdotal accounts across different media outlets and platforms produce and stabilize a new truth beyond verified facts. Individual descriptions of what happened at Belchhi did not coincide, and the circumstances of the elephant ride remained unclear. For instance, Indira Gandhi was variously described as having requested an elephant from party members; accepted an offer of an elephant from a resourceful local; and commandeered an elephant herself from a surprised villager. But as some version or other of the broader elephant story continued to be retold, the discrepancies in these details ceased to matter. The narrative stabilized around its two key poles of the intrepid elephant-riding leader, and the visible enthusiasm of the waiting people.

A specific act of violence experienced by particular caste bodies had brought Belchhi into the public spotlight. But the dominant narrative did not dwell on this detail. The Belchhi story is remembered today as a story about Indira Gandhi's visit to the site of the massacre, rather than the story of the massacre itself, or of its origins in the structural cruelties of caste society. Displacing the memory of the violent deaths that first brought it to public consciousness in the aftermath of the emergency, Belchhi has mostly lived on as an iconic moment of political rebirth and legitimation for Indira Gandhi as the popularly acclaimed leader of the people. In its recounting, Belchhi has been transfigured from a scene of mass death and charred corpses to a stage for the political legitimation of a figure standing tall outside the electoral fray. It is a story about an electoral loser who very visibly commanded the love of her people precisely through her location outside the zone of electoral politics.

Such public displays of Gandhi's intense and passionate communion with the people began to attract increasing media attention in the post-emergency period. Media commentary emphasized how she enthusiastically "went to the people"—a common formulation that further accentuates the idea of exteriority—and how the people in turn embraced her with love and devotion. The snarling hostility of the press toward the emergency's main author had dominated media coverage of Indira Gandhi in the immediate aftermath of the emergency. Quite soon this morphed into a grudging and skeptical acknowledgment and even admiration of Indira Gandhi's popular legitimacy.

As we have seen in the iconic case of the Belchhi visit, initially the idea of Indira Gandhi's popular legitimacy was conveyed in media imagery of the enthusiastic and devoted crowd at moments unrelated to the electoral cycle. As media reports and public discussions waxed eloquent on Gandhi's mass appeal, the *ur*-democratic concept of the sovereign will of the people was disconnected from the electoral institutions and processes that made up Indian democracy. In fact, as the Belchhi incident illustrates, Indira Gandhi's mass appeal and her electoral success were presented as opposing forces. She had lost the elections and she had won the people's love.

Subsequently, however, this idea of popular sovereignty as a form of electoral exteriority and radical disconnection from the constraints of electoral spaces and times was reworked. Indira Gandhi's crowd-pulling abilities became the highlight of press coverage during her electoral campaigns for by-elections in 1978. Following her victory in the Chikmagalur by-elections, a constituency in the southern state of Karnataka in November 1978 that returned her to parliament after an electoral campaign, she was seen to be "deluged" and "overwhelmed" by the overflowing emotions of large crowds everywhere she went. Evidence of visible displays of crowd enthusiasm became a press bellwether for electoral success.

The idea of visible public passion is key here.[74] Crowd sizes at election rallies have routinely informed media predictions of popular legitimacy and electoral success. With the Chikmagalur by-elections, evidence of some kind of collective performative excess also entered the calculus. The visible surfeit of publicly expressed emotions, and displays of irrational fervor and devotion, became a staple of electoral commentary. They were hailed as signs of successfully commanding the people's love.

To summarize: Modes of political legitimation expanded during the post-emergency years. Repeatedly emphasizing its meticulous attention to due procedure even at the expense of delivering justice, the Shah Commission tried to secure the legitimacy of the post-emergency government by emphasizing the procedural and lawful nature of its actions. The Janata government made a second type of legitimacy claim based on the individual moral conduct of party leaders, with morality defined by "saintly idioms" and Gandhian themes of material divestment, sexual chastity, simplicity, and self-denial. The media attention attracted by Indira Gandhi's "passion plays," or the dramatic displays of popular devotion that were said to attend her forays in public life toward the end of the 1970s, introduced a third mode of legitimation. Authority claims were now linked to collective and visible expressions of popular sentiment.[75]

Despite the obvious differences between these ideals of institutional proceduralism, individual probity, and public passion, the idea of the political outside served as a common normative foundation. The constitutive distance of institutions and actors from the rough-and-tumble of politics was the central theme of legitimacy claims in this period. They spotlighted how the Shah Commission was staffed by nonpolitical bureaucrats; how the Janata leadership was uninterested in material or political power; how Indira Gandhi was (very literally) traveling in the political wilderness. The consecration of an outsider politics that invested legitimacy and authority in institutions and actors distant and disconnected from the electoral system emerged as the main legacy of the post-emergency years.

The normative ideal of the political outside was shaped and honed by institutional initiatives such as the Shah Commission's inquiry into the excesses of the emergency as well as by strategic maneuvers on the part of political parties (the Janata coalition) and individual political actors (Indira Gandhi). It continues to animate and authorize the field of democratic politics today, many decades after the formal end of the emergency. When we recall that the wielding of power by political outsiders situated beyond formally sanctioned channels and systems was in fact one of the emergency's cardinal sins, this continuity seems paradoxical, if not outright perverse.

CONCLUSION: DEMOCRATIC MODULATIONS

There have been multiple public remembrances of the Indian emergency in recent years. Initially linked to memorialization efforts on the symbolic occasion of the emergency's fortieth anniversary in 2015, the remembrance of this nondemocratic moment in India's political history is also presented as an urgent political act in the context of ascendant authoritarianism in India and elsewhere in the world. Moving away from such appeals to the symbolic and political importance of emergency memories, I have argued in this chapter that remembrance projects miss the point. Far from being a forgotten and distant historical aberration that requires recuperation, the emergency has influenced and grounded contemporary Indian democracy in substantial ways.

To see and understand this historical connection and continuity, a generative rather than a recuperative approach to the emergency is in order. How to engage this political formation as neither metaphor nor memory? How to see the emergency not as a distant and exceptional past that we need to remember and analogize from the vantage point of an altogether different present, but as the enabling ground, continuing presence, and horizon of our normal democratic everyday?

To understand the generative emergency, this chapter has focused on the immediate post-emergency period (spanning the end of the 1970s and the beginning of the 1980s, roughly 1977–84), a surprisingly neglected moment in political histories of India. Revisiting the prevailing common sense about the restoration of democracy that followed the formal end of emergency rule in the spring of 1977, it has taken a closer look at the actual terms and logics of this conclusion.

What happened after the emergency ended, and what did the project of democratic restoration actually look like? Addressing these questions, I concluded that we should revise the idea of a democratic restoration or return of some kind of pre-emergency status quo. We should consider instead the emergence of a *new* democratic normal at the end of the 1970s: how Indian democracy was transformed and modulated by the historical event of the emergency. Condemning and undoing the emergency was the main task at hand at this time. However, many of the salient norms of democratic politics in the aftermath of the emergency—about political legitimacy, public interest, representative government—and the actions of state and non-state institutions like commissions, the judiciary, and media and civil society groups, adapted and carried forward or modulated the emergency's political logics in several significant ways.

The rise of outsider politics was foremost among these modulations. The post-emergency years witnessed the growing political authority and influence of actors and institutions that were not connected to the electoral political system, who claimed legitimate authority on the basis of their political-electoral distance and exteriority or the fact that they were political naïfs and outsiders. This was a historical irony. A similar formation of outsider authority had been a notorious feature of the emergency regime. The exercise of personalized power by extraconstitutional authorities such as the prime minister's son Sanjay Gandhi, who had never contested a single election nor been formally appointed to a governmental position, was among the primary excesses that the state-appointed Shah Commission was charged to investigate in the emergency's aftermath, as part of the "never again" consensus that shaped post-emergency political culture in the country.

How to explain the rise of outsider politics in post-emergency India? This chapter has offered an historically contextualized explanation and related it to the contingent political exigencies of the time. For instance, although the Shah Commission and other post-emergency commissions of inquiry were established with the explicit intention of delivering a "true justice" to the people, this aim was quickly overshadowed and sidelined by efforts to establish the credibility of the Commission and the new government. In turn, this dominance of the credibility imperative, and the ensuing prioritization of proceduralism over justice, were responses to the particular dilemmas of political power in the late 1970s. Soon after assuming office, the new Janata government was beset by a series of internal rivalries and splits that emboldened its political opposition. And so, even though the sweeping electoral mandate that it had just received should have authorized the new government to effect substantial changes, this just didn't happen. Instead, the policies of the Janata government were subject to intense criticism, and the Shah Commission became a prime target of opposition.

As the Congress party leadership publicly challenged the authority of the Shah Commission on the grounds that it was politically biased, countering this charge by establishing the Commission's nonpolitical character—how it was a political outsider manifestly disconnected from partisan ambitions—became an urgent task for the Janata government as well as for commission officials. This in turn led to an increasing emphasis on the procedurally and legally constrained actions of the Commission, and a demonstration of all the ways in which it could not and did not deliver justice. This was a paradoxical outcome. Discourses and displays of official limitations and failures were produced by state agencies themselves, and the legal and procedural calculus of the state and the moral reckoning of the people were placed on separate tracks.

Although it played a key and formative role, the Shah Commission was not the sole agent of outsider politics in post-emergency India. Other contemporaneous developments also contributed to the normative salience of the political outside, whether the Janata government's efforts to present its leaders as saintly figures uninterested in political power and material rewards, or Indira Gandhi's strategies for gaining public attention through dramatic acts like goodwill visits to former political rivals or her elephant ride to Belchhi.[76] Together these consolidated the vision of a pure space of popular-moral sovereignty where true democracy could be founded and renewed: a space set apart from the instrumental calculations of electoral politics as well as from the stiff proceduralism of lawful governance.

It is not surprising that electoral politics was criticized and condemned in the aftermath of the emergency, a period and regime that was directly linked to the political ambitions and insecurities of politicians like Indira Gandhi. Neither was such condemnation entirely new. As many scholars have observed, the normative ideal of anti-politics and the call for political transcendence were familiar themes of colonial and postcolonial political culture. What distinguished the post-emergency embrace of the political outside was the differentiation or split between justice and law, popular morality and procedural governance that it effected. The resulting formation of democratic disappointment is an enduring legacy of India's generative emergency. In the narrative of post-emergency democracy, lawful and procedural governance is estranged from popular-moral coordinates and somehow always lets the people down. Democracy is seen to require for its cure the extra-electoral and extra-institutional interventions of a political outsider.

POSTSCRIPT: THE NAGARWALA MYSTERY

A postscript to end the chapter like it began, with the contents of a file from the National Archives of India. Ever since the notoriously elusive Shah Commission files were made available to researchers in 2011, they have attracted a fair amount of attention from journalists and scholars. The "requested by" log pasted to the inside cover of each Shah Commission file that I received from archive librarians was rarely empty, reminding me to my considerable disappointment that I was hardly traversing an unexplored research terrain.

But two moments of discovery stood out in this otherwise unoriginal pursuit. The first was the file about Raghumane's suicide that I stumbled upon by mistake. As I have recounted in the opening sections of this chapter, the dry yet chilling account of this "commissioned death" pushed me to inquire into how and why proceduralist and legal-formal imperatives overshadowed the promise of redemptive justice in the aftermath of the emergency. It got me to think about the broader political consequences of this shift, and of the gap between state sovereignty and popular-moral sovereignty that it illuminates. What does it mean when the legitimacy of state institutions is linked to their manifest *in*ability to conform to and satisfy the people's desire for justice and their moral senses of punishment, revenge, and atonement?

A second archival discovery led me to an answer. While studying the Shah Commission files at the National Archives in the summer of 2016, I came across a collection of documents from the Jaganmohan Reddy Commission, another commission of inquiry that had been set up by the Janata government after the emergency ended.[77] In contrast to its contemporaries who focused on the misdeeds of the emergency regime, the Reddy Commission addressed an event that preceded the emergency by several years.

The subject of the Reddy Commission was the Nagarwala case, an eponymous political scandal involving Prime Minister Indira Gandhi that had caused considerable public controversy in the early 1970s. In the summer of 1971, a story about an astonishing financial swindle made the headlines. The improbable details resembled the plotline of a thriller film or some other piece of fantasy fiction.

One day in May 1971, Ved Prakash Malhotra, the head cashier at central Delhi's Parliament Street branch of the State Bank of India, received a phone call at his desk. The caller identified himself as P. N. Haksar, the principal secretary to the prime minister, and asked Malhotra to withdraw sixty million rupees in cash from the bank and hand it over to a courier waiting outside. The money was for a "top-secret Bangladesh mission," he was told, and the paperwork required for the bank's records would be provided shortly.[78]

Malhotra was initially reluctant and suspicious, but agreed to carry out the instructions after a female voice came onto the phone and confirmed the details. Malhotra immediately identified this as the voice of Prime Minister Indira Gandhi, and greeted her as *Mataji* (honorific for mother). The voice confirmed the orders and added a set of "secret code words" that would allow Malhotra to identify the courier. Malhotra withdrew the money, placed it in a suitcase, and informed his colleagues at the bank that the required documentation would be provided shortly. He drove to the designated drop-off, where a "tall, burly, fair-complexioned man"[79] was waiting for him. Malhotra handed over the suitcase to him after the correct code words *Bangladesh ka babu* (gentleman from Bangladesh) were provided, and drove to the prime minister's residence to pick up the promised receipt from Haksar.

Haksar had no idea what he was talking about. No such call had been made by anyone, least of all the prime minister. Malhotra immediately notified the police, who had in the meantime been contacted already by his suspicious colleagues from the bank. Displaying unusual alacrity and efficiency, the police launched Operation Toofan (hurricane), tracked down the man on the same day, and recovered all but five thousand rupees of the missing money. Apprehended at the Parsi Dharamshala (guesthouse) in the city, he identified himself as Rustom Sohrab "Jimmy" Nagarwala, an ex-military officer.

Nagarwala confessed to the police that he had imitated the prime minister's voice. He was sentenced to four years of rigorous imprisonment after what is arguably the shortest trial in Indian legal history (it lasted ten minutes). He subsequently recanted his confession and filed an appeal on procedural grounds, but this was rejected. Nagarwala spent the next few months in prison writing letters to personal acquaintances and journalists. He said that he had some very important information with national security consequences that he needed to share. He insisted that he was a secret agent with connections to RAW, the Indian intelligence agency. The entire operation was part of a secret plan to realize the covert Bangladesh liberation operation that Indian military and intelligence were engaged in at the time.[80] The prime minister, the head cashier, and even the police were all in on the alleged swindle, Nagarwala claimed. He was no con man, but a hero working valiantly to realize the greater national good.

About five months into his prison term, Nagarwala suddenly fell ill and died soon after he reached the hospital. The police officer who had investigated the case, D. D. Kashyap, died in a car crash while on his way to his honeymoon. These incidents further fanned the flames of public speculation. Rumors of Indira Gandhi's involvement in the Nagarwala affair proliferated. Speculations ranged from financial embezzlement to allegations of organized killing.

The declaration of the emergency four years after Nagarwala's mysterious death interrupted but did not end the swirl of accusations. Soon after the Janata government came to power in 1977, the Nagarwala case, comprising the original incident at the bank as well as the circumstances surrounding his sudden death, was taken up for formal inquiry by the state-appointed Reddy Commission. For the new Janata government, solving the Nagarwala mystery appealed as a potent symbol of institutional transformation, and perhaps even a means to establish the criminal culpability of Indira Gandhi.

But the Reddy Commission went the anticlimactic way of its contemporaries. After sixteen months and thousands of pages of documentation that yielded an 820-page final report, the story remained murky. The Commission concluded that there were insufficient evidentiary grounds to reach any conclusion about culpability. In fact, it was not possible even to determine the nature of the wrongdoing in the first place. Was it a clever individual heist for financial gain, or a grand conspiracy to further national and even global political ambitions? Who was Nagarwala, what did he know, and why did he die? The questions remained unanswered.

The Reddy Commission's files show how such a (non)conclusion was reached, and what calculus of wrongdoing allowed *l'affaire Nagarwala* to not be ruled a punishable crime.[81] A diverse set of testimonies piled up before the Reddy Commission. They reflected the complex and protracted nature of a case that included events ranging from a bank heist in 1971, to the sudden deaths both of the chief accused, Nagarwala, and of the chief investigating officer. Although they addressed very different issues and concerns, nearly all spoke of some kind of deep-seated systemic rot. In just about every stage of the Nagarwala case, institutions and systems did not function as they were supposed to and let the people down.

The Commission took these accusations on board. It concluded, quite reasonably, that if each of the problematic aspects of the Nagarwala case could be explained by an institutional or systemic failure of some kind, the question of individual culpability was moot. Thus the medical neglect that led to Nagarwala's death was not part of any deliberate plan. It was caused by the institutional malfunction and indifference that routinely prevailed in Indian prisons and hospitals. Similarly, the mysterious fire at the record room in the Tis Hazari court complex that destroyed key documents seized from the State Bank of India was the result of a careless error by underqualified security personnel,[82] and not a grand conspiracy.

Instead of delivering the promised verdict on the former prime minister's guilt, the Reddy Commission highlighted the endemic dysfunction of the system as a whole. It confirmed this as the baseline of normalcy against which the exceptionalism of crimes and excesses were to be measured. It was not surprising that institutions didn't work, that people were routinely mistreated, that there was neglect, suffering, and sometimes even death. Why would we expect otherwise? These were not prosecutable crimes. Rather, they were "tolerable lapses" and "tendencies" that, although unfortunate, did not constitute grounds for prosecution. A minimalist set of remedies would suffice, according to the Reddy Commission. Government officials should strive to avoid the "dereliction of duty," people shouldn't smoke in archive rooms, government hospitals should have a few more beds for patients. No dramatic action involving punitive or radical transformative measures of any kind was required.

* * *

As I read the Nagarwala files in the new millennium, the dry and resigned tally of the broken things, failed institutions, and unkept promises that constitute the everyday normal, and the tinkering-at-the-edges quality of its proposals for change, leap out of the pages like an old familiar friend. The language of democratic disappointment from more than four decades ago remains our common sense today. The invocation of procedural constraints is also very familiar. Like the Shah Commission, the Reddy Commission repeatedly emphasized its deliberate choice to uphold procedural consistency and evidence-based reasoning at the expense of delivering any kind of definitive answer that could put public speculation to rest. The Shah Commission had separated procedure and justice. It had placed its work of restoring institutional credibility and the rule of law in the domain of the former and not the latter. In a similar move, the Reddy Commission differentiated procedure from the clamor of public opinion and perceptions.

In the name of producing rational, evidentiary truths, the Reddy Commission chose not to engage any of the emotionally charged speculations and fears that gave the Nagarwala mystery its intense affective charge. As Reddy concluded,

> [t]here were several lacunae and to supply an answer to these would force me to leave the safe haven of facts which [are] required to be established by evidence and enter the realm of conjectures and speculation.[83]

But conspiracies and innuendos continued to swirl and even intensify in the wake of this retreat to the "safe haven of facts." The noncommittal position of the Commission fueled ever-more-elaborate stories about the various hidden forces and intentions that must have been at work behind the strange tale of Nagarwala.

In the summer of 2016, something falls out of the typewritten pages of a Reddy Commission file. It is a blue inland letter, the standard-issue prepaid envelope of the Indian postal services. The letter is signed by Dr. S. D. Misra, "MA (Lond), Ph.D. (Lond)," from Ujjain in the central Indian state of Madhya Pradesh, and has an arresting subject heading: "Subject: Sex game/Power Politics vis-à-vis Nagarwala Kand [episode]."[84]

Tiny handwriting covers every inch of paper. A crazed jumble of words stands the official narrative of the Reddy Commission on its head. For the Commission, the Nagarwala mystery was all about governmental malfunction. It was related to an unfortunate set of lapses on the part of governmental institutions and actors. There was no malice or avarice at play; no evidence of dark forces and hidden hands whatsoever. Its roots could be clearly mapped and isolated. The cause thus identified, "dereliction of duty" by government officials, was discrete and confined to the dysfunctional government of Indira Gandhi. All else was deemed unverified conjecture and speculation, as we have seen already.

In S. D. Misra's account however, everything is implicated. His narrative about Nagarwala refuses boundaries. There is no distinction between speculation and fact. Conspiracy is truth. State and citizen are intimately entwined. The letter details how the dark play of political forces connect the most personal aspects of his life—from his divorce as a result of his wife's affair with his father, to the loss of his job—to the highest levels and decisions of the state. His wife's affair, the Nagarwala mystery, an assassination attempt on the Janata prime minister: everything is part of the same giant conspiracy.

I find several other letters like it in the file. Not all are as delusional. But like Misra's inland letter, each is a voluntary act of citizenship by individuals who have come forward for their own reasons, to address their state in the manner and matter of their choosing.[85] Detailing elaborate theories about hidden influences at work, and the near-magical powers of political leaders, they refuse the dominant terms of cynical citizenship and democratic resignation. They deny the difference between fact and speculation, truth and conspiracy, law and morality. There is no pure space outside politics, they whisper. All is power. Like Raghumane's suicide, these are the forgotten traces that call for our remembrance.

FOUR

OUTSIDER AGENCY

THIS CHAPTER, LIKE THE one before it, approaches the emergency as a generative rather than a deviant event in India's political history. A generative approach accounts for why, more than four decades later, several of the authoritarian regime's legacies are alive in the rhythms and textures of ordinary *democratic* politics in India. Here, too, I make the case for the generative emergency by focusing on the post-emergency period, that is, the years from the late 1970s to the mid-1980s. Both contemporaneous participants and later observers have described this as the time of the emergency's decisive reversal, when democracy returned to the country. But as we've seen in the previous chapter, democracy's return journey after 1977 traced a rather crooked line that looped back along older grooves. Many of the actual practices of politics and statecraft undertaken in the name of restoring democracy during these years in fact carried forward, albeit in altered form, many of the ideas and policies that were associated with the emergency itself.

The political outside was one such idea. As the preceding discussion of the Shah Commission of Inquiry and its aftermath has shown, post-emergency democratic restoration projects reinforced a hard division between politics and the people, and set up binaries between law/justice, state sovereignty/popular sovereignty, and moral conviction/political compulsion. The moral power of the people was held to lie squarely outside the domain of electoral politics, as something that exceeded the grasp of corrupt political representatives and indifferent bureaucrats. This vision of a distant popular-moral sovereignty[1] was paired with a countervision of what I've dubbed the rotten state: of how India's power-hungry elected representatives and the officials they appointed invariably let the people down. Of course, the belief that an extra-political and morally charged people-power was the substance of real democracy had long animated political ideologies and movements in India and elsewhere. Yet after the emergency this was no longer simply a normative ideal. It now took the form of actual political interventions. The political outside became the ground on which new kinds of non-electoral agents and institutions, and new assertions of extra-political agency, gained visibility, legitimacy, and power.

This chapter is about the exercise of outsider political agency after the Indian emergency. Through a discussion of an important innovation that emerged in the late 1970s and early 1980s, the new legal-jurisprudential form of public interest litigation (or PIL, as it is popularly known today) and the distinctive kinds of public and political actions that it precipitated, I chart the authoritative emergence of political outsiders—individuals as well as institutions—and the lasting effects of outsider politics in and on Indian democracy. Two arguments anchor the discussion. First, I track the *extra-electoral mediations of democracy*, that is, how a new set of intermediaries came to exercise curative agency and representative authority in the late 1970s and early 1980s. Hailed as political-electoral outsiders, these individual and institutional actors were charged with the urgent work of curing the ills of the political system.

Some background context is helpful to understand the significance of this development. In the first few decades after independence, the state was the main institutional vehicle of popular representation in India, and its legitimacy was firmly tied to its electoral mandate. Public discourse repeatedly emphasized how, in marked contrast to its colonial predecessor, the sovereign Indian state after 1947 was freely chosen by its citizens in the largest exercise of full suffrage that the world had ever known. This changed after the emergency. Starting in the late 1970s, the dyad of electoral representation that linked the state to its people was interrupted by various non-electoral intermediaries. They promised to truly represent the people and fulfil the promise of democracy by countering the misdeeds of elected representatives and the governmental functionaries that they had appointed. Focusing on two prominent institutional intermediaries, the judiciary and the media, this chapter traces how a surge of beyond-the-ballot representative claims mediated the restoration project of post-emergency Indian democracy. I also consider the distinctive networked form that outsider political agency took, as "concern networks" brought together journalists, judges, lawyers, academics, and social activists in a common cause of democratic remedy or repair.

Concern networks drew upon a distinctive set of normative ideas about *wounded citizenship* and practiced a politics of *civic anger* that form my second line of inquiry. I use the term *wounded citizenship* to describe a repertoire of public reasoning that became popular in the post-emergency period. The quintessential ordinary citizen of a polity—the main subject in whose name democratic politics justifies itself—was defined as a victim of political wrongdoing, a bearer of a wound inflicted by the political establishment. The idea of wounded citizenship was elaborated in public cultural discourse and in the legitimation vocabularies of state institutions. From the late 1970s onward, state and non-state actors publicly justified their actions in terms of meeting the needs of wounded and victimized citizens.

The post-emergency political imagination leaned away from the developmentalist dreams of state-guided progress that had dominated national discourse since independence. It spoke instead of the broken promises and dashed hopes of nation-building, and configured the present as a crisis time of failed utopia.[2] The misdeeds and failures of the state/the system—named as a lethal mix of venal cruelty, indifference, and inefficiency—came to dominate the public agenda and displaced the "statist sublime" of Nehruvian India.[3] Along with the revaluation of the postcolonial state (from a source of hope to disillusion) and the contraction of political time (from future progress to present crisis), a new and socially expansive understanding of victimhood and injury also took hold. Staging their angry interventions around a wide range of issues, from the unpaid pensions of government servants to the custodial torture of prisoners by state officials, concern networks addressed a universal subject of wrongdoing. We the wounded people.

This chapter explores the implications of defining peoplehood as a common experience of injury—of approaching citizenship through a "wrongs framework" rather than a rights framework, we might say. Several key elements of present-day Indian democracy were shaped by these generalizations of wounded citizenship from the late 1970s. The elite-as-everyman syndrome, where elite and middle-class Indians blithely speak in the name of the ordinary citizen or common man; the frequent eruptions of outrage politics in contemporary public culture; the urgent "crusades" of curative democracy to heal and purge the diseased body politic and restore democracy to an original state of pristine health through the expert interventions of a political outsider—all these familiar markers of our political everyday are linked to the post-emergency formations of wounded citizenship, civic anger, and outsider political agency, as we will now see.

THE PIL REVOLUTION

Public interest litigation is a distinctive judicial and legal instrument that was first used in India in the late 1970s, in the post-emergency context of democratic restoration. It has been widely credited with ushering in a juristic and social revolution that reshaped litigation pathways and, at a more fundamental level, rewired the circuitry of state-citizen relations in India.[4] PIL merits discussion not only because it is an iconic marker of the particular historical moment of the Long 1970s that I am interested in, but because it was centrally invested in the project of curative democracy that is the subject of this book. It was a tool and technique that aimed to repair the broken democratic system.

Hailed in hyperbolic terms as a revolution, public interest litigation is a specific type of litigation that can be moved in an Indian court by an individual, group of citizens, or even the judiciary itself *suo moto* (on its own cognizance) to challenge acts of illegality, lawlessness, or neglect by state institutions and officials. The main innovation here is the nondirect character of the challenge, which is presented in the name of someone separate and distinct from the physical petitioner who actually moves the courts. A PIL thus involves an assertion of distance. Unlike civil, criminal, and constitutional litigation, public interest litigation separates the litigant and the injury. In a PIL the litigation is always for another, whether a person or a nonpersonified collective interest. This could be a specific and named injured party who is unable to litigate for reasons that often stem from the harm itself, for example, exploited construction workers on public works projects, or unlawfully detained or tortured prisoners. PILs can also be moved in the name of a more general and amorphous sense of the public and its injured interest, as for instance when PILs challenge the location of polluting industries on the grounds of harm to essential public goods such as health and environment.

Standing

The distinguishing innovations of public interest litigation can be grouped into four categories.[5] First, it transforms rules of standing (*locus standi*). In the framework of Anglo-Saxon adversarial jurisprudence that has been adopted by former British colonies like India, the determination of who has the right to bring a case before a court is made on a private and individualized basis. An individual complainant has to prove that she is the directly aggrieved party with "real interests" at stake. Moreover, as Jamie Cassels has observed, in the capitalist contexts in which Anglo-Saxon law has evolved, real interests invariably mean individual property and financial interests. As a former British colony, Indian law also reflects these "proprietary and fiduciary interest" principles of colonial British law.[6]

After independence, these colonial principles melded with postcolonial commitments to a judicially minimalist interpretation of the separation of powers doctrine that reflected the hold of Nehruvian socialism in the new republic. In the postcolonial dispensation that prevailed after 1947, it was deemed ideologically sound to keep the judiciary within a relatively constrained terrain, to prevent it from obstructing the social transformation agendas of institutions like the elected legislature that embodied the will of the newly sovereign people.[7] Additional pragmatic considerations about keeping the judicial caseload manageable further ensured a narrow interpretation of legal standing in the early years of the new republic. As Cassels has noted, the conservative interpretations of standing that dominated judicial discourse in the founding period were usually accompanied by observations about how any diversion from the direct-injury principle would either cause chaos for the courts by "opening the floodgates" of litigation,[8] or else would violate the delicate institutional balance of the separation-of-powers doctrine enshrined in the Indian constitution.

In a substantial departure from these existing conventions of direct standing, the Indian Supreme Court after the emergency began to admit petitions from third parties who clearly did not have any direct interest-based involvement in the matter that they brought to the court's attention. In fact, their manifest disconnect from the injured subject was usually the basis for the admission of their petitions. From the late 1970s and early 1980s onward, standing expanded beyond conventional frameworks of individualized direct injury to encourage the petitioning agency of strangers and outsiders. PIL petitions joined together an unlikely cast of characters. Academics living in Delhi could successfully petition the court about the mistreatment of women in a state care facility located two hundred kilometers away in Jaipur. The plight of prisoners in Bihar was heard through the petition of a lawyer in Delhi who had never met them. The surprise of standing that resulted as strangers connected to work together became one of the most distinctive features of PIL in its early years.

By expanding the principles of judicial standing, public interest litigations did not only change the identity of the petitioner who could appear before the courts (from direct to indirect or "representative"). They also redefined the very subject of interests that formed the core of the litigation. Unlike the conventional judicial recognition of injuries to individualized private interest, post-emergency PIL petitions defined interests in collective terms. A distinctive juridical-political subject, the public and the people, gained legibility in Indian democracy. And, as we will soon see, the defining feature of this public subjectivity was its representational dependence on electoral outsiders. It could only be expressed through the interventions of intermediary agents located outside the system of electoral representation.

Procedure

Second, PILs relaxed legal and juridical procedures. Just as the expansion of standing was justified on the grounds of making justice accessible to the weak and oppressed, the main arguments for procedural relaxation marshaled similar ideas about judicial unblocking in order to reach marginalized and vulnerable populations who were outside the circuits of the law. Formal-legal procedures were contrasted to, and said to thwart, the normative promise of justice.[9] Increasingly, legal and judicial action in the name of the people came to mean action that was procedurally unconstrained in some fashion. "Epistolary jurisdiction," or the admission of petitions on the basis of handwritten letters and even postcards mailed to individual justices, was one such procedural innovation.[10] The material difference of these documents marked in physical form the shift away from the ponderous and daunting languages and rituals of justice-seeking, whose successful negotiation required an entire apparatus of specialized professionals that only a few could access and afford. The frequent exercise of the court's *suo moto* powers was another example. In the PIL era, it was not only civilian third parties who could claim to represent the public interest before the judiciary. The justices of the Supreme Court and high courts could perform this role as well, admitting petitions "on their own accord" after receiving a letter or reading a news report about a horrific incident.[11] The signal-and-action relay between courts and media, in which media attention sparked legal and judicial action in the name of the people and public interest, soon became an integral part of the PIL process.

A final set of procedural innovations involved changes in evidentiary practices that reflected the distinctive conciliatory logic governing public interest litigations. Public interest litigation charged the state and its agencies with various kinds of wrongdoing. However, this was not the zero-sum adversarial encounter staged by civil and criminal justice, which must conclude with a winner and a loser. In a PIL, both the petitioner and the accused or respondent—the Indian state—had a common stake in the public interest. As Justice P. N. Bhagwati would observe in his judgment on the landmark *ASIAD workers* case of 1982:

> The State or public authority against whom public interest litigation is brought should be as much interested in ensuring basic human rights, constitutional as well as legal, to those who are in a socially and economically disadvantaged position, as the petitioner who brings the public interest litigation before the court.[12]

In the aftermath of the emergency, public interest litigation framed the contract of citizenship as a relationship of mutual obligation between state and citizen. Instead of an adversarial contest between inimical interests, public interest litigation was a joint venture between state and citizen that furthered a mutual commitment. Although the state was a respondent, the main charge of the litigation was not against the state as such. Rather, it was against the illegalities that were committed on its behalf, that harmed the legitimacy of the state as much as they harmed the immediate injured party. Equally, then, the state as respondent stood to benefit from the PIL. The disclosures and remedies of public interest litigation would allow the state to improve its administrative performance and would also salvage or shore up the normative "myth of the state."[13] As legal scholar G. L. Peiris has pithily summed up, "respondents . . . [are] protagonists in the collective quest for social justice."[14]

Evidentiary standards for public interest litigation were accordingly quite different from those that applied to the adversarial contexts of conventional litigation. PIL involved a unique form of collaboration between the petitioner and the respondent (the state) in a joint effort to "help the court to find the truth."[15] When adjudicating a PIL, Supreme Court judges relied quite heavily upon reports produced by fact-finding expert committees that they themselves appointed. Courts also relaxed existing evidentiary standards and often admitted news reports as evidence.

Duration

The third set of changes that public interest litigation introduced had to do with the temporal horizon of judicial concern. Public interest litigation expanded the duration of the judiciary's involvement in a case. Unlike traditional litigation, which exits the courtroom when a final decision pronounced by the judge concludes a case, public interest litigation involved courts in the ongoing monitoring and implementation of outcomes, and saw them pass a large volume of interim directions that applied close judicial attention to administrative details.

According to some critics, by authorizing such close and continuous judicial involvement in an issue, the instrument of PIL has effectively enabled the judiciary to contravene the constitutional separation-of-powers doctrine. The judiciary has transformed itself from a passive institution of judgment to an active lawmaker and administrator, resulting in the phenomenon of "judicial legislation."[16] The judiciary also intervenes in existing societal arrangements by involving social actors of its choosing in a PIL process. As noted earlier, the appointment of fact-finding commissions by courts is a common practice. By exercising these appointment prerogatives, the judiciary can substantially redefine the main issue at hand—effectively redefining the public interest itself—through decisions to involve specific kinds of experts. For instance, in hearing a case involving a stone quarry in the Dehradun valley of northern India, the *Rural Litigation Kendra* case of 1983, the Supreme Court appointed a committee comprising town planners, environmental scientists, and geologists to study the environmental consequences of stone crushers and limestone kilns.[17] The court's appointments effectively endorsed and strengthened the petitioner's argument that the environment was a public interest. They also created an institutional pathway for the "scientization" of environmental advocacy. Following *Rural Litigation Kendra,* the convening of similar bodies of expertise and the presentation of similar constellations of scientific evidence became a standard practice for future generations of environmental activists.[18]

Doctrine

Finally, public interest litigation introduced significant changes in doctrinal interpretations. These were usually in the direction of broad or "permissive" readings of the constitution. They involved what Cassels describes as "creative adjudication and the elaboration of rights" beyond legal positivism.[19] Court decisions in PIL cases have generally involved an expansive interpretation of constitutional articles, especially Articles 14 and 21, the equality-liberty dyad that forms the democratic core of the Indian constitution.[20] There has also been a concerted move toward reading Parts III and IV of the constitution together, that is, the respective provisions for justiciable fundamental rights and nonjusticiable directive principles.[21]

Pre-emergency judicial practices of constitutional interpretation approached these as contending and hierarchical principles. Courts generally upheld fundamental rights with their liberal commitments to individual freedoms, over the vision of socioeconomic transformation through active state intervention that was enshrined in the directive principles section of the constitution. This constitutional hierarchy, along with the balance between the transformative legislature and conservationist judiciary that it prescribed, was challenged during Indira Gandhi's tenure. As the previous chapter has noted, starting in the late 1960s, Indira Gandhi's attempts to legitimize her position as the new leader of a divided Congress party saw her deploy an instrumentalist version of populist socialism. Sidestepping institutional intermediaries and party organizations, she directly appealed to mass electoral constituencies. The elevation of constitutional directive principles and their grand promise of socioeconomic change was central to this effort.[22] This was achieved both through constitutional amendments that prevented the judicial review of any legislation that was enacted to fulfil a directive principle, and through governmental initiatives like the Twenty-Point Programme that borrowed quite heavily from the constitutional text of directive principles.[23]

After coming to power in March 1977, the new post-emergency Janata regime called for a widespread reversal of emergency policies and practices. But as the previous chapter has noted, the actual reversal that took place was neither as absolute nor as sweeping as the "never again!" rhetoric of the 1977 election campaign had promised. Instead of being annulled, many emergency-era policies and precepts were recalibrated after the emergency ended. For instance, the emergency regime's prioritization of directive principles was reworked in the post-emergency period, and public interest litigations aided this effort. From the late 1970s on, judicial orders and decisions on PIL cases frequently offered up new interpretative hybrids that linked and fused the collective and transformational vision of directive principles with individualist and liberal ideas of fundamental rights and freedoms.[24]

LINEAGES OF PUBLIC INTEREST LITIGATION

Judicial Expiation

In most discussions of Indian public interest litigation, the post-emergency Supreme Court is given the main credit as the originator and main mover. In Upendra Baxi's memorable phrase, PIL was a product of the judiciary's "expiatory syndrome" after the emergency. It reflected the fervor that gripped the country's apex court as it sought to make amends for its failure to live up to its constitutional obligations of protecting the fundamental rights of citizens during the emergency.[25]

As I've noted earlier, post-independence India witnessed an institutional tussle between the elected legislature and the unelected judiciary as competing loci of representational authority. The issue of land reform in the 1950s is an exemplary instance of this institutional competition, when judicial interventions in the name of protecting individual property rights countered legislative efforts in the name of socioeconomic redistribution and reform. In some instances, the judiciary gained the upper hand by marshaling the power of judicial review to strike down laws as unconstitutional. At other moments, parliamentary legislators pushed back through legislative innovations such as the creation and expansion of constitutionally specified schedules or lists of legislative issues that were protected from judicial review.[26]

Starting in the late 1960s, this seesaw of power was replaced by concerted efforts to secure executive dominance over all branches of government. For instance, in the early 1970s a series of governmental measures such as bank nationalization and the abolition of "privy purses" or payments to the erstwhile rulers of Indian princely states were publicized as representative actions that realized the true interests of the people. Judicial efforts to stay and reverse these legislative actions were, in turn, dismissed with righteous rhetoric from the incumbent regime that pitted the allegedly conservative judicial tendency to uphold the "vested interests" of the "propertied classes" against the popular sovereignty embodied in Indira Gandhi's government.

The Indira Gandhi government's challenge to judicial authority was not only at the level of rhetoric. In the run-up to the emergency, efforts to create a "committed judiciary"[27] led to the transfer of judges and the suspension of seniority conventions of judicial promotion. The declaration of the emergency in June 1975 secured for the legislature and the executive a clear dominance over the judiciary. Indeed, for many contemporary observers, the main motivation for the declaration, coming as it did right after an unfavorable judicial decision against Indira Gandhi, was to curb judicial power and reassert the political authority and primacy of Gandhi and her government. During the emergency, the Gandhi government passed constitutional amendments that further enhanced its discretionary power. The omnibus forty-second amendment, passed in 1976, drew down the safeguards of individual fundamental rights and authorized the legislature to fulfil the directive principles of the constitution. Earlier in the year, the Swaran Singh Committee was constituted to consider amendments to the constitution and appraise the relationship between the "three pillars" of government. Included among its terms of reference was the parliamentary system of government itself, and whether this should be "abandoned" in favor of a presidential system. Many of the committee's recommendations enhanced the authority of the central executive at the expense of other check-and-balance institutions such as the judiciary.[28]

The Supreme Court played a supportive role in all these developments. It threw out constitutional challenges to emergency rule and passed numerous judgments that supported the Gandhi government. For instance, in the infamous *ADM Jabalpur* case, which challenged the government's power of arbitrary detention, Supreme Court justices handed down a majority opinion favoring the government.[29] Several sitting justices also extended their support to the Gandhi regime beyond the courtroom. They participated in governmental projects of legal aid during the emergency and enthusiastically affirmed their commitment to the official governmental agenda of "justice for the poor."[30]

When the emergency ended in March 1977, the new Janata government promised a new era of democratic restoration. It became incumbent upon the Supreme Court to carve out a substantially different institutional identity for itself. In the immediate aftermath of the emergency, the court had to reclaim its public legitimacy by showing how, despite the fact that many of the emergency-era judges continued in office, it was now an altogether different and democratic institution. According to Baxi, the innovation of PIL served this end of democratic reinvention. As he puts it, the "judicial populism" of post-emergency PIL was "an attempt to refurbish the image of a court tarnished by a few emergency decisions, and also an attempt to seek new, historical bases of legitimation of judicial power."[31] In Baxi's account, the post-emergency judiciary rejected its earlier role as an advocate of authoritarian rule and claimed the mantle of popular representation and democratic agency. The pioneering use of PIL allowed the Supreme Court of India to remake itself as a Supreme Court *for* Indians, to use Baxi's famous phrase.[32]

Baxi's thesis of PIL's expiatory provenance has also been extended to an earlier historical moment, to place public interest litigation in a redemptive relationship with pre-emergency judicial behavior. For instance, several scholars have contrasted the judicial idea of public interest that gained ground in the late 1970s and early 1980s with the apex judiciary's spirited defense of individual interests and property rights in the 1950s and 1960s. From this perspective, PIL did not just redeem the court's dubious emergency-era democratic record. The explicit pro-people thrust of public interest litigation also allowed the Supreme Court to distance itself from its older pre-emergency reputation of socioeconomic conservatism, and to rework public memories of how, in the name of protecting individual rights to property, the apex judiciary had in fact thwarted several pieces of redistributive socioeconomic legislation during the peak years of Nehruvian socialism.[33]

Finally, albeit more in a corrective rather than an expiatory vein, some scholars have seen the apex judiciary's turn to PIL in the post-emergency years as an effort by sitting socialist judges such as Bhagwati and V. R. Krishna Iyer to cut through the dross of the "top-heavy socialism" of the Indira Gandhi regime.[34] In this reading, PIL was a corrective judicial maneuver that aimed to revive the spirit of "genuine" socialism by investing agency and meaningful authority in the true representatives of the people. Starting in the late 1960s, Indira Gandhi had steadily accumulated and centralized governmental power in the name of progressive change and social justice. The rapid realization of socialist goals was one of the main public justifications she offered for the emergency, whose signature

Twenty-Point Programme was suffused with high socialist language and imagery. But as the legal scholar Rajeev Dhavan has concluded,

> this had meant no more than giving more power to the State agencies in the name of socialist justice. . . . [P]eople were weary of this theory of law and social change. It was top-heavy. It cheated the people by making promises which were fulfilled to the extent that they filled the pockets of administrative and political intermediaries who pocketed the dividends of welfare.[35]

The apex judiciary was often a direct target of the Congress's instrumental socialism, and judges were called out for their class bias by Gandhi and members of her party on numerous occasions. These were among the ghosts that the post-emergency judiciary sought to exorcise by adopting a new judicial course of PIL-enabled "genuine" social change.

Judicial Populism and Social Contexts

All the accounts of public interest litigation's origins as an expiatory or corrective form of judicial action make the case for a sharp rupture between the emergency and its aftermath. As the language of innovation and even revolution makes clear, public interest litigation is seen to mark and constitute a substantial change in Indian jurisprudence, one that swerved the path of Indian democracy away from its recent authoritarian tracks.

But not everyone agrees. Legal scholar Anuj Bhuwania has recently argued in his provocative account of PIL lineages that this thesis of judicial disjuncture is mistaken. According to Bhuwania, the judiciary's eager embrace of public interest litigation did not disrupt emergency-era norms and practices. Rather, it extended them. Public interest litigation, he notes, advanced a distinctive form of judicial populism that allowed a range of different actors, including the apex judiciary itself, to make representative claims on behalf of the people.[36] This populist logic, Bhuwania argues, was borrowed or adapted from the preceding emergency regime, ironically the very regime that PIL was supposed to counter and disavow. Public interest litigation's distinctive institutional and procedural bypasses that liberalized prevailing rules of standing, relaxed evidentiary standards, and granted judicial recognition to handwritten postcards and newspaper reports so that the downtrodden could access justice—all of these echoed the emergency's main justifying principle of suspending the institutional and procedural constraints of electoral democracy in order to protect and save the people.

Many features of public interest litigation were foreshadowed during the emergency itself. The commitment to free legal aid was enshrined as a constitutional principle (Article 39A) by the notorious emergency-era forty-second amendment. The law to abolish bonded labor enacted by the emergency government (the Bonded Labour Abolition Act of 1976) subsequently became a major legislative touchstone of PILs in the post-emergency years. The core PIL precepts of liberalized standing and expansive constitutional interpretation were also elaborated during the emergency. Ruling on the *Mumbai Kamgar Sabha* case in 1976, Justice Krishna Iyer concluded that the "spacious construction of locus standi in our socio-economic circumstances and conceptual latitudinarianism permits taking liberties where the remedy is shared by a considerable number, particularly when they are weaker."[37] This judicial logic would continue to shape the idea of the public interest long after the emergency had come to an end.

Bhuwania's continuity thesis can also be taken further to link public interest litigation to an older judicial history that predates emergency populism. For instance, if we approach PIL as a particular kind of representative claim, then we can easily see how it repeats an ongoing tussle of divided sovereignty between courts and legislatures. Is democracy sustained and deepened by electoral or by constitutional authority? Who best represents the people: elected legislatures or courts; political insiders or political outsiders? These unresolved conflicts roiled the Indian republic from its founding moment. They led to several momentous institutional standoffs, such as the judicial intransigence over land reform legislation that we have discussed earlier, and the landmark constitutional cases of *Golaknath* and *Kesavnanda Bharati*, which established the respective scope and parameters of judicial review and legislative autonomy.[38] Public interest litigation was but the most recent version of this ongoing contest of representation. It did not break with the judicial and political past. Rather, it took forward many preexisting assumptions about the role and relationship of the judiciary to political democracy and the people.

Although they diverge on the question of how public interest litigation relates to Indian judicial and political history, both the expiatory and the continuity theses on the origins of public interest litigation share a common judiciary-centric approach. Both emphasize the actions and intentions of individual justices[39] and present PIL as a planned outcome of a deliberate decision by judges—a "judge-led and even judge-induced" phenomenon.[40] But the empirical record of the actual course of public interest litigation presents a rather different story. For instance, Rajeev Dhavan has observed how the judges' admission of a letter petition in the landmark *Sunil Batra* "prisoners case" PIL was more of an ad hoc, instinctive response to a specific moment and issue than it was the product of a concerted and preplanned campaign to expiate the judicial sins of the emergency by deliberately inventing epistolary jurisdiction.[41] A fuller account of PIL origins must therefore move beyond the narrow arena of judicial intentions and actions. It must consider the broader social-political milieu and the diverse constellation of actors and forces within but also outside the courtrooms, which shaped this new formation of the public interest.[42] To quote Dhavan again,

> the social politics that led to this initiation cannot just be traced to a seeming crisis of conscience among judges who had refrained from accepting judicial review of administrative detention during the Emergency. It was part and parcel of a deeper crisis in the untidy discourse of the Indian State. Indian socialism had perjured itself many times over. An alliance of protest and thinking was overdue, both amongst India's extremely articulate middle class intellectuals as well as the disadvantaged whose cause some of them espoused.[43]

In sum, the rise of public interest litigation is explained neither by the expiatory intentions of individual judges, nor by their reproduction of emergency-era populist logics. Instead, social and historical context matters. There is a reason why the idea of public interest litigation gained traction at this particular historical moment of the late 1970s and early 1980s in India, and why it diverged from its counterparts in other countries.[44] As Sanjay Ruparelia has argued, in order to explain the "puzzle of progressive juristocracy" in post-emergency India we need to look beyond the judiciary to the "groundswell of diverse social movements" that shaped and drove public interest litigation at the time.[45] The democratic ferment and political experimentation that followed the end of the Indian emergency; the influence of new media and publicity technologies; the increasing public salience of non-state organizations such as social movements and NGOs; and the rise of new social actors, specifically a new generation of lawyers, academics, journalists, and self-described social activists with distinctive life and work trajectories and ideological-political orientations that were quite different from those of the preceding nationalist generation, all played a crucial role in birthing the PIL revolution.

The idea of public interest championed by political outsiders emerged out of a fissured political field, where a diverse ideological range of activists challenged the ability of elected politicians to truly represent the people. It was shaped by a tangle of competing influences and motivations. Progressive activists and the post-Naxalite "new left" in India undoubtedly played a role.[46] But so did the less-acknowledged forces of consumer activism and middle-class political assertion. Defying easy categorization as either a progressive judicial revolution or a regressive judicial populism, public interest litigation, along with its associated ideas of wounded citizenship and outsider intermediaries of the people, would be put to work in varied ways.

A Different Justice

Embedding PIL in a wider social and political context also recasts it as an evolving and piecemeal process, rather than a preplanned initiative with a singular post-emergency birthdate. The various elements that we consider to be signature features of PIL today, whether the liberalization of traditional standing rules or the non-adversarial juridical approach that it encouraged, did not appear all at once. Instead, these gradually sedimented over time, around a core idea of a "different justice" that predated the emergency. The idea of different justice had two meanings. At the first level, it involved an assertion of a nationally or even civilizationally constituted difference from Anglo-Saxon judicial orders. At the second level, it called attention to the distinctive justice needs of a particular social group within India, variously named as the weak, the vulnerable, the backward, the downtrodden, or the poor. Both these meanings were related. In other words, India's justice needs were held to be different from those of the West *because* there were weak, poor, and backward masses in India.

Discussions about India's unique social and political order and the distinctive justice conditions that it created had an older history. From the moment of republican founding in the late 1940s, when Bhimrao Ambedkar presented his draft of the Indian constitution to the Constituent Assembly with a somber warning about the "life of contradictions" between political equality and social inequality that confronted the new republic, the distinctive character of Indian reality, and the gap between ideal-typical visions and the lived experience of democracy, were running themes in national debates. In the early years after independence, several commentators pointed to the divergent pathways of actually existing justice in the country. They observed how the prevailing widespread poverty and socioeconomic inequality placed demands upon the Indian judicial system that were very different from those in the advanced industrial democracies of the West.

India's normative traditions of law and justice were also heralded as unique. For instance, Supreme Court justices Krishna Iyer and Bhagwati, widely credited as the intellectual forces behind public interest litigation, frequently remarked on the historical and culturally sedimented norms of non-adversarial conflict resolution that prevailed in India. In marked contrast to the adversarial frameworks of Anglo-Saxon justice that enjoyed global hegemony, Indian norms of justice were seen to involve consensus, compromise, and collective mediation. More than professional lawyers and individualized contractual relationships based on payment and profit, *panchayats* or village councils constituted by bonds of respect, trust, and face-to-face familiarity were identified as the main forums for the delivery of justice in the country. These alternative and "indigenous" historical norms and practices had to be recuperated in order to meet the distinctive challenges of the Indian present, it was urged.[47]

Efforts to realize this normative order of judicial difference by reviving supposedly indigenous traditions of justice preceded the post-emergency period of public interest litigation by several decades. Already in the 1950s, political elites and governmental commissions had confronted the problem of judicial exclusion. How to overcome the formidable economic, educational, and geographic barriers that blocked judicial access for the poor and backward masses who constituted the vast majority of India's citizens? Chief among the solutions proposed was the creation of a new set of judicial institutions called Nyaya Panchayats (indigenous law councils). Exercising optional jurisdiction over petty cases, these village justice councils were supposedly based upon older indigenous judicial institutions and systems that enjoyed social legitimacy in rural India.[48]

Indigenous justice did not receive formal constitutional sanction as a legally enforceable idea that the state was constitutionally compelled to pursue. Nevertheless, Nyaya Panchayats remained on the policy agenda of the new Indian state in the 1950s and were taken up as institutional experiments by several state governments. Endorsed both by the Indian government and by international development agencies such as the Ford Foundation as culturally appropriate institutional options for the "new nations" of the postcolonial world, Nyaya Panchayats took their place alongside village cooperatives, *gram sabhas*, community development projects, and rural contact schemes that encouraged urban university students to undertake short stints of reconstructive rural labor in Indian villages.[49] They were all part of the midcentury project of modernization and reflected its central injunction to secure a stable "political order in changing societies" by adapting or synthesizing Western modernity and non-Western custom and traditions.[50]

As the Nyaya Panchayat program's idealization of a distinctive normative and institutional form of a consensual village justice administered by wise village elders made clear, the postcolonial program of adapted modernity was based upon an idea of Indian tradition that braided Gandhian mythologies about the Indian village as an exemplar of self-reliant community with colonial Orientalist ideas about the unchanging recalcitrance of the Indian rural. Nyaya Panchayats and their successor institutions such as Lok Adalats or people's courts, established in the 1970s, mostly exercised modernist-statist forms of agency. As Marc Galanter and Jayanth Krishnan point out in their review of *panchayat* justice projects from the 1970s, the institutional norms for *panchayat* justice were aligned with the bureaucratic rationality of the modern state. For instance, in the 1973 Krishna Iyer Committee report on legal aid, the proposal to establish the *panchayat* model of justice delivery had state functionaries such as retired judges presiding over these alternative indigenous courts rather than cultural-customary "traditional authorities."[51]

The idea of a different justice tailored to the unique contexts of India, and accessible to the country's vast population of vulnerable citizens, was also taken forward during the period of the Indian emergency.[52] Populist legitimation during the emergency included the promise of a new kind of people's justice that would transform existing Western modular templates to bring law and justice within reach of the "common man." Legal aid for the poor and the weak was an established priority of the emergency regime. It gained official endorsement as one of the points of the Twenty-Point Programme, the guiding policy charter of the national state during the emergency. The promise of free legal aid was formally introduced into the constitution as well, with the forty-second amendment adding it to the list of newly invigorated directive principles (as Article 39A) that were protected from judicial review.

The institutional contours of emergency-era legal aid projects continued to be cast along the lines of indigenous justice commitments from earlier years.[53] Drawing upon many of the provisions of these previous reports, the 1976 Bhagwati Committee Report on National Juridicare advocated for a "locally based 'indigenous' forum under the guidance of an educated and benevolent outsider."[54] The model remained that of a "paternalist indigenous justice," emulating the scenario sketched by the legal academic Upendra Baxi in his account of a local forum of dispute resolution in Gujarat that was published that same year.

Baxi's multilayered description of an innovative alternative dispute resolution process and forum in the north Indian village of Rangpur that transformed "*takrar* to *karar*" and gave rural citizens in remote areas of the country access to the constitutional promise of justice identified numerous features that made the local system effective.[55] The Bhagwati Report selectively highlighted two of these as the primary means by which the unique problem of limited judicial access for India's "weaker sections" could be resolved. These were the institutionalized informality of the dispute-resolution processes at Rangpur, and the mediating agency and authority of the insider-outsider Hariballabh Parekh, a spiritual leader who coordinated and presided over the Rangpur forum. In future years these two features would go on to orient the PIL process as well. The creation of informal procedures and the intermediary agency of insider-outsiders came to be seen as vital to the realization of the public interest: the twin keys that would unlock the power of the people. Let us take a closer look at each of these.

Procedural Bypass

Institutionalized informality was already a feature of Nyaya Panchayat projects in the 1950s.[56] The emergency-era Bhagwati Report made this an explicit goal.[57] It called for an "institution-directed approach to the problem of poverty." Informal judicial and legal arrangements would respond flexibly to the distinctive and urgent needs of Indian justice. They would supplement but not override existing institutional coordinates, and leave the overall orientation and mandate of rule unchanged. By putting the "problem of poverty" at front and center, the Bhagwati Report also referenced the second meaning of different justice that I have alluded to earlier, that is, a form or system of justice that was specifically attuned to the needs of the poor and the weak and their distinctive "suffering," to use another of Baxi's memorable phrases.[58] The trope of indigeneity linked the call for a different justice to a claim of national difference, and contrasted Indian judicial norms and empirical experiences to Western and colonial norms and realities. The trope of poverty and suffering fragmented the national frame to highlight the uneven character of justice within the Indian nation.[59] From this perspective, making justice accessible to those presently excluded from its ambit—the primary task of legal aid programs, in other words—called for processes and systems that were attuned to the ontologically different needs and meanings of justice for different kinds of Indians, namely the poor, the weak, the vulnerable, and the backward.[60] This would be achieved through the relaxation and circumvention of existing formal procedures. In all the differentiated justice projects, judicial difference involved bypassing existing procedures. Pitting technical-bureaucratic procedures against the needs and interests of the suffering poor as the main obstacles to their realization, the Bhagwati Report proposed to give the poor access to justice by removing the daunting obstacles that stood in their way, whether the considerable financial costs of legal access, the lack of legal-professional expertise that was required to navigate the existing system, or the long delays in dispensing justice that placed a particularly heavy burden on the precarious lives of the working poor.

Similar ideas of a different justice that had to relax procedures in order to give voice to the distinctive problems of the poor carried over to the post-emergency context of PIL. The dominant view expressed in legal aid initiatives from the 1960s and 1970s, that the interests of the marginalized could only be secured by circumventing formal procedures and "technicalities," continued to gain ground after the emergency. So too did the emergency-era opposition between the authentic expression of popular sovereignty and the alienating effects of procedure that had been deployed by the Indira Gandhi regime to justify the suspension of democratic procedure. As Bhuwania has noted, PIL advocates invariably framed existing legal-judicial procedures as obstacles to popular participation. For instance, several justices closely associated with the PIL innovation in the early 1980s explicitly made the case for a differentiated justice in their account of why public interest litigation matters, and upheld procedural relaxation as the main solution. Only by removing the barriers of procedural formalism, they argued, would the voice of suffering be heard.[61] As Justice Krishna Iyer explained in the *Ratlam* judgment of 1980, PIL was a way to ensure "access to justice" beyond the "blinkered rules of standing of British Indian vintage."[62] The judgment in another landmark PIL case, *Bandhua Mukti Morcha* from the 1980s, made a similar point. Public interest litigation called for more relaxed procedures in order to "make basic human rights meaningful to the deprived and vulnerable section of the community and to ensure them socio-economic justice."[63]

These procedural changes came about in a piecemeal and gradual manner. For instance, "epistolary jurisdiction," the procedural change that is widely hailed a signature innovation of PIL, was introduced in 1978 when judges admitted letter petitions during the *Sunil Batra* case. A few years later, the *Hussainara Khatoon* case introduced the radically new practice of representative standing by allowing an unconnected third party to stand for an aggrieved subject. The practice of court-appointed inquisitorial commissions was deployed in the 1983 *Bandhua Mukti Morcha* case, and the *ASIAD workers* case of 1982 saw the Supreme Court formalize the principle of collaborative justice or the distinctive mode of cooperation between the defendant/state and complainant/citizen as joint custodians and beneficiaries of the public interest.

Several unexpected outcomes resulted from these changes. To begin with, procedural relaxation meant not so much the end of formal procedures as such, but rather the invention of new ones and the creation of an alternative system of "poor justice" that was governed by a distinctive set of rules and conventions. To use Galanter and Krishnan's critical term for the creation of alternative informal fora and mechanisms of justice delivery such as tribunals, Lok Adalats, and Nyaya Panchayats, a logic of "debased informalism" structured India's judicial reform initiatives. These included pre-emergency attempts to constitute Nyaya Panchayats as alternative forums for dispute resolution, emergency-era proposals for "national juridicare" and legal aid for the poor, and the post-emergency phenomenon of public interest litigation. In all these instances, instead of equipping excluded subjects with the necessary resources and skills to negotiate the existing terrain of formal justice, a parallel system of institutions and procedures was created for the exercise of discretionary authority by putative political outsiders, judges chief among them.

Next, justice was linked to the values of urgency and immediacy. Neither the "never again" vision of justice as a redemptive dialogue with the past, nor the transformative vision of justice as the realization of a new future, took hold. Efforts to create a different justice for the poor primarily addressed the present. The call for justice in post-emergency India was mainly a demand for actions in the here and now. Moreover, these justice acts had to be tangible or publicly visible. Public interest litigation and other differentiated justice initiatives placed a high premium on justice delivery as a publicly witnessed form of action. As a result, technologies of communication and publicity and the agency of media actors became integral to the justice process. We will explore the role of media in the formation of the public interest in later sections of this chapter.

Third, although it undoubtedly empowered and benefited marginalized citizens, the call for a different kind of justice that addressed the suffering of the poor was a technique of statist incorporation. It is important here to recognize the mixed motivations of such projects. As various committee reports and governmental deliberations clearly attest, the policy frameworks of legal aid projects and related initiatives reflected both a strong commitment toward empowering excluded citizens by recognizing their distinct concerns and needs, and statist concerns of order and stability. Conceived under conditions of increasing social discontent and mass mobilizations against the government in the 1960s, Indian legal aid initiatives worked to bring the potentially rebellious poor into the safe and known ambit of the judicial-legal system by channeling their discontent along institutional routes. The problem of the "lawless poor" was a problem of legal exclusion, but it was also a problem of disorder and insurgency that threatened the stability of Indian democracy. Legal aid initiatives were developed to address this latter concern as well.

During the emergency, the Bhagwati Committee announced a legal services program that would "provid[e] representation to 'groups of social and economic protest'" and "encourage [a] group-oriented and institution-directed approach to the problem of poverty." New "legal techniques and methods," such as class action or group-interest litigation, were needed to bring to the court the "problems of the poor," the Committee further observed.[64]As the Bhagwati Committee report makes clear, a key aim of the legal aid initiatives and the wider project of emergency socialism was to align the statist goals of stability, order, and security with socialist commitments to social progress and uplift. Poverty alleviation required an "institution-directed" approach, in its words.[65] The later, post-emergency innovation of PIL would draw upon this mixed legacy.

Public interest litigation is hailed as a weapon of the weak that gave voice to the distinctive experience of suffering by providing a different kind of responsive justice. However, it also drew on the statist legacy of differentiated justice, and mirrored and expressed state rationality. As Susan Susman has observed, one of the reasons why there was support for the expansion of standing in PILs was that the "legal community" saw an opportunity to "defuse political and social movements by channelling them into a legitimate forum."[66]Other scholars such as Peiris concur, seeing PIL as a response to "societal conditions in the subcontinent which pose the danger of significant alienation of a large section of a community from the values infusing the legal system." Public interest litigation is an opportunity to "alleviat[e] tensions and preserv[e] the social fabric."[67] In Justice Krishna Iyer's words, "if the courts cannot, or will not, give relief to people who are in fact concerned about a matter then they will resort to self-help, with grave results for other persons and the rule of law."[68] To combine Upendra Baxi's famous aphorisms on PIL, "taking suffering seriously" was an "establishment revolution."[69]

Intermediaries of the People: Political Outsiders and Concern Networks

Although they feature prominently in accounts of public interest litigation, the liberalized criteria of standing that allowed the suffering of the "weaker sections" to be voiced in Indian courtrooms are only one part of the PIL story. Public interest litigation also introduced new practices of mediation and invested political authority in a new class of "socio-legal" representatives of the people.[70] As we have already noted, the Indian project of making justice accessible did not enable direct access to judicial institutions by equipping underresourced litigants with the financial or legal resources that they lacked. Instead, it introduced and legitimized a new kind of representational agency. Public interest litigation was a practice of representative claims-making. It called for new and better representatives of the people rather than for direct popular participation.[71] Representational authority was invested in political outsiders: networked formations of individuals and organizations located outside the arena of electoral politics. Repeatedly contrasted to the "meddlesome interloper or busybody," the public-spirited bystander[72] emerged as a key actor within Indian democracy as a result of the PIL revolution.

Even a cursory look at the corpus of cases from the early years of public interest litigation confirms the central role played by intermediary third-party actors. Although they engaged a diverse range of issues that ranged from the inhumane and illegal treatment of prisoners to the livelihood concerns of pavement dwellers facing eviction, they entered the judicial arena in a similar way. Many of the early PIL petitions were brought into the courtroom by individuals with a similar social and professional profile, who had no prior or current relationship with the actual aggrieved subject. Indeed, Susman notes that in order to get a preliminary injunction or "direction" from the court as soon as possible, some lawyers read a news article and filed the PIL before they contacted the injured parties.[73] For instance, in the *Hussainara Khatoon* case of 1979, the litigation over the prolonged detention of "undertrials" in Bihar jails—those who had been confined to prison for multiple years while awaiting trials, sometimes for periods longer than the maximum punishment for their alleged crime—was brought by Kapila Hingorani, a lawyer practicing in Delhi.[74] The case of the *Agra Homes* in 1981 relied upon the interventions of two Delhi-based academics with legal expertise, Upendra Baxi and Lotika Sarkar, who brought the terrible living conditions in state-run facilities for women to the Supreme Court's attention. A Bombay-based journalist named Olga Tellis moved the courts for representative standing in the case of pavement dwellers in Bombay who were facing eviction. Sheela Barse, another Bombay-based journalist, filed a landmark PIL on the mistreatment of children in state-run juvenile homes. Bonded laborers in Faridabad were represented by Swami Agnivesh, a social worker, along with his organization, Bandhua Mukti Morcha.

These and other examples attest to the unique "alliance of protest and thinking"[75] that initiated and sustained public interest litigation and transformed the act of litigation into a wider social activity.[76] The term *alliance* is important here. One of the distinctive features of public interest litigation was its networked form. Public interest litigation brought together institutions and individuals who did not share formal organizational ties but were moved to action by the particular issue at hand. The affective solidarities of these "concern networks" did not seed enduring organizational structures such as lobby groups, platforms, and associations. Their temporal horizon was often finite. The public outrage and flurry of concerned activity that erupted around particular events and issues were eventually replaced by fresh cascades of concerned action sparked by revelations of other horrors.

A review of landmark PIL cases shows that concern networks and outrage cascades involved two kinds of social actors. The first group comprised professionals in the fields of law, academia, and journalism who were located mostly in Delhi and Bombay. Social activists belonging to "social action groups" with an explicit agenda of social and structural change,[77] and NGO and civil society components of the developmental and social reform sector in India, also featured prominently in the lineup of litigants.[78] In many instances, individual petitioners had a legal background of some kind, whether as practicing lawyers and legal academics, or as social activists who used legal strategies in their work.[79] A significant proportion of PIL petitioners were journalists who specialized in the newly popular craft of investigative journalism. Moreover, individual petitioners usually had significant reputational resources of social-intellectual capital, and were described as "eminent persons" in media and public discussions. Examples included D. C. Wadhwa, professor at the Gokhale Institute of Economics; Shivaram Karanth, a Kannada writer and social activist; Kamaladevi Chattopadhyay, a cultural activist noted for her efforts to revive traditional handcrafts and artisanal work; and the legal scholar and law professor Upendra Baxi. In all, a relatively small and select group of individuals advanced representational claims in the name of the people/the public interest.[80]

The second group of PIL petitioners consisted of organizations from the field of social action, civil society, and social movement activism that flourished in the post-emergency period. The field spanned a very wide range of ideological positions, and was organizationally diverse as well. It comprised both grassroots groups that directly worked with different local communities in participatory ways and national-level organizations that were more bureaucratized and professionalized. The varied groups that took up the PIL cause reflected this ideological and organizational diversity. Some, such as the Consumer Action Education Centre, based in Ahmedabad, and the Common Cause Foundation of Delhi were urban consumer action groups and organizations that worked with and for middle-class citizens and their concerns. Others, such as the Bandhua Mukti Morcha, were advocacy and participatory groups that worked toward the goals of empowerment and socioeconomic transformation or "uplift" of marginalized constituencies of slum residents, informal workers, urban homeless populations, and marginalized rural communities. Still others were social action groups that did not work directly with communities but assisted other civil society organizations with various tasks (for example, legal assistance, assistance with public communications).

Unsurprisingly, a large proportion of these were groups that specialized in various forms of legal work. Several PILs were filed by organizations such as the Lawyers Collective, whose work involved engaging the law by providing legal education and legal assistance to underprivileged citizens, spearheading efforts at law and judicial reform, and activating constitutional frameworks to enforce citizens' rights.[81]

The PIL arena was also populated by organizations with specific commitments to issues of human rights, civil liberties, feminist struggle, and, in later years, environmental issues. Organizations such as the People's Union of Civil Liberties (PUCL) were among the petitioners in early PILs filed in the late 1970s and early 1980s. When it wasn't directly involved, PUCL lent considerable legal and organizational support to other petitioners on areas of shared concern such as the rights of prisoners and the prevalence of custodial abuse in state institutions. The growth of public interest litigation also coincided with the growing political and social salience of the women's movement in India. Feminist individuals such as the law professor Lotika Sarkar would play a leading role in both these arenas of legal as well as social action, indexing the close engagement of the Indian women's movement of the time with governmental and legal-constitutional frameworks.[82]

As the list above shows, there was considerable ideological diversity among the organizations that filed PILs, and organizational goals were quite divergent. For example, environmental groups petitioning to "clean and green" the city by relocating industries and restricting rickshaw traffic collided quite directly with organizations supporting the urban livelihood rights of informal workers and rickshaw pullers.[83] Despite these differences, many of the organizations professed a common nonpolitical orientation and framed their PIL work as nonpartisan and nonprofit actions undertaken to realize common social values and interests. Their appeals to the nonpolitical replayed older political themes. These included Gandhian ideas of decentralized projects of self and societal transformation; Jayaprakash Narayan's call for *sampoorna kranti*, or total revolution, to realize "partyless democracy" that had mobilized significant sections of the citizenry in the years leading up to the emergency; and the post-Naxalite variant of left politics ascendant in the 1970s and beyond that emphasized institutional engagement with status quo political structures over the antisystemic revolutionary violence of the Maoist-inspired Naxalbari movement of the late 1960s.

All these historical currents fed into the activist norm of nonpolitical intervention that gained prominence in post-emergency India. In contrast to the "saintly idiom" of political renunciation and abdication,[84] the mandate of post-emergency activism was both to go outside politics, and to intervene actively in politics from this putatively pure space of the political outside. Leveraging the normative position of the political outsider, activists advanced representative claims about their political agency—about how they could represent the will of the people and the public interest.[85] Concern networks drew on this logic of nonpolitical intervention in their public petitions. As the arguments advanced in the *Bandhua Mukti Morcha* case show, the main plea to grant representative standing to the petitioners was linked both to their identity as political outsiders—their manifest lack of a political stake in the issue at hand; their involvement solely on grounds of public concern—and to their mission of reforming the political system and fulfilling the original constitutional promise of citizenship rights.

The representative claims made by petitioners in PIL cases did not only hold up new representatives of the people, the political outsiders who could more authentically represent the public interest. They also presented new "depictions or portraits of the represented,"[86] and made claims about the subject of representation, that is, who the real people really were. The idea that there were new and diverse constituencies of real people in need of representation reflected a wider political consensus. PIL claims about representing the real people were made in the specific historical context of the late 1970s and early 1980s. This was a time of considerable representational pluralism, when new practices of political mobilization that activated new kinds of social constituencies and new domains of political action were gaining salience across India.

For the first time since independence, the national government was formed by a coalition of political parties that did not include the Congress party. The Janata coalition brought new political actors into government, and gave national political legitimacy and voice to a range of new social groups, from the petty bourgeois supporters of the Hindu right Jan Sangh party to the intermediate-caste "bullock capitalists" of the Lok Dal. The ensuing changes in the cultures and practices of national electoral politics were mirrored by significant shifts in regional (that is, subnational) political cultures. In fact, a significant development of this period was the emergence of the regional arena as a space of political mobilization. Along with the rise of regional politics, the social categories of religion, ethnicity/language, and caste became politically salient in the 1980s. The decade witnessed the establishment and electoral success of identitarian parties in several parts of the country. Rejecting national frameworks of political representation, parties such as BSP, JMM, and Shiv Sena championed the interests of specific caste, language, ethnic, and regional groups, asserting that these were the essential, basic units of social and political life.[87]

It is against this backdrop of diverse and competing representations of the "real people" that PIL petitioners advanced their claims. At the same time that regional autonomy movements in different parts of the country asserted the primacy of subnational identity and new regional political parties made caste and ethnic identities politically salient, intermediaries in PIL cases offered to represent specific population segments in the name of the public interest: the urban homeless, female prisoners, oppressed-caste bonded laborers, construction workers, trafficked tribal women.

Bona Fides and Public Spirit

What made these representative claims credible and legitimate? Contrasted with "meddlesome busybodies" and people motivated by personal and instrumental concerns of profit, publicity, and power, PIL petitioners were admitted to the court as "bystanders" who acted with genuine, bona fide intentions.[88] A closer look at early cases shows that this in turn meant three things. First, there had to be a demonstrable lack of individual, direct interest in the litigation. Many public interest litigations proceeded without any direct contact being established between the petitioner who moved the court and the actual victim of the injury under discussion. In the landmark case of *Hussainara Khatoon*, for instance, Kapila Hingorani did not visit the Bihar jail to witness the plight of the prisoners herself. Instead her main source of knowledge of the matter was a series of news reports that she had chanced upon. In numerous other instances as well,

PIL petitioners did not have firsthand knowledge of the individuals and social contexts that were the subject of their petition, and used this deficit to established their bona fide credentials. To quote Susman's review of early PIL petitioners:

> The members of Bandhua Mukti Morcha were not current or past bonded laborers. Rather, they were people who shared outrage at the institution of bonded labor and had investigative and reporting skills lacking in the illiterate people whose rights they sought to further.
>
> Similarly, Dr. Baxi had no relationship whatsoever with the women's custodial center in Uttar Pradesh; he was an appalled and informed observer and familiar of the Supreme Court. While Khatri was a blinded pre-trial detainee, the lawyer who had clipped and sent the newspaper expose of his plight to the Supreme Court was not; and Sheela Barse was not an inmate of an insane asylum or a slum dweller living on the pavement, but a concerned journalist who became the petitioner in several unrelated public interest cases.[89]

Second, at the same time as the petitioner had to demonstrate her lack of prior personal knowledge and direct connection to the aggrieved party named in the PIL, she had also to establish her expert knowledge and professional experience with the broad subject of the litigation (for example, women's empowerment; human rights). Judicial recognition for bona fide petitioners was also granted on the basis of judicial familiarity. Many petitioners were legal professionals known to presiding judges, for example lawyers, legal academics, and individuals who had previously appeared as PIL petitioners in other cases. As Susman has remarked, the practice frequently reinforced existing gendered hierarchies, and the public interest credentials of senior male lawyers were accepted with relative ease.[90] Along with gender, age, and legal experience, the judicially known petitioner also possessed social or reputational capital as an "eminent person."[91] In sum, representing the public interest called for both distance/disconnection (from individual injured parties) and embeddedness (in the socio-legal establishment). Concern networks were embedded in social contexts and structured around hierarchies of reputation, respectability, gender, education, and professional experience. The political outsider was usually a social insider of some kind or other.

Finally, public interest litigations mandated a specific form of affective engagement. Each case saw petitioners and concern networks moved to action by intense cascades of publicly expressed outrage, and these affective intensities of "civic anger" were quite central to the public interest narrative. The language of petitions as well as retrospective recollections of landmark cases by petitioners were saturated with normative emotions like anger, shock, horror, and anguish that attested to the bona fide intentions of the petition. Petitioners affirmed their deep emotional investments in the matter at hand, and the churn of sentiments that had propelled them to action. If establishing the lack of direct ties to the injured parties of a PIL was vital, it was equally important to demonstrate the profusion of emotional ties and the ineffable workings of "public spirit" that drove each case forward.

I use the term *normative emotions* to distinguish between an experiential ontology of emotions (the actual feelings experienced by individuals) and a socially and politically sanctioned repertoire of emotional expression in public contexts. In other words, whether a political actor really feels angry is a separate question from whether she can act angry, that is, perform and express anger publicly, and as a political stance. The latter has to do with the historical-institutional contexts that structure the affective idioms of political legitimation. These vary across time, and the political affect of Indian democracy has been quite differently configured in different historical moments. The affective orientation of the democracy-rebuilding paradigm in the post-emergency period diverged from both the affective politics of "diffident hope" in the Nehruvian nation-building era[92] and from the paranoid styles of emergency-era fear and conspiracy politics.

A new politics of civic anger distinguished the curative democratic initiatives of the late 1970s. Strident expressions of outrage and indignation at the intolerable state of affairs accompanied and justified the urgent actions to repair the system. Enough is enough! Public interest litigation was a prime example of the post-emergency's distinctive genre of angry politics. Through the 1980s, as PIL became a familiar socio-legal technology, its signature languages of righteous indignation diffused through the wider political field. They recast the relation of citizen and state in terms of injury and disillusionment—the wounded people versus the cruel and indifferent establishment—and called for immediate remedial action by public-spirited outsiders. Diverging quite sharply from the dispassionate norms of deliberative rationality that liberal democracy endorses, curative democracy invested political agency with an urgent and moral-ethical charge and fanned "the white heat of anger,"[93] as a newspaper op-ed of the time would describe it.

The op-ed citation directs us to one of the prime drivers of the curative democracy project: the Indian news media. As the pioneering public interest lawyer Kapila Hingorani's recollections of the *Hussainara Khatoon* case illustrate, media played a vital role in the PIL process. In a detailed interview a few years before her death, Hingorani recalled how one morning, after her children had left for school, she and her husband, Nirmal Hingorani, also a lawyer, settled down to their morning routine of reading the newspapers. Struck by an article in the *Indian Express*, Nirmal asked Kapila to read it, too. Written by a retired police officer, the piece was the second part of a two-part series that chronicled "the plight of undertrial prisoners languishing in various jails in Bihar for cruelly long periods of time for no crime other than their poverty."[94]

The lawyer couple was "sickened and revolted" by what they read, and decided on the spot to file a habeas corpus writ. Kapila Hingorani reached the Supreme Court the same day. She could not establish conventional standing based on kinship connections as "next friend" of the injured parties, she did not have any direct interest in the matter, and she could not prove delegation of authority via a power of attorney granted by the aggrieved party. But Hingorani was known to the court registrar, and she was able to convince him to admit the petition. After initially rejecting Hingorani's proposal, he finally agreed to place the petition before the court along with a list of his objections. Appearing before the bench in plain clothes rather than in her usual lawyer's robes, Hingorani successfully argued the case of Hussainara Khatoon in a new and distinctive role of representing the public interest—a labor of representation that involved speaking for a distant other as a "public spirited person."[95]

After hearing the arguments, the court ordered the immediate release of forty thousand prisoners without a bail bond, declaring its "anger and anguish" at the "shocking state of affairs." Inaugurating a new pathway of non-adversarial justice, Hingorani was directed to collaborate with state counsel to prepare lists of prisoners. Reading together constitutional article 21 (the right to life and liberty) and directive principle 39A (the right to free legal aid and right to speedy trial), law was named as a "positive and constructive social device for the poor." "Inject[ing] equal justice into liberty" was hailed as the main mandate for democracy.

In this landmark PIL widely recognized as one of the first in the country, the media did not just raise public awareness by providing factual information. They also engaged in "affective attunement"[96] through their choice of news frameworks and semiotic vocabularies of shock, outrage, and grief. Hingorani's description of how after reading a story in the morning papers, she was sickened and revolted and *had* to do something about it, attests to the affective mediations at work in the PIL process, and the varied representational labors that constituted the sense of a wounded public interest:

> I started reading the article while sipping my tea. I felt choked. How can such a situation exist in our country? We are lawyers of so many years' standing and we are not even aware of it, we must do something about it.[97]

News media played an important role in the rise and growth of civic anger and outsider politics. Newly freed from the constraints of censorship and fear that had shadowed the eighteen months of the emergency, Indian media worlds pulsed with political life in the late 1970s. Along with the heralded PIL revolution, the revolutionary moniker was also bestowed on the news media of this period. They were recognized as vital influences in the post-emergency landscape, and as counterparts to the judiciary in quite a literal sense. As influential institutional actors in high politics, they shaped and co-created the outsider political imagination. As technologies of communication, they amplified and diffused outsider politics across social space. Let us takc a closer look.

MEDIATIZED DEMOCRACY[98]

Indian democracy was increasingly "mediatized" from the late 1970s onward. Media institutions and actors were incorporated into the field of democratic politics as active participants and players. Media forms patterned political expression. This was largely related to changes in the political economy and technologies of Indian mass media at the time, which amplified the social reach and presence of the media in everyday lives. For instance, technological innovations such as desktop and offset printing allowed newspapers to publish new local editions. There was also a surge in vernacular news publications, as computer-based print technologies offered cheap and efficient alternatives to the laborious hand-crafted production of individual metal typeface letters for non-Roman alphabets.

Media growth after the emergency was also fueled by the availability of new sources of capital. Many new entrepreneurs set up media businesses, eager to capture the expanding streams of advertising revenue generated by the growing consumer goods economy.[99] All of this led to a dramatic increase in the size of Indian reading publics (television and radio audiences also increased during this time). Moreover, the rapid growth of vernacular media and the launch of numerous niche media publications meant that news media coverage was more socially expansive and reached more diverse populations in the post-emergency years. Well before the much-discussed satellite revolution of the 1990s and the social media revolutions of our twenty-first-century present, India witnessed a time of sustained "communicative abundance."[100]

Changes in the professional worlds of post-emergency Indian journalism were also consequential. In the 1970s, a new postcolonial cohort of journalists born mostly after independence joined the ranks of journalists whose firsthand experience of colonial rule and the anticolonial struggle had been reflected in the nationalist tenor of their journalism, and their strong alignments with the Nehruvian national project. In contrast, the journalists who began their careers around the time of the emergency had lived through student militancy and state repression. They were socialized in political and cultural milieus where in place of the optimism and hope sparked by midcentury utopias of national liberation and statist development, state-led projects attracted sustained criticism.[101]

Media were among the main targets of the emergency regime. In fact, it began with a blunt and dramatic act of media suppression. Right after the emergency declaration was signed by the Indian president late at night on June 24–25, 1975, state officials shut off the electric supply to the areas of Delhi where most of the major national newspapers (and their printing presses) were located, so that news reports about the midnight developments could not be published. This furtive maneuver of censorship was soon replaced by a formal structure of censorship rules that mandated prepublication authorization and established a chief censor's office for the print media.[102]

A few months into the emergency, the direct censorship system was supplemented by a set of more informal and subtle measures that got media practitioners to willingly participate in their own censorship. These included conducting sudden income tax raids on media owners, withdrawing government advertising from newspapers, restructuring the governing board of a national newspaper to place a regime-friendly figure at its helm, harassing proprietors of independent presses that printed publications deemed critical of the government, and the infamous "phone call tactic" whereby political leaders would call editors and media owners to convey a seemingly innocuous message with a tacit threat that was clearly understood. Most large media houses managed to work around and compromise with these informal pressure tactics without endangering their institutional and financial survival. However, smaller media organizations were vulnerable to these pressures, and several magazines that were known for their critical journalism shut down during the emergency.[103] The international media were not spared, either. Numerous journalists working with international media organizations had their press accreditations canceled and were made to leave the country, while several others were denied permission to enter India.

Along with the negative prohibitions of censorship and threat, the emergency government also invested heavily in propaganda. Both state and non-state media were used for this purpose. State television and radio coverage focused mainly on the beneficence of the Congress government and lavished fawning praise on the Gandhi mother-and-son duo. Tacit and not-so-veiled hints and threats combined to ensure that government activities were covered in a positive light. State advertising budgets handled by the Directorate of Advertising and Visual Publicity (DAVP) were also directed toward the same end of regime promotion. The efforts to monopolize media narratives culminated with the merger of existing news agencies to create a single organization, Samachar, that would supply news feeds to all national and international media organizations. Together the combination of formal and informal, prohibitive and propagandistic measures that were in place between June 1975 and January 1977 produced a largely pliant media that eagerly conformed to the regime's will. In the apocryphal description attributed to L. K. Advani, a Hindu nationalist politician from the Jan Sangh party who was imprisoned during the emergency and subsequently joined the Janata government as its minister of information and broadcasting, during the emergency the Indian media crawled when it was asked to bend.[104]

After the formal end of emergency rule in the spring of 1977, journalists and media organizations began to assert their political and public voice and authority in new ways. They differed not just from the submissive media of the recent emergency past, but also from the longer arc of postcolonial media history that went back to the post-independence era. Moving away from the restrained tones of press discourse that had mostly aligned with state and national leadership in the first few decades after independence, journalists in the late 1970s and 1980s took up increasingly critical and angry stances against the political system. Media publications frequently featured damning exposés of state violence, neglect, and failure.[105]

A distinctive new media ideology and institutional-political identity was also formed at this time, of media as a political force in its own right. Diverging from the conventional liberal fourth-estate parameters of media as neutral providers of information and communication, journalists and media organizations became political actors who were actively involved in the legislative, policy, and even in the judicial work of the state. Several journalists and editors in the late 1970s and 1980s also acted as informal mediators and connectors during this time of volatile coalition politics and quick-changing political alliances. The journalist Prabhash Joshi of the *Indian Express* group, for instance, parlayed his long association with JP Narayan and his relationship with individual RSS leaders like Nanaji Deshmukh to become a key figure in the behind-the-scenes activity of the Janata alliance formation in the mid-1970s.[106] Informal or back-channel political networks remained salient and in fact gained in importance after the Janata government collapsed and Indira Gandhi returned to power in

1980. A new era of state-business collaborations unfolded in the decade of the 1980s. Journalists continued to leverage their connections and access to multiple social worlds, and consolidated their role as active and significant players in the political game.

Investigative Journalism and Curative Democracy

A powerful wave of investigative journalism swept Indian media worlds after 1977.[107] The media revelations drew attention to a diverse range of concerns. The "Kamala story" of 1981, about the sale of a woman in a north Indian town, exposed the social practice of human trafficking. The Bhagalpur exposé of the mass blinding of prisoners in the eastern state of Bihar in 1980 disclosed a shocking account of police torture. Investigative journalism in the late 1970s also drew attention to incidents of political corruption. Several notable stories from the post-emergency period implicated prominent politicians in "scams" where political benefits were traded for personal financial gains. The Antulay cement scam was one such story, broken by *Indian Express* executive editor Arun Shourie in the autumn of 1981. On the basis of documents leaked to him by an anonymous source, Shourie alleged that the chief minister of Maharashtra, A. R. Antulay, had extorted funds for the Congress party's campaign from construction companies through the fictive sale of cement (hence the eponymous cement scam). Likened to the Watergate revelations in the United States, the story created a stir in the Indian parliament, and Antulay was forced to resign a few months later.

Although the specific issues of torture, trafficking, and graft were unique, they were all presented in similar ways. India's new journalism after the emergency had a distinctive style and idiom. A few common themes were woven through all the media scandals that shook up public and political culture in the late 1970s and early 1980s. Most post-emergency media exposés implicated the political system. No matter the specifics of the incident at hand, journalists offered the same diagnosis: elected representatives, bureaucracy, and police were invariably identified as the main cause of the problem. Often the culpability of the political system was not immediately clear,[108] and elaborate narrative explanations and moralized conclusions about the causes of specific incidents would be quite important to the genre of post-emergency investigative journalism. Media exposés offered up empirical details of events, but also provided preferred readings of them. What the story was really about was a very important part of the story. Another related theme was that of the unresponsive state. In many instances, the fallout of the media exposé, and the fact that after the revelations and the public outcry that followed, the state still did nothing and nothing changed, were folded into the narrative to deepen the indictment of the system.

Second, media exposés highlighted the heroic agency of the individual journalist and the role of media as the people's crusader.[109] The main protagonist of most media stories, particularly those that had involved undercover covert investigations, was the daring journalist who battled the system in the name of the people. His[110] interventions were presented as bold and dramatic acts that broke the fetters of bureaucracy and legal convention to respond to the higher moral imperative of democratic redemption. A related theme was that of the media-judiciary partnership, or how journalists and courts could work together to redeem the people. For instance, the media revelations about the Kamala case led to a public interest litigation filed by the journalists who had covered the story, in which they petitioned the Supreme Court "qua citizens . . . to ensure that the executive takes steps to end the inhuman traffic in women."[111] This pattern of public interest litigation following media exposés would be repeated across a variety of different cases in the years to come.

Post-emergency investigative journalism presented stories about representatives who failed the people and those who saved them. The elected representatives and government officials who did nothing to help the victims; the daring outsider journalist who battled the political system in the name of the people; the unresponsive state that remained unmoved but nevertheless the journalist persevered, enlisting the help of other like-minded political outsiders like the judiciary—these were the stock themes of investigative journalism after the emergency. They resonate with our contemporary present as well. Across much of the world today, political discourse is framed by a triangular set of relations. The virtuous people are pitted against an indifferent, corrupt, cruel, and broken system until the redemptive political outsider, the third protagonist, cures democracy through his decisive and daring actions. As the example of India's new journalism shows us, this populist triangle, associated today with the authoritarian specters of strongman politics, was traced out several decades ago in the context of democratic restoration in the late 1970s, a time with a very different political and normative charge.

Wounded Citizenship

A final common theme of the investigative journalism of the post-emergency era was that of wounded citizenship, that is, presenting the generic citizen as an injured victim of the political system. If the unresponsive state and elected representatives were the villains of investigative news stories, the citizen was the victim whose suffering and exploitation the media bore witness to. The theme of suffering as such was not unknown to Indian political and public culture. Literary and cinematic texts of the post-independence period were steeped in dark and troubled representations of the contemporary Indian condition. As I have documented in earlier work, the political discourse of the Nehruvian era was equally haunted by specters of an Indian darkness.[112] In marked contrast to the triumphalist rhetoric of the twenty-first century that hails India's arrival on the stage of global recognition, official nationalism in the mid-twentieth-century decades dwelled on the many difficulties and failures that confronted the newly minted Indian nation-state. In post-independence India, the figure of the impoverished, backward, and needy citizen was repeatedly evoked to legitimize the state-led project of national development.[113]

The official nationalist discourse of citizenship as victimhood did not uniformly encompass all Indians. There were specific victims who bore specific kinds of wounds. In Nehruvian India, wounded citizens were primarily specified as ascriptive minorities, that is, numerically small communities subjected to historical practices of discrimination and exploitation because they had been born into a particular identity group. Religion and caste were the main ascriptive identities recognized by the state. The Nehruvian state introduced a variety of constitutional and legal measures that recognized the distinctive concerns of religious minorities and caste groups at the lowest end of the caste hierarchy (the former Untouchables).[114] Moreover, as developmentalist discourse about the "hungry masses" and the "humble peasant" shows, statist concern about citizen-victims also had a strong class dimension in the early post-independence years. In the Nehruvian national imagination, economically marginalized citizens, religious minorities, and oppressed castes bore the wound of citizenship.[115]

These specifications would change in the late 1970s. Post-emergency media narratives built upon the theme of suffering and deprivation, but it was increasingly presented as a general condition that affected all "ordinary Indians" in some way or another. Some post-emergency media exposés continued in the Nehruvian vein. They highlighted the extreme atrocities that the political system inflicted upon particular marginalized subjects: Dalits, poor rural women, inmates of mental asylums, bonded labor, child labor. Others took up a new cause, namely the suffering of urban middle-class citizens at the hands of the same system.[116] For instance, the angry journalism of the late 1970s and 1980s also foregrounded stories related to urban crime and lapses in urban security (for example, the notorious Chopra children murder case of 1982), state failure to provide expected public services and entitlements (for example, state pensioners who had not received their just dues), inadequacies in civic infrastructure, and everyday encounters with the indignities of petty corruption. The idea of the specific, historical wound borne by a particular caste-class victim was generalized to include all kinds of injuries inflicted by the establishment, from the mass blinding of prisoners to graft and embezzlement, to unpaid pension contributions. In post-emergency media discourse, we were all repositioned as wounded citizens. A "logic of equivalence"[117] connected the grievances of individuals and groups who were often from very different social locations, and brought their singular experiences of injury into a common framework of commensuration.

The logic of wounded equivalences extended beyond media worlds. It also shaped the normative imagination of the public interest. Most discussions of the formative era of public interest litigation highlight the exclusion and deprivation faced by socioeconomically marginalized individuals and groups as the main concern. But the problems of the salaried middle classes were on the agenda as well. The imagination of wounded citizenship encompassed both the wound of suffering borne by tortured and deprived bodies, and the wound of civic disenchantment, of the citizen let down by her state as a victim of bureaucratic indifference and neglect. The *Pensions* case, which laid claim to the public interest at around the same time that the plight of Hussainara Khatoon and her fellow prisoners prompted Hingorani's pioneering PIL, illustrates these dual meanings of wound and interest that prevailed at the inception of public interest litigation.

A writ petition concerning pension rules was filed in the Supreme Court in December 1980, alleging the violation of the fundamental constitutional right to equality before the law (Article 14). The petitioners were D. S. Nakara and Satyindra Singh, a retired civil servant and a rear admiral. They were assisted by a newly formed "social service organization" called Common Cause, which published letters to the editor in leading national dailies, soliciting additional information and additional petitioners from the wider public.[118] Two years later, in December 1982, a Supreme Court bench led by Justice Y. V. Chandrachud ruled in favor of the petitioners. The central government filed a review application four months later (April 1983), but it was denied by the Court.

However, the court decision remained unimplemented and by July 1985 an estimated eight thousand petitioners who might have benefited from the petition had died. Media attention turned to this matter of continued governmental neglect despite judicial orders, and highlighted the continued suffering of petitioners more than five years after the courts were first moved on the matter. The media outrage struck a judicial chord. The Allahabad High Court quickly issued an interim order directing the central government to pay family pensions to widows of former high court judges within thirty days. These signal-and-response relays between media and judiciary continued over the next months. In August, a *Times of India* report about pensioner Thanawalla's "harassment with regard to nonpayment of pension"[119] led to a Bombay High Court judge, H. H. Kantharia, taking *suo moto* cognizance. He issued a show-cause notice on the matter to the accountant general and the central government. Adding to the mediatized relay, the news story about Thanawalla's case was itself the outcome of another news story. Thanawalla had written in to the newspaper with details of his case after reading a story in the *Times of India* about the similar plight of another pensioner, Chandrasekhar Ramasubra Mani. The pension case marked the entry of a new actor in the PIL arena, the

Common Cause organization. Common Cause's continued efforts to represent the public interest over subsequent decades would take forward the curative democracy project and its idea of a commonly wounded people.

MAKING COMMON

Founded in Delhi in 1980 by a retired Punjabi civil servant, Hari Dev (H.D.) Shourie, the social action organization Common Cause has been a vanguard of the PIL revolution since its inception. At the time of Shourie's death in 2005, Common Cause had filed more than seventy petitions in the name of the public interest in the Supreme Court and Delhi High Court. The official origin story of Common Cause narrates how Shourie and his neighbor and friend U. C. Dubey, a retired military officer, came up with the idea after a series of frustrating visits to the Delhi electricity supply company offices to clear up a billing dispute. Repeatedly encountering incompetent and unhelpful governmental officials, they found that there were many other citizens with similar experiences. Scores of retired taxpayers were being callously treated by the very state they had served dutifully throughout their professional career. Determined to change things, Shourie, Dubey, and a few other like-minded individuals decided to establish a "non-political, non-profit and voluntary organization" that would pursue "the cause of the common man" and "seek redress for problems of the people."[120]

The founders of Common Cause came from similar social backgrounds. Most were retired older men living in middle-class and elite residential areas in Delhi such as West End and Defence Colony. They had retired as senior state officials or professionals. The group included a former finance secretary of the central government, a former auditor general of India, a military officer, a senior advocate, and an internationally prominent editor and writer.[121] Members worked on a voluntary basis and ran the organization with the modest subscription fees contributed by members (individuals could join the organization by paying a subscription fee of one hundred rupees). Common Cause engaged primarily with the media and the judicial system, and used the new instrument of public interest litigation to achieve its aims. Even though most of the founders were not trained lawyers, they quickly gained legal competence and expertise in what was at the time a new and evolving field. Common Cause members garnered recognition and respect in the country's apex courtroom, as the posthumous tribute to Shourie by a former chief justice of the Supreme Court would attest.

Shourie filed Common Cause's first writ petition in the public interest in 1980, about a discrepancy in the payment of government pensions to retired public servants. Following several unsuccessful attempts to get a response from elected representatives and the prime minister's office, he turned to the media and the judiciary. After the publication of his letter to the editor of a national daily had elicited more than 15,000 complaints and testimonies from aggrieved pensioners, Shourie filed a petition in the Supreme Court, urging the court to take action on this matter of public interest. The court responded favorably. Its decision benefited at least 100,000 pensioners around the country, according to organizational estimates, although the implementation of the decision met with further governmental obstacles, as we have already seen. Nevertheless, the positive judicial response encouraged the organization to embrace the PIL strategy. It would shepherd many more petitions through the Supreme Court and various high courts of the country over the next decades.

At the time of a commemorative review in 2005, after a quarter century of existence Common Cause had produced a substantial body of litigation that offered a distinctive definition of the public interest and of the related ideas of people, state, and citizen. Table 1 below lists the various writs that the organization filed in the Supreme Court and Delhi High Court between 1980 and 2005, categorized according to the main subject of each petition.

As the table shows, the largest number of petitions filed by Common Cause were about problems with the quality, cost, efficiency, and access to public services. Presenting the state-citizen relationship as that of a rational, fee-paying consumer who expects high-quality services delivered to her by an accessible and efficient service provider, they linked the "common cause" of the ordinary citizen to a particular service-delivery model of consumer citizenship. Further, as the list of service deficiencies in Table 4.1 shows, the normative consumer-citizen in whose name Common Cause fought the good fight was located in a metropolitan middle-class social

TABLE 4.1 *Common Cause petitions, 1980–2005*

Category	Subjects of *Common Cause* writs in the Indian Supreme Court and Delhi High Court
Urban, middle classes *Property* *Taxes*	Pensions
	Postretirement medical facilities under ESIC Act (Employees' State Insurance Corporation Act)
	Income tax deductions (TDS, tax deducted at source)
	Property tax
	Introduction of unit area method for property tax
	Rateable value (property assessment)
	Relaxations for allowing constructions in DDA colonies (government-regulated residential housing in Delhi)
	Conversion of leasehold into freehold property
	Apartments Ownership Act
	Rent control
	Regulating unauthorized colonies
	Misuse of farmhouses in Delhi
	Animal hazards on roads
	Operation of beauty parlors and massage parlors
Consumer	Consumer Protection Act[122]
Corruption *Discretionary power* *Personal gain*	Lokpal proposal (national ombuds authority)
	Allotment of petrol pumps
	Out-of-turn Maruti allotments (car)
	Telephone freebies
	Discretionary quotas
	Appointments in Board for Industrial and Financial Reconstruction
	Appointment of the comptroller and auditor general
	Reservations in educational institutions and services in Tamil Nadu
	Arbitrary transfer of officers affecting efficiency
	MPLADS (discretionary development funds for parliamentary representatives); parliamentary pensions
	Nonperforming assets
	Proliferation of fake universities
	Nonbanking finance corporations
	Exemption of public sector units from MRTP (price regulations)
	Infructuous investment on nonfunctioning airports
	Lottery scam
	Sale of spurious drugs
	Sale of illicit liquor

Category	Subjects of *Common Cause* writs in the Indian Supreme Court and Delhi High Court
Public	Lawyers' strikes
services	Pending criminal cases
Efficiency	Pendency of cases in courts
Quality of	Problems relating to the functioning of the judiciary
services	Too many holidays
Urban focus	Two time zones
(some) Targeted	Post and Telecom workers' strike
services for the	Strike threat by NTPC executives (public energy company)
poor	Pollution by slaughterhouses
	Postal service
	Conditional access system (cable television)
	Electricity billing (defective meters)
	Electricity load; load shedding (electricity theft)
	Installation, maintenance and replacement of water meters
	Change in billing system of MTNL (telephone)
	Phasing out of blue line buses (Delhi public transport)
	Railway accidents
	Accidents on roads and highways
	Condition of mortuaries
	Infrastructural facilities in burn ward of Safdarjung Hospital (Delhi)
	Recruitment of ineligible lab technicians in Safdarjung Hospital
	Use of incinerators for disposal of hospital waste unregulated blood banks
	Prevalence of AIDS in the country
	Lifting of ban on sale of non-iodized salt
	Introduction of astrology and *purohitya* (training of Hindu priests) in universities; primary education
	Education of poor children
Antipolitics	Elections and political parties
Electoral politics	Large-scale advertisements in newspapers projecting image of politicians and political parties
	Frequent elections
	Maintenance and audit of accounts by political parties
	Jumbo cabinet in Uttar Pradesh
Social reform	Communal harmony
	Frequent projection of crime and violence on television
	Ritual of burying of children in some villages in Tamil Nadu
	Two-child norm
	Female feticide
	Euthanasia

Source: *Great Crusader for People's Causes H. D. Shourie* (New Delhi: Common Cause, 2005), 84–85.

milieu. Many petitions addressed problems that were unique to Delhi. These included the illegalities of urban farmhouses, a form of urban encroachment practiced by Delhi elites; rebuilding rights in residential colonies regulated by the Delhi Development Authority; and the "menace" of stray cows on the crowded streets of the national capital.

Given the physical location of the organization in Delhi, the Delhi-centric focus of the petitions was hardly surprising. What stood out, however, was how a geographically specific set of issues were re-presented and reframed as matters of general national concern. From the very outset of the PIL revolution, through the 1980s and beyond, the public interest petitions filed by Common Cause frequently reinforced a partial vision of the commons. Appeals to the judiciary to get rid of the unsightly sores of illegal slums, the cow menace on Delhi streets, or the polluting effects of (Muslim-run) slaughterhouses targeted the urban populations that depended on these illegal and informal practices and places for their survival. They reflected ideals of civic order that were grounded in particular caste-class realities. There was a particular social location from which stray cows were perceived as a traffic nuisance. There was a particular social location where the main problem with illegal slums was their ugliness rather than their absence of basic public utilities.[123] Nevertheless, these exclusionary demands were presented in a universal and disinterested register, as something that all of the people wanted and needed.

The conventional academic narrative about India's experiences with public interest litigation describes a decisive chronological shift toward the end of the twentieth century, when the political culture of neoliberal economic reform replaced the mass-welfarist themes of the Nehru era with a new emphasis on the middle classes. According to this view, PIL "Mark 1" addressed the suffering of the marginalized and dispossessed in the post-emergency years, while PIL "Mark 2" in the late 1990s and beyond focused on class-selective issues like corruption and environmental degradation.[124] However, the work of Common Cause in the aftermath of the emergency suggests that this neat chronology of post-liberalization transition, and the thesis of neoliberal disjuncture, is inaccurate. A preoccupation with middle-class subjectivity, and the political metonymy of a narrow class-caste elite—urban, middle class, upper caste standing in for the people as a whole—was also present in the pre-liberalization era.

Already in the late 1970s, the idea of the public interest encompassed both general and specific constituencies, the wound of suffering borne by marginalized citizens as well the wound of disappointed expectations inflicted on the urban middle classes. Alongside the concern networks that mobilized around the atrocities of custodial violence and other incidents of extreme exploitation and dispossession, similar configurations of the media-judiciary-civil-society network drew attention to a different set of wrongs. These ranged from the nonpayment of pensions to the widows of public servants, to the unhygienic conditions of unregulated blood banks and the discretionary "out of turn" allotment of telephone connections to powerful people by the state-run telephone company. The issues were distinct. However, Common Cause engaged them in equivalent ways, as subjects of similar kinds of public interest litigation petitions. The judicial authorities concurred. They granted to both the iodization of salt and the trafficking of women—to take two random subjects of PILs filed in the early 1980s—the identical status of a matter of public interest. In the capacious and amorphous name of the public interest and the people, the logic of equivalence that Ernesto Laclau identifies as the main enabling condition of populism "chained" disparate social demands along a single fault line.[125] A commonly wounded people was pitted against the same corrupt, cruel, and incompetent establishment.

This in turn had implications for how the form and terms of popular redemption—the solution to the people's problems—was imagined. What was to be done? The PIL work of Common Cause shows us that the equivalences of wounded citizenship were applied to ideas of wrongdoing as well as remedy. As we have already seen, a distinctive feature of public interest litigation was its placement of seemingly incommensurable acts and situations within a common framework of justiciable injury. Iodized salt and human trafficking, the problem of mass blindings, and that of stray cows were all adjudicated as public interest matters. This evenhandedness also applied to the remedial interventions proposed for different wrongs. The concern networks that Common Cause assembled to expose civic problems mirrored the media-judiciary-civil-society alliances[126] that came together around issues of extreme violence and exploitation. They drew upon similar sets of public-spirited individuals and organizations.[127] They also proposed similar kinds of cures. Like the atrocity PILs, Common Cause petitions invoked the remedial agency of political outsiders. They sought solutions from people who were purportedly outside the corrupt sphere of electoral politics but were at the same time influential and resourceful enough to make a political difference. The active role of retired government servants and military officers in the Common Cause petitions attests to this insider-outsider position of distance-yet-leverage that the curative democratic initiatives of the post-emergency era relied so centrally upon.[128]

However, even as it replicated a familiar form of outsider politics, Common Cause also put on the table a distinctive set of normative ideals that have become ever more influential in the years since. As Table 1 shows, a large number of Common Cause petitions were about the abuses of discretionary power. These included out-of-turn allotments, personal enrichment, the corrupt excesses of electoral politics (for example, underhanded financial dealings, inappropriate advertisement that blurred lines between government and party),[129] and regulatory inefficiencies on the part of state authorities (for example, unregulated blood banks, overregulated building plans). The remedies demanded were, in turn, about transparency, monitoring, and regulatory reform. One of the most prominent issues that dominated Indian politics in the 1990s and 2000s, the right to information, was championed by Common Cause in the 1980s itself. Monitory democracy values of efficiency, transparency, and accountability were embraced at this time, well before the era of economic liberalization with which they are usually associated.

CONCLUSION: ON CHANGING CHANGE

Nation-building was an important keyword in the mid-twentieth-century Indian political lexicon. Compressing and conflating processes that had unfolded in a gradual sequence over a long period of time in Europe and North America, the term described how the newly independent nation-state simultaneously engaged with democratization, state formation, capitalist development, and cultural nationalization. This was not unique to

India. The compressed urgencies of nation-building appeals anchored numerous projects of postcolonial sovereignty around the globe. Urgent calls to citizens to participate in state-led efforts to build the nation resounded across much of Asia and Africa at the time. However, by the late 1970s and early 1980s, a new set of normative ideas had gained public salience. In the aftermath of the Indian emergency, the call to restore, cure, or renew the political system of democracy came to dominate public life, displacing the older language of nation-building.

The political consequences of this shift from nation-building to democracy-rebuilding has been the focus of this chapter. How was the problem of democratic breakdown defined and what kinds of solutions were offered in the late 1970s and beyond? Who were the principal agents and protagonists of democracy's proposed cure? What remedies were offered, and—to keep going with the medical metaphor—what were their side effects? Addressing these questions, I have continued the exploration of outsider politics and curative democracy that is the main purpose of this book. The previous chapter focused on the origins of outsider politics. It tracked how the political outside was configured as the normative location of democracy and popular sovereignty in the specific context of the Indian emergency and its aftermath. This chapter has looked at the exercise of outsider political agency in post-emergency India, and the tangible political actions and practices that the outsider norm enabled. Through a discussion of public interest litigation and the interventions of socio-legal and media "concern networks," I have shown how democratic representation was taken outside the electoral system. Starting in the late 1970s, a range of different intermediary institutions and agents claimed the moral authority to represent the true interests and desires of the demos.

The Long 1970s were a momentous and formative period in post-independence India's political history, when democracy was both suspended and restored. It is not just that numerous political, social, economic, or cultural changes took place at this time. Rather, the idea of change itself was profoundly reimagined. Change is far from self-evident. It is made as much as it is found. It is a political idea, a claim, and a proposition of a particular kind. One such proposition about change came to hold sway in the Long 1970s, pushed forward by a unique mix of media, judicial, and civil society institutions and actors. In the new light of curative democracy, ideas of democratic political agency were recrafted in substantial ways: what it means to act in the name of the people; who should undertake such action and for whom; what the goals and measure of democratic change should be; what its social and political costs and exclusions are.

CONCLUSION

CROOKED LINES

After the uprising of the 17th of June
The Secretary of the Writers' Union
Had leaflets distributed on the Stalinallee
Stating that the people
Had forfeited the confidence of the government
And could only win it back
By increased work quotas. Would it not in that case be simpler
for the government
To dissolve the people
And elect another?

—Bertolt Brecht, *Die Lösung*/The Solution (1959)

IN PLACE OF A summative conclusion that ties up loose ends, this final chapter reflects on why outsider politics and curative democracy may be good to think with. I begin with a brief reflection on these two concepts. Replicating the zigzagged research process that produced this book, taking me from the present to the 1970s, I then ask about the lineages of the present. What can our temporal detour to the contexts where the redemptive energies of curative democracy and outsider politics were first activated tell us about the state of contemporary democratic politics in India?

This book has traced how a particular political project of curative democracy became influential in India in the Long 1970s. *Curative democracy* is my term for a particular way of saying, seeing, and doing politics. It is a distinctive vision and language of politics that is materialized in tangible sets of policies, institutions, and public practices. Curative democracy projects express two core ideas. First, they offer a reformist and remedial vision of political change: the call is for a *cure*, not a revolutionary upheaval nor a renunciation of politics. Second, they legitimize a distinctive form of outsider politics that configures political agency around an ideal of political exteriority and authorizes an outsider as the main agent of political change. In the diagnosis that curative democracy projects offer, the curative democrat—democracy's doctor, the agent of healing and repair—is someone who stands outside the political fray. Only an outsider can heal the sick body of the political system, it is held. When such an individual is objectively involved in politics, for example, a politician vying for votes or an incumbent of state office—Modi, Trump, Berlusconi come to mind here—their claims to outsider status emphasize the distinctive values, conduct, and identities that allegedly separate them from the dirt and disrepair of "the system."

The curative democratic imagination and the figure of the outsider have imprinted Indian political cultures and public life for more than four decades. As the preceding chapters have shown, they have been sustained by different sets of forces traversing diverse public realms: thus, the mobilizing efforts of new political parties such as the AAP (chapter 1); news-making practices in "new" as well as "old" media worlds (chapters 2 and 4); emergency-era populism and post-emergency initiatives of democratic restoration (chapter 3); civil society activism and public interest litigation (chapter 4). In bringing together these varied expressions in a common framework as this book has done, three notable social and political implications of curative democracy and outsider politics come to light.

First, these are contingent formations that became legible in a particular historical context. They were shaped in and by the conjunction of specific sets of social and political forces and events in late-twentieth-century India. A line of Indological argumentation that has recently enjoyed a revival of sorts in some quarters of contemporary anthropological writing explains features of Indian politics by invoking an enduring cultural essentialism of some kind. From this perspective, the attractions of curative democracy and the political outsider could be explained by culturalist assertions such as "Indians are naturally predisposed to acts of transcendence and renunciation" or "Indians are inherently hierarchical."[1] In marked contrast, an emphasis on the contingency of these formations reflects a broader view that culture is itself politically and historically crafted and modulated, and evolves across time and circumstance. From contemplations of enduring cultural essence, our attention is redirected to the specific political genealogy of curative democracy, and to the historically contingent (and hence mutable) pathways of its rise and influence.

Second is the resolutely pragmatist character of such a politics and the sharp contrast with other imaginaries of political change that have held sway in India. There is a striking divergence between the reformist contours of the curative projects discussed in this book and the revolutionary utopias and "world-making" impulses of left socialisms that have a strong historical presence in the country, or the right-wing utopias that are currently ascendant. It reminds us that curative democracy projects and outsider politics have a status quo–ist or establishment core. The stated aim of such a politics is to restore a putative political-social equilibrium, to put matter back in place rather than to make alternative and new worlds possible. In many instances, this restorative impulse is also a hierarchical one. Curative democracy often invests in a fantasy of return to an unequal order where everyone knows (and cheerfully accepts) their place.

Third, curative democracy and outsider politics are embedded in the uneven sociological landscape of Indian democracy. Each of the chapters has drawn attention to an unequal social world in which such a politics flourishes. In the examples we have discussed, from the investigative journalists of the post-emergency era to the Aam Aadmi Party workers of the new millennium, certain kinds of social subjects endowed with certain forms of class-caste capital have exercised curative agency. We have seen that gendered, religious, and ethno-regional considerations matter as well. Curative democrats in India have mostly been male, and those who attract media and public recognition as nationally relevant political agents who have the capacity to fix and heal India's sick democracy are often from northern Indian, caste Hindu milieus. Not everyone is, or can be, a curative democrat. To take these sociological dimensions seriously is to confirm Ambedkar's famous observation that, *pace* Arendt, the political question is always a social question.[2] Considerations of democratic futures must reckon with the matrix of historically sedimented social relations that distribute scarce political resources and power, striating political horizons and bending arcs of change along crooked lines.

It is to such a consideration of Indian democracy's present and future that I now turn. Can the older formations of curative democracy and outsider politics help us understand the political condition of India today?

STRONGMEN

This is the time of the strongmen. In recent years, they have come to govern many different countries around the world with a decisive electorate mandate, flexing their authoritarian muscle in raw displays of boastful power and upending democracy's core precepts in the name of restoring power to the people. Brazil, the Philippines, Russia, Turkey, India, Egypt, Hungary, Indonesia, the United States, Slovenia, Poland, we can go on. A common type of leader is at the helm of national politics across this varied geopolitical terrain. Nearly always, it is a singular male figure who promises to break the vise grip of elites over the diseased and corrupt system of political democracy and restore the people to their due place of power. The concentration of political authority in a self-fashioned outsider to "the system" who fires up a disillusioned electorate with his agenda of decisive action is a familiar feature of our present times.

Some scholars have related the strongman's rise to the widening social inequalities and precarities created by the predatory reign of financialized capitalism and the failures of existing governments to mitigate its disastrous effects, from the relentless commodification of all human relations to the irreversible depletion of natural resources that imperils planetary futures. Strongman rule is a system-stabilizing reaction to this crisis, some argue.[3] It is a structural recalibration of contemporary disorder around the promise of redemptive action. It is an attempt to divert the insurrectionary potential of mass anger away from the capitalist order and toward scapegoats, usually weak minorities, that strongmen leaders target as the cause of the people's despair.

Taking a less functionalist approach, others have related the rise of strongman politics to the "crumbling of social foundations" and the steady decay of democracy's organizational, institutional, and procedural features over the past decades.[4] Strongmen political entrepreneurs thrive in the wastelands of imploded democracies in this telling. They seize the political opportunities opened up by the collapse of traditional political parties, and the availability of new kinds of media technologies for mass mobilization. The normative political languages and distinctive modes of publicity that strongmen deploy resonate widely with citizens who are disappointed and thoroughly disenchanted with democracy-as-usual. They ignite popular hope and belief that the messianic leader will make things great again.

Strongman regimes are not new. Ruth Ben-Ghiat emplots a century-long series that begins with Benito Mussolini in the 1920s. Twenty-first-century "new despots" resemble these earlier avatars but also stand out in several important ways. Chief among these is the context of political democracy in which contemporary strongman rule flourishes as a specific form of "elective despotism," to use John Keane's term.[5] Unlike their predecessors, all the contemporary regimes included within the category are formal and constitutional democracies, although their specific attributes, dominant ideological orientations, levels of institutional consolidation, and substantive democratic records may differ. Millennial strongmen have emerged from *within* democracy; they morph rather than kill democracy. Strongmen regimes are hybrid political forms that combine democratic and authoritarian elements of rule and legitimation. Drawing upon the arguments of this book, this chapter traces how this combination was produced in India, and its implications for democratic futures.

The authoritarianism-within-democracy mix means that consent as well as coercion is used to legitimize strongman rule. But this is not just about influencing individual belief and conviction. Elective despots strive as much to pervade as to persuade, to be publicly encountered as much as to be believed. As Esra Özyürek, Ruth Ben-Ghiat, and other scholars of twentieth-century strongmen regimes have shown, Atatürk and Mussolini cults proliferated their monumental and miniaturized replicas across a wide range of public and domestic arenas, from the embroidery profile on a handkerchief to giant murals along public avenues.[6] Close to a century later we see similar fractal effects at work. Innumerable statues, hoardings, masks, holograms, digital streams, and algorithms disperse, mirror, and multiply the strongman as a familiar everyday presence.

Strongmen regimes thus rely quite heavily on publicity, performance, and multisensory spectacles to constitute their political authority. There are often sharp ideological and political differences between regimes. Political Islam and "Christianism" respectively fuel the strongman politics of Erdogan and Trump;[7] the socialist worldview of a Chavez is very different from the militarist-right nationalist orientations of a Putin.[8] Despite these differences, strongman performances reproduce a common set of themes. The first is personalization. Strongman imaginaries are usually anchored to a singular figure who embodies and incarnates the true spirit of the people. Power is concentrated in both institutional-procedural and symbolic ways. The institutional checks and balances of democratic government are circumvented using a variety of means. These include the evisceration of parliamentary deliberation procedures that have historically served to counterbalance executive authority, and discretionary appointments to bureaucratic positions on the basis of personal loyalty to the leader rather than professional criteria of selection and promotion.

The strongman also centers himself in the symbolic narrative of people and nation, conflating love and loyalty to the people and the nation with himself. Nationalist ideologies promote abstract and collective forms of passion and devotion—the love for land, religion, language, or community. Strongman regimes cultivate love for the individual leader as the true and the only incarnation of the people. The idea of incarnation is quite different from representational claims about the relationship between the leader and the people/nation. The leader's work of expressing and safeguarding the consciously determined and fully formed will of the people is emphasized by the latter. In contrast, the figure of strongman-as-avatar showcases the leader's fidelity to a core essence that eludes popular awareness and knowledge. The claim of popular incarnation is thus a claim about a different and a better access to the authentic truth of the people that they themselves do not know. Asserting the superior knowledge and agency of the leader, the strongman is placed in a hierarchical relation to the people. We will come back to this point about hierarchy later in the chapter.

The second recurring theme is that of masculine power and virility. As the publicity campaigns around leaders like Trump, Putin, Duterte, and

Bolsonaro make abundantly clear, strongman authority is expressed and legitimized through heteronormative displays of "toxic masculinity" and violent misogyny.[9] The leader's fit and muscular body (Putin), sexual prowess and unconstrained sexual enjoyment (Berlusconi, Duterte), and easy and abundant access to women (Trump) are among the sexualized metonymies of political authority that proliferate quite freely in strongman regimes, endorsed by state functionaries and party supporters as well as by non-state media and private citizens. Reflecting national variations in sociocultural norms, in some instances the gendering of strongman authority as male requires performances of celibacy and austerity rather than virile swaggering. The publicity around Modi and Erdogan foregrounds their sober respectability as paterfamilias figures, not their sexual excesses. However, this does not challenge the basic normative premise of masculinity as the defining attribute of strongman leadership.

Third, the strongman is invariably identified as an outsider to the system and to the tightly knit circles of elites who are seen to have usurped power from the people. The idea of the outsider, like that of the system and the elites, is multifaceted. The strongman asserts his distance from the status quo in social, political, and economic terms. Moreover, outsider claims do not have a single and stable class referent. In some cases, the humble background of the strongman distinguishes him from the wealthy elites who have usurped power from the people. In others, it is exactly the opposite. It is *because* he is wealthy that he can stand apart from the corrupt temptations of political office. The divergent strongman narratives around Modi and Trump illustrate the doubled construction of outsider identity. Modi the humble *chaiwala* and Trump the billionaire both claim their legitimate authority as outsiders to the system. They are leaders untainted and fundamentally disinterested in the sordid hustle of politics because they, like the people, inhabit moral and social worlds that are outside the closed and corrupt system.

Finally, strongmen usually come across as larger-than-life protagonists. They are lone figures who are (literally) seen to thoroughly shake up the system with their forceful interventions. Strongmen boldly undertake decisive actions that shatter social and political conventions in all kinds of unexpected ways and capture public attention with their unfettered originality. In a variety of different strongman regimes around the world, the political theater of "eventocracy" is a familiar recurrence.[10] Aligning with prevailing commercial and social media logics of sensation and stimulation, policy decisions and the ordinary and even mundane business of governance are repackaged as unique events that dominate media interest and confirm leader-centric narratives about political authority and agency. Examples include Narendra Modi's demonetization policy announcement (discussed below), Rodrigo Duterte's dramatic declarations of a war on drugs in the Philippines, and Jair Bolsonaro's national addresses from a hospital bed during the Covid-19 pandemic in 2020, which visually conveyed both his ordinary vulnerability and his extraordinary powers of control and survival over the dreaded disease.

Enacted as dramatic surprises, like thunderclaps and skyfalls, events shore up the normative ideal of the unconstrained leader who breaks free of convention and conformity and transforms the status quo with his bold actions. The much-discussed contemporary phenomenon of "post-truth" that characterizes strongman regimes the world over has an analogous role.[11] It is a set of public interventions that asserts the leader's autonomy from all kinds of conventional restraints, including that of facticity and consistency. When critics lament the gap between facts/truth and the fantasies and conspiracies spun by strongman regimes, they fail to understand its legitimation functions. The existence of such a gap conveys the strongman's transformative, rule-bending capacities and his ability to create and shape realities. In other words, it is *because* the strongman performances are fantastical and patently untrue that they legitimize the strongman as a transformational agent of popular redemption.[12]

INDIAN VAUDEVILLE

All these features of strongman rule are replicated in contemporary India, where national politics is dominated by the distinctive governance style of Prime Minister Narendra Modi and the incumbent BJP government. Ever since the BJP's decisive parliamentary win in 2014 (repeated again in 2019), the centralization and personalization of power in and around Modi has proceeded apace. After coming to power, the BJP filled a large number of important state offices with people who were ideologically aligned with the party credo of Hindu nationalism and were personally loyal to Modi.[13] These included cabinet ministries, gubernatorial offices, cultural, research, and educational institutions, and technocratic, regulatory, investigative, and watchdog state agencies such as NITI Aayog, the Securities and Exchange Board of India (SEBI), the Election Commission, the Central Information Commission, the Auditor General, the Central Vigilance Commission, the Central Bureau of Investigation, and the public broadcaster Prasar Bharati. Significantly, several of these, such as the Election Commission, the Central Information Commission, and the Comptroller and Auditor General, were check-and-balance institutions invested with powers of oversight and veto over the exercise of governmental power. Controlling these "institutions of accountability" facilitated a process of "executive aggrandizement" or the unconstrained exercise of power by the national executive.[14]

The judiciary and the bureaucracy were also targeted for personnel changes. One of the first legislative attempts of the BJP government in August 2014 targeted the National Judicial Appointments Commission (NJAC). Although it was ultimately unsuccessful, the measure aimed to replace the existing collegium system of judicial appointments, where judges themselves determined the composition of the Supreme Court and high courts, with a system in which the national executive would play a decisive role. In the case of bureaucratic appointments, the new government paid special attention to the staffing of the prime minister's office (PMO) and brought in new officers of its choosing to serve as principal secretaries and close aides to the prime minister. These were intra-bureaucracy transfers that conformed to existing civil service rules and conventions of seniority. But in subsequent years, the BJP also appointed several outsiders to senior bureaucratic positions. In 2018, the central government announced a new scheme of "lateral entry" into the civil services that brought nine new joint secretaries from outside the tightly specialized ranks of elite civil service to key ministries. In July 2020, the government proposed to hire another four hundred directors and deputy directors of state agencies under this scheme.[15]

Along with the institutional realignment of governmental authority around a single individual, the incumbent BJP government has also reworked symbolic imaginaries to foreground an individual leader-centered vision of nation and people. Modi's tendency to talk about himself in the third person[16] is an apt reflection of the great leader cult that has stabilized around his singular presence. Fantastic, exaggerated claims about his god-like omnipotence have proliferated within state and social media circuits. Like his counterparts, Modi's power is constituted in gendered terms as a specifically masculine form of power. However, this is differently inflected. As I have noted earlier, sexual braggadocio and virility are notably absent from the masculinist performances of Modi's strongman authority. They make use of other kinds of symbols and affects that are reproduced and dispersed through reverential propaganda as well as satirical memes. Modi appears before his adoring audiences as the strong leader with an impressive fifty-six-inch chest. He is Bal Narendra, the fearless child who nonchalantly wrestled crocodiles by the river. He is the dashing fighter pilot; the bejeweled king; the meditating ascetic; the avuncular teacher. He is the energetic "bro" greeting ecstatic crowds at the Howdy Modi rally in Houston, Texas, his buddy Donald Trump at his side.[17]

Strongman eventocracy is a defining feature of the Modi regime as well. Modi's surprise broadcast on the evening of November 8, 2016, that 500- and 1,000-rupee currency notes would cease to be legal tender in the country within four hours of his televised announcement is a classic example. As I noted in the Introduction, the announcement had an immediate material impact on the lives and livelihoods of the vast majority of Indian citizens as it removed from circulation the very denomination of currency notes with which daily wages were paid and quotidian essentials were bought. Carefully crafted as an attention-grabbing public spectacle—a prime-time address to the nation that interrupted regular programming to be simultaneously broadcast on all television and radio channels—demonetization was also distinguished by an "intimate aesthetic." As the journalist Steve Coll has astutely noted, *notebandi* (literally, note-closing) allowed Modi to "reach into the pocket of almost every Indian."[18] The suddenness of the announcement was highlighted in the speech itself. Modi described how the announcement had taken government officials and political insiders completely by surprise. Like the ordinary citizens who were listening to his broadcast, they too were completely unaware of the impending policy decision, he explained. The secrecy and stealth was necessary in order for his masterstroke to be effective. The remedy that Modi promised, of how demonetization would clean up the corrupt system of electoral politics and vanquish the specter of black-money-fueled terrorism, was premised on this distinction between the leader's unique foresight and the ignorance of ordinary citizens and government officials. The ability to surprise—to stage events that were completely unexpected and unknown—anchors the legitimation claims of the strongman. It is a sign of his extraordinary distinction.

Constituted as the ultimate public surprise, the demonetization policy placed Modi at the center of media narratives, as the prime author of the nation's present and future. Post-truth cascades have further intensified his authorial claims. He is someone who can not only dominate media narratives, but can shape and even create truth and fact. In critical discussions about the post-truth alternative realities, concerned scholars and citizens often make a binary distinction between truth and lies. They wonder and worry about how and why patently false narratives that fly in the face of empirical and experiential reality are able to gain social traction. Why do Modi fans believe clearly incorrect and often absurd narratives that have been conclusively proved to be untrue by fact-checkers? Why aren't they skeptical about the wild inconsistencies in even the basic biographical details that he provides?[19] Why don't they question the shape-shifting chimera of his public performances where he continually says different things to different people? These stark oppositions between falsehood and truth, and the presumption that fact-checking and truth-telling can enlighten gullible and duped citizens, misunderstand the public effects and legitimation work of Modi's *bahurupiya*,[20] his quicksilver shape-shifting public masquerades.

In the social media echo chambers of Modi supporters, the empirical veracity of Modi-related memes is not the issue. Rather, it is how they confirm the authorial power of the great leader to varnish and tarnish truth, to bend and invent facts from scratch. Modi's capacities of performative excess and abundance are affirmed when he changes his public persona with dizzying speed, morphing from a dandy in a bespoke suit to a silent sage in a cave, from a gentle nature lover feeding peacocks to a muscled, hard-hatted figure striding through a construction site; when he styles his hair, body, clothes, and comportment to resemble the nationalist icons Mahatma Gandhi and Rabindranath Tagore. The political scientist John Keane has coined the felicitous term "vaudeville government" to describe the diverse and dynamic political promises that contemporary strongmen make in the course of "being different things to different people at different times."[21] Nineteenth-century vaudeville theatrical performances in Europe and the United States drew in varied audiences with their entertaining mix of genres and styles: "strongmen and singers, dancers and drummers, minstrels and magicians, acrobats and athletes, comedians and circus animals."[22] As it prioritizes the instrumental goal of maximum popular outreach over ideological and political consistency, the twenty-first-century political vaudeville routine endorses a similar, capacious and flexible "big tent" approach. Keane identifies the confusing public effects of "kaleidoscopic" modes of governance as an additional advantage for new despots. Opposition is harder to mobilize in the ever-changing vaudeville of strongman regimes where rule is constantly being reorganized in new configurations.

To these strategic advantages, we might add that the performative elements of vaudeville government are important as well. As the example of Modi's many metamorphoses shows, the issue is not that his costumes are convincing and authentic and that people take the fictions for truth. Rather, the dexterous excess and fakery of the masquerade pervade and constitute circuits of publicity. Modi memes multiply through economies of digital sharing, turbocharged by the very absurd incredulities that make them patently untrue. The economy of social media attention and engagement, expressed through digital actions such as sharing, liking, and forwarding, is fueled by mendacity rather than veracity. Lies, more than verified truth, attract public notice and gain traction in social media worlds. Strongman legitimation relies more on presence and pervasion than persuasion and conviction. Meshing with the logics of commercial and digital media, the obvious fakery of the *bahurupiya* vaudeville that has taken center stage over the past decade in India fulfils these goals rather well.

REPERTOIRES

Why are strongmen in power today? Since most strongman regimes are established within formal democracies, this is usually framed as a question about popular consent and support. One line of inquiry focuses on the duped and ignorant voter, and the various communicative tricks and strategies of media and public opinion manipulation that strongmen and their image industries successfully deploy. But as we have already noted, ideological persuasion and efforts to win the hearts and minds of individual citizens are not the main priorities of strongman rule. The economy of appearances in which strongman authority materializes as an abundant and ubiquitous public presence does not only require cognitive ignorance. The public identification of strongmen authority does not exclusively rely on mechanisms of mass psychological deception. A second set of explanations focuses on the cultural-religious foundations of strongman legitimacy. For instance, in discussions of the Indian case of societal support for Narendra Modi, the "Hindu voter" is usually identified as the prime subject. In this line of argumentation, a default natural religiosity is ascribed to India and Indians, and the performative practices of the strongman are seen to resonate with these preexisting and (what are presumed to be) hegemonic religious identity frames. These are also majoritarian frames. They reflect the religious beliefs of the demographic majority, a category that is conceived in naturalized and monolithic terms (Hindus as a seamless and invariant/transhistorical community).

A recent news article about Modi's pandemic performance is a good example of this religiosity-centric approach. In the months of April and May 2021, the second wave of the global Covid-19 pandemic battered India with sudden and fierce intensity. Daily infection rates and death tolls escalated rapidly even as health infrastructures collapsed. In the first days and weeks of this national crisis, visuals of mass cremations dominated national and international news. Social media relayed millions of panicked pleas for emergency assistance, and citizens scrambled to access hospital beds and oxygen cylinders. The Indian state was conspicuous by its absence and silence. Neither was essential public infrastructure made available at even the most rudimentary and minimal level, nor did government officials appear in public to offer information, reassurance, or condolences to bewildered and bereaved citizens. Instead, civil society organizations and spontaneously assembled social media networks of ordinary Indians improvised essential pastoral care and emergency relief.

Their self-provisioned actions stood in sharp contrast to the mediatized spectacle of pandemic action. In an age of globally interconnected social and digital media circuits, Indian audiences were familiar with normative templates of how governments could and should respond to the Covid-19 crisis. They saw how in many other countries there were daily briefings by public health experts and regular press conferences held by pandemic crisis management teams appointed by the state. There were relatively prompt public responses from elected representatives who would regularly address national audiences with varying degrees of reassuring and purposeful resolve. Even when leaders like Bolsonaro and Trump used these occasions to downplay and deny the pandemic, they did not overlook the importance of public communication and engagement at this crisis time.

Social/media criticism grew louder and ever more derisive and angry about the Indian state's failure to respond to the biggest public health crisis that the country had ever known. The Modi regime attempted a course correction with a national televised address by the prime minister. It turned out to be an exemplary moment of *bahurupiya* masquerade. On April 20, 2021, Modi appeared on national television in a guise that was altogether different from his previous pandemic appearance, the infamous national lockdown announcement of March 24, 2020. At the onset of the pandemic in 2020, the Modi regime had enacted a classic piece of eventocratic political theater. Emulating the surprise of the demonetization announcement of November 2016, Modi announced an immediate nationwide lockdown scheduled to go into effect within a few hours, and which would have an enormous and direct impact on the lives of ordinary citizens.[23]

In April 2021, however, even as the pandemic's second wave exponentially surpassed the infection, death tolls, and public panics of its first wave, there were no governmental displays of immediate and decisive action. No grand announcements were made in the course of the prime minister's address to the nation that evening. Instead, Modi's speech repeated platitudes and stilted phrases of condolence. Speaking rather stiffly, he announced a change in vaccination policy that was decidedly anticlimactic and minimalist in its scope. Henceforth, the central government rather than the states would take responsibility for the delivery (and funding) of vaccines at public health institutions and facilities across the country, Modi announced.

Modi's physical appearance and affect that evening were starkly different from all that had gone before. He spoke in a monotone at far remove from the passionate emotional cadences that usually suffused his oratory. The great leader addressed his nation as an otherworldly elderly man dressed in nondescript white clothes, with a long, straggling beard and untamed bushy eyebrows. Commenting on the visible and dramatic change in the prime minister's public performance, the *New York Times* journalist Amy Kazmin emphasized the Hindu religiosity of Modi's new performance style. The political scientist Christophe Jaffrelot, a key interview subject for the article, amplified this into a broader set of reasoned observations about the enduring importance of religious, specifically Hindu majoritarian, tropes and idioms in Indian politics.[24]

Kazmin effectively answers the question of "Modi magic"—why popular support and loyalty toward Modi has not wavered despite the government's spectacular mismanagement of the pandemic—in the register of religious essentialism. "Hindu devotees" buy into Modi's guru image, the article concludes. His popular backing can be explained by the enduring power of "India's ancient myths and historic Hindu kingdoms" that legitimize the figure of the all-powerful "spiritual advisor" of the king.[25] The discussion confirms a sense of India's primordial Hinduness, and understands legitimacy and political authority in India to be determined by and derived from long-standing and even timeless religious beliefs. The idea of a religiously constituted politics is not limited to this news article. It frames general discussions of the Modi regime and its Hindutva project of political religion as well. The main lens through which India's contemporary strongman politics and Modi's leadership style is viewed is that of Hindu majoritarianism. The regime's ideological commitments to and location within the Hindutva social-cultural milieu of the Sangh Parivar, the Hindu nationalist "family of organizations," is regarded as its primary and most distinctive feature.

However, the Hindutva project understood as an insular formation with an exclusive focus on religion, identity, and normative community is not the only ground of strongman political authority. An exclusive focus on Hindutva fails to recognize that Indian strongman politics is a *governmental project* that is centrally engaged in the tasks of rule and governance.[26] The question of Modi's legitimacy must also be approached beyond the analytical terrain of religious politics, its resonances with normative Hinduness, and the holy aura of the guru leader. What is the broad field of legitimation vocabularies that the Modi regime draws on, combines, and remixes? What is the range of idioms in which Modi's strongman authority is expressed? These questions relate the Hindutva exception to the establishment norms of Indian democracy, and direct our attention to the terms of political engagement that exceed the familiar paradigm of religious politics. Modi's strongman performances illustrate how governmental Hindutva is placed within and improvises upon existing themes and vocabularies of political democracy in India. *Bahurupiya* Modi is both guru and political outsider. He is an authority figure combining multiple idioms and modes of political legitimation, interweaving older and mainstream themes of politics with Hindu majoritarian symbolism.

To summarize. The rise of the strongman is not so much a political caesura, a sharp break from politics-as-usual that conventional accounts of the "strongman freak show" foreground in tones of amazement and horror. In India and other countries where strongman regimes have won large electoral mandates and widespread societal support in recent years, legitimation strategies draw upon many of the resources of conventional, accepted, and legitimate political repertoires. Strongmen leaders (and the political parties behind them) harness and repurpose many establishment political norms and precepts. Their authority claims resonate with familiar political conventions of the sayable, the visible, and the sensible[27] rather than with essential cultural and religious beliefs whose hold over "Indian hearts and minds"—another aggregate truism—remains an open empirical question. Even if we are to accept the thesis of the intrinsic religiosity of Indians (and accept as well that a specifically north Indian caste-Hindu variant of Hinduism is the natural religious identity for the country at large), we do not know how and why this works at the level of political determination. What are the mechanisms and pathways that translate religious belief and identity into political support for a leader, political party, or government? This question remains unanswered.

Moving away from the imputation of religious beliefs and cultural predispositions as the prime movers of Indian politics, legitimacy should be related to publicly articulated (and hence documented and documentable) *political* repertoires. These comprise the languages of public justification that have been used to explain, authorize, and claim political power and agency. The institutional and normative "bounds of the permissible" must be taken into account. Normative tropes; blind spots and red lines that structure public discourse in institutions of social reproduction and rule—educational institutions, judicial institutions, legislative and policy bodies, bureaucratic forums, and media—matter as well. Seen from this angle, processes of mainstreaming and normalization are central to the rise and consolidation of strongman regimes. The strongman as a figure of governmental authority and an agent of rule is as much about political fit and articulation with established political repertoires as it is about disruption and breakdowns of the existing democratic order.

The concept of a political repertoire helps to clarify the specific character of strongman authority. The term derives from *repertorium*, the late Latin word for list. When used in ordinary language, it describes a set of theatrical knowledges and skills—thus, the repertoire of an actor or a theater company (repertory)—that actors select from when they perform before different audiences. Repertoire has been used as a social science concept in at least two fields of scholarship: theories of social movements and contentious politics, and the sociology of culture. Charles Tilly deployed the term in the late 1970s to convey the repetition, regularities, and the historical embeddedness of contentious politics. A decade later, in *The Contentious French*, he elaborated upon the idea of repertoires as marking out the "bounds of the permissible" and forming the distinctive political cultures of a place.[28] In scholarship on the sociology of culture, repertoires and "toolkits of culture" were used as conceptual currency in the 1990s and beyond. They were defined as a set of diverse resources for strategic action, a "stable cultural script or set of routines that facilitates, naturalizes, and encourages . . . political action,[29] or, more pithily, a "bag of tricks."[30] Although there are differences in the two scholarly approaches, there is a shared understanding of a repertoire as a strategically designed set of remixed and repurposed elements, a configuration that both repeats and innovates. Repertoires are also seen to be variably deployed and hence are ideologically and politically ambivalent and polysemic. The same elements can be combined with new ones or rearranged in different formations. When the concept of a political repertoire is applied to strongman regimes, their strategic design, remixed and repurposed constitution, and political-ideological ambivalence come into focus.

Strongman politics in contemporary India interweaves and mixes Hindu majoritarian themes with favored themes of democratic politics that predate the "saffron wave" of our present times. Chief among these are the themes that have been tracked in this book: curative democracy and the valorized agency of the political outsider. In an ironic twist of history, the antidemocratic edifice of the contemporary Indian strongman regime rests on foundations that were laid during the golden age of democratic reclamation and restoration more than four decades ago. The crooked arc of curative democracy connects the Long 1970s to our present times. The *bahurupiya* vaudeville performances of Modi's political theater harness the aura and legitimacy of the political outsider, a figure valorized by secularists and Hindu nationalists alike.

OUTSIDER POLITICS

When, why, and how did the idea of the political outsider as the authentic representative and redemptive agent of the people, rescuing them from the corrupt depredations of establishment institutions and electoral politics, become influential in modern democracies? Where is the political outside and who is an outsider? Addressing these questions in the context of India, this book has traced the rise of the political outsider, the politics/extrapolitics divide, and the project of curative democracy that frames these ideas of political partition, to the specific historical moment of the Long 1970s—the time before, during, and after the infamous Indian emergency of 1975–77. I have argued that the distinctive historical experience of a "parabolic transition" during this period when democratic and authoritarian political forms mutated into each other firmed the hold of the outsider political repertoire in the country.

The series of regime shifts that marked the long decade of the 1970s, from democracy to emergency authoritarianism in the mid-1970s, to democracy again in the late 1970s, plot an arc of parabolic transition, to use an image described by the political scientist Colin Crouch.[31] According to Crouch, "when you trace the outline of a parabola, your pen passes one of the coordinates twice: going in towards the center of the parabola, and then again at a different point on the way out."[32] The parabolic movement of political time means that there is no circular return to a point of origin or a before. Neither is there a decisive rupture from which an entirely new after emerges. Instead, a parabolic transition marks both difference and connection across time. "We are located in a different point in historical time [and we also] carry the inheritance of our recent past with us."[33] India's Long 1970s traced such a parabolic arc. The emergency regime of 1975–77 built on the preceding inheritance of democratic government, and the project of democratic restoration in the late 1970s and early 1980s modulated the emergency experience. Outsider politics was one of the main outcomes of these parabolic transitions. The modulations of democracy into emergency, and emergency into democracy, crystallized political authority around the figure of the political outsider.

Outsider politics emerged in three phases. The first was in the context of the protest movements of the late 1960s and early 1970s, a time of significant social and political churn when India witnessed fierce struggles for political succession after the death of the first prime minister and icon of the anticolonial movement, Jawaharlal Nehru. New social actors entered the political arena as active rights-bearing subjects who made assertive and voluble demands upon the state. Militant mass agitations erupted in multiple locations across the country, unsettling the elite compact of "passive revolution"[34] that had stabilized postcolonial democracy in its formative years. The normative ideal of the political outside exercised a powerful hold on the "demand politics" of this period.[35] As the mobilizations of the fabled JP movement show, the themes of institutional inadequacy and a pervasive sense of distrust and disappointment with electoral democracy, political parties, and state-led developmental initiatives were central to the agitations.

In the early 1970s, socialist activist Jayaprakash "JP" Narayan's call for a *sampoorna kranti* to realize *lok niti*, a "total revolution" to realize "people power," ignited mass protest movements across the country. The JP movement revived the anti-statist themes of older political projects such as Gandhian and radical nationalisms from the early decades of the twentieth century, and midcentury postcolonial initiatives of social construction and voluntarism such as the Bhoodan or land gift movement popularized by the Gandhian activist Vinoba Bhave.[36] It located popular sovereignty and real democracy in the realm of the "nonpolitical." This was an imagined space of moral purity, separated from the corrupt mess of electoral politics. Other social movements of the time advanced different ideological visions. For instance, demanding the "annihilation of the class enemy," the Maoist-inspired Naxal movement in eastern India advocated sweeping and violent changes in social relations and political order.

Despite these differences, all of these interventions in the name of the people commonly highlighted the failures of the state and electoral politics. In these utopian visions, the sovereign power of the people found expression in the angry swirl of insurgent bodies, in spaces and forms that were distant from ponderous bureaucracy and from the cunning of electoral politics. In the insurrectionary imagination of this period, it was neither state nor political party, but rather, the moral virtue of the political outside, and the interventions of individuals and groups manifestly uninterested in political power and privilege, that paved the path to real democracy.

The second phase of outsider politics was linked to the rise of authoritarian populism in the early to mid-1970s. Facing the cascades of popular discontent across the country, the ruling Congress party, under the leadership of Prime Minister Indira Gandhi, turned to modes of populist legitimation that mirrored the extra-institutional logics of the very movements that were arranged against it. Congress populism was centered on the redemptive agency of the singular great leader, Indira Gandhi. This vision of populist incarnation embraced the logic of political separation and placed leader and people in the sublime and pure space of the political outside.

By the mid-1970s, outsider rule was a tangible reality. The declaration of a national emergency at the end of June 1975 suspended the normal work of everyday politics and centralized power in Indira Gandhi and her small coterie of loyal followers.

The emergency years also saw the intensification of normative appeals to the ideal of the political outside/the political outsider. Going outside electoral politics in the name of the people in order to rescue and redeem a broken and failed democracy was the main justification for the emergency. The regime's main claim of providing virtuous and effective governance turned on the fact of political distance or exteriority, on how the suspension of parliamentary democracy with all of its attendant chaotic and corrupt politicking would reflect and restore the will of the people. Indeed, the emergency regime very literally authorized the rule of political novices and unaccountable, "extra-constitutional" outsiders like Indira Gandhi's son Sanjay Gandhi and his "Gang of Four," whose main qualification was their personal loyalty to the Gandhis.[37]

Emergency rule came to an abrupt end with the surprise announcement of elections in early 1977 and the defeat of the Indira Gandhi regime in March that year. Outsider politics now entered a third phase, as a distinctive language of antipolitics was popularized by state and social actors working to rebuild Indian democracy in the late 1970s and early 1980s. Drawing on pre-emergency discourses of *lokniti* and "non-party political formations," these post-emergency efforts of democratic restoration linked legitimacy and virtue to distance from electoral politics. The divide between morality and politics that the Congress regime had used to justify the suspension of electoral democracy and the imposition of the emergency was validated, not overturned. The credibility dilemmas confronted by the new Janata government in the aftermath of the emergency saw an officially sanctioned narrative about the "people outside" gain traction: how a representative government constrained by law and procedure cannot fulfil the expectations of popular sovereignty; how there is always and necessarily a popular gap at the heart of electoral representation. From the late 1970s, India's new democratic normal was structured around this discursive divide that opposed law and procedure to morality, justice, and the people.

The post-emergency years also witnessed several notable changes in the institutional architectures and practices of political representation. Non-electoral or extra-parliamentary actors, both individuals and institutions, became increasingly important in public life, and there was a surge in beyond-the-ballot claims of popular representation. Contesting the representative authority and legitimacy of elected politicians (and of the bureaucracy they had installed), the media, the judiciary, academics, social movements, and nongovernmental organizations took up the mantle of popular representation and claimed that they could address the interests and needs of the real people in more effective and more authentic ways. The initiatives of public interest litigation, investigative journalism, and social movement and civil society activism that flourished in this period and are widely hailed as vital democracy-enhancing innovations of the time all reproduced the common sense that the broken political system could only be fixed from places outside it, that only political outsiders could rebuild Indian democracy. The mantle of popular representation now shifted to non-electoral actors like the "eminent citizen," the brave journalist, and the wise judge. Democratic accountability was reconfigured as well. It was largely turned into a matter of individual moral judgment and conduct on the part of individuals who were moved, on their own accord, to act in the name of the people. The outsider called for us to believe in the sincerity and authenticity of her representative actions, without giving us independent grounds to test and sustain this belief beyond the representative claim itself.

In sum, the figure of the outsider was claimed by different political projects and invested with new attributes and meanings at different historical moments. In the initial assertions of outsider politics during the protest movements of the 1960s and early 1970s—the first plot point of our parabolic curve—the main attributes of the political outsider were moral and ethical purity. These were expressed through individual and publicly visible acts of sacrifice, austerity, probity, and saintly conduct. As the narratives that built up around JP Narayan show, the extraordinary distinction of the outsider, the fact that he was a man unlike any other, was another key theme. The next iteration of outsider politics in the authoritarian populism of the early to mid-1970s layered a new set of attributes onto the political figure of the outsider. The populist narratives about Indira Gandhi and Sanjay Gandhi showcased their swift and bold decisions and transformative interventions. The outsider in the populist imaginary of the emergency was the quintessential strongman, with Sanjay Gandhi exemplifying this muscular ideal and its valorization of instinctive action and immediacy over rational debate and collective deliberation.

Post-emergency initiatives in the late 1970s and early 1980s modulated the outsider ideal in yet newer ways. As the media, judicial and legal actors, civil society and social movement activists, and academics took up the mantle of popular representation, the authority and legitimacy of the political outsider was linked to professional expertise and knowledge, especially of the legal-judicial kind. Outsider agency also took on performative and visible attributes in post-emergency India. Political outsiders performed big and bold public acts, around moments and events of immediate and urgent crisis. Journalists and print media publications also played a central role, and outsider political agency gained meaning and authority through the extensive media coverage that it commanded in the post-emergency years.

The modulations of outsider politics continued through the 1980s. The political outsider continued as an authority figure beyond the time of democratic restoration, when political and social concerns other than the "expiation" of emergency rule dominated the national agenda. These included challenges to federal unity that were mounted by secessionist movements in the 1980s, the rise of Hindu nationalism as a social and electoral force in Indian democracy from the mid-1980s onward, and the assertions of regional political movements that mobilized around identity categories (region, language, ethnic belonging, caste).[38]

Substantial economic changes also took place in these years. A gradual process of economic "reforms by stealth"[39] that restructured the state-planned national economy along "pro-business" lines unfolded through the 1980s.[40] They laid the groundwork for more extensive and high-visibility economic changes in subsequent decades. By the end of the twentieth century going into the early decades of the twenty-first, India's reinvention as a free-market economy fully integrated into the circuits of global capitalism was embraced as the main national agenda. Spectacular displays of the rapid and irreversible changes under way in a "brand-new India" now dominated the public imagination.[41]

The rebranding of India as the favored destination of global capital substantially impacted social, cultural, and political relations in the country. The new millennium saw the rapid and decisive consolidation of middle-class political agency and authority in national politics. In the context of India's highly unequal social order, this was essentially an assertion of elite power. As numerous studies of the new Indian middle classes have shown, the mantle of the ordinary citizen and the common man in whose name national laws and policies are enacted has been claimed by a narrow social fragment with very specific caste, class, religious, spatial, and gendered attributes.[42]

Through all of these varied changes and challenges of the past decades, the norm of the political outsider, the condemnation of dirty politics, and the seemingly paradoxical claim that political skill and virtue come from political ignorance and innocence have continued as prominent themes of national discourse. The ideal political leader is the newcomer, the naïf, and the stranger to the murky worlds of politics and power. However, like its evolving trajectory through the Long 1970s, the political outsider has also been a mutating figure in subsequent decades. Different historical contexts have added on their own nuances or layers to the figure of the political outsider. Outsiderness has been invested with multiple meanings as it has been claimed by varied political and social forces. In present-day India, we can identify at least four main avatars of the political outsider that circulate in national discourse. As outlined in the ideal-typical sketches below, each links a different set of idealized outsider attributes to claims of popular representation and virtuous leadership.

The CEO

Ever since the early churn of economic transition in the 1980s and the imagination of a new Indian techno-modernity associated with the tenure of Prime Minister Rajiv Gandhi (1984–90), the professional-managerial CEO has been valorized as an effective political agent and leader—someone whose work ethic is sharply opposed to the inefficient and corrupt ways of elected officials. Several individuals have taken up important leadership roles in government and policy worlds over the years on the basis of CEO identity-claims. The CEO figure is also a favored media trope that attracts considerable and positive coverage in commercial news media.

The CEO is a literal outsider to the world of politics. She is someone who has established a reputation and a career by other means. Their considerable professional experience and success both establish their distance from political worlds and equip them with the right skills for national leadership. Idealized qualities associated with the CEO outsider archetype include managerial command-and-control abilities; a proven track record in running a successful corporate enterprise (preferably a leading "high-tech" or knowledge-economy firm with a global presence) and a reputation for making bold and risky decisions; technological and technocratic expertise; and the moral probity that stems from the considerable economic success that these individuals invariably enjoy. As the sociologist Max Weber noted a century ago, political honesty and immunity to the temptations of political pelf are usually the dividends of "plutocracy." Only the independently wealthy can afford to "live for politics"; all others must "live off politics."[43]

Examples of CEO outsiders celebrated in India include Satyan "Sam" Pitroda and Nandan Nilekani. Pitroda, a nonresident Indian, returned to India from the US in the late 1980s and joined Rajiv Gandhi's government as a technology advisor. He has been widely hailed as one of the main enablers of India's "leapfrogged" modernity via the "IT revolution."[44] About two decades later, Nilekani, the cofounder of the global IT corporation Infosys, would play a similar governmental role that transferred his professional and technological expertise into policymaking and administrative arenas. Nilekani was given a cabinet-rank status as the chairman of the Unique Identification Authority of India, a governmental agency that aimed to enroll the Indian population in a universal biometric identification program. Nilekani, like Pitroda, was hailed as a public authority figure with a manifest and substantial "technomoral" difference from conventional political representatives, that is, someone whose life and globally recognized professional success exemplified both technological skill and ethical integrity.[45] Some politicians without any actual experience in corporate management have also been hailed as CEO leaders because they purportedly embody these qualities, for example Andhra Pradesh chief minister N. Chandrababu Naidu, Gujarat chief minister and later prime minister Narendra Modi, and the chief election commissioner of India in the 1990s, T. N. Seshan.[46]

The Showman

The film star politician is a familiar figure in national and regional political arenas. Since independence, several popular movie actors, such as M. G. Ramachandran and J. Jayalalithaa in Tamil Nadu, and N. T. Rama Rao in Andhra Pradesh, have contested and won elections and risen to positions of high political office.[47] The showman stands out for their performative and charismatic qualities. They are well-known celebrities, mostly from the commercial film industry, and command a massive fan following. Like the CEO, the showman's long record of professional success establishes their political independence and their public purpose. They do not need to enter politics for fame or fortune. Rather their entry into politics entails the altruistic sacrifice of fame and fortune to serve the people. The showman's visible popularity among the masses is another sign of her democratic potency. The voluntary commercial transaction that each purchase of a film ticket represents is an expression of popular consent and will formation.[48]

For all outsider archetypes, but especially for that of the showman-outsider, the performative and public character of their political agency is of prime importance.[49] The showman-outsider inhabits and creates an "eventocracy," as we noted earlier. The actions of the showman are invariably big and dramatic, and even banal policy announcements are transformed into theatrical spectacles that are announced with grand flourishes. This in turn means that the showman is a singular and extraordinary figure. Their charisma, aura, and superhuman abilities set them apart not just from their nemesis of the corrupt politician, but from the people themselves. Similar to the CEO archetype, the appeal of the showman and the terms of his redemptive political agency are framed in terms of leadership rather than identification. The showman-outsider commands the devotion and obedience of the people, and her promise of representation and popular redemption is expressed in hierarchical, one-way terms.

The Innocent

Over the first decades of the new millennium, narratives about a politically innocent subject who acts to redeem and save Indian democracy have prominently featured in national media and public discourse. Almost always figured as a young, middle-class, urban and urbane or cosmopolitan individual, the innocence/naïveté of these protagonists is their defining feature. They are individuals who do not have any prior experience with organized politics and public service, and who lack specialized knowledge or interest in political issues as such. Despite their political innocence and ignorance and in fact because of it, the narrative goes, they are ignited to public action when they encounter egregious incidents of wrongdoing and injustice. The political innocent suddenly becomes a visionary and daring public activist, a tireless "crusader" for the "ordinary citizen" and the "common man."[50] Like the other outsider figures of the CEO and the showman, the innocent is also figured as a subject who has no connection to political worlds, and it is precisely this distance that enables her to become a powerful and meaningful agent of political change. However, in an important difference from the idealized attributes invested in other outsider figures, the innocent outsider does not have a wealth of professional experience and knowledge, nor a unique performance skill. Instead their agency is shaped by the mediatized play of emotions and instincts. They are usually outraged and moved to act by a shocking media revelation. Immediacy, spontaneity, and mediatized visibility are the defining features of her agency.

The figure of the innocent outsider is closely associated with the surge of middle-class activism and media activism in the new millennium. Examples include the multiple media-mobilized *Justice for* campaigns of the mid 2000s we have reviewed in chapter 2, which demanded justice for victims of crimes involving politically connected perpetrators; the Youth For Equality movement of 2006, which agitated against the extension of caste-based reservations in professional educational institutions; and the widespread street protests across many Indian cities that erupted in the aftermath of the infamous Delhi gang rape case of 2012.[51] All these extensively relied upon innocent outsider narratives to legitimize their actions as truly representative of the real people.

The demographic composition of the campaigns, as predominantly young, urban, and middle-class, shored up their claims of political exteriority. As chapter 1 has documented, the India Against Corruption Movement and the new political party that emerged out of it, the Aam Aadmi or Common Man's Party (AAP), foregrounded the youthful innocence of their membership. Along with the impressive technocratic and professional profiles of its leaders and volunteers, its youth profile also distinguished the AAP from the aging cohorts of other political parties. The party highlighted this demographic difference in its (ultimately successful) attempt to convince voters that it presented a meaningful political alternative to establishment political parties.

The Bootstrapper

In the bootstrapper avatar, the political outsider appears as a non-elite individual with a memorable life story of self-made social mobility and an exceptional, against-all-odds ascent to political power. The standard narrative presents a person who is an outsider to the narrow and closed ranks of the Indian (political, social, and cultural) elite, and who rises to a position of great national responsibility and public prominence by their "bootstraps" alone, that is, by relying solely on her own individual merit, effort, and determination. She stands out from the ruling establishment in all kinds of ways, from her attire, accent, habits, and preferences, to the values and vision of the greater public good that she tirelessly works to realize. The bootstrapper's individual life story is frequently hailed as a national metaphor, as proof that a manifestly new India will triumph over the old.

Examples of actual political leaders who are perceived as bootstrappers in the public imagination, in large part because they have actively participated in the crafting of such a self-image, include Mamata Banerjee, current chief minister of West Bengal; Laloo Prasad Yadav, former chief minister of Bihar; and Narendra Modi, current prime minister of India. They are designated—and also style themselves—as simple, "vernacular," and "subaltern" subjects who are outsiders to the cosmopolitan enclaves of Lutyens' Delhi, the fabled seat of elite power in the capital city.[52] Their ascent to political power is presented as an exemplary tale of democratization. In this story, the outsider's trailblazing march through establishment citadels that he replaces with his upstart visions shows the long-excluded people that their time will surely come.

Repurposing Outsider Politics

The political repertoire of the contemporary Modi regime includes all of these variants of outsider politics. Its strongman performances and carefully curated public images showcase one or other outsider avatar: CEO, Film Star, Innocent, Bootstrapper, sometimes in jarring combination. The repurposing of outsider politics is not limited to the visual domain. Although it is overshadowed by the strident flourish of the saffron wave, the theme of curative democracy has featured prominently in the legitimation claims of the BJP government. Its status as a normative touchstone of Indian democracy continues to be affirmed in the age of Hindutva. The discourse of anti-corruption, the familiar diagnosis of democracy's sicknesses, and the corresponding call for urgent remedial interventions by political outsiders featured quite centrally in the electoral campaign of the Modi-led BJP in 2014 that inaugurated the contemporary era of strongman rule. The 2014 campaign in fact foregrounded the call for democratic reform and cure, and made a calculated decision to soft-pedal the party's explicit commitments to its Hindu-first ideology. The latter was communicated in a coded register of dog whistles. For instance, even as he presented a sanitized and salutary public persona as *vikas purush*, man of development, Modi spoke of the dangers of a "pink revolution," code for the allegedly widespread practice of cow slaughter by Muslims.[53]

In a very literal example of repurposed tropes of political cleansing that have a history and context that predates the political time of Hindutva's millennial resurgence, Modi's 2014 campaign centrally featured the theme of anti-corruption. The campaign featured him wielding a broom as he announced the launch of his new Swachh Bharat (Clean India) Mission for a garbage-free India. The metaphorical reference to cleaning up the dirty cultures of Indian politics was not a unique maneuver. The imagery was directly lifted from the Aam Aadmi Party, whose debut electoral campaign two years earlier had featured the broom (and broom-wielding party workers) since it was the official symbol of the party. The point here is not to point out the mimetic plagiarisms of the BJP's political praxis. Rather, it is to draw attention to Hindutva's braided and entangled presence in the field of Indian democratic politics-as-usual, where it draws upon many of the normalized and mainstream themes of Indian democracy to legitimize its rule. In an ironic twist of politics and history, these are often the "good" norms that we are urged to revive, in order to defeat "bad" Hindutva.

Other legitimation idioms drawn from different political and ideological formations, including those of Hindutva, are deployed by the Modi regime in its quest for popular assent and regime stabilization. What results is a curious amalgam shot through with internal contradictions, and which cannot be reduced to a singular political-ideological essence or orientation. It is thus not enough, either as an explanatory or a political move, to focus only on the religious-ethnic supremacism that so obviously marks the incumbent authoritarian populism of our times. Our attention must turn as well to the uneasy fact of the suture, fit, or articulation of Hindutva politics with India's democratic political order. This has institutional, policy, and discursive aspects.[54] For instance, several of the BJP government's initiatives upon assuming office in 2014 have seen the regime exercise its legitimate power "as per rule." The flurry of state appointments on the basis of personal loyalty to Modi and ideological sympathy with the cause of Hindu nationalism, noted earlier in this chapter, is one example of the legally and constitutionally sanctioned terms of Hindutva's advancement within Indian democracy. The existing system of constitutional democracy readily makes available such discretionary powers of executive appointment. As I have argued elsewhere, because of its large electoral majority and the lack of an effective parliamentary opposition, the BJP government has been able to use these powers in an unconstrained way, and has made many more appointments, and done this far more swiftly, than its predecessors.[55]

In other instances, we see the continued deployment of repressive laws and technologies of rule that long predate the BJP government, from colonial-era anti-sedition laws, to the Armed Forces Special Powers Act of the Nehru era, and the "anti-terrorist" Unlawful Activities Prevention Act, which was legislated by a Congress government in the Long 1970s. Their intensified use in present times, and their instrumentalization for explicitly authoritarian purposes and for shoring up the strongman rule of Narendra Modi in particular, is of course unprecedented. Nevertheless, the institutional-legal scaffolding predates the current moment and is linked to other "ideas of India"[56] that otherwise have little in common with Hindu nationalist visions.

To summarize. The making of an "ethnic democracy" may well be the main goal of the BJP government, as Christophe Jaffrelot, a longtime observer of Hindu nationalism, has recently pointed out.[57] But as the repurposing of curative democracy and outsider political repertoires by the incumbent regime shows, the routes run through the ordinary and acceptable terrain of democracy as much as that of ethnic assertion.

DIE LÖSUNG, THE SOLUTION?

In closing, the trail of curative democracy and outsider politics leads me back to the populism-democracy relationship that the book opened with. Several compelling accounts of populism's recent rise have drawn attention to its democratic implications and value. Veering away from the somber assessments of strongman populism, they urge us to take seriously the idea of popular sovereignty and its restoration that is at the heart of the populist appeal. Across the world, the timing of populist movements coincides with the manifest bankruptcy of existing democracies, whether in the form of unresponsive governments that are indifferent to the vast and increasing economic inequalities that sunder their societies; the manifest disconnect between political parties and popular interests; or the inability of ordinary citizens to find avenues of expression within the existing political system. Against this backdrop, the populist promise to inaugurate a new and true democratic order is worth heeding. Although populism's slide into strongman authoritarianism is a frequent occurrence, it is neither necessary nor inevitable. The "royal road" or "mirror" of populism inaugurates democratic openings as well, Ernesto Laclau, Chantal Mouffe, Thea Riofrancos, and a host of others persuasively have argued.[58]

At one level, the Indian example confirms these arguments about the positive and corrective/balancing relationship of populism and democracy. The people emerged as political subject at times of deep democratic malfunction and crisis in the country, whether marked by the growing gap between the popular struggles of a "demand polity" and the institutional responses that the "command polity" made available in the late 1960s, or by the increasing public perception that the existing array of political parties do not represent the interests and identities of millennial citizens. Separated by four decades, popular mobilizations in the name of the *janata* and the *aam aadmi* similarly invested democratic hopes in redemptive visions of political transformation. The political history of post-independence India provides ample empirical evidence for democracy and populism's proximate and twinned connection.

At another level, however, the specific forms in which Indian populism has found expression—the interventions of outsider politics and curative democracy documented in this book—temper our democratic optimism. The intrinsically hierarchical constitution of outsider politics, and the conclusion that the redemptive outsider is invariably a social insider of some kind, have been common themes across all the chapters. The proprietorial claims of AAP supporters inspecting infrastructure projects for Delhi's "lower class" in chapter 1; the coded caste dog whistles of television journalists in chapter 2; the "extra-constitutional authorities" and the procedural commissioners in chapter 3; and the "concern networks" formed by "eminent citizens" in chapter 4 all reflect the distinctive configuration of an ownership democracy where legible political claims are socially specified. Curative democrats and political outsiders come from certain social positions and locations and not others. Contra Rancière, democracy in India is about the rule of *some* bodies.[59]

The distinctive trajectories of India's curative democracy and outsider politics also draw attention to populism's representative claim. This book has shown how, from the Long 1970s to the present, Indian visions of democratic change have been centrally invested in the question of representative leadership. The character, identity, and agency of representatives more than the participation and actions of the represented have been the main pivots of political concern. Curative democracy projects have called for different kinds of leaders; for new institutions to monitor the actions of representatives; for extraordinary and eminent citizens to represent the interests of ordinary people. Brecht's epigraph to this chapter is a satirical extreme of the kinds of intermediated solutions that have been proposed for democracy's cure. The resulting location of populism within the frame and terms of a representational politics—one that is structured around a specifically vertical hierarchy of proprietorial representation, as we have already noted—belies the loud critiques that populism has long mounted against representative democracy. At least in the Indian context studied here, and possibly in others as well, contemporary populist visions of the people bear the pedagogical or instructional imprint of developmental and colonial projects of people-making from earlier eras, and remind us that new political forms are entangled with ones that they set out to replace. Although they are propelled by different political motivations, the twenty-first-century strongman; the millennial "crusader" for new politics; the "nonparty political" outsider and the "extra-constitutional authority" from the Long 1970s; the goddess leader-redeemer who declared an emergency in order to save democracy; the concern networks that mobilized around the wounded people in order to restore democracy after the emergency ended—all collide and glance off each other.

Could it be otherwise? In recent times, a few glimmers of other possibilities have thinned out the strongman's fog, if only briefly. In December 2019, the name of the people and the charge of democratic change were attached to a public occupation in the streets of the Shaheen Bagh neighborhood in Delhi. For three months, a remarkable public gathering of thousands of people, many of them ordinary Muslim women and men, asserted their constitutional rights and identities as Indian citizens and protested the Modi regime's announcement of a controversial new citizenship law, the Citizenship Amendment Act of 2019 (CAA) and an accompanying population register, the National Register of Citizens (NRC). Fulfilling an enduring vision of Hindu nationalist supremacy, the CAA-NRC combination proposed religious criteria for the determination of Indian citizenship that would render the status of Muslims suspect and potentially even stateless.

The anti-CAA-NRC protests were continually evolving mobilizations that inspired supporters and worried the regime with their unpredictable dynamism and their constantly renewed popular energies. New sets of people kept arriving at the protest site from all around Delhi and India through the cold Delhi nights. Over the ensuing weeks and months, diverse activities and protest infrastructures filled the Shaheen Bagh intersection, from passionate impromptu speeches delivered by visitors to rousing protest songs and poetry, public art projects, volunteer libraries, and child care and health care arrangements. After a protracted episode of organized mass violence against Muslims that broke out in early 2020 in Delhi and in which BJP supporters and the Delhi police were directly implicated, the Shaheen Bagh protests continued in a precarious and more tentative register, absent the massive crowds and media attention of earlier months. The protest site was cleared once the Covid pandemic lockdown came into effect in March 2020, by which time media narratives had successfully reframed Shaheen Bagh as a "Muslim uprising," attaching an "anti-national" label on a protest formation whose most visible public icon was the Indian national flag.[60]

Later that year, in November 2020, another public occupation started in the border areas surrounding Delhi. Lasting much longer than Shaheen Bagh and reaping a remarkable political victory, this also opened a path beyond the well-worn terrain of outsider politics and curative democracy. Dubbed the farmer's movement by the media, but involving a wide cross section of agrarian and urban workers who could not be defined by the "farmer" label, large numbers of people launched a sit-in to protest a series of agricultural reform laws that aimed to commercialize and privatize India's agrarian economy (specifically allowing large monopoly corporations to dominate production, exchange, and price determinations for agricultural labor, inputs, and produce).

Lasting almost a year, the protest camps at border sites like Tikri and Singhu were distinctive for their decentralized organization that brought hundreds of thousands of people with myriad political and social interests and identities together under a broad common demand of a total repeal of the farm laws. Intricate arrangements for food, shelter, and warm clothing and blankets for the protesters during the cold winter months, and innovative media platforms such as the *Trolley Times*, a newspaper printed and circulated at the protest site, sustained the protests and ensured their physical and also narrative survival within the otherwise regime-friendly circuits of mainstream media. In a remarkable display of political resolve and patience, the Tikri-Singhu camps continued for almost a year. The protests culminated in an unprecedented political victory when the government backed down in November 2021. Modi publicly apologized for the legislative missteps, and the laws were withdrawn. Like in Shaheen Bagh, the farm protest camp sites soon emptied out and returned to their mundane everyday status as nondescript thoroughfares once again.[61]

Both the Shaheen Bagh protests of 2019–20 and the farmers' protests of 2020–21 replayed the familiar dramaturgy of the people rising up against the system to reclaim their constitution and assert their place in the nation. However, there were three distinctive aspects that stood them apart from the populist repertoires of outsider politics and curative democracy traced in these pages. First, the hierarchical and tutelary logic of representative "on-behalf-of" leadership that has shaped assertions of people power in India was conspicuously absent from both protest scenes. The calls for reclaiming the constitution and the assertion of citizenship rights in Shaheen Bagh, and the demand for repealing the farm laws voiced at the Tikri and Singhu camps, were embodied, fully presenced acts of particular bodies that spoke for and as themselves. The demands were at once deeply personal and individual—the stakes of their own individual survival had brought most protesters to Shaheen Bagh, Tikri, and Singhu—and open, partial, and unrestricted/nonexclusive. In a semantic emphasis that invites further reflection, both sets of protests used metaphors of "joining in" and "coming to" an ongoing, larger, and open-ended process rather than those of ownership, control, and recuperation of a putatively lost political order.

Second, unlike either the curative democratic initiatives of AAP workers and television journalists, where ordinary citizens are exhorted to rise up and cleanse Indian democracy, or the redemptive narratives of outsider agency that were advanced during, before, and after the emergency, the protest imaginaries of Shaheen Bagh and Tikri-Singhu veered away from the political/nonpolitical distinction. The people were identified and called up not in terms of their political purity and exteriority, nor their victimhood and innocence. Instead, the continually evolving character of organized but decentralized formation presented the people as so many discordant and incomplete presences, demands, and ideas that could not be stabilized around a single political ideology, identity, or individual leader.

A final point of contrast was provided by the extended temporal arc of the protests and the quality of political patience that they conveyed. Where the call for immediate action and a sense of urgent crisis fuels the outrage politics helmed by political outsiders, the demands of farmers and citizens drew upon a politics of waiting and expectation. The mobilizing powers of the protests derived in fact from the extended rhythms and elastic intervals of political change that allowed newer bodies to keep joining in and remaking the people in different configurations. Muslim women, children, artists, citizens, farmers, Dalits, Jats, *maulvis*, professors, comedians, they, us, I.

Are these alternative ways of making the people politically sustainable? What difference do they make, and do they constitute alternatives at all (many believe otherwise)? Inviting further attention, these questions push us to consider democratic change that is neither restoration nor cure; to imagine democratic futures decoupled from the political outsider.

NOTES

Introduction

1. See Judith Butler, *Notes Toward a Performative Theory of Assembly* (Cambridge, MA: Harvard University Press, 2018).

2. Portions of this section are drawn from Paula Chakravartty and Srirupa Roy, "Mediated Populisms: InterAsian Lineages—Introduction," *International Journal of Communication* 11 (2017), https://ijoc.org/index.php/ijoc/article/view/6703.

3. A small sample would include works such as Hans-Georg Betz, *Radical Right-Wing Populism in Western Europe* (New York: Palgrave Macmillan, 1994); Rogers Brubaker, "Populism and Nationalism," *Nations and Nationalism* 26, no. 1(2020): 44–66; Partha Chatterjee, *I Am the People: Reflections on Popular Sovereignty Today* (New York: Columbia University Press, 2019); Jason Frank, "Populism Isn't the Problem," *Boston Review*, August 15, 2018, https://bostonreview.net/articles/jason-frank-populism-not-the-problem/; Ghita Ionescu and Ernest Gellner, eds., *Populism: Its Meaning and National Characteristics* (New York: Macmillan, 1969); Michael Kazin, *The Populist Persuasion: An American History*, rev. ed. (Ithaca, NY: Cornell University Press, 1998); Ernesto Laclau, *On Populist Reason* (London: Verso, 2006); William Mazzarella, "The Anthropology of Populism: Beyond the Liberal Settlement," *Annual Review of Anthropology* 48 (2019): 45–60; Benjamin Moffitt, *The Global Rise of Populism: Performance, Political Style, and Representation* (Stanford, CA: Stanford University Press, 2016); Chantal Mouffe, *For a Left Populism* (London: Verso, 2018); Cas Mudde, "The Populist Zeitgeist," *Government and Opposition* 39, no. 4 (2014): 541–63; Cas Mudde and Cristóbal Rovira Kaltwasser, *Populism: A Very Short Introduction* (New York: Oxford University Press, 2017); Cas Mudde and Cristóbal Rovira Kaltwasser, "Studying Populism in Comparative Perspective: Reflections on the Contemporary and Future Research Agenda," *Comparative Political Studies* 51, no. 13 (2018): 1667–93; Jan-Werner Müller, *What Is Populism?* (Philadelphia: University of Pennsylvania Press, 2016); Francisco Panizza, ed., *Populism and the Mirror of Democracy* (London: Verso, 2006); Margaret Canovan, *Populism* (New York: Harcourt Brace Jovanovich, 1981); Pierre Rosanvallon, *The Populist Century: History, Theory, Critique* (Cambridge: Polity Press, 2021); Yannis Stavrakakis et al., "Populism, Anti-populism, and Crisis," *Contemporary Political Theory* 17 (2018): 4–27; Paul Taggart, *Populism: Concepts in the Social Sciences* (Philadelphia: Open University Press, 2000); Nadia Urbinati, "Political Theory of Populism," *Annual Review of Political Science* 22, no. 6 (2019): 111–27.

4. See, for instance, Pankaj Mishra, *Age of Anger: A History of the Present* (New York: Macmillan, 2017).

5. Within the field of media studies, this has been a primary area of focus with a disproportionate emphasis on the volume of media coverage of populist leaders like Donald Trump. See Claudia Alvares and Peter Dahlgren, "Populism, Extremism and Media: Mapping an Uncertain Terrain," *European Journal of Communication* 31, no. 1 (2016): 46–57; Julia Azari, "How the News Media Helped to Nominate Trump," *Political Communication* 33, no. 4 (2016): 677–80; Yochai Benkler et al., "Study: Breitbart-led Right-wing Media Ecosystem Altered Broader Media Agenda," *Columbia Journalism Review* 4, no. 1 (2017), https://www.cjr.org/analysis/breitbart-media-trump-harvard-study.php; Jacob Groshek, "Helping Populism Win? Social Media Use, Filter Bubbles, and Support for Populist Presidential Candidates in the 2016 US Election Campaign," *Information, Communication & Society* 20, no. 9 (2017): 1389–1407; Issie Lapowski, "Donald Trump Supporters Are More Susceptible to Clickbait," *Wired*, October 31, 2015, https://www.wired.com/2015/10/donald-trump-supporters-are-more-susceptible-to-clickbait/; Pippa Norris, "Why Populism Is a Threat to Electoral Integrity," *LSE European Politics and Policy (EUROPP) Blog*, 2017, http://blogs.lse.ac.uk/europpblog/2017/05/16/why-populism-is-a-threat-to-elector al-integrity/; Brian Ott, "The Age of Twitter: Donald J. Trump and the Politics of Debasement," *Critical Studies in Media Communication* 34, no. 1 (2017): 59–68.

6. For example, neither Pankaj Mishra's popular take on the angry working-class voters in the UK and the US nor sociologist Arlie Hochschild's account of southern Tea Party supporters marshals much empirical evidence about the concrete institutional mechanisms that translate or convert anger over economic exclusion into electoral support for populist political movements and parties driven by racism and xenophobia. Arlie Hochschild, *Strangers in Their Own Land: Anger and Mourning on the American Right* (New York: New Press, 2016). On the concept of the "low information voter" see Richard Fording and Sanford Schram, "The Cognitive and Emotional Sources of Trump Support: The Case of Low-Information Voters," *New Political Science* 39, no. 4 (2017): 670–86.

7. Matt Wilde, "Populism, Right and Left," *Public Books*, 2017, https://www.publicbooks.org/populism-right-and-left/.

8. See Mudde, "The Populist Zeitgeist."

9. Albert Hirschman, *Exit, Voice, and Loyalty: Responses to Decline in Firms, Organizations, and States* (Cambridge, MA: Harvard University Press, 1970), 1.

10. Using the example of Alexis de Tocqueville's comparative sociology of democracy (in France and in America), Sudipta Kaviraj distinguishes between Tocquevillean "sociologically consequent" modes of analysis that focus on the effects of democracy over extended periods of time, and "causal" analyses that are concerned with the rise of democracy. See Sudipta Kaviraj, "The Empire of Democracy," in *Anxieties of Democracy: Tocquevillean Reflections on India and the United States*, ed. Partha Chatterjee and Ira Katznelson (New York: Oxford University Press, 2012), 20–49, 22.

11. I have analyzed in detail these nation-building initiatives, and the distinctive imagination of a nation-statist identity that emerged out of Nehruvian nation-building, in earlier work. See Srirupa Roy, *Beyond Belief: India and the Politics of Postcolonial Nationalism*. (Durham, NC: Duke University Press, 2007).

12. On India's unique "simultaneous" transition to democracy, in contrast to the sequential pathways of democratization in Europe and the United States, see Kaviraj, "The Empire of Democracy."

13. Indian Constituent Assembly Debates XI, November 25, 1949, https://indiankanoon.org/doc/792941/.

14. The concept of the "Congress system" was contemporaneously theorized by the political scientist Rajni Kothari. See Rajni Kothari, "The Congress System in India," *Asian Survey* 4, no. 12 (1964): 1161–73. On the pacted or negotiated character of power in Nehruvian India, see Pranab Bardhan, *The Political Economy of Development in India* (Oxford: Basil Blackwell, 1984); Francine Frankel, *India's Political Economy: The Gradual Revolution*, 2nd ed. (New York: Oxford University Press, 2006); Susanne Hoeber Rudolph and Lloyd Rudolph, *In Pursuit of Lakshmi: The Political Economy of the Indian State* (Chicago: University of Chicago Press, 1987).

15. A perceptive analysis of this period is available in Sudipta Kaviraj, "Indira Gandhi and Indian Politics," *Economic and Political Weekly* 21, no. 38–39 (1986): 1697–1708.

16. On the economic imaginary of India in the colonial and postcolonial periods, see, respectively, Manu Goswami, *Producing India: From Colonial Economy to National Space* (Chicago: University of Chicago Press, 2004), and Satish Deshpande, "Imagined Economies: Styles of Nation-Building in Twentieth Century India," *Journal of Arts and Ideas* 24, no. 5 (1993): 5–35.

17. Hindi commercial cinema from the Long 1970s is a rich repository of this discursive and affective style. The stock figure of the smuggler-villain, and the "angry young man" vigilante hero who transgressed institutional and legal boundaries in the name of popular redemption, proliferated across the films of this period, diffusing the themes, fears, and fantasies of outsider politics and curative democracy through the everyday worlds of public culture. For a close discussion of these tropes in the cinema of the time, and their subsequent mutation, see Ranjani Mazumdar, *Bombay Cinema: An Archive of the City* (Minneapolis: University of Minnesota Press, 2007).

18. On the condemnations of "dirty politics" in India, and the normative distinction between the political and the nonpolitical, see among others Thomas Blom Hansen, *The Saffron Wave: Democracy and Hindu Nationalism in Modern India* (Princeton, NJ: Princeton University Press, 1999), and Prathama Banerjee, *Elementary Aspects of the Political: Histories from the Global South* (Durham, NC: Duke University Press, 2020).

19. For a rich and nuanced account of the role that renunciatory and sacrificial themes (and the difference between them) play in the "political theology of Indian democracy," see Thomas Blom Hansen, *The Law of Force: The Violent Heart of Indian Politics* (Delhi: Aleph Books, 2021), especially chapter 3.

20. On the political economic transformations of this period, see Stanley Kochanek, *Business and Politics in India* (Berkeley: University of California Press, 1974); Atul Kohli, *India's Democracy: An Analysis of Changing State-Society Relations*, rev. ed. (Princeton, NJ: Princeton University Press, 1990); Atul Kohli, *Democracy and Discontent: India's Growing Crisis of Governability* (Cambridge: Cambridge University Press, 1991); Rudolph and Rudolph, *In Pursuit of Lakshmi*.

21. On the Navnirman and JP movements, see Christophe Jaffrelot and Pratinav Anil, *India's First Dictatorship: The Emergency, 1975–77* (New Delhi: Oxford University Press, 2021); Dawn Jones and Rodney Jones, "Urban Upheaval in India: The 1974 Nav Nirman Riots in Gujarat," *Asian Survey* 16, no. 11 (1976): 1012–33; Ghanshyam Shah, *Protest Movements in Two Indian States* (Delhi: Ajanta, 1977); John Wood,

"Extra-Parliamentary Opposition in India: An Analysis of Populist Agitations in Gujarat and Bihar," *Pacific Affairs* 48, no. 3 (1975): 313–34.

22. There is a large literature on the emergency, from both academic and political perspectives, including a substantial genre of autobiographical accounts of what it was like to live through this period. For comprehensive and innovative accounts that include useful against-the-grain appraisals of existing scholarship and present hitherto unknown and unpublished primary material that sheds new light on the emergency, see Jaffrelot and Anil, *India's First Dictatorship* and Gyan Prakash, *Emergency Chronicles: Indira Gandhi and Democracy's Turning Point* (Princeton, NJ: Princeton University Press, 2019). See also Arvind Rajagopal, "The Emergency as Prehistory of the New Indian Middle Class," *Modern Asian Studies* 45, no. 5 (2011): 1003–49, and Emma Tarlo, *Unsettling Memories: Narratives of the Emergency in Delhi* (Berkeley: University of California Press, 2003).

23. This can cut both ways. On the one hand, transparency reforms have made it more difficult for ration shop owners to divert supplies to the open market by monitoring stocks and daily sales practices. On the other hand, the biometric and surveillance technologies have exclusionary effects. They can burden ordinary citizens who are marginalized on grounds of education, caste, class, and gender, and can increase their dependence on new sets of intermediaries and brokers. On the ambivalent power relations of transparency reforms, see Guillaume Dandurand, "The Techno-Politics of Food Security in New Delhi: The Re-Materialization of the Ration Card" (PhD diss., York University, 2018); Rob Jenkins and Anne-Marie Goetz, "Accounts and Accountability: Theoretical Implications of the Right-to-Information Movement in India," *Third World Quarterly* 20, no. 3 (1999): 603–22; Ursula Rao and Vijayanka Nair, eds., "Special Section: Aadhaar: Governing India With Biometrics." *South Asia* 42, no. 3 (2019): 469–81.

24. See NDTV, "Arvind Kejriwal Launches 'Bijli Paani Satyagraha' in Delhi," October 6, 2012, https://www.ndtv.com/india-news/arvind-kejriwal-launches-bijli-paani-satyagraha-in-delhi-501078.

25. For an analysis of the demonetization policy as an "eventocratic" performance, see Rohan Kalyan, "Eventocracy: Media and Politics in Times of Aspirational Fascism," *Theory & Event* 23, no. 1 (2020): 4–28. I discuss demonetization in relation to Modi's strongman politics in chapter 5.

26. On the strong presence of electoralist tropes in discourses of Indian democracy see Mukulika Banerjee, *Why India Votes* (New York and London: Routledge, 2014), and David Gilmartin, "Towards a Global History of Voting: Sovereignty, the Diffusion of Ideas, and the Enchanted Individual," *Religions* 3, no. 2 (2012): 407–23. While Banerjee gives us a celebratory account of Indian elections that emphasizes the democratizing experiences of voting, Thomas Hansen offers a sobering counter that draws attention to how electoral majorities constitute and express the "violent heart of Indian politics," seeing in elections not so much democratic inclusion as the constitution of permanent majoritarian power. See Hansen, *The Law of Force*.

27. W. H. Morris Jones, *The Government and Politics of India.*, 2nd ed. (London: Hutchinson University Library, 1967).

28. For a comprehensive account of the braided logics of capitalism and democracy that define the "new India," and the powerful role of corporate capital in setting national

agendas, see Ravinder Kaur, *Brand New Nation: Capitalist Dreams and Nationalist Designs in Twenty-First-Century India* (Stanford, CA: Stanford University Press, 2020). For a discussion of the broader global logics of a "pro-poor capitalism" that exert influence well beyond India, see among others Anand Girihardas, *Winners Take All: The Elite Charade of Changing the World* (New York: Knopf, 2018); Ananya Roy, *Poverty Capital: Microfinance and the Making of Development* (New York and London: Routledge, 2010).

29. See John Keane, *Power and Humility: The Future of Monitory Democracy* (Cambridge: Cambridge University Press, 2018); Sonia Alonso et al., eds., *The Future of Representative Democracy* (Cambridge: Cambridge University Press, 2012).

30. Amrita Basu, *Violent Conjunctures in Democratic India* (Cambridge: Cambridge University Press, 2015); Angana Chatterji et al., eds., *Majoritarian State: How Hindu Nationalism Is Changing India* (New York: Oxford University Press, 2019); Thomas Blom Hansen and Srirupa Roy, eds., *Saffron Republic: Hindu Nationalism and State Power in India* (Cambridge: Cambridge University Press, 2022); Christophe Jaffrelot, *Modi's India: Hindu Nationalism and the Rise of Ethnic Democracy* (Princeton, NJ: Princeton University Press, 2021).

31. James Ferguson, *The Anti-Politics Machine: Development, Depoliticization, and Bureaucratic Power in Lesotho* (Minneapolis: University of Minnesota Press, 1994).

32. Cited in Ferguson, *The Anti-Politics Machine*, 255.

33. See Wendy Brown, *In the Ruins of Neoliberalism: The Rise of Antidemocratic Politics in the West* (New York: Columbia University Press, 2019); Colin Crouch, *Post-Democracy: A Sociological Introduction* (Cambridge: Polity Press, 2014); Eric Swyngedouw, "Where Is the Political? Insurgent Mobilizations and the Incipient Return of the Political," *Space and Polity* 18, no. 2 (2014): 122–36.

34. See Peter Burnham, "New Labour and the Politics of Depoliticisation," *British Journal of Politics and International Relations* 3, no. 2 (2001): 127–49; Matthew Flinders and Jim Buller, "Depoliticisation: Principles, Tactics, and Tools," *British Politics* 1 (2006): 293–318; Colin Hay, *Why We Hate Politics* (Cambridge: Polity Press, 2007).

35. Corey Robin, *Fear: The History of a Political Idea* (New York: Oxford University Press, 2006), and Corey Robin, *The Reactionary Mind* (New York: Oxford University Press, 2011).

36. Jacques Rancière, *Hatred of Democracy*, trans. Steve Corcoran (London: Verso, 2006), 46–47.

37. See Chantal Mouffe, ed., *The Challenge of Carl Schmitt* (London: Verso, 1999), especially the chapter by Slavoj Zizek, "Carl Schmitt in the Age of Post-Politics," 18–37.

38. Swyngedouw, "Where Is the Political?"

39. See, for instance, the well-known lament by Robert Putnam on the decline of civic associational life in the United States. Robert Putnam, *Bowling Alone: The Collapse and Revival of American Community* (New York: Simon & Schuster, 2000).

40. Jonathan Dean, "Tales of the Apolitical," *Political Studies* 62 (2014): 452–67.

41. György Konrád, *Antipolitics: An Essay* (New York: Harcourt, 1984).

42. David Marcus, "Memory as Homeland," *Dissent* 230 (2008): 120–24, 123.

43. Václav Havel, *The Power of the Powerless* (New York: Vintage Classics, 2018).

44. Gil Eyal, "Anti-Politics and the Spirit of Capitalism: Dissidents, Monetarists and the Czech Transition to Capitalism," *Theory and Society* 29, no. 1 (2000): 49–92.

45. Suzanne Berger, "Politics and Antipolitics in Western Europe in the Seventies," *Daedalus* 108, no.1 (1979): 27–50, 30.

46. Originally a research institution in Delhi with close ties to the Congress government and Indira Gandhi herself, CSDS intellectuals reversed their allegiances during the 1970s and especially during the emergency to come out in strong support of JP Narayan, the iconic leader of anti-Congress protest movements and subsequently of emergency resistance. In the late 1970s, researchers at the CSDS sharpened their intellectual focus on the idea of an indigenously rooted or vernacular modern. Developing wide-ranging critiques of top-down statist models of developmental modernity—both state capitalist and state socialist variants were targets of sustained critique—and the instrumental and power-serving calculations of party politics, founder Rajni Kothari and his colleagues advocated for a new and moral political order structured around "non-party political formations" and "people's movements" that were organically embedded in and directly accountable to local contexts and communities. Explicitly eschewing models of revolutionary resistance, academics, activists and the state were envisioned as partners in a new moral project of democratic renewal and expansion. Along with *Seminar* magazine core intellectuals Romesh and Raj Thapar, CSDS scholars played a leading role in developing a manifesto for the Janata party ("An Agenda for India"), where their idea of a non-party political formation committed to a new, grassroots process of democratization and development was elaborated and explained to wider political and public constituencies. See Daniel Kent-Carrasco, "A Battle Over Meanings: Jayaprakash Narayan, Rammanohar Lohia, and the Trajectories of Socialism in Early Independent India," *Global Intellectual History* 2, no.3 (2017): 370–88; Rajni Kothari, "The Non-Party Political Process," *Economic and Political Weekly* 19, no. 5 (1984): 216–24; Rajni Kothari, *Memoirs: Uneasy Is the Life of the Mind* (Delhi: Rupa, 2002); Aditya Nigam, "The Non-Party Domain in Contemporary India," unpublished paper prepared for the project on State of Democracy in South Asia report, Lokniti; Srirupa Roy, "The Death of the Third World Revisited: Curative Democracy and World-Making in Late 1970s India," in *Inventing the Third World: In Search of Freedom for the Postwar Global South*, ed. Jeremy Adelman and Gyan Prakash (London: Bloomsbury, 2023), 239–60; Harsh Sethi, "The Immoral 'Other': Debate between Party and Non-Party Groups," *Economic and Political Weekly* 20, no. 9 (1985): 378–80, and the fiftieth-anniversary commemorative reflections on the history of CSDS that were published in *Seminar* magazine (vol. 639, 2012) and on the CSDS website (http://www.csds.in).

47. See Pierre Rosanvallon, *Counter-Democracy: Politics in an Age of Distrust* (Cambridge: Cambridge University Press, 2008).

48. See Alonso et al., eds., *The Future of Representative Democracy*; Keane, *Power and Humility*; Rosanvallon, *Counter-Democracy*.

49. Dean, "Tales of the Apolitical," 459.

Chapter One

1. Portions of this chapter were previously published in an earlier essay. See Srirupa Roy, "Being the Change: The Aam Aadmi Party and the Politics of the Extraordinary in Indian Democracy," *Economic and Political Weekly* 49, no. 15 (2014): 45–54.

2. In a bit of clever wordplay, the acronym *AAP* means "you" in Hindi.

3. Delhi is the national capital and also a state in the Indian federation with its own legislative assembly. It has limited federal autonomy; unlike other Indian states the Delhi government does not control law and order, a federal design feature that is fiercely contested by incumbent state governments, especially when they are formed by political parties that are not in power at the central level.

4. There is a large body of scholarship on anti-establishment or anti-party parties like AAP, but it is focused mostly on Europe. See, for instance, Amir Abedi, *Anti-Political Establishment Parties* (London: Psychology Press, 2004); Gissur Erlingsson and Mikael Persson, "The Swedish Pirate Party and the 2009 European Parliament Elections," *Politics* 31, no. 3 (2011): 121–28; Thomas Poguntke and Susan Scarrow, "The Politics of Anti-Party Sentiment," *European Journal of Political Research* 29, no. 3 (1996): 257–62; Andreas Schedler, "Anti-Political-Establishment Parties," *Party Politics* 2, no. 3 (1996): 291–312; Allan Sikk, "Newness as a Winning Formula for New Political Parties," *Party Politics* 18, no. 4 (2012): 465–86; Paul Taggart, "New Populist Parties in Western Europe," *West European Politics* 18, no. 1 (1995): 34–51.

5. On Kejriwal's career, see among others Anuradha Sharma, "New Brooms and Old: Sweeping Up Corruption in India, One Law at a Time," *Current Anthropology* 59, no. S18 (2018): S72–S82. Pran Kurup, *Arvind Kejriwal and the Aam Aadmi Party: An Inside Look* (Delhi: Bloomsbury India, 2016); Samanth Subramanian, "The Agitator," *New Yorker* (August 26, 2013).

6. https://www.youtube.com/watch?v=1m_XCPVGlSo.

7. The unusual scene of an incumbent chief minister undertaking a public *dharna* (sit-in protest) was widely covered by the media. But the images of the chief minister huddled in blankets sleeping on the street did not circulate for very long. Kejriwal ended his strike after one night, claiming victory after dialogues with the central government yielded an agreement on the suspension of a few police officers and a promise to work on police reform measures in the near future. See NDTV, January 21, 2014, "Arvind Kejriwal, on Dharna Against the Police, Spends Night on the Road," https://www.ndtv.com/photos/news/arvind-kejriwal-on-dharna-against-police-spends-night-on-the-road-16978.

8. See, for instance, Aastha Chauhan, "Somnath Bharti and the Terrible, Everyday Racism of a South Delhi Mohalla," *Kafila* (2014), https://kafila.online/2014/01/21/somnath-bharti-and-the-terrible-everyday-racism-of-a-south-delhi-mohalla-aastha-chauhan/. There were critics within the party as well, although the disagreements were not made public. Despite AAP's official defense of the action, in internal discussions several leaders conveyed their displeasure to Bharti and his team in no uncertain terms. Interview with Bharti's former campaign manager Pawan Kumar, Malviya Nagar, March 5, 2015.

9. As anthropologist Bani Gill has noted in her ethnographic research on African migrants in Delhi, the "shadow of illegality" falls on anyone who "looks African" in the city. Their everyday lives, the constraints that they navigate daily, as well as the horizons of expectations that they strive toward, are textured and molded by this presumption of their unauthorized status. As Gill has astutely noted, this is not just a legal-juridical presumption but equally a moral and ethical judgment that constitutes the African migrant as a monstrous and nonhuman figure of fear, loathing, and absolute difference. See Bani Gill, "In the Shadow of Illegality: The Everyday Lives of African Migrants in Delhi" (PhD diss., University of Copenhagen, 2019); Chauhan, "Somnath Bharti"; Gabriel

Dattatreyan, *The Globally Familiar: Digital Hip Hop, Masculinity, and Urban Culture in Delhi*. (Durham, NC: Duke University Press, 2020).

10. The research on Shazia Ilmi's election campaign in the RK Puram constituency in 2013 was conducted in collaboration with Lalit Vachani, who was making a documentary film on the AAP's electoral debut. See Lalit Vachani, *An Ordinary Election* (Wide Eye Film, 2015), https://lalitvachani.com/film09.html.

11. In Hazare's home state of Maharashtra, "Anna" is an honorific for elder brother.

12. Aheli Chowdhury's dissertation on the politics of the anti-corruption movement documents how Hazare was strategically selected by Kejriwal and his colleagues to be the "public face" of the anti-corruption agitation. Her interviews with key organizers of the movement reveal a hardheaded calculation about the choice of Hazare. In these recollections, he is a literal mouthpiece/figurehead of the movement. Although the specific terms are not used by Chowdhury's informants, it is clear that the selection of Hazare is based on his public appeal as the quintessential political outsider who embodied all the norms of curative democracy. See Aheli Chowdhury, "Social Movements Post 1990s in India: A Sociological Analysis of Changing Modes of Political Mobilisation" (PhD diss., University of Delhi, 2017), especially chapter 5.

13. The specific demand was for civil society participation in drafting the Jan Lokpal Bill, a piece of pending parliamentary legislation for the creation of a national ombuds authority to monitor and punish corrupt (and derelict) government officials. For a discussion of the ambivalent politics of Hazare's movement, see Partha Chatterjee, "Against Corruption=Against Politics," *Kafila* (2011), https://kafila.online/2011/08/28/against-corruption-against-politics-partha-chatterjee/; Nivedita Menon and Aditya Nigam, "If Only There Were No People Democracy Would Be Fine," *Kafila* (2011), https://kafila.online/2011/08/22/if-only-there-were-no-people-democracy-would-be-fine/; Roy, "Being the Change"; Aradhana Sharma, "Finding Women Among Common Men," *Kafila* (2012), https://kafila.online/2012/12/12/finding-women-among-common-men-aradhana-sharma/; Mukul Sharma, *Green and Saffron: Hindu Nationalism and Environmental Politics* (Delhi: Orient Blackswan, 2011); Vinay Sitapati, "What Anna Hazare's Movement and India's New Middle Classes Say About Each Other," *Economic and Political Weekly* 46, no. 3 (2012): 39–44.

14. This was a motley crew with diverse ideological affiliations, and included active adherents of Hindu nationalist causes. The involvement of volunteers from the Hindu paramilitary organization Rashtriya Swayamsevak Sangh (RSS, National Volunteer Corps) attracted critical attention at the time, calling into question the IAC's self-description as a nonpartisan movement. On the IAC's diverse constituencies, see Sitapati, "Anna Hazare's Movement." On the organizational role that the right-wing Hindutva think tank, the Vivekananda International Foundation, and the "godman" Baba Ramdev are alleged to have played, see Manoj CG, "At Centre of Stirs Against Graft, a Body with RSS Links, Ex-Babus," *Indian Express* (August 20, 2012), http://archive.indianexpress.com/news/at-centre-of-stirs-against-graft-a-body-with-rss-links-exbabus/990502/.

15. After a long and intensive period of popular/mass mobilization and governmental lobbying by social movements and civil society groups from the early 1990s onward, India's landmark Right to Information act (popularly known by its acronym, RTI) was

promulgated by parliament in 2005. The Indian version of the "sunshine legislation" promised governmental transparency and accountability by giving citizens the right to demand copies of governmental records on all matters except those classified for national security, and to receive these within a specified time period or else receive a written explanation about their nondelivery. On the RTI movement, see Chowdhury, "Social Movements Post 1990s in India"; Amita Baviskar, "Winning the Right to Information in India: Is Knowledge Power?" in *Citizen Action and National Policy Reform*, ed. John Gaventa and Rosemary McGee (London: Zed Books, 2010), 130–46; Jenkins and Goetz, "Accounts and Accountability"; Prashant Sharma, *Democracy and Transparency in the Indian State: The Making of the Right to Information Act* (London and New York: Routledge, 2015).

16. For a discussion of historical-conceptual genealogies of antipolitical transcendence in India, see Hansen, *The Saffron Wave*; Srirupa Roy, "The Political Outsider," in *The People of India: New Indian Politics in the Twenty-First Century*, ed. Ravinder Kaur and Nayanika Mathur (Delhi: Penguin Viking, 2022), 66–87.

17. See, for example, Chatterjee, "Against Corruption"; Suhas Palshikar, "Of Radical Democracy and Anti-Partyism," *Economic and Political Weekly* 48, no. 10 (2013): 10–13.

18. Yogendra Yadav interviewed by Ajaz Ashraf, December 24, 2013, https://www.oneindia.com/india/delhis-politics-is-much-more-class-politics-than-caste-yogendra-yadav-1364049.html.

19. Prashant Bhushan, Google Hangouts session with AAP supporters, November 16, 2013.

20. The *jhadu* or broom was a multivalent symbol that communicated different meanings, such as the campaign theme of political cleansing and the idea of the ordinary (the broom as a familiar household object recognized across the spectrum of social classes). There were tacit associations with Dalit identity as well, and the party's decision to begin its inaugural campaign with a public event at a Dalit (Valmiki) neighborhood, where party leaders carried brooms, amplified this meaning. See Gopal Guru, "Two Conceptions of Morality: A Political Reading," *Economic and Political Weekly* 49, no. 17 (2014): 112–17.

21. In his public appearances, Kejriwal usually wore open-toed slippers (*chappals*), a short-sleeved "bush shirt" with a couple of pens in the front pocket, and a scarf or "muffler" in the winter that earned him the moniker Mufflerman on social media (subsequently repurposed by the AAP in its own campaign publicity). All of these are sartorial choices that signify middle-class identity (specifically, middle-class respectability) to Indian audiences. See Subramaniam, "The Agitator."

22. The Wagon R, built by the Maruti Suzuki automobile company, is a five-seater hatchback that is marketed to Indian middle-class consumers as a quintessential middle-class car: affordable, practical, and apparently designed with the normative middle-class family in mind. Videos and photographs of Kejriwal often showed him driving a Wagon R with other AAP leaders inside, an image that was intended to project the leader's ordinariness and "down-to-earth" accessibility, as well as the party's principled avoidance of the trappings of political power. For a close analysis of AAP's symbolic communication practices, and the specific role of objects such as the Wagon R, see

Jyotirmaya Tripathy, "The Broom, the Muffler and the Wagon R: Aam Aadmi Party and the Politics of De-elitisation," *International Quarterly for Asian Studies* 48, nos. 1–2 (2017): 77–95.

23. Field notes, Chhattarpur campaign's Jan Sampark (public interaction) with Kumar Vishwas, MCD Park (60 Foot Road, Chhattarpur), September 5, 2013.

24. Parts of this discussion are captured in Lalit Vachani's *Ordinary Election* documentary film on Shazia Ilmi's election campaign.

25. Conversation with Omendra Bharat, RK Puram campaign office, August 10, 2013. According to Bharat, slum dwellers just have a "habit" or *aadat* to live in *gandagi*. He cited the example of a slum improvement scheme that was undertaken in Mumbai to make his case. According to Bharat, the residents of the demolished slums were given new apartments as compensation, but instead of moving in they rented them out and went to live in another slum.

26. These are also the main emphases of anti-corruption politics and the right-to-information movement. See Baviskar, "Winning the Right to Information in India"; Jenkins and Goetz, "Accounts and Accountability"; Sharma, "New Brooms and Old."

27. Julia Eckert, "Introduction: Subjects of Citizenship," *Citizenship Studies* 15, nos. 3–4 (2011): 309–17, 313.

28. Parivartan soon took up the more general cause of protesting the corruption of government agencies and elected officials, particularly those responsible for ensuring fair distribution and efficient delivery of public goods and services such as electricity, water, and subsidized food ("ration" supplies, as they are called in India). The organization's Ghoos ko Ghoosa, or Drive Against Bribes, campaign was in many ways the precursor to the anti-corruption movement of 2011. Like the Ghoos Ko Ghoosa campaign, the 2011 anti-corruption movement forged alliances between civil society/social movements and mainstream media organizations and involved many of the same individuals in leading positions, Arvind Kejriwal chief among them.

29. Kabir video, interview with Saurabh Sharma and Aheli Chowdhury of Kabir, Delhi, September 18, 2013.

30. Keane, *Power and Humility*.

31. JJ colony is the abbreviated version of *jhuggi-jhopri* colony, or formerly unauthorized urban settlements that have since been regularized (hence "colony"). According to proposed parliamentary legislation, the Slum and Jhuggi Jhopri Areas (Basic Amenities and Clearance) Bill (2015, 2010), a *jhuggi jhopri* is defined as "a small roughly built house or shelter usually made of mud, wood or metal having thatched or tin sheet roof covering."

32. Recall that its chief demand was for the arrogation of authority outside the electoral system: a non-elected group of civil society representatives should play a leading role in drafting legislation for the establishment of another non-elected institutional authority, the Jan Lokpal.

33. Yadav frequently invoked this distinction between "alternative" and "substitution" politics in speeches and media interviews. See, for instance, "AAP Does Not Believe in Any Isms, Says Yogendra Yadav," *Live Mint*, January 13, 2014, https://www.livemint.com/Politics/1bZ8xwxxvBEixvx3DzgcRK/AAP-does-not-believe-in-any-isms-says-Yogendra-Yadav.html.

34. This term peppered speeches by Anand Kumar and Yogendra Yadav at public gatherings organized by AAP's US chapter in Chicago in the summer of 2013.

35. AAP ticket seekers in each constituency had to collect one hundred signatures endorsing their candidacy. They also had to provide contact details for each of the signatures so that they could be verified by the party. The party's political affairs committee then prepared a short list of up to five candidates after soliciting public input through various channels including social media, and conducting independent verification checks into the credentials of each applicant. The basic biographical details of all the short-listed candidates, including details of their income and assets and criminal records, were posted on the AAP website. The final choice was announced following an interview by the selection committee, and a vote on the short list by active volunteers in the constituency. With each carefully thought-out step of this apparently transparent, participatory, and meritorious procedure of candidate selection, the AAP strove to establish its difference and distance from other political parties that distributed tickets on the basis of narrow and instrumental considerations of votebank politics.

36. These include a comprehensive website with details on all aspects of the campaign, from donor lists to socioeconomic profiles of candidates; Facebook pages for each constituency; multiple Twitter streams and hashtags about the party; the availability of downloadable "self-print" party publicity material such as stickers, posters, and so on; AAP TV, a streamed web channel hosted on MyStream; YouTube channels devoted to the party; the use of Google+ (Google Hangouts sessions) to enable interactions with party leaders and candidates, which was particularly popular among non-resident communities. Mobile technologies are used as well, for instance, the practice of automated "robocalling" and bulk SMS (text message) campaigns. The party's use of social media builds upon practices adopted during the earlier anti-corruption effort of 2011, where, much like recent popular mobilizations in other parts of the world such as the Arab Spring or the Gezi Park uprisings in Turkey, observers have noted considerable synergies between online and offline mobilizational practices.

37. Despite this disavowal, the careful cultivation of relationships with mainstream journalists and media owners was a central plank of the party's communication strategy. Party leaders, several of whom were former journalists, were widely perceived by reporters as being readily accessible and "media savvy" or well versed in the ways of delivering camera-friendly sound bites. The party's efforts to rely on new media rapidly became a newsworthy story, and the news of the AAP's "media bypass" proliferated in the very traditional media that it was said to avoid. As several journalists who covered the AAP campaign have since noted, the media cell of the party in the run-up to the 2013 elections served as a very helpful and efficient resource for journalists in search of stories on the campaign trail, and contributed to the generally positive tenor of media coverage of the party's first campaign.

38. Subramanian, "The Agitator."

39. For a sustained engagement with the political implications of "unmarking" and the "general category," see Satish Deshpande, "Caste and Castelessness: Towards a Biography of the 'General Category,'" *Economic and Political Weekly* 48, no. 15 (2013): 32–39.

40. Farmhouses are iconic estates belonging to Delhi's political and economic elites that dot the landscape of Chhattarpur.

41. Pseudonym. At the time that we interviewed him (between July and November 2013), the informant's family did not know about his role as an AAP party worker.

42. Field notes, AAP Chhattarpur office (Ayanagar), September 1, 2013.

43. Its lineages can be directly traced to the mobilizing efforts of the anti-colonial nationalist movement, and to earlier historical and mytho-historical formations as well. See W. H. Morris-Jones, *The Government and Politics of India* (London: Hutchinson, 1964); Hansen, *The Saffron Wave*; Roy, "The Political Outsider."

44. Martin Webb, "Success Stories: Rhetoric, Authenticity, and the Right to Information Movement in India," *Contemporary South Asia* 18, no. 3 (2010): 293–304.

45. Bisht's intervention story focused on page 4 of the voter registration form. We can find the solution to the voters' problem on the very form that is routinely rejected by electoral authorities because address proofs are missing, he explained. Page 4 explicitly states that where documents such as bank papers and utility bills are not available, any envelope addressed to the applicant bearing a canceled stamp as proof of delivery by the Indian postal service will suffice as an acceptable proof of address. Moreover, page 4 also authorizes election officers to make personal visits at least twice to the locations of those who lack even this kind of postal evidence. Election officers must personally make, and document, efforts to visit any individual who submits a form, even if it is a homeless person who lists "under X Flyover" or "next to Y temple" as his address. See Election Commission of India, Voter Registration Form (Form 6), Page 4, Point 8, (II) and (III): explanations of Item (h) about "Place of current ordinary residence."

46. This is related to the "optical turn" in contemporary democracies. As the heightened political salience of media exposés and leaks suggests, sight and the attendant dimensions of visibility and spectatorship are supplanting speech, voice, and deliberation as important modes of democratic expression across the globe. See Jeffrey Green, *The Eyes of the People: Democracy in an Age of Spectatorship* (New York: Oxford University Press, 2009).

47. The party also relied heavily on the practice of the media sting during its first campaign. Hidden-camera investigations or stings were used to document so-called political scams that were disclosed during weekly *pol khol* (exposé or debunking) press conferences organized by the AAP, when journalists would be presented with evidence of various kinds of governmental wrongdoing at a venue and time carefully chosen to coincide with the news-cycle compulsions of print as well as electronic media. While the *pol khol* press conferences were soon discontinued, the sting continued as a key technology. In December 2013, the party introduced a new innovation of "citizen-stings" after forming the Delhi government. Citizens were encouraged to use their smartphones cameras to carry out their own covert filming and submit the evidence by calling a dedicated hotline. Here again the emphasis was on visual evidence that would quite literally capture the alleged crime and criminal on camera. Chapter 2 examines the broader social and political significance of the "sting operation," a prime instrument of the curative democracy project in contemporary India.

48. For an overview of the BJP's "long-distance nationalism" projects, see Christophe Jaffrelot and Ingrid Therwath, "The Sangh Parivar and the Hindu Diaspora in the West: What Kind of Long-Distance Nationalism?" *International Political Sociology* 1, no. 3 (2007): 278–95.

49. On the AAP's NRI supporters and party workers in the United Kingdom, see Martin Webb, "Digital Politics in the Diaspora: U.K. Aam Aadmi Party Supporters Online and Offline," *Television and New Media* 21, no. 4 (2020): 420–33.

50. I borrow this term from Sikk, "Newness as a Winning Formula."

51. The plastic donation jar carried around by party workers on their daily door-to-door campaigns is another example of how the party uses the language and visual props of *chanda* collection or the commonplace practice of soliciting voluntary petty cash household contributions for neighborhood festivities and events (usually of a religious nature), to differentiate AAP from its partisan counterparts.

52. Claims of uniqueness are inaccurate: this is a long-standing practice of Indian communist parties, for whom such visible practices of "mass" funding set them apart from the foreign funding and capitalist dependency that marks bourgeois political parties.

53. Publicity events that were described as "freeze mobs" and "metro waves" offered further opportunities to stage voluntarism and free will. These events involved pairs of AAP volunteers, identified by their AAP *topi* or white Gandhi cap with the slogan *main hoon aam admi* (I am the common man) printed in black, engaging in forms of unusual public action—for example, standing like frozen statues—in crowded urban locations such as metro stations or the central park at Connaught Place. The idea behind these events, as the volunteer Rajesh Singh explained, was to pull supporters "on their own" to the AAP. "We don't approach anyone, *they* approach us, *they* start asking us questions and only then do we reply."

54. Leader of the Congress party Sonia Gandhi's renunciation of the prime ministerial position in 2004 is the latest in a series that goes back to Jawaharlal Nehru's periodic threatened resignation dramas in the 1950s, or Mahatma Gandhi's decision to remain physically far away from the formal political stage at the moment of independence in August 1947.

55. AAP's emphasis on the extraordinary actions of its leaders and activists resonates well with Prathama Banerjee's observations on how the long-standing theme of transcendent sacrifice in Indian political thought reflects and constitutes particular hierarchies of power. See Banerjee, *Elementary Aspects of the Political*.

56. See Lisa Björkman, "You Can't Buy a Vote: Meanings of Money in a Mumbai Election," *American Ethnologist* 41, no. 4 (2014): 617–34; Frederic Schaffer, *The Hidden Costs of Clean Election Reform* (Ithaca, NY: Cornell University Press, 2008).

57. Vachani's documentary depicts this contrast vividly. The action abruptly shifts from campaign meetings in a plush living room in Vasant Vihar to the winding lanes of Bhanwar Singh Camp.

58. The term *colony* is commonly used in India to describe settled residential localities in urban areas. It is used in class-specific ways, such that working-class informal "slum" settlements are not considered "colonies."

59. I use this noun deliberately, as less than 1 percent of the AAP legislators were women (only 6 of the 67 AAP legislators were women).

60. AAP vote share in 2013: 29 percent; 2015: 54 percent; 2020: 54 percent (rounded).

61. Prominent founder-leaders who quit the party include Yogendra Yadav, Prashant Bhushan, Anand Kumar, Shazia Ilmi, Ashutosh, Ashish Khetan, and Meera Sanyal.

Yadav and Bhushan went on to form their own movement, Swaraj Abhiyan, in 2015, and a new political party, Swaraj India, in 2016. In their words, it was an "alternative political vehicle" to realize the goals of anti-corruption and *swaraj* that the AAP had failed to deliver. The implosions and disruptions registered within my own research experience as well. Shortly after my encounters with AAP candidates and party workers Shazia Ilmi and Omendra Bharat during my first research stint in 2013, they left the party and joined the BJP. Munish Raizada, an NRI doctor who had moved to India from Chicago to play an active role in the party's inaugural campaign, was seated in the AAP health ministry office in the Delhi Secretariat building when I visited the government office after the 2015 elections, working as an unofficial consultant-advisor to the new government. However, by the end of November that year, he had parted ways with the party after a very public disagreement wiith the leadership that was amplified on social media channels and websites. Raizada went on to play an active role as a media opponent of AAP, circulating newsletters, emails, and YouTube videos in which he indicted the party for a sweeping range of offenses. On each of my return visits to former research field sites, I met numerous other former informants like Raizada who had quit the party and now described themselves as disgruntled and betrayed ex-volunteers.

62. Many of these events have occurred in Delhi, from the attacks on universities (and the campus uprisings that resulted) in 2016, the citizenship protests in 2019–20, and the so-called "riots" in February 2020, to the global COVID-19 pandemic in which Delhi was the major national hot spot in the deadly second wave of April–May 2021.

63. Interview with Sanjeev Kumar, February 26, 2015.

64. The political consultancy firm I-PAC, headed by Prashant Kishor, was hired by Kejriwal to work on the 2020 elections. This belied the "new politics" claims of AAP, as it resorted to a tactic used by all other political parties: Kishor and I-PAC had in fact worked for AAP's main rivals, the BJP and Congress, in previous elections.

65. See Srirupa Roy, "Target Politics: Digital and Data Technologies and Election Campaigns—A View from India," in *Media and the Constitution of the Political: South Asia and Beyond*, ed. Ravi Vasudevan (Delhi: Sage, 2021), 285–310.

66. Interview with Sanjeev Kumar, February 26, 2015.

67. Ajaz Ashraf, "A Capital Test for Muslim Candidate Defying Votebank Politics," *The Hindu*, October 5, 2013, https://www.thehindu.com/opinion/op-ed/a-capital-test-for-muslim-candidate-defying-vote-bank-politics/article5201866.ece.

68. During the 2020 campaign, Kejriwal repeatedly deployed religious discourse and imagery of the Hindu monkey god Hanuman, and presented himself as a Hanuman *bhakt* (Hanuman devotee), at once distinct from but also aligned with the Hindutva worldview of the BJP. Recall that in Hindu mythology, Hanuman is a devotee of Ram, the mythological figure at the center of Hindu nationalist mobilizations. As the establishment newsmagazine *India Today* noted, "The message was that he was an ardent Hindu, but his politics wasn't a copy of BJP's Hindutva." See Rahul Shrivastava, "Populism Mixed with Soft-Hindutva Makes Arvind Kejriwal a Force to Reckon With," *India Today*, February 12, 2020, https://www.indiatoday.in/elections/delhi-assembly-polls-2020/story/populism-mixed-with-soft-hindutva-makes-arvind-kejriwal-1645626-2020-02-12.

69. The pilgrimage sites were Badrinath, Kedarnath, Puri (Jagannath), Dwaraka, Haridwar, Amarnath, Vaishno Devi, Kashi, Tirupati, Ajmer Shareef, Gaya, Shirdi,

Rameshwaram, Amritsar (Sikh), and Sammed Shikhar (Jain). See Gaurav Bhatnagar, "Kejriwal Government Expands Religious Outreach in Election Year," *The Wire*, July 31, 2019, https://thewire.in/politics/kejriwal-government-expands-religious-outreach-in-election-year.

70. Here the Hindutva affiliations of the AAP's predecessor movement, the IAC, are of significance (see note 14). In recent years, the BJP has instrumentalized these convergences and freely borrowed from the AAP's mobilizational repertoire. For instance, Modi's 2014 electoral campaign prominently featured the broom, a signature theme of the recently concluded AAP campaign in Delhi. The digital campaign strategies of the two parties also closely mirror each other, with the active recruitment of diaspora subjects to mobilize votes an innovation that both parties claim credit for. On the digital politics of the BJP campaigns, see Rohit Chopra, *The Virtual Hindu Rashtra: Saffron Nationalism and New Media* (Delhi: HarperCollins, 2019), and Roy, "Target Politics."

71. Conversely, other parties apparently fielded *anpar netas* (illiterate leaders), as AAP worker Sandeep Bisht dismissively described the Samajwadi Party politician, Azam Khan. Field Notes, Connaught Place, September 16, 2013.

72. Field Notes, Malviya Nagar, September 20, 2013.

73. In Chhattarpur, as in other constituencies, AAP membership was almost exclusively male: we encountered only about a dozen women party workers over the course of three months of daily visits to one or more of the constituencies.

74. In 2006, YFE emerged as an urban social movement to protest the proposed extension of caste-based affirmative action policies in public institutions of professional higher education (medical and engineering universities). On the reproduction and transformation of caste power in and through higher educational institutions, see Satish Deshpande and Usha Zacharias, eds., *Beyond Inclusion: The Practice of Equal Access in Indian Higher Education* (New Delhi: Routledge, 2013); Ajantha Subramanian, *The Caste of Merit: Engineering Education in India* (Cambridge, MA: Harvard University Press, 2019). On YFE politics and mobilizational styles, see Nandini Chandra, "Young Protest: The Idea of Merit in Commercial Hindi Cinema," *Comparative Studies of South Asia, Africa and the Middle East* 30, no. 1 (2010): 119–32.

75. See Webb, "Success Stories."

76. The *mohalla sabha* or neighborhood council process was an initiative of decentralized neighborhood governance introduced by the AAP. Each assembly constituency was to be divided into around forty units comprising around 3,000–6,000 residents each, and invested with decision-making powers over certain budget allocations that concerned immediate and everyday life concerns (for example, street lighting and street repairs, construction of public libraries, "beautification" of parks, etc.) The Delhi Dialogue process was launched in the run-up to the 2015 assembly elections as a participatory "bottom-up" consultation process to engender responsive governance. The idea was for small groups of locally informed party workers to convene neighborhood-level meetings with residents to brainstorm ideas for inclusion in the party manifesto, and get a sense of citizens' priorities and needs. Dialogues were organized around various themes (for example, women's safety, education, health) that channeled discussions along particular expected tracks.

77. Even though the party's official publicity emphasized the public consultations and participatory processes such as Delhi Dialogue, as Stéphanie Lama-Rewal has recently shown, these have worked as spaces of intermediation and pedagogical instruction as much as arenas where "ordinary citizens" could express and exercise their civic agency and identity in any direct or unmediated sense. See Stéphanie Lama-Rewal, "Metropolitan Democracy from Below: Participation and Rescaling in Delhi," *Territory, Politics, Governance* 11, no. 2 (2023): 338–53.

78. See Sagar, "Caste Away: The Aam Aadmi Party's Perpetuation of Upper Caste Politics," *Caravan Magazine* (2019), https://caravanmagazine.in/reportage/aam-admi-party-perpetuation-upper-caste-politics.

79. Pseudonym.

80. He describes his job in very general terms; he "helps businesses to skill."

81. Pseudonym.

82. For instance, Hindu migrant workers from Bihar and Jharkhand can conduct their ritual prayers for the annual Chhath religious festival (widely celebrated in their states) in a specially designated Chhath area by the pond that has been built just for this purpose.

83. Hannah Arendt, *The Human Condition*, 2nd ed. (Chicago: University of Chicago Press, 1998).

84. Hanna Pitkin, *The Attack of the Blob: Hannah Arendt's Concept of the Social* (Chicago: University of Chicago Press, 1998).

85. See Frank Mehring, "All for the Sake of Freedom: Hannah Arendt's Democratic Dissent, Trauma, and American Citizenship," *Journal of Transnational American Studies* 3, no. 2 (2011): 1–32, http://escholarship.org/uc/item/7j88q162; Elisabeth Young-Bruehl, *Hannah Arendt: For Love of the World*, 2nd ed. (New Haven, CT: Yale University Press 2004), especially chapter 5.

86. Young-Bruehl, *Hannah Arendt*, 165.

87. Pitkin, *The Attack of the Blob*, 101.

88. However, attending to the social lineaments of political action does not mean that we endorse the thesis of social determination. To question the ideal of the autonomous political is not to replace it with a model of politics as the predetermined reflection of social relations. Rather, even as they are socially forged, political acts have unanticipated and unlikely effects that exceed both instrumentalist political intention and social determination. For instance, Bharti's midnight raid seeded some unexpected developments and created new openings for social and political transformations that were neither intended nor foreseen. Although the AAP officially defended Bharti, in the aftermath of the Khirki raid several leaders privately conveyed their displeasure to Bharti and his team in no uncertain terms. This pushed Bharti's campaign manager, Pawan Kumar, to take action. Kumar was anxious to redeem the reputation of his constituency within the party, and the reputation of the party to a broader public. So, without Bharti's knowledge, Kumar returned to Khirki in February 2014, this time to "talk to Africans," as he put it to me, to "understand their point, to explain ours."

His visit eventually led to the establishment of an Indo-African *shanti vahini*, a "peace vehicle" or forum where several of the African residents of Khirki communicated their experiences of everyday racism. Over a series of meetings, Khirki residents and AAP volunteers were confronted with uncomfortable accounts of how landlords routinely charge African tenants extortionate rents, cut off water and electricity, and enter their rooms to confiscate laptops and passports if they are more than two days late on rent; how they are pelted by stones and called abusive names by young children as they walk down Khirki's lanes. Some AAP volunteers went on to organize meetings with landlords and resident welfare associations in Khirki, and to create the beginnings of structures of mediation around what were previously impassable problems.

The aftermath of the Khirki raids also created an opening for a new assertion of political agency. Out of another series of conjunctural events and happenstance, a Nigerian migrant named Olamilekan Jason Ojora claimed the role of what he described as the "super-leader of the African community." Following the raids, Ojora became the main interlocutor of the AAP, of the media correspondents who flocked to Khirki to report on stories about African migrants, and of civil society groups like the Khoj International Artists Association. When I met him in 2015, Ojora was leveraging his contacts with Somnath Bharti and the AAP to launch a career as a model in television and internet advertisements and eventually in film. He was also hopeful that his connections to the AAP political leaders would prove beneficial for his church, Christ Consulate, a pentecostal mission serving the expatriate African community in Delhi.

The unexpected twists and turns have continued since then. In 2019, Ojora was arrested at Delhi airport while on his way to a film shoot in Goa, and was charged with overstaying his visa. He was kept in custody at an immigration detention center for several weeks, and eventually deported to Nigeria. I read about his arrest in the newspapers and contacted two researchers who had also interviewed Jason during the course of their research on African migrants in Delhi, Gabriel Dattatreyan and Bani Gill. We were able to get in touch with Jason via Facebook, and kept in touch with him using WhatsApp and other social media while he was in the detention center. We consulted lawyers and NGOs to see if Jason could continue to stay in India, but this did not work out. Jason was eventually deported to Lagos, leaving behind all his possessions and his life in Delhi.

Jason remains in Nigeria at the time of writing (June 2023) and is trying to launch a media and entertainment career there. He positions himself as an "ambassador" to international media worlds, Bollywood and India in particular. He remains in sporadic touch with his AAP contacts, especially Pawan Kumar.

Chapter Two

1. A note of clarification: This chapter has a specific and limited focus on the production worlds, work norms, and professional practices of liberalized media institutions and actors. A more comprehensive consideration must engage with the affective cultures of liberalized media, and examine how media practices engage and refract the subjectivities of media users and audiences. Due to space constraints, and an overarching analytical commitment to the view that ideas, ideologies, and media "messages" can be understood in terms of their material manifestations and pervasiveness rather than through claims about their persuasiveness, I have limited the scope of my inquiry to what liberalized media professionals do, and how they understand and justify the purpose of their work.

For a detailed statement on approaches to ideology "beyond belief," see Roy, *Beyond Belief*, Introduction.

2. There is a voluminous and compelling body of scholarship on "mediatization" as a dominant process of our times, which explores how the distinctive logics of (commercial) media diffuse across and determine other social and political fields. This chapter takes a close look at the terms and contours of these "media logics" and "affordances" that have usually been glossed in market-derived and commercialized terms; for example, mediatization is conflated with the commodification of news and the rise of a populist "consumer citizenship." I argue here that such generalized perspectives overlook the complex political terrain and the diverse political influences that structure liberalized media worlds both in India and elsewhere, and which cannot be reduced to market imperatives alone. On mediatization (and the mediatization-populism relationship in particular) see Frank Esser and Jesper Strömbäck, eds., *Mediatization of Politics: Understanding the Transformation of Western Democracies* (New York: Palgrave Macmillan, 2014); Peter Lunt and Sonia Livingstone, "Is 'Mediatization' the New Paradigm for Our Field? A Commentary on Deacon and Stanyer (2014, 2015) and Hepp, Hjarvard and Lundby," *Media, Culture & Society* 38, no. 3 (2016): 462–70; Gianpetro Mazzoleni, "Towards a 'Videocracy'? Italian Political Communication at a Turning Point," *European Journal of Communication* 10 (1995): 291–319; Robert Samet, *Deadline: Populism and the Press in Venezuela* (Chicago: University of Chicago Press, 2019); Colin Sparks and John Tulloch, eds., *Tabloid Tales: Global Debates Over Media Standards* (Lanham, MD: Rowman & Littlefield, 2000).

3. On neoliberal normative cultures or what we might term "free market moralities," see, among others, Lauren Berlant, *Cruel Optimism* (Durham, NC: Duke University Press, 2011); Luc Boltanski and Eve Chiapello, *The New Spirit of Capitalism* (London: Verso, 2007); Andrea Muehlebach, *The Moral Neoliberal: Welfare and Citizenship in Italy* (Chicago: University of Chicago Press, 2012); Gizem Zencirci, "Affective Politics of Structural Adjustment: 'Cruel Optimism' and Turhan Selçuk's Cartoons in Turkey, 1983–1986," *Journal of Social History* 53, no. 1 (2019): 53–75.

4. For a comprehensive look at the liberal paradigm of media as the fourth estate of democracy, see Michael Schudson, *Why Democracies Need an Unlovable Press* (Boston: Polity Press, 2008).

5. Several Indian television news anchors and journalists have a political celebrity status and command widespread public recognition well beyond their immediate professional circuits. Examples include Prannoy Roy, Ravish Kumar, Rajdeep Sardesai, and Barkha Dutt.

6. I borrow this pithy phrase from Usha Rodrigues and Maya Ranganathan, *Indian News Media: From Observer to Participant* (Delhi: Sage, 2014).

7. The situation changed by around 2008–2009, when the effects of the global financial crisis dried up the advertising revenue streams that had powered media growth, and the availability of new kinds of digital technologies substantially restructured broadcast media production processes and work relations. The size of the television news media workforce also shrank substantially as companies laid off thousands of workers.

8. Drawing upon his Hindu nationalist interlocutors' distinction between factual and emotional truths, Hansen directs attention to the distinctive affective and political

constitution of the latter. See Thomas Blom Hansen, "Babri Masjid and Its Aftermath Changed India Forever," *The Wire*, December 7, 2017, https://thewire.in/communalism/babri-masjid-aftermath-changed-india-forever.

9. This chapter studies the enabling relationship between media and populism through a specific focus on the normative news values that orient the professional worlds of liberalized/commercial news media, and their reproduction and consolidation of the curative democracy and political outsider themes that are central to the populist political imagination. Mediatized populism can of course be approached through other avenues of inquiry as well, and there is a rich and useful body of scholarship on the affective and social "affordances" that media technologies, and digital and social media technologies in particular, offer to populist projects. See, for instance, the collection of essays in Chakravartty and Roy, eds., "Mediated Populisms"; Chowdhury, *Paradoxes of the Popular*; Cody, "Populist Publics"; Paolo Gerbaudo, "Social Media and Populism: An Elective Affinity?" *Media, Culture & Society* 40, no. 5 (2018): 745–53; Moffitt, *The Global Rise of Populism*; Mazzoleni, *Populism and the Media*; Samet, *Deadline*.

10. On the changing social profiles of elected representatives in India across the different levels of the political system, see Christophe Jaffrelot and Sanjay Kumar, eds., *Rise of the Plebeians? The Changing Face of the Indian Legislative Assemblies* (New York and London: Routledge, 2009); Christophe Jaffrelot and Gilles Verniers, "The Reconfiguration of India's Political Elite: Profiling the 17th Lok Sabha," *Contemporary South Asia* 28, no. 2 (2020): 1–13.

11. Laclau, *On Populist Reason*.

12. Laclau famously defines populism not as a political aberration or pathology, but as the constitutive form and mode of the political—the "royal road to the political" (67) in his words.

13. Portions of this section have been drawn from a previously published essay. See Paula Chakravartty and Srirupa Roy, "Media Pluralism Redux: New Frameworks of Comparative Media Studies 'Beyond the West,'" *Political Communication* 30 (2013): 349–70.

14. One hundred twenty-two of these were active as of March 2011, the date of the decadal review of the TV news industry. See Chakravartty and Roy, "Media Pluralism Redux," 350.

15. Revised estimates from 2018 document a total of 866 private television channels in the country, of which 383 are classified as news and current affairs channels. See Geeta Seshu, "No, Republic TV-led News Broadcasters Federation Is Not Fighting 'Lutyens Media,'" Newslaundry, July 31, 2019, https://www.newslaundry.com/2019/07/31/no-republic-tv-led-news-broadcasters-federation-is-not-fighting-lutyens-media. In 2021, the Reuters Institute at the University of Oxford reported a total of 392 news channels in India. See Anjana Krishnan, "India," in *The Reuters Institute Digital News Report 2021*, ed. Nic Newman et al. (Oxford: Reuters Institute for the Study of Journalism, 2021), 134–36.

16. Atul Kohli, "Politics of Economic Growth in India, 1980–2005: Part II, The 1990s and Beyond," *Economic and Political Weekly* 41, no. 14 (April 8–14, 2006): 1361–70.

17. Rob Jenkins, *Democratic Politics and Economic Reform in India* (Cambridge: Cambridge University Press, 1999).

18. To take just one example, privately produced broadcast news first entered the Indian arena in the form of half-hour weekly capsules that were commissioned by the Ministry of Information and Broadcasting for the state television channel Doordarshan in 1988. As Nalin Mehta has documented in his history of satellite news television in India, the entry of non-state actors into the tightly controlled arena of broadcast news was enabled by a low-stakes decision that did not challenge the state's existing authority in any way. The news production company NDTV proposed a program on international news that would not interfere with Doordarshan's existing monopoly on the politically valuable genre of domestic news. Nalin Mehta, *India on Television: How Satellite News Channels Have Changed the Way We Think and Act* (Delhi: HarperCollins, 2008).

19. Ravinder Kaur has compellingly analyzed the political implications of the *jugaad* idea as a shorthand for an authentic Indian modernity that became increasingly popular among corporate and management circuits in the country in the early decades of the new millennium. See Ravinder Kaur, "The Innovative Indian: Common Man and the Politics of *Jugaad* Culture," *Contemporary South Asia* 24, no. 3 (2006): 313–27.

20. For multidisciplinary engagements with the political economy of Indian media liberalization, see Adrian Athique et al., eds., *Indian Media Economy*, vols. 1 and 2 (New Delhi: Oxford University Press, 2018); Somnath Batabyal, *Making News in India: Star News and Star Ananda* (London and New York: Routledge, 2012); Chakravartty and Roy, "Media Pluralism Redux"; Mehta, *India on Television*; Sahana Udupa, *Making News in Global India: Media, Publics, Politics* (Cambridge: Cambridge University Press, 2015).

21. Padmaja Shaw, "News Television and Democracy," *Revista de Economia Politica de la Tecnologias de la Informacion y Comunicacion* 11, no. 2 (2019), http://www.eptic.com.br/arquivos/Revistas/vol.XI,n2,2009/09-PadmajaShaw.pdf. On the structures of news media ownership in the era of media liberalization, see also Paranjoy Guha Thakurta, "Media Ownership in India—An Overview" (2012), https://paranjoy.in/article/media-ownership-in-india-an-overview; Vibodh Parthasarathi and Adrian Athique, "Market Matters: Interdependencies in the Indian Media Economy," *Media Culture & Society* 42, no. 3 (2020): 431–48.

22. Although there is limited disclosure of media ownership in India, from the data available in the public domain, supplemented by my interviews with media organizations, it appears that television channel ownership was more diffuse than concentrated in the initial phases of media liberalization. Prior to the deceleration of 2009–10, large national and transnational corporate media houses owned a minority—approximately 40 percent—of the 268 news channels registered in the country over the past decade (Government of India, Ministry of Information and Broadcasting, 2010). Complicating conventional understandings of media liberalization as a corporate takeover process of sorts, a provincial entrepreneurial class—a term that references both the geographic provenance of many of India's new entrepreneurs and their social distance from national symbolic imaginaries—played a significant role in the news media field.

23. On the "newspaper revolution," see the pioneering work of Roger Jeffrey, *India's Newspaper Revolution: Capitalism, Politics, and the Indian Language Press, 1977–99* (Delhi: Oxford University Press, 2000). Updated discussions include Taberez Neyazi, *Political Communication and Mobilisation: The Hindi Media in India* (Delhi: Cambridge

University Press, 2018); Sevanti Ninan, *Headlines from the Heartland: Reinventing the Hindi Public Sphere* (Delhi: Sage, 2007).

24. On the dynamics of political regionalization in India, see Yogendra Yadav, "Electoral Politics in the Time of Change: India's Third Electoral System, 1989–99," *Economic and Political Weekly* 34, no. 34/35 (August 21, 1999): 2393–99.

25. As Jaffrelot and Kumar have shown, from the 1990s onward, Indian parliamentary representatives have come from socioeconomic and regional backgrounds that are quite different from the upper-caste, upper-class, and metropolitan lineages of parliamentarians from previous decades. See Jaffrelot and Kumar, *Rise of the Plebeians*.

26. These vignettes draw upon extended ethnographic field research on the everyday work cultures of television news in India during the "boom period" of media liberalization. In 2007–2008, I conducted approximately 120 open-ended interviews with employees in news media organizations: production houses that were directly engaged in producing broadcast news, as well as a range of allied organizations (for example, apex industry associations, training institutes, "media watch" civil society organizations). I also spent time on the "news floor" observing a range of different activities that went into the production of news, from daily edit meetings to "breaking news" coverage, crime beats, and election coverage by field reporters.

27. Pseudonym.

28. Many thanks to Ayesha Kidwai for her translation.

29. Pseudonym.

30. See Tejaswini Ganti, *Producing Bollywood: Inside the Hindi Film Industry* (Durham, NC: Duke University Press, 2012).

31. There was no connection between the alleged incidents of sex work, the distribution of alcohol before elections, and the mobile phone thieves—these were three separate events that had occurred in the vicinity of the Sarita Vihar police station. The police's attempt to leverage media publicity by staging them together in a single "photo parade" seemed to have created a larger and connected story in the minds of the assembled reporters. They talked about these as linked incidents and even as different moments of the "same crime."

32. Pseudonym.

33. The "just in time" nature of the news production process is also notable, with the assembly of news stories taking place after the "order" is placed, that is, after audience interest in a story is registered by its emergence on a competitor channel's news cycle.

34. A common newsmaking practice around the world, a *vox pop*, abbreviation of the Latin phrase *vox populi*, is the term used for the act of gauging and representing public opinion by soliciting a quick comment from an "ordinary person."

35. In fact, two opposing temporal rhythms marked television news during my research period. On the one hand, there was the "speeding up" phenomenon, of news bulletins being squeezed into smaller time bands as the proportion of advertising time grew. During interviews in April 2008, reporters and editors at CNN-IBN estimated that for every twenty-four-hour news cycle, there are only six hours available of news programming, and this includes studio shows. In other words, the total amount of time available for live news broadcasts was only four hours daily, that is, around 15 percent of total broadcast time (the rest goes to advertisements). On the other hand, there was the

phenomenon of *khabar talna*, or drawing out the news. In order to minimize newsgathering costs, the same story would be repeated multiple times with minor changes and embellishments (the introduction of "new angles," as producers described it), and news production ended up being more "desk driven" than "beat reporter" driven.

36. The research head of the leading Hindi news channel, Aaj Tak, Sanjay Pathak, expressed a similar view about the importance of narrative distinction: "everyone has the content, research is about making it unique." Interview, April 2007.

37. In this regard, I was also struck by the fact that independent validation and cross-checking of details did not form part of the daily beat routine. On the contrary, journalists tended uncritically to reproduce the information handed out by state officials (police, for example), and there was a clear imprint of state-centrism on the commercial news media field.

38. Rahul Pandita, an ex–Aaj Tak journalist, described journalists' preferences for police and army briefings in an interview with me in April 2007. He recollected the "media savviness" of certain senior police officers and army public relations officers (PROs) he had encountered during his journalistic career, and how "journalists do not question their word." Pandita's observations also apply to media attitudes toward the Indian armed forces. There is a palpable sense of awe and reverence toward uniformed personnel that cuts across language media as well as party lines, and any criticism of military actions is immediately condemned by television news journalists—often in a stern, hectoring tone—as an "antinational" act. The news coverage of the Kargil war with Pakistan in 1999 by prominent television news journalists such as Barkha Dutt is an example of how an open endorsement of the "patriotic" military is perceived as a perfectly legitimate journalistic stance.

39. The news media's interest in high politics or formal politics was harnessed and cultivated by the BJP, whose media strategy was carefully calibrated around this focus. In a visit to the BJP media cell in March 2007, and a meeting with Saurabh Malviya, the media cell spokesperson, I noticed the many ways in which the party anticipated and provided for the prosaic and material needs of newsgathering, thereby increasing the likelihood that BJP-focused stories would make it to the news. For instance, Malviya and others in the BJP cell were well aware of work compulsions such as the need to provide quick bites and the importance of "being first" with the news. To meet these needs, the media cell would provide ready-made "reaction bites" to journalists on important issues of the day, and had also set up charging stations where journalists could power their cell phones, their essential work equipment. As Malviya described it to me, the work of "news facilitation" was very important to the BJP. Interview with Saurabh Malviya, March 2007.

40. The "angle" of a news story often generated a distinctive attention economy as popular stories prompted a cascade of imitations and spin-offs around the same theme by rival channels. As Sachin Jain, the founder of the Bhopal-based alternative/grassroots media education and training organization Vikas Samvad, explained in an interview, at times these commercially driven "angles" provided opportunities for alternative versions to be introduced into the media landscape by civil society actors who sought to alter the news agenda. Interview with Sachin Jain, Bhopal, May 2008. Rakesh Diwan of CNN-IBN recounted a related episode, of how he had "bent" the news angle around the

coverage of Bollywood superstar Amitabh Bachchan to introduce a discussion of "social anger" during the Indian emergency. (Bachchan was famous for portaying an "angry young man" in films set in the emergency/post-emergency context, and Diwan used this information to segue from celebrity news into a discussion about politics.) Interview with Rakesh Diwan, February 2007.

41. Interview with Satyashree Gandham, Cobrapost, October 2014.

42. See Shaunak Sen, "Sting Videos: Everydayness as Truth Aesthetic," *Marg*, September 1, 2018, https://www.thefreelibrary.com/Sting+Videos%3a+Everydayness+as+Truth-Aesthetic.-a0558532446.

43. The practice of sting journalism in India has been analyzed by Anirban Gupta-Nigam, "How Systems Cohere: Niira Radia in 2017," *Bioscope: South Asian Screen Studies* 8, no. 2 (2017): 244–67; William Mazzarella, "Internet X-Ray: E-Governance, Transparency, and the Politics of Immediation in India," *Public Culture* 18, no. 3 (2016): 473–505; Maya Ranganathan, "Sting Journalism: A Sign of the Times," in *The Indian News Media: From Observer to Participant* (Delhi: Sage, 2014): 65–94; Ravi Sundaram, "Publicity, Transparency and the Circulation Engine: The Media Sting in India," *Current Anthropology* 56, no. 12 (2015): 297–305; and Sen, "Sting Videos." With the exception of Sen's production-based ethnography, most of the existing scholarship focuses on the discursive and visual content of the sting and the political discourse generated around it.

44. Bahal's first sting was an exposé of "match fixing" by the Pakistani cricket team that he carried out for a British tabloid, the *News of the World*, in 1997. See Aniruddha Bahal, "Tale of the Sting," *Open Magazine*, September 2, 2010, https://openthemagazine.com/sports/tale-of-the-sting/.

45. Tarun Tejpal, "Sleaze, Senseless Greed, and Dirty Heroes," *Tehelka*, March 13, 2001, https://archive.tehelka.com/channels/Investigation/tarun.htm. See also the detailed discussion of Operation West End in Madhu Trehan, *Tehelka as Metaphor: Prism Me a Lie, Tell Me a Truth* (Delhi: Roli Books, 2001).

46. Several commentators have noted that it may not have been a coincidence that the only head that rolled in the wake of the Operation West End revelations was that of a Dalit political leader. See, for instance, the discussion in Kaur, *Brand New Nation*, chapter 5, note 83.

47. As sting journalism became popular and lucrative, and attracted increasing political attention, a range of allied practices were invented that sought to appropriate its perceived power. These included intriguing phenomena such as "fake stings" and "counter-stings." The former entailed the pretense of carrying out a sting in order to blackmail someone, or staging evidence in order to falsely implicate someone. See, for instance, the Uma Khurana "fake sting" of August 2007, where manipulated footage of a government schoolteacher was used by a local television channel to claim that she was involved in a "prostitution racket." Mannika Chopra, "Year of the Fake Sting," *The Hoot*, December 30, 2007, http://asu.thehoot.org/media-watch/media-practice/year-of-the-fake-sting-2867. Counter-stings or "reverse stings" involve "stinging back" at the media by covertly recording journalists engaged in nonlegal activities. In 2012, the Jindal Power and Steel Corporation released hidden-camera footage that allegedly showed journalists from the Zee News television channel engaging in extortion. See Amit Bhardwaj, "Zee-Jindal and Sudhir Chaudhary Tapes: The Battle That

Never Was," Newslaundry, July 19, 2018, https://www.newslaundry.com/2018/07/19/zee-naveen-jindal-sudhir-chaudhary-tapes-subhash-chandra.

48. The specific visual conventions of the sting are noteworthy. The requirement of covertness and secrecy enhances the importance of the technomaterial infrastructures of sting operations. As Shaunak Sen has shown in his research on journalists and video editors responsible for creating sting packages for television broadcast, the availability of particular kinds of technological formats and machines determines the scope and the eventual content of stings. The particular visual imagery that comes to define wrongdoing in the climactic "gotcha!" moment of each sting, the use of out-of-focus shots and muffled audio, the reliance on rather heavy-handed video-editing effects to enhance the visual legibility of a sting (for example, the common visual effect of using arrow graphics to draw attention to a particular section of a fuzzy image)—all of these reflect the technological affordances (and limitations) of the equipment that was used for each sting operation. For instance, Operation West End was filmed using a large and rather unwieldy hidden camera with limited recording space. In his discussion with Sen, the West End journalist Mathew Samuel recounted how the difficulties of turning the camera on without being detected by the subjects they were filming restricted the sting journalists to recording only the moments in which a tangible activity was taking place. As other journalists emulated Operation West End using similar kinds of hidden camera equipment and tactics, a recognizable visual repertoire stabilized that came to associate corruption and wrongdoing with "action visuals" of certain kinds, for example, handing over and receiving a bundle of cash (or a briefcase). It is only in later years, with the adoption of digital formats and technologies that offered enhanced recording and storage capacity and the availability of more unobtrusive cameras that were hidden in pens and tie clips rather than large handbags, that sting journalists could let their hidden cameras roll undetected for longer periods. In contrast to Operation West End, the later stings were able to capture banal conversations and interactions. These were mostly uneventful and nonspectacular—dramatic climactic moments along the lines of the cash handout or the briefcase transfer were usually missing from these stings. However, they provided a window into the wider networks and practices that enabled and embedded corruption as a set of long-term, ongoing processes rather than a one-off event involving discrete individual culprits. See Sen, "Sting Videos," and Shaunak Sen, "Decoding the Big Indian Sting," *Sarai* (2014), https://sarai.net/decoding-the-big-indian-sting/.

49. For a political theory perspective on the distinctions of voice and vision, see Green, *The Eyes of the People*.

50. At the time of my research, multiple news channels engaged in the promotion of stings through frequent teasers and trailers, and programmed follow-up stories after the sting was broadcast.

51. The emphasis on "sting optics" and "sting vision" by Mazzarella and Gupta-Nigam overlooks this didactic, expository aspect of sting praxis.

52. On the concept of a "poor image," see Hito Steyerl, "In Defense of the Poor Image," *e-Flux Journal* 10 (2009), https://www.e-flux.com/journal/10/61362/in-defense-of-the-poor-image/. On the indexical truth value of "poor images," where the diminished quality of an image references the "undoctored" nature of footage and therefore its correspondence with reality, see Sen, "Decoding the Big Indian Sting."

53. As Sen has noted, the visual elements of the sting serve mainly as "image templates" and "styles." Instead of indexing a particular object, the fast-moving blur of pixels and the muffled diegetic (and in many instances altogether absent) sound that characterize most sting videos constitute the "language and syntax of the real." The footage recorded and disseminated by a sting video indexes reality as such, and the fact that the image quality is poor makes it a raw and "undoctored" or unmediated reflection of the real. Sen, "Decoding the Big Indian Sting."

54. At the time of my research in 2007, one of the stings broadcast on national news television very literally exposed the popular Hindi pop singer Himesh Reshammiya by secretly filming him without the cap that he always wore, in order to show audiences that he was bald.

55. Sen, "Decoding the Big Indian Sting."

56. For instance, sting journalist Jamshed Khan's stories cast a comprehensive net over contemporary social and political life and showed how there was "crisis time" and corruption, dysfunction, and venality in nearly every sphere of life. His resumé of sting operations at the time of my interview with him included stories on an asylum in Agra (for *Tehelka*); "fatwas for sale"; a scandal around state subsidies for the Haj pilgrimage; fake godmen; trafficking of human organs; and unscrupulous auditors. Interview with Jamshed Khan, April 2008.

57. This is an emic term used by media practitioners.

58. See, for instance, Gupta-Nigam, "How Systems Cohere," and Mazzarella, "Internet X-Ray."

59. Stings are instrumentalized to accumulate social capital and power at the local level as well. In the course of my research with stringers in Bihar, I was frequently recounted anecdotes about stings (sometimes even the threat of one) being used as leverage. On stringer work cultures, see Srirupa Roy, "Television News and Democratic Change in India," *Media, Culture & Society* 33, no. 5 (2011): 761–77.

60. The highlights of these memories were invariably the risky and daring acts of the journalists, and the "big public impact" of the exposure, which usually remained a declarative or assertive statement disconnected from any specific criteria of such impact, for example, legislative or policy change.

61. There has been considerable regulatory leeway for stings in India. According to Sanjay Chandra, then-producer of the crime segment of Zee News, which specialized in sting operations, "there are no regulations on the sting in India, you can even enter the court with cameras after getting prior approval." Chandra noted the irony of using these concessions to focus on mundane matters: "the problem with crime stings is that they are focusing on very trivial things, like people asking for Rs. 500 bribes. It's like *atomic weapon se machhar marna* (killing a mosquito with an atomic weapon)." Interview with Sanjay Chandra, April 2008.

62. According to Jamshed Khan of the Star News Special Investigations Team (interview, April 2008): "Sting journalists have their own unwritten rules, for example that they should not force money on someone; *they* should be asked for money. They also have to get proof of the wrongdoing." Khan gave the example of how he was able to actually send two people on a Haj pilgrimage by paying a bribe, and used this as proof for his sting story about "bribes for Haj."

63. Interview with Jamshed Khan, April 2008.

64. For instance, the Operation West End story emerged out of a chance encounter and a casual conversation on a bus between Mathew Samuel and a fellow passenger. Samuel's personal curiosity and "gut instincts" led him to pursue the story after the journey had ended.

65. "Media cascades" also play a role, and the choice of sting topics is also shaped by the mimetic competition that prevails in the news media industry. For instance, Jamshed Khan observed that "they are always making decisions on which stings to run based on TRPs," and gave the example of how news stories about recent celebrity marriages had encouraged the production and broadcast of a sting on Islamic marriage practices (the program was titled *Nikahnama*). Khan also noted that *Nikahnama*'s failure to attract sufficient TRPs affected future programming decisions. Because of the TRP failures of programs like *Nikahnama* and another story about an Islamic cleric who accepted bribes to pronounce "fake *fatwas*," Star News decided not to support Khan's "dynamite story" for a sting on "*hawala* (black) money from Johannesburg and Durban going to *madrasas* (Islamic schools)." Although Khan did not spell this out explicitly, he indicated that the programming decision involved "Muslim themes" in some fashion. Interview with Jamshed Khan, April 2008.

66. Mazzarella, "Internet X-Ray."

67. Jamshed Khan shared vivid descriptions of his sting experiences. The use of fake names and fake mobiles was of course a standard practice; sometimes the levels of deception got so complex, especially when they were simultaneously working on multiple sting stories, that the journalist forgot what name they were using for which story. In Khan's account, the main element of a sting was finding the right "broker." He gave the example of the "Operation Theater" sting, on how major private hospitals in Delhi were admitting politicians in conflict with the law as their patients, in order to help them evade arrest on medical grounds. The journalists were able to cover the story because they found brokers in the hospital canteens and in the tea stalls outside the hospital, who provided them with the necessary information and leads. Similarly, for Operation Chakravyuh, another sting that Khan had worked on in 2005 about corruption among members of parliament who diverted constituency development funds for their personal use, the information came from a broker whom Khan had met in the canteen of North Block, a government building that housed multiple central ministries. Interview with Jamshed Khan, April 2008.

68. Monetary transactions are an intrinsic feature of all stings, but we lack public and verifiable information about the amounts that are exchanged and the budgets that media organizations authorize for stings. Jamshed Khan shared the information that Operation Chakravyuh was the most expensive sting that he had worked on, and cost approximately 400,000–500,000 rupees (approximately $5000.).

69. On October 25, 2007, *Tehelka* hosted a press conference at the Press Club in Delhi to publicize Operation Kalank (Stain/Ignominy), a sting conducted by the journalist Ashis Khetan, who had captured on hidden camera the alleged perpetrators of the Gujarat pogroms of 2002 boasting about their violent actions against Muslim residents of the state. I attended the press conference and was struck by the fact that not a single question was asked of the *Tehelka* team regarding the modalities of the sting, or any questions concerning the actual process or the backstory.

70. This raises the question of choice. What determines the specific subject of a sting? Why are some kinds of wrongdoing brought to light while others are overlooked? The answer lies in a combination of intermediary-driven initiatives, the exercise of individual journalistic discretion, and unplanned encounters. For instance, a chance conversation on a bus between Samuel and a middleman for the defense ministry, documents provided by people working in the ministry, and Bahal, Samuel, and the *Tehelka* editorial team's ideas about organizational priorities and directions produced Operation West End. However, these coincidences, interests, and the role of individually exercised discretion in decision-making (whether by the individual journalist or the individual media house) were not acknowledged in the sting's claim to popular representation (how it arose out of a sense of general public concern and fidelity to the general interests of the people).

71. See Chandra, "Young Protest," on the deliberate emulations of *Rang de Basanti* by middle-class youth mobilizations in the early decades of the twenty-first century.

72. In 2018, there were news reports that Sharma was eligible for parole. Jessica's sister Sabrina, who was by then the only surviving member of the Lall family, told journalists in search of a "reaction bite" that she had forgiven Sharma and the issue of his incarceration or release didn't really didn't matter to her any more. Sharma was finally released in 2020 and said that he is "deeply sorry for the pain [he has] caused the Lal family." See Prawesh Lama, "I'm Deeply Sorry for Pain I've Caused to Jessica Lal's Family, Says Manu Sharma," *Hindustan Times*, June 5, 2020, https://www.hindustantimes.com/india-news/i-am-deeply-sorry-for-the-pain-i-have-caused-the-lal-family-manu-sharma/story-bf1wQPtlDdJqnX4IHonc4N.html.

73. Narayanan made this comment in a speech addressed to the Supreme Court on the occasion of its golden jubilee in January 2000. http://www.krnarayanan.in/html/speeches/others/jan28_00.htm.

74. Media coverage emphasized that he was a "criminal-politician," amplifying the negative association with political power with additional allegations of criminality and illegality. The Yadavs were powerful *and* lawless.

75. Boltanski and Chiapello, *The New Spirit of Capitalism*.

76. For a compelling account of the new India imaginary, see Kaur, *Brand New Nation*.

77. John Keane, "Communicative Abundance," in *Democracy and Media Decadence* (Cambridge: Cambridge University Press, 2014), chapter 1. On the "fantasy of abundance" that "communicative capitalism" promotes, see Jodi Dean, "Communicative Capitalism: Circulation and the Foreclosure of Politics," *Cultural Politics* 1, no. 1 (2005): 51–74.

78. Interview with Q. M. Naqvi, March 2007.

79. These conceptions of democracy were not confined to the spaces of media activism, and seeded political currents beyond the time-space of early millennial media worlds. For instance, chapter 1 has documented how the themes of responsiveness, democratic listening, and "action politics" informed the political discourses and mobilizations of the IAC and the AAP. The political common sense about the emotional people—the view that democracy must represent the people's "real feelings" and "hidden aspirations"— also structures the mobilization strategies of Hindu nationalism.

80. In the campaign narratives, the crime of the violent killing of three innocent people was compounded and repeated many times over by their family members' subsequent failure to gain a fair and timely hearing. It was their unmet quest that fueled the campaign's fire. Justice had to be delivered to Jessica's sister, and to all India's overlooked ordinary citizens that she symbolized.

81. Media responsiveness was mostly described in "techno-democratic" terms, that is, by citing the unique affordances of media technologies. These included the intermedial relays that allowed audiences to send text messages and make phone calls to television news help lines during live news broadcasts—feedback that was scrolled on live tickers to yield further sets of (technologically mediated) public responses. They were upheld by journalists as evidence of the interactive, responsive, and essentially democratic nature of the campaigns, and by extension, of media itself as an institutional and political force and presence.

82. Capital punishment is of course the most overt and extreme form of "decisive action."

83. On media coverage in the era of economic reform, see Paula Chakravartty and Dan Schiller, "Neoliberal Newspeak and Digital Capitalism in Crisis," *International Journal of Communication* 4 (2010), https://ijoc.org/index.php/ijoc/article/view/798; P. Sainath, "India Shining Meets the Great Depression," India Together, April 2, 2006, https://indiatogether.org/depress-op-ed.

84. The term comes from Butler, *Notes Towards a Performative Theory of Assembly.*

85. The candlelight vigil is a sign of the general or unmarked and undifferentiated character of the people. They become legible as a flickering constellation of candles that cannot be distinguished from each other. Candles are also a quintessential ordinary and quotidian object, at the same time as they are a global protest commodity that signifies affinity and parity/equivalence with global protest cultures.

86. Several commentators have noted the marked divergence between the media attention that was directed toward the gang rape of a young woman in Delhi in December 2012, widely described as an act of violence against "India's Daughter," and the relative media silence around the equally horrific gang rape of Dalit women in Khairlanji village in Maharashtra in 2006. See, for instance, Dhrubo Jyoti, "December 16 Gangrape: The Real Reason why Bilkis Bano and Khairlanji Don't Trigger a 'Tsunami of Shock,'" *Hindustan Times* May 6, 2017, https://www.hindustantimes.com/analysis/december-16-gang-rape-the-real-reason-why-khairlanji-or-bilkis-bano-don-t-trigger-a-tsunami-of-shock/story-QoSaEpHCqFotIb4xfgfYXM.html.

87. Interview with Aditya Raj Kaul, March 2007.

88. The sociological composition of the movement provided further evidence of its socially exclusive character. In the course of my interviews with YFE activists in their South Delhi office (in South Extension) and on the Jawaharlal Nehru University campus in March and April 2007, I found that all its members were from dominant-caste backgrounds.

89. Virendra's account of his educational background emphasized its individualized qualities, that is, his individual talents and preferences such as "reading a lot" and "writing well," rather than the social and historical opportunities and networks that had enabled his educational opportunities and achievements.

90. Anil Chamaria et al., *Survey of the Social Profile of the Key Decision Makers in the National Media* (New Delhi: Media Study Group, 2006).

91. A majority expressed explicit preferences for "merit-based" educational and professional recruitment procedures, another coded concept for caste ideology. See Subramanian, *The Caste of Merit*, on "the caste of merit."

92. The single-issue focus of discussions about upper-caste dominance in the media overlooks these intersections and articulations. The problem is not simply that of the erasure or marginalization of Dalit issues by the absence of Dalit journalists in the newsroom. It is equally a problem of transposition and analogy, or the indirect and tacit ways in which caste gets called out and named, and the fact that only certain kinds of issues get named as "caste issues" (for example, reservations, violence, discrimination faced by Dalits and not property ownership, land rights).

93. Rajesh Talwar was my dentist at the time. I had followed the story since the discovery of Aarushi's body on the morning of May 16, 2008, made national headlines, but had not seen a photograph of Talwar until a few days later. I continued to visit the Talwars' dental practice for the next couple of years. We never discussed the case.

94. The Talwars lived in the Noida area of Delhi, a suburban conglomeration located in the neighboring state of Uttar Pradesh, and their dental practice was in South Delhi (in the Hauz Khas neighborhood).

95. For a rare academic analysis of "cultures of servitude" in India, see Raka Ray and Seemin Quayum, *Cultures of Servitude: Modernity, Domesticity, and Class in India* (Stanford, CA: Stanford University Press, 2009).

96. K. K. Gautam, a retired police officer, dropped by the apartment on his own initiative while the Talwars were away to immerse Aarushi's ashes in the Ganga River near Haridwar, and discovered the body. For a vivid account of Gautam's role, see Avirook Sen, *Aarushi* (Delhi: Penguin India, 2017).

97. However, the visuals continued primarily to be about Aarushi, and the "backstories" or background information about the life of the victim were also about Aarushi rather than Hemraj.

98. A suburb of Delhi, Noida is part of the state of Uttar Pradesh, and the UP police has jurisdiction over the area.

99. On the fateful night of May 15, said the inspector general, Rajesh Talwar came home to find Aarushi and Hemraj in an "objectionable" but "not compromising" position." In the story he told, an enraged Talwar lured Hemraj to the terrace on the pretext of a conversation, and then proceeded to kill him. Dr. Talwar then returned to his apartment, drank a few whiskies, and killed his daughter. The next morning, he called the police, claiming that he had just discovered Aarushi's body.

100. The inspector general announced that the "background cause" of the murder was the knowledge that Aarushi and Hemraj had of Dr. Talwar's ongoing extramarital relationship with a colleague. Aarushi's disapproval and Hemraj's penchant for gossiping about this with other domestic workers in the neighborhood had allegedly angered Dr. Talwar for a while. But what angered him even more, the IG revealed, was the fact that Aarushi and Hemraj had "grown close" to each other in the course of discussing Dr. Talwar's affair.

101. Nupur Talwar's interview with Sonia Singh, an anchor on the English-language channel NDTV, was minutely analyzed in media and public discussions. A main point

of controversy was her lack of tears and relative composure during the interview, which was interpreted, Lady Macbeth style, as a telling sign of her cold and calculated ways and even as proof of her involvement in the murder.

102. For example, Hindi-language media stories commented on the peculiarity of Aarushi sending emails to her parents even though they all lived in the same home. The fact that she was planning a "sleepover" with friends to celebrate her upcoming fourteenth birthday was seen as another odd and even suspicious detail. See Sen, *Aarushi*.

103. Interview, July 2018.

104. Mayawati and Chowdhury belonged to polarized class-caste and linguistic milieus. The former was the Hindi-speaking Dalit leader from Uttar Pradesh, the latter an English-speaking upper-caste politician based in Delhi.

105. See Jinee Lokaneeta, *The Truth Machines: Policing, Violence, and Scientific Interrogations in India* (Ann Arbor: University of Michigan Press, 2020), for an incisive analysis of India's adoption of forensic technologies, including a discussion of the Aarushi case.

106. As we've already seen, this announcement triggered a series of momentous investigative and judicial actions, for instance the decision to transfer the case to the CBI.

107. The controversy generated by Singh's press conference prompted the transfer of the case to the CBI; Talwar's television interview was cited in prosecution arguments as proof of her coldblooded killer instincts.

108. Condemnations of "politicization" dominated media narratives about the double murders. For media critics of the Talwars, the case proved how political connections and pressure could be used by powerful elites to exonerate themselves. For media supporters of the Talwars, the case shone a light on the capture of law and order institutions by vested political interests. Unsurprisingly, neither side acknowledged that the boundaries between political and *media* institutions and actors were porous and blurred as well.

109. Media discussions identified a mixed set of motivations, including class antagonism and resentment (for example, the "rural-feudal mindset" of the UP police), institutional preservation instincts (for example, in order to cover up their errors and inefficiencies, the investigative and prosecutorial agencies escalated their actions well beyond legal and moral limits), and petty dislikes (for example, the second investigative officer, Kaul, was held to "dislike" Nupur Talwar's cold attitude). See Sen, *Aarushi*.

Chapter Three

1. See, for instance, the collection of essays in Niraja Jayal, ed., *Re-forming India: The Nation Today* (Delhi: Penguin Random House, 2019); Kaur, *Brand New Nation*.

2. Michel Foucault, "Nietzsche, Genealogy, History," in *The Foucault Reader*, ed. Paul Rabinow (New York: Pantheon, 1984), 76–100, 82.

3. Amita Malik, "Dressing up for Shah," *Times of India*, December 2, 1977, 8.

4. National Archives of India, Ministry of Home Affairs (1978). "Lok Sabha Short Notice Q. No. 507 by Shri Keshavrao Dhongde, MP regarding suicide by a person before the Shah Commission." File II/13012/43/78/ComSec. The narrative in this section has been compiled from the documents in this file, and in File II/13012/32/78 ComSec ("Notice of calling attention regarding suicide by one K. Raghuman Rahudane in the premises of Shah Commission"). Attesting to the irrelevance and unimportance of this case for the official post-emergency narrative, even the name of the victim is not recorded

correctly. In MHA file II/13012/32/78 ComSec ("Notice of calling attention regarding suicide by one K. Raghuman Rahudane in the premises of Shah Commission") he is referred to variously as K. Raghuman Rahudane; Kundalik Raghu Mane; and Shri Mane.

5. Examples include Jagmohan, head of the Delhi Development Authority and lead figure in the Delhi slum demolition programs, who went on to become lieutenant governor of Delhi, governor of Jammu and Kashmir, cabinet minister and member of parliament (for the BJP), and recipient of one of the highest state honors, the Padma Vibhushan, in 2016; Navin Chawla, secretary of Delhi lieutenant governor Kishan Chand during the emergency, who was indicted for "emergency excesses" by the Shah Commission but then went on to serve as the chief election commissioner of India from 2005 to 2010; and Pranab Mukherjee, Indira Gandhi's close confidant and cabinet minister during the emergency, who was appointed as the president of India in 2012.

6. Mark Sawyer, *Racial Politics in Post-revolutionary Cuba* (Cambridge: Cambridge University Press, 2006), 7; William Sewell, "Historical Events as Transformation of Structures: Inventing Revolution at the Bastille," *Theory and Society* 25, no. 6 (1996): 841–81.

7. Philip Oldenburg's metaphor of the emergency as an "immunization shot" for Indian democracy, that introduced a "mild form of the autocracy virus" to Indian democracy and secured its future health, captures this sense of the emergency's continued relevance in the post-emergency era. See Philip Oldenburg, "The Emergency: An Immunization Shot Against Autocracy," *Mint*, June 22, 2015, https://www.livemint.com/Opinion/J1kCLXq1HcQmTjdH5BLwM/The-Emergency--An-immunization-shot-against-autocracy.html.

8. For a classic account of the structural compulsions that shaped the emergency decision, see Kaviraj, "Indira Gandhi and Indian Politics."

9. Gandhi's flurry of policies during this period included bank nationalization, the abolition of privy purses or statutory payments made to the titular heirs of erstwhile princely states, and the increasing use of explicit socialist rhetoric targeting the "monopoly classes" of economic and social elites.

10. Cited in B. N. Tandon, *PMO Diary II: The Emergency* (Delhi: Konark Press, 2006), xlvii.

11. Several contemporary observers have described the material and spatial contours of this shift in power, and pointed to the emergence of a literal new center of power. During the emergency, government officials had to change their daily walking routine and go to the prime minister's house rather than the offices of the cabinet in order to show their files and receive instructions from Mrs. Gandhi, since this is where her son and his advisors were ensconced! The importance of the Prime Minister's Office, with its independent secretariat, has remained unchanged in the intervening years, as yet another example of the emergency's continued, living legacy for Indian politics. The memoirs of B. N. Tandon and P. N. Haksar provide vivid and contemporaneous accounts of the power wielded by Sanjay Gandhi and his "coterie" during the emergency years.

12. Derisively referred to as the "gang of four," the "palace guards," and the "wolf pack," Sanjay Gandhi's group consisted of Bansi Lal, who held the cabinet defense portfolio during the emergency; Om Mehta, junior minister of home affairs, and V. C. Shukla, the minister of information and broadcasting. Youth Congress workers Jagdish

Tytler, Kamal Nath, and Ambika Soni; Jagmohan, the head of the Delhi Development Authority; P. S. Bhinder, a senior police official; and B. R. Tamta, the municipal commissioner, were others in Sanjay Gandhi's inner circle.

13. See Uday Mehta, "The social question and the absolutism of politics," *Seminar Magazine* 615 (2010): 23–27, on the historical context of constitution-framing and the imperatives of "political absolutism" and nation-making that gave rise to the fundamental rights/directive principles structure.

14. As reported in *India Today*, September 15, 1976, 10.

15. The twenty points were: (1) Reduce prices by government action (procurement, production, and distribution); display price lists and stock statements; punish hoarders; (2) Ceiling on urban property; (3) Personal income tax exemption limit raised from Rs. 6000 to Rs. 8000; (4) Textile items for mass consumption (dhotis, saris) at regulated prices (controlled cloth scheme: quality and distribution improved); (5) "Smuggler asset grab;" penalizing tax evasion; (6) Essential commodities for student hostels at controlled prices; (7) Textbooks at fair prices and book banks; (8) Raising of license-free investment limit for industries not requiring imported machinery, simplification of industrial license policy (and increasing penalties for violations); (9) Workers' participation in industry (shop floor) and production programs; (10) National permits for trucks; (11) Implementation of land ceiling laws and redistribution of land to landless; (12) Rights of tribal folk; (13) Abolition of bonded labor; (14) Home sites for landless; (15) Moratorium on execution of decrees for recovery of rural debt; liquidation of rural indebtedness; (16) Alternative sources of rural credit (banks and credit cooperatives) to help artisans, small and marginal farmers, landless laborers; (17) Regulation and/or enhancement of minimum wages for rural poor (agricultural labor); (18) Irrigation, drinking water, power projects (superthermal stations, streamlining of state electricity boards); (19) Handloom industry: supply of inputs to weavers at reasonable prices; rationalize reservation policy for handlooms; appoint separate development commissioner for handlooms; (20) Amend Apprenticeship Act to provide work opportunities for educated youth; minorities, SC and ST, handicapped persons.

16. This distinctive hybrid was a leitmotif of emergency-era publicity, which presented disciplined action as voluntary and even joyous or enjoyable for individual citizens.

17. The symbolism of transport condensed all of these desires. In both state publicity efforts and independent media coverage during the emergency, it was repeatedly represented as a time of smooth-flowing traffic, punctual public transport, good roads, and affordable cars and fuel.

18. The ideal of decisive governmental action was projected onto the international arena as well. Discussions of the emergency's various achievements included admiring accounts of India's "muscle-flexing" on the global stage that regularly appeared in the non-state media.

19. The selection is significant not only because it illustrates reigning perceptions about public goods and political virtues (what the emergency was good for), but because the magazine's carefully curated choice of respondents reveals its social imagination of the people to be primarily urban and middle-class. *India Today* inaugural issue, December 15, 1975: "What People Say," 12–13.

20. *India Today*, December 15, 1975.

21. As their appearance in the pages of *India Today* suggests, these ideals were hailed by private media as much as by official publicity. Reflecting Lloyd and Susanne Rudolph's *gleichschaltung* or compliance thesis of the Indian emergency, of how a range of pragmatic and instrumental calculations related to profit-seeking, power-seeking, or even simple survival yielded high levels of public compliance and conformity with the emergency regime, there was often considerable overlap between the propagandist exhortations of the Directorate of Advertising and Visual Publicity and representations of the emergency in the independent media. See Lloyd Rudolph and Susanne Hoeber Rudolph, "To the Brink and Back: Representation and the State in India," *Asian Survey* 18, no. 4 (1978): 379–400.

22. See the work of Patrick Clibbens on the idea of economic crimes during the emergency, and Rohit De for a longer historical trajectory of this normative-political formation. Patrick Clibbens, "Mrs. Gandhi's Buried Treasure: 'Economic Offenders' in Emergency India," paper presented at the CeMIS Colloquium, University of Göttingen, 2015; Rohit De, "Commodities Must Be Controlled: Economic Crimes and Market Discipline in India (1939–1955)," *International Journal of Law in Context* 10, no. 3 (2014): 277–94.

23. This is not unique to India. As many scholars have argued, paranoid fear-mongering rhetoric and accompanying practices distinguish the populist style of politics.

24. Myron Weiner's contemporaneous documentation of election graffiti includes "Our pledge, bread and liberty—vote for Janata," and "Save democracy, vote for Janata party." Myron Weiner, *India at the Polls: The Parliamentary Elections of 1977* (Washington, DC: American Enterprise Institute Press, 1978).

25. "Janata Party Poll Campaign begins," *Statesman*, January 31, 1977.

26. For an analysis of these events and the election defeat of Mrs. Gandhi, see Tariq Ali, "The Fall of the Congress in India," *New Left Review* 103, no. 1 (1977): 43–58.

27. Weiner, *India at the Polls*, 17.

28. Jyotirindra DasGupta, "The Janata Phase: Reorganization and Redirection in Indian Politics," *Asian Survey* 19, no. 4 (1979): 390–403.

29. See Weiner, *India at the Polls*, and Georges Lieten, "Janata as a Continuity of the System," *Social Scientist*, 9, no. 5/6 (1980–81): 14–35.

30. DasGupta, "The Janata Phase," 392.

31. Lee Schlesinger, "The Emergency in an Indian Village," *Asian Survey* 17, no. 7 (1977): 627–47, 639.

32. Former Congress Socialists who joined the Janata were led by so-called "Young Turks" like Mohan Dharia, Chandrashekhar, and Krishan Kant.

33. Lieten, "Janata as a Continuity of the System."

34. Rudolph and Rudolph, "To the Brink and Back," 386. The phrase "stealthy political accommodation" is from Lieten, "Janata as a Continuity of the System," 26.

35. The Janata government's policy decision in 1977 to deny licensing facilities to the Coca-Cola Company in India unless it agreed to cede majority control to its Indian partner, and the subsequent release of a government-produced cola to replace the foreign brand that was named "Double Seven" (77), a supposed reference to the year of the party's grand victory, were among the high-visibility public signals of its commitment to an "India-first" economic policy.

36. The "looking right, talking left" economic policies of the Gandhi regime before and during the emergency shored up the role of organized private capital as a key partner of the developmentalist state and active player in the planned command economy. The Janata government continued along much the same lines and further cemented this partnership of state and capital. Often overlooked in discussions of the Janata government's expressed ideological preference for Gandhian socialism and its emphasis on national self-sufficiency and small-scale economic activities, several large and "joint ventures" (public-private economic enterprises) were launched in the post-emergency years that strengthened the position of private capital. Examples include the influential role granted to the private company Hindustan Lever in development aid, and the development of commercial agriculture in the name of promoting Gandhian decentralized development. Lieten, "Janata as a Continuity of the System," 26–28. As Lieten reminds us, "the small-scale industry is not necessarily a small-capital industry, but quite often comes under the direct or indirect control of the monopoly houses" (33). The Janata period also saw the further development of joint sector projects as a result of which the influence of private monopoly houses grew in sectors that previously had been reserved for state-led industrial development. For example, Janata signed a major, and controversial, agreement for technical cooperation between the Indian public sector power equipment manufacturer Bharat Heavy Electricals Limited (BHEL) and the West German firm Siemens AG, and granted a license to the private industrial house Tata for imports related to power generation (30–31).

37. As the Rudolphs note, "the Gandhian legacy is compatible with state corporatism. Gandhians emphasize class collaboration, consensual modes of handling conflict, and the social origins of private wealth that entails stewardship in its disposition, commitments not incompatible with the stateness of a version of state corporatism." Rudolph and Rudolph, "To the Brink and Back," 399–400.

38. Stanley Kochanek, "Review of L. N. Sharma, The Indian Prime Minister: Office and Powers," *Journal of Asian Studies* 37, no. 4 (1978): 785–86, 785.

39. See *India Today*, September 30, 1977, on the banning of textbooks, and Lloyd Rudolph and Susanne Rudolph, "Rethinking Secularism: Genesis and Implications of the Textbook Controversy, 1977–1979," *Pacific Affairs* 56, no. 1 (1983): 15–37. As the Rudolphs observe about the Janata government's effort to manage the writing of history textbooks shortly after assuming office in 1977, "both Congress and Janata governments assumed they could and should intervene in a tutelary and patrimonial manner on behalf of their very different world-views and priorities" (17).

40. "Fear of Big Brother at Secretariat Persists," *Statesman*, May 10, 1977. The Janata government was well aware of this problem and the difficulties it posed for the inquiry process. In at least one case, a commission set up to inquire into the misdeeds of the emergency complained about the issue of post-emergency continuities of personnel: "The secretariat part of the work of the Dass committee was left entirely to the discretion of the officers of the ministry. There was no knowing whether the officers had preserved all the files and had presented all the available evidence. It was bad procedure to make those who were part of Shri Shukla's apparatus responsible for processing matters for the purposes of the White Paper." Deposition of KG Ramakrishnan, Chief Editor, *Yojana*. In "Proceedings of the Shah Commission: New Media Management Policy of

the Government During the Period of the Emergency," National Archives of India, Ministry of Home Affairs (1978), File VI/11034/80/56(105) ISDVI.

41. DasGupta, "The Janata Phase," 391.

42. *India Today*, March 31, 1977

43. *India Today*, July 15, 1977.

44. "Excesses Committed by Overzealous Officers," *India Today*, March 15, 1977.

45. Weiner, *India at the Polls*, 12–13.

46. "Fernandes Decries Talk of 'Forgive and Forget,'" *Statesman*, March 24, 1977.

47. See Margaret Canovan on these two "faces" of democracy. Margaret Canovan, "Trust the People! Populism and the Two Faces of Democracy," *Political Studies* 47 (1999): 2–16.

48. For a critical perspective on the resolution of this dilemma in favor of credibility rather than redressal and the cause of justice, see Sadhan Ghose, "Probe Commissions." *Opinion*, March 7, 1978, 5–8. "[Soli Sorabjee, Additional Solicitor-General of India] said that an Enquiry Commission was meant to analyse events that had shaken the confidence of the people in the administrative system and help in restoring it. 'It is not to rake up the past but redeem the future'" (5). Ghosh refers to Shah Commission as a "decoy operation": "Besides being unduly permissive about Indira and Sanjay, it is spending too much time on inessential matters and unimportant men. It does not appear to distinguish between technical lapses (which can be called 'excesses' only by stretching the language) and real atrocities" (6).

49. This is the title of John Dayal and Ajoy Bose's incisive contemporaneous account of the Shah Commission's proceedings. See John Dayal and Ajoy Bose, *The Shah Commission Begins* (Delhi: Orient Longman, 1978).

50. Dayal and Bose, *The Shah Commission Begins*, 1.

51. Dayal and Bose, *The Shah Commission Begins*, 2.

52. Shah's appointment was announced on April 29, 1977.

53. Dayal and Bose, *The Shah Commission Begins*, 2.

54. In addition to the Shah Commission, these included the Gupta Commission to inquire into the malpractices and corruption charges against Maruti, a set of car manufacturing enterprises headed by Sanjay Gandhi; the Reddy Commission to inquire into charges of corruption and abuse of power against former defense minister Bansi Lal; the Reddy Commission to inquire into the "Nagarwala conspiracy" from the early 1970s involving Indira Gandhi (the postscript of the chapter discusses this in further detail); and the Grover Commission to inquire into corruption charges against Karnataka chief minister Devraj Urs. See "Commissions: A Growth Industry," *India Today*, November 30, 1977, and A. G. Noorani, "Commissions of Inquiry: Skeletons in the Cupboard," *India Today*, June 15, 1977.

55. The Commission had no real precedent to fall back upon. Regime-level investigations where the conduct of the highest leadership of the country would be scrutinized had never previously taken place. Procedures kept evolving over the course of events as the Commission adapted to its ongoing experiences.

56. Dayal and Bose, *The Shah Commission Begins*, chapter 1.

57. The first postcolonial commission of inquiry was the Chagla Commission, constituted in 1958 to inquire into charges of financial impropriety and misuse of public

authority in the Mundhra corruption case. Subsequent commissions followed a similar format, of inquiring into cases involving specified government officials, both bureaucrats and elected representatives, who were accused of some kind of rent-seeking activity. Soon the proceedings, especially in the case of the Das Commission in 1963, which looked into allegations of political corruption against Partap Singh Kairon, the chief minister of Punjab, came to closely resemble judicial hearings. Formally and constitutionally, the Commission remained a nonpunitive body that issued nonbinding recommendations to the government regarding the validity of the charges that it investigated. But increasingly, the self-representation of postcolonial commissions, as well as public perceptions of their work, saw them as judicial institutions that worked within adversarial procedural frameworks to investigate public servants accused of specified misdemeanors.

58. According to the Commission, emergency excesses were defined as the subversion of lawful processes, conventions, and procedures; the misuse of power of arrests and detention; maltreatment and atrocities on arrested and detained persons; compulsion and use of force in the implementation of the family planning program; and "indiscriminate, high-handed or unauthorized" instances of slum demolition. At an experiential level, these were of course incommensurable. Media censorship, slum demolitions, and the imprisonment of citizens without due cause involved neither the same logistical modes, nor the same physical suffering. In the serial logic of the Commission, however, these would be considered equivalent, even equal, crimes against democracy and the people.

59. Rupa Viswanath, "Commissioning Representation: The Misra Report, Deliberation and the Government of the People in Modern India," *South Asia* 38, no. 3 (2015): 495–511.

60. The first interim volume of the report was published in March 1978, the second in May 1978, and the final in early August 1978.

61. Although there is no documentary evidence of the order, it is widely held that the newly elected Congress government ordered the seizure and destruction of all copies of the Shah Commission report in 1980, and the one surviving copy was located at an unnamed Australian university. In 2011, Era Sezhiyan, an elderly politician from the Janata party (formerly of the DMK party of Tamil Nadu), republished his personal copy of the report along with a lengthy introduction, titled *Shah Commission Report: Lost and Regained* (Chennai: Aazhi Press, 2018). The report has subsequently been made available as a digital text on several websites, and can be easily downloaded today.

62. Viswanath, "Commissioning Representation."

63. *India Today* cover story on "Human Rights: Terror through Torture," May 31, 1977.

64. Officials from these state agencies had directly participated in controversial emergency-era actions such as the imprisonment and mistreatment of political prisoners; police-coordinated slum demolitions; and income tax raids.

65. In later years, efforts to apprehend political wrongdoing did not engage in these forms of deliberate downscaling. For instance, contemporary instances of investigative sting journalism and the anti-corruption campaigns of the Aam Aadmi Party often go after the highest levels of political authority, and have named and blamed the Indian prime minister on several occasions, something that the Shah Commission never did.

66. *India Today* cover story, November 30, 1977, "India's Watergate." Media coverage frequently contrasted Shah's professionalism and diligence with the churlish and high-handed behavior of Congress regime officials at Commission hearings that exemplified the authoritarian indifference of the emergency regime. For instance, a report on the Shah Commission concluded that "[t]he session offered the people an opportunity to have a close look at the physiognomy of the middle-aged egg heads of India's bureaucracy—almost archaic, very political and highly arrogant." "Shah Commission: Accused Offers Excuses." *India Today*, November 30, 1977.

67. Iqbal Narain, "India 1977: From Promise to Disenchantment?" *Asian Survey* 18, no. 2 (1978): 103–16: 112.

68. In 1978, *Surya*, a magazine published by Maneka Gandhi, the wife of Sanjay Gandhi, ran a two-page spread of photographs of Suresh Ram, the son of the deputy prime minister and Janata leader Jagjivan Ram, in a so-called "compromising position" with a young college student. The sensationalist headlines that accompanied the piece, "Sushma [the student] Pawn in International Spy Ring!" and "Defence Secrets Leaked to Chinese Embassy?" sold over 120,000 copies of the special print run ordered by Maneka Gandhi and triggered a swirl of rumors and allegations that brought Jagjivan Ram's quest for prime ministerial office to an abrupt end.

69. "100 Days of Janata Rule: Contradictions between Practice and Precept," *India Today*, July 15, 1977.

70. In addition to these acts of invention, Indira Gandhi also enlarged existing repertoires of legitimation by accentuating existing themes that had been deemphasized and largely avoided in the Nehruvian official cultural imaginary. The religious ethos or constitution of political leadership was one of these themes. Indira Gandhi's public displays of religious fervor and devotion in the post-emergency period are legion. Examples include the derisively described "temple tour frenzy" in the immediate aftermath of the emergency, when she traveled to temples across the country; her close consultation and reliance on a series of charismatic "god men" and gurus; and the *rudraksha* religious beads that she wore with increasing frequency during her public appearances.

71. This quote from a contemporaneous journalistic account in *India Today* is exemplary: "[W]hatever her intentions, she received a tumultuous welcome at Nagpur Airport by a 7000-strong crowd on July 24th. Mrs. Gandhi stopped twice to give spontaneous speeches. She said in one of her speeches that she knew the people were waiting for her to move. 'But you should move,' she told the public. 'Unless you move, no movement can succeed. I will follow.'"

72. Pranab Mukherjee, *Indira Gandhi Centennial Lecture* (Delhi: Press Information Bureau, 2016).

73. See the dramatic description of the Belchhi visit in *India Today*, 1978: http://indiatoday.intoday.in/story/indira-gandhis-visit-to-belchhi-a-well-calculated-political-move/1/435706.html.

74. Although his specific focus is on crowd violence, Francis Cody's discussion of the performative publicity of crowds as democratic agents is very relevant here. See Francis Cody, "Print Capitalism and Crowd Violence Beyond Liberal Frameworks," *Comparative Studies of South Asia, Africa, and the Middle East* 35, no. 1 (2015): 50–65, and Nusrat

Chowdhury, *Paradoxes of the Popular: Crowd Politics in Bangladesh* (Stanford, CA: Stanford University Press, 2019).

75. After Belchhi, Indira Gandhi increasingly assumed the public role of an empathetic and determined/fearless savior of the downtrodden (a different incarnation than her emergency role as the Hindu goddess Durga).

76. Technological and sociological changes in Indian media had a role to play here. New printing and design technologies and the presence of new (and younger) journalists in the newsroom in the late 1970s and 1980s transformed prevailing norms of newsworthiness and brought these events to media and public attention. Chapter 4 discusses post-emergency journalism in further detail.

77. National Archives of India, Ministry of Home Affairs, "Proceedings of the Reddy Commission," 1978, File Series VI/11022.

78. "The Nagarwala Case: Is the Truth Buried?" *India Today*, April 30, 1977

79. "The Nagarwala Case: Is the Truth Buried?"

80. India went to war with Pakistan over the issue of East Pakistan's independence and the establishment of the sovereign nation-state of Bangladesh about six months later, in December 1971.

81. As we've already seen, the Shah Commission had also engaged in a similar evaluative exercise, determining, among other things, that the Raghumanes' experience of suffering was not an excess that merited further governmental inquiry.

82. With the bad habits of smoking and littering (it was concluded that an improperly extinguished cigarette or matches thrown away by a security guard had started the fire in the record room).

83. *Report: P. Jaganmohan Reddy Commission of Inquiry Regarding Nagarwala Case* (Delhi: Ministry of Home Affairs, Government of India, 1978).

84. National Archives of India, Ministry of Home Affairs, "Proceedings of the Reddy Commission," 1978, File series VI/11022.

85. For example, letters from Major Sheel and Markandeya Singh, and the published pamphlet *Story of Indira 1975*, which was sent to the Reddy Commission by Thamizh Naadan. "Proceedings of the Reddy Commission," 1978, National Archives of India, Ministry of Home Affairs, File VI/11022/4/80/ISDVI (part 91) and File VI/11022/4/80 ISDVI (Part 113).

Chapter Four

1. Another conception of popular-moral sovereignty associates it not with distance from politics per se but with the (actual or potential) exercise of force by a numerical majority. In this version, the people are a numerically preponderant, forceful, and even violent presence who embody the "law of force" beyond the amoral institutional scaffolding of representative politics. Since the 1990s, this idea of popular-moral sovereignty as a forceful rather than a "sublime" or "transcendent" presence has gained considerable ground. For an incisive elaboration of popular sovereignty as majority force, see Hansen, *The Law of Force*.

2. For a compelling account of how the idea of "failed utopia" gained global traction in the 1970s, see Samuel Moyn, *The Last Utopia: Human Rights in History* (Cambridge, MA: Harvard University Press, 2012).

3. On the statist sublime and the distinction from "dirty politics," see Hansen, *The Saffron Wave*, chapter 1.

4. There is a vast body of work on PIL. Notable scholarship includes Monika Ahuja, *People, Law, and Justice: Casebook on Public Interest Litigation*, vols. 1 and 2 (Delhi: Orient Blackswan, 1997); Monika Ahuja, "Public Interest Litigation in India: A Socio-Legal Study" (Diss., London School of Economics, University of London, 1996); Carl Baar, "Social Action Litigation in India: The Operation and Limitations of the World's Most Active Judiciary," *Policy Studies Journal* 19, no. 1 (1990): 140–50; Upendra Baxi, "Taking Suffering Seriously: Social Action Litigation in the Supreme Court of India," *Third World Legal Studies* 4, no. 6 (1985): 107–32; Prashant Bhushan, "Supreme Court and PIL," *Economic and Political Weekly* 39, no. 18 (2004): 1770–74; Anuj Bhuwania, *Courting the People: Public Interest Litigation in Post-Emergency India* (Cambridge: Cambridge University Press, 2017); Jamie Cassels, "Judicial Activism and Public Interest Litigation in India: Attempting the Impossible?" *American Journal of Comparative Law* 37 (1989): 495–519; Jill Cottrell, "Courts and Accountability: Public Interest Litigation in the Indian High Courts," *Third World Legal Studies* 11 (1992): 199–213; Clark Cunningham, "Public Interest Litigation in Indian Supreme Court: A Study in the Light of American Experience," *Journal of the Indian Law Institute* 29 (1995): 494–523; Rajeev Dhavan, "Law as Struggle: Public Interest Law in India," *Journal of the Indian Law Institute* 36, no. 3 (1994): 302–38; Marc Galanter, *Law and Society in Modern India* (Delhi: Oxford University Press, 1989); Jayanth Krishnan, "Social Policy Advocacy and the Role of the Courts in India," *American Asian Review* 21, no. 2 (2003): 91–124; G. L. Peiris, "Public Interest Litigation in the Indian Subcontinent: Current Dimensions," *International and Comparative Law Quarterly* 40, no. 1 (1991): 66–90; Sanjay Ruparelia, "A Progressive Juristocracy? The Unexpected Social Activism of India's Supreme Court," Working Paper 391 (2013), Kellogg Institute, University of Notre Dame; S. P. Sathe, *Judicial Activism in India: Transgressing Borders and Enforcing Limits* (New Delhi: Oxford University Press, 2003); Susan Susman, "Distant Voices in the Courts of India: Transformation of Standing in Public Interest Litigation," *Wisconsin International Law Journal* 13, no. 1 (1994): 57–103.

5. Sanjay Ruparelia offers a related, threefold classification or summary of the key features of PIL. According to him, these are (1) changes in standing and the identity of aggrieved persons; (2) court appointment of fact-finding and monitoring commissions to engage in "socio-legal" work (similar to Brandeis briefs in the United States); and (3) administrative tasks undertaken by commissions' appointment by court. See Ruparelia, "A Progressive Juristocracy," 15.

6. See Cassels, "Judicial Activism and Public Interest Litigation in India," 498.

7. On the role of the judiciary in Nehruvian India, beginning with the Constituent Assembly's vision for a limited judiciary, see Granville Austin, *The Indian Constitution: Cornerstone of a New Nation* (Oxford: Clarendon Press, 1966), and Granville Austin, *Working a Democratic Constitution: A History of the Indian Experience* (Oxford: Oxford University Press, 2003); also Galanter, *Law and Society in Modern India*. Rohit De offers an alternative account of the significant role that law, the judiciary, and the constitution played in the transformational projects of Nehruvian India. However, De relates this to the actions and initiatives of ordinary citizens rather than to the intentions and design of

leaders and constitution framers. See Rohit De, *A People's Constitution: The Everyday Life of Law in the Indian Republic* (Princeton, NJ: Princeton University Press, 2018).

8. Cassels, "Judicial Activism and Public Interest Litigation in India," 498, and Susman, "Distant Voices in the Courts of India," 81–82. Citing Cassel's research, Susman concludes that the "floodgates" thesis about a massive increase in the volume of petitions following the relaxation of standing rules was confirmed by Supreme Court statistics. Over a fifteen-month period between 1987 and 1988, 23,772 letter petitions were received by the public interest cell of the Supreme Court (however, only 110 of these, that is, less than half a percent, were admitted as writ petitions and actually impacted the workload of the court). See Susman, "Distant Voices in the Courts of India," 81–82.

9. See Bhuwania, *Courting the People*, for an extended and nuanced discussion of the "procedure vs. democracy" distinction, building on the Supreme Court's own commentary in *S. P. Gupta v. President of India and Others* on December 30, 1981. AIR 1982 SC 149, 1981 Supp (1) SCC 87, 1982 2 SCR 365: "Procedure is but a handmaiden of justice and the cause of justice can never be allowed to be thwarted by any procedural technicalities."

10. On the origins of epistolary jurisdiction (literally, jurisdiction about an epistle or letter), see G. L. Peiris, "Public Interest Litigation in the Indian Subcontinent: Current Dimensions," *International and Comparative Law Quarterly* 40, no. 1 (1991): 66–90, 67–68, and Baxi, "Taking Suffering Seriously," 116. Rajeev Dhavan has compiled a list of early PIL cases that established epistolary jurisdiction as precedent. See Dhavan, "Law as Struggle," 307, note 36.

11. The shocking story of custodial torture, of the police pouring sulfuric acid into the eyes of prisoners, was first reported as a minor news item by the *Indian Express* newspaper in October 1979 and then extensively investigated by journalist S. N. M. Abdi for the *Sunday* magazine with the support of editor M. J. Akbar. Abdi's investigations sparked a media storm and brought several other journalists to the case, including Arun Shourie, whom we will see more of in this chapter. The case was taken up by the Supreme Court and became "the first case in which compensatory damages for human rights violations were considered." See Marc Galanter, "Snakes and Ladders: Suo Moto Intervention and the Indian Judiciary," *FIU Law Review* 10, no. 1 (2014): 69–83, 74.

12. *People's Union for Democratic Rights and Others vs. Union of India and Others*, September 18, 1982, 1982 AIR 1473, 1983 SCR (1) 456, 1:4.

13. Thomas Blom Hansen, "Governance and State Mythologies in Mumbai," in *States of Imagination: Ethnographic Explorations of the Postcolonial State*, ed. Thomas Blom Hansen and Finn Stepputat (Durham, NC: Duke University Press, 2001), 221–56, 222.

14. Peiris, "Public Interest Litigation in the Indian Subcontinent," 72.

15. Sathe cites the example of *Azad Rickshaw Pullers Union v. Punjab* in his discussion of collaborative, non-adversarial partnerships between state, court, and petitioner, and the centrality of cooperative disclosure to the process. The case concerned a challenge to the Punjab state government's law prohibiting owners from renting out their rickshaws to individuals who would actually ply them (in order to prevent the exploitation of the non-owner pullers). The court decision found a mediated solution that suited all parties. The Punjab National Bank was ordered to provide loans to rickshaw pullers to buy their own rickshaw, thus preserving the original legislative intent of preventing rickshaw rental without obstructing either the rickshaw pullers' source of livelihood or

the rickshaw owner's source of profit. See S. P. Sathe, "Judicial Activism: The Indian Experience," *Washington University Journal of Law and Policy* 6 (2001): 29–107, 78.

16. Sathe, "Judicial Activism," 84–85. See also Bhuwania, *Courting the People*, on the phenomenon of PIL "creep," that is, how the courts are increasingly ready to redefine the original scope of the PIL. The innovation of omnibus PILs, where the court clubs together individual petitions, thereby introducing all kinds of other issues into the space of litigation, is another example of the court's prerogative action.

17. Peiris, "Public Interest Litigation in the Indian Subcontinent," 78.

18. In the *Wangla* case from 1988, concerning levels of radioactive substance in milk, the Supreme Court appointed a committee comprising members of the Planning Commission, the Atomic Energy Centre, and the Economic and Planning Council. As Peiris has observed, the selection choices reflected and further consolidated the "development-science-planning" nexus of Nehruvian India. Peiris, "Public Interest Litigation in the Indian Subcontinent:" 78, discussing *Dr. Shiv Rao Shanta Rao Wangla and Others vs. Union of India and Others*, January 20, 1988, JT 1988 (1) SC 144, (1988) 1 SCC 452.

19. Cassels, "Judicial Activism and Public Interest Litigation in India," 501.

20. Article 14 guarantees the fundamental right to equality before the law, and Article 21 protects life and personal liberty.

21. Ruparelia, "A Progressive Juristocracy," 11.

22. For a discussion of the constitution as a future promise and its distinctive imaginary of hope, see Uday Mehta, "Constitutionalism," in *The Oxford Companion to Politics in India*, ed. Niraja Gopal Jayal and Pratap Bhanu Mehta (Delhi: Oxford University Press, 2010).

23. Emergency-era constitutional amendments also added to the list of directive principles (for example, Article 39A on free legal aid) and introduced a new section, Article 51A, listing eleven "fundamental duties" for Indian citizens. https://doj.gov.in/sites/default/files/Fundamental-duties_0.pdf.

24. The constitutional guarantee of the right to life (Article 21) emerged as a particularly prominent constitutional locus for such practices of normative fusion. Several PIL cases, such as *Olga Tellis* (on the rights of homeless pavement dwellers), redefined this classically liberal individual precept of liberty to align with the socioeconomic collective welfare commitments and responsibilities of the state as outlined in the directive principles (Part IV) of the constitution. Judicial readings of the concept of life expanded its meaning to include livelihood, education, hunger, and human dignity. Conversely, legislative acts framed in terms of realizing and securing right to life, such as the law that formalized citizens' right to education (Right to Education Act, 2009) and the National Rural Employment Guarantee Act (2005), received constitutional sanction. On the creation of a social rights constitutional framework through the expanded reading of Article 21 that PILs provided, see Madhav Khosla, "Making Social Rights Conditional—Lessons from India," *International Journal of Constitutional Law* 8, no. 4 (2010): 739–65, and Shylashri Shankar and Pratap Bhanu Mehta, "Courts and Socioeconomic Rights in India," in *Courting Social Justice: Judicial Enforcement of Social and Economic Rights in the Developing World*, ed. Varun Gauri and Daniel Brinks (Delhi: Cambridge University Press, 2009), 146–82.

25. Baxi, "Taking Suffering Seriously," 108.

26. On the judiciary-legislature contest over land reform, see Austin, *The Indian Constitution* and *Working a Democratic Constitution*; Rajeev Dhavan, *The Supreme Court of India: A Socio-Legal Critique of Its Juristic Techniques* (Delhi: N. M. Tripathi, 1977).

27. This was an explicit goal in the 1971 election manifesto of the Congress party. On Indira Gandhi's push for a "committed judiciary" see Diego Maiorano, "India's Institutions in the Early 1980s: The Pre-history of the Great Transformation," *Modern Asian Studies* 48, no. 5 (2014): 1389–1434, 1398–99.

28. For the full text of the Swaran Singh Committee Report (1976), see https://www.ebc-india.com/lawyer/articles/76v2a4.htm, accessed on December 9, 2021.

29. *Assistant District Magistrate Jabalpur vs. Shivkant Shukla and Others*, April 28, 1976, 1976 AIR 1207, 1976 SCR 172.

30. Upon Indira Gandhi's return to office in 1980, Justice Bhagwati wrote her a fawning letter that attracted a fair amount of media and public attention when the contents were revealed: "May I offer you my heartiest congratulations on your resounding victory in the elections and your triumphant return as prime minister of India? It is a most remarkable achievement of which you, your friends and well-wishers can be justly proud. It is a great honour to be the prime minister of a country like India." See "Serenity of Supreme Court Jarred by Letter Sent by Justice P.N. Bhagwati to Indira Gandhi on Her Election Victory," *India Today*, April 15, 1980, http:/www.indiatoday.in/magazine/indiascope/story/19800415-serenity-of-supreme-court-jarred-by-letter-sent-by-justice-pn-bhagwati-to-indira-gandhi-806597-2014-02-04. See also Ruparelia, "A Progressive Juristocracy," 26.

31. Baxi, "Taking Suffering Seriously," 113.

32. Baxi, "Taking Suffering Seriously," 107.

33. Land reform was a prime example, but there were numerous other legislative actions as well that were challenged by the Supreme Court. Ruparelia has noted that the Supreme Court struck down 128 pieces of Directive Principles–inspired legislation that threatened the private property regime between 1950 and 1967. Ruparelia, "A Progressive Juristocracy," 11.

34. Dhavan, "Law as Struggle," 317.

35. Dhavan, "Law as Struggle," 317.

36. See Bhuwania, *Courting the People*, and Sathe, "Judicial Activism," for the distinction between judicial populism and judicial activism: "Activism is populism when doctrinal effervescence transcends the institutional capacity of the judiciary to translate the doctrine into reality." Sathe, "Judicial Activism," 42.

37. *Mumbai Kamgar Sabha, Bombay vs. M/S Abdulbhai Faizullabhai and Others*, March 10, 1976, 1976 AIR 1455, 1976 SCR (3) 591.

38. From 1950 to 1967, the apex judiciary intervened several times to check the social reform zeal of the government on issues such as land reform. In the famous *Golaknath* decision of 1967, the Supreme Court asserted its power of judicial review over parliament and struck down as unconstitutional any legislation or constitutional amendment that restricted the scope of fundamental rights (Part III of the constitution). In turn, the Indira Gandhi government responded to *Golaknath* by asserting legislative and executive supremacy over the judiciary through a spate of constitutional amendments and legislative enactments that whittled down judicial review. Executive actions such

as the transfer and supersession of judges were also undertaken with the express aim of constituting a cooperative or "committed judiciary." In fact, this was named as an explicit goal in the Congress party's manifesto during the 1971 election campaign. The contest between legislature and judiciary continued for the next six years, through the emergency, and each branch of government scored emphatic but momentary victories in a seesaw balance of power. To take just one instance of this alternation, the judicial decision on *Kesavananda* in 1973 that elaborated the constitutional "basic structure" doctrine restricting the ambit of legislative action was met with an immediate governmental response. On the very next day, the government intervened in the appointment of judges and superseded the conventional principle of judicial seniority in nominating a new chief justice. See *C. Golaknath and Others vs. State of Punjab and Others*, February 27, 1967, 1967 AIR 1643, 1967 SCR (2) 762; *Kesavananda Bharati & Others vs. State of Punjab and Others*, April 24, 1973, Writ Petition (civil)135 of 1970.

39. In particular, the role of Justices Bhagwati and Krishna Iyer are foregrounded in most accounts of PIL.

40. Arvind Narrain and Arun Thiruvengadam, "Social Justice Lawyering and the Meaning of Indian Constitutionalism: A Case Study of the Alternative Law Forum," *Wisconsin International Law Journal* 31, no. 3 (2014): 525–65, 529, citing Upendra Baxi, "The Avatars of Judicial Activism: Explorations in the Geography of (In) Justice," in *Fifty Years of the Supreme Court of India: Its Grasp and Reach*, ed. S. K. Verma and Kusum Kumar (Delhi: Oxford University Press, 2000).

41. Dhavan, "Law as Struggle," 317.

42. See also Rohit De's important recent work on bringing the citizen-litigant back into constitutional history. De rightly notes that the "first mover" in a courtroom is the legal subject or litigant who brings the case to the notice of the court. The judicial story must begin with this figure rather than from the conventional locus of the judge and lawyer. De's recentering of the judicial narrative frames judicial action as a *response* to the initiating agency of the ordinary citizen, who "compel[s] an unwilling state to speak to him." Rohit De, "Beyond the Social Contract," *Seminar Magazine* 615 (2010): 43–47, https://www.india-seminar.com/2010/615/615_rohit_de.htm.

43. Dhavan, "Law as Struggle," 306.

44. Baxi has famously argued for different terminologies of "public interest litigation" in the US versus "social action litigation" in India. According to Baxi, in contrast to the transformative impulses of social action litigation in India, "[T]he PIL movement in the United States involved innovative uses of the law, lawyers and courts to secure greater fidelity to the parlous notions of legal liberalism and interest group pluralism in an advanced industrial capitalistic society. . . . PIL activism has instead of generating pressures for structural changes in law and society ended up servicing the much exposed ideology of interest group pluralism and legal liberalism." Baxi, "Taking Suffering Seriously," 109.

45. Ruparelia, "A Progressive Juristocracy, 8–11.

46. After the Maoist-inspired Naxalite insurgency of the late 1960s–early 1970s had been quashed by the state, and communist political parties became increasingly "embourgeoised" through their increasing involvement in electoral politics and the business of governance (the Communist Party of India (Marxist)–led Left Front coalition formed

the state government in West Bengal in 1977), a new space opened up in post-emergency India for a nonparliamentary new left that engaged with social movements and ideas beyond the conventional class politics framework of classical Marxism. For an illuminating history of the Indian left, see Praful Bidwai, *The Phoenix Moment: Challenges Confronting the Indian Left* (Delhi: HarperCollins, 2005), and on the social movement–left intersections in the 1980s see Gail Omvedt, *Reinventing Revolution: New Social Movements and the Socialist Tradition in India* (London and New York: Routledge, 1994).

47. For a critical appraisal of the idea of an "indigenous law," see Marc Galanter, "The Aborted Restoration of 'Indigenous Law' in India," *Comparative Studies in Society and History* 14, no. 1 (1972): 53–70.

48. Some members of the Indian constituent assembly had advocated for the inclusion of such alternative judicial institutions in the constitution itself. However, there was considerable resistance to the idea, not the least from the main constitution drafter, B. R. Ambedkar, who argued against the proposal in very firm and direct terms, and against the broader romanticized vision of village community that drove this and other Gandhian-inflected premises. Ambedkar's argument won the day, and the call for this restoration of indigenous practices of law and justice was relegated to Part IV, the Directive Principles section of the constitution, as a non-justiciable mission statement.

49. On the evolution, distinctive political imagination, and transnational lineages of community development programs in "new nations," see Daniel Immerwahr, *Thinking Small: The United States and the Lure of Community Development* (Cambridge, MA: Harvard University Press, 2015); Subir Sinha, "Lineages of the Developmentalist State: Transnationality and Village India, 1960–1965," *Comparative Studies in Society and History* 50, no. 1 (2008): 57–90.

50. For the most part, the critical scholarship on modernization theory overlooks this idea of "synthesis" and emphasizes instead the erasures that were effected by modernization projects in the midcentury developing world.

51. Marc Galanter and Jayanth Krishnan, "Bread for the Poor: Access to Justice and the Rights of the Needy in India," *Hastings Law Journal* 55 (2004): 791–97, 793–94.

52. Indeed, the project of legitimizing or justifying the emergency in the mid-1970s drew quite heavily upon the vocabulary of Indian difference. Government pronouncements stressed the unique and exceptional dangers that India faced, which called for an equally distinctive measure, of suspending democracy in order to save it. As the specter of the "foreign hand" that threatened to destabilize the Indian polity made clear, and the addition of "national integrity" to the preamble of the Indian constitution by the forty-second constitutional amendment of 1976 further underscored, the national delimitation of politics and democracy was a central precept of the emergency regime.

53. With the same judicial agents at the helm, this was unsurprising. The emergency-era report on legal aid was authored by Justices Krishna Iyer and Bhagwati, each the author of two previous committee reports on the subject (Bhagwati's 1970 report was on legal aid in Gujarat, and Krishna Iyer's report from 1973 was on national legal aid). After the emergency, these two figures would be the main protagonists of the PIL revolution and have been widely hailed as the pioneering "fathers" of the innovation.

54. Galanter and Krishnan, "Bread for the Poor," 794.

55. Upendra Baxi, "From *Takrar* to *Karar*: The *Lok Adalat* at Rangpur—a Preliminary Study," *Journal of Constitutional and Parliamentary Studies* 10 (1976): 53–64.

56. The term describes an effort by the state to create and control a new kind of judicial arrangement that dispenses with prevailing common law institutions and procedures in order to emulate so-called indigenous or traditional modes of law and justice. As the phrase suggests, it involves a formally designed and executed set of changes that authorize new institutional coordinates and procedures.

57. See Ahuja, "Public Interest Litigation in India," 73.

58. Baxi, "Taking Suffering Seriously."

59. The two meanings of different justice were in fact linked; justice for the poor was an indigenous justice and vice versa. India's past traditions of indigenous justice from the past were hailed as being especially responsive and receptive to the present requirements of India's poor. See, for instance, Justice Chandrachud's judgment in the *Raj Narain* case, which cited the example of the Mughal "bell of justice" that could be rung outside the emperor Jahangir's court by a "common man" to "draw the attention of the ruler to his grievances and sufferings." *Indira Nehru Gandhi vs. Shri Raj Narain and Others*, November 7, 1975, Appeal (civil) 887 of 1975.

60. In 1973, the Krishna Iyer Committee recommended the *panchayat* model for "weaker sections," those with "limited means," and those who were "socio-economically backward."

61. As Aman Hingorani has summarized, "Since its inception in 1979, it [public interest litigation] has been used to mould state law into an instrument of socio-economic justice by discarding from the formal legal system precisely those elements which induce legal formalism and 'neutrality' of law." Aman Hingorani, "Indian Public Interest Litigation: Locating Justice in State Law," *Delhi Law Review* 17 (1995): 159–203, 162. Further emphasizing its procedural departures, PIL has also been described as a "home-delivery system of justice" by a scholar (G. S. Lodha, cited in Dhavan, "Law as Struggle," 303), a metaphor that has also found favor with others: "it was as if, in the estimate of a lawyer, otherwise known for sober judgement, 'the Supreme Court had brought justice to the door of those who live a hand-to-mouth existence and are illiterate and unorganized.'" Anand Prakash, "Public Interest Litigation," *Annual Survey of Indian Law*, 20 (1984): 324–32, 332, cited in Dhavan, "Law as Struggle," 303, note 12.

62. Cited in Ahuja, "Public Interest Litigation in India," 64.

63. *Bandhua Mukti Morcha* judgment, cited in Ahuja, "Public Interest Litigation in India," 60. In these and other instances both meanings of different justice—indigenous justice as well as poor justice—were referenced and interlinked. Thus procedural relaxation was simultaneously the hallmark of a distinctive Indian (and non-Anglo-Saxon) form of justice, and the vehicle or means of delivering justice to and for the poor. According to Justice Bhagwati, these judicial innovations were necessary because "Anglo Saxon law is transactional, highly individualistic, concerned with an atomistic justice incapable of responding to the claims and demands of collectivity, and resistant to change. Such law was developed and has evolved . . . essentially . . . to deal with situations involving the private right/duty pattern. It cannot possibly meet the challenge raised by . . . new concerns for the social rights and collective claims of the underprivileged."

Sarbani Sen, *Public Interest Litigation in India: Implications for Law and Development* (Calcutta: Mahanirban Calcutta Research Group, 2002), 82.

64. Ahuja, "Public Interest Litigation in India," 69.

65. Ahuja, "Public Interest Litigation in India," 69.

66. Susman, "Distant Voices in the Courts of India," 70. A different modality of quelling insurgent action that threatened political order, the notorious Terrorist and Anti-Defamation Activities Act, was passed in the same post-emergency context in which PIL and legal aid were introduced as a means of co-opting and channeling protest. Susman, "Distant Voices in the Courts of India," 99–100.

67. Peiris, "Public Interest Litigation in the Indian Subcontinent," 89.

68. *Fertilizer Corporation Kamgar Union and Others vs. Union of India and Others*, November 13, 1980, 1981 AIR 344, 1981 SCR (2) 52.

69. Baxi, "Taking Suffering Seriously," 415. Aman Hingorani concurs that PIL "offers . . . a paradigm of law which locates the content of informal justice within the formal system." Hingorani, "Indian Public Interest Litigation," 162.

70. Baxi, "Taking Suffering Seriously," 117.

71. Most discussions of the field of post-emergency "new politics" define it negatively as a "non-party" space. They overlook the institutional structures and representational claims that are in fact foundational to the practice of new politics. See chapter 1 on the idea of the nonparty political formation in India.

72. As Aman Hingorani summarizes the judgment in *Ayaaubkhan Noorkhan Pathan v. State of Maharashtra*, "The court must maintain strict vigilance to ensure that there was no abuse of the process of court and that 'ordinarily meddlesome bystanders are not granted a visa.'" Aman Hingorani, "Public Interest Litigation," *Annual Survey of Indian Law* (2013): 969–1000, 997.

73. Susman, "Distant Voices in the Courts of India," 85. PIL lawyers often justify this "paternalism" in terms of the logic of number. If a large group is the subject of the petition, then less consultation is justified. Susman, "Distant Voices in the Courts of India," 88.

74. Hingorani was networked to legal and social activist communities within India and in a wider transnational milieu that stretched from East Africa to Southeast Asia, as the historian Rohit De has recently shown. Rohit De, "Rights from the Left: Decolonization, Diasporas, and the Global History of Rebellious Lawyering," presentation at the InterAsia Fellows Conference, Chiang Mai, Thailand, Social Science Research Council, 2014.

75. Dhavan, "Law as Struggle,"306.

76. Dhavan, "Law as Struggle," 299.

77. On social action groups in India, see S. L. Sharma, "Social Action Groups as Harbingers of Silent Revolution," *Economic and Political Weekly* 27, no. 47 (1992): 2557–61.

78. According to Baxi's critical appraisal, their involvement makes "social action litigation . . . an aspect of third-party, professional adjudication and thus reduces the space for creative experimentation of people's power." Baxi, "Taking Suffering Seriously," 65.

79. PIL soon developed into a professional niche within the legal profession, and some individuals came to be known as PIL lawyers, akin to the phenomenon of "cause lawyering" in the United States. M. C. Mehta is one such individual, who has developed

an international reputation as a PIL lawyer specializing in cases involving the environment. See Bhuwania, *Courting the People*, chapter 2.

80. In the caustic appraisal of Upendra Baxi, the field of Indian social action and activism was an "introspect estate of the select few," and activists resembled a self-anointed "priesthood." See Baxi, "Taking Suffering Seriously," 65.

81. On the role of the Ford Foundation in endorsing the legal activism turn through its financial support to organizations such as the Consumer Education Research Centre, and as a significant actor in the field of legal education, see Dhavan, "Law as Struggle," 305, and Jayanth Krishnan, "Professor Kingsfield Goes to Delhi: American Academics, the Ford Foundation, and the Development of Legal Education in India," *American Journal of Legal History* 46 (2004): 447–99.

82. This did not mean a gender-just court, by any means. The Supreme Court was simultaneously the betrayer and the redeemer of gender rights and justice. It handed down its retrograde judgment on the *Mathura* rape case in 1979, at the same time as its self-consciously progressive innovation of public interest litigation was taking shape. In fact, the petitioner in *Mathura* was the same individual, Lotika Sarkar, who would meet with a very different response to her petition about the rape of a Dalit woman in a police station than her PIL about the mistreatment of women in state-run institutions.

83. On the social and spatial biases of the environmental turn in urban civic activism and judicial politics, see Amita Baviskar, *Uncivil City: Ecology, Equity, and the Commons in Delhi* (Delhi: Sage, 2020).

84. Morris-Jones, *The Government and Politics of India*. His notion of the "saintly idiom" has been discussed in chapter 1.

85. As Upendra Baxi has observed in his discussion of "voluntarism" and "activism," the former mostly involves ad hoc actions motivated by sentiments of pity toward the less fortunate, and religious-moral considerations about "doing good." The focus of voluntarism has mostly been on the direct provisioning of the social demand by the volunteer groups and individuals. In contrast, activism is a programmatic and organized activity that engages state structures and "the political system" to realize socioeconomic change, and is directed toward the ultimate goal of political change and reform (the system has to be "fixed" and changed in some fashion so that present conditions can improve). See Upendra Baxi, "Activism at Crossroads with Signposts," *Social Action* 36, no. 4 (1986): 378–89.

86. Michael Saward, "The Representative Claim," *Contemporary Political Theory* 5 (2006): 297–318, 300.

87. This converges with the grassroots/locality/community focus of civil society and social movements in the same period, what Marcus Franda describes as their "small politics" approach. Marcus Franda, *Small Is Politics: Organizational Alternatives in India's Rural Development* (Delhi: Wiley Eastern, 1979).

88. *S. P. Gupta*, also known as the *Judges Transfer Case*. Interestingly, the petitioners whose genuine public interest motivations the Supreme Court endorsed in *S. P. Gupta* were lawyers, and this was specially noted as the main reason for admitting their petition.

89. Susman, "Distant Voices in the Courts of India," 75–76.

90. See also Susman, who quotes an interview with a Supreme Court lawyer, P. Rathinam, who was readily recognized as a petitioner in high court PIL cases. In

sharp contrast, when a younger female colleague presented a petition about a woman who had been raped and her husband killed, such judicial recognition was not forthcoming. "[T]he Court gave her a week to revisit the village and get the signatures of the injured parties assuring that they consented to this action." Susman, "Distant Voices in the Courts of India," 75.

91. Sathe observes that petitioners Sunil Batra and Vasudha Dhagamwar were "known social activist(s)" and Bandhua Mukti Morcha and PUDR were "known organizations." Sathe, "Judicial Activism," 77. Peiris describes another petitioner, D. C. Wadhwa, as a "well-qualified volunteer" whose research on ordinances received praise from Bhagwati for its "assiduous and painstaking efforts." Peiris, "Public Interest Litigation in the Indian Subcontinent," 71.

92. I have written elsewhere about the "diffident hope" of Nehruvian India. See Srirupa Roy, "India 2030 and the Limits of Competitive Futurism," in *Germany and the World 2030*, ed. Stephan Mair et al. (Berlin: Econ Press, 2018), https://deutschland-und-die-welt-2030.de/en/article/india-2030-and-the-limits-of-competitive-futurism/.

93. This phrase was used by Hiranmay Karlekar, a former editor of the *Hindustan Times* newspaper, to describe the outrage of media and "ordinary citizens" at the incompetence and callousness of state authorities in failing to prevent the murder of two teenagers in Delhi in the early 1980s (the "Chopra children" murder case, which created a media storm in the post-emergency period). See Srirupa Roy, "Angry Citizens: Civic Anger and the Politics of Curative Democracy in India," *Identities* 23, no. 3 (2016): 362–77.

94. Hingorani, "Indian Public Interest Litigation," 163. The articles were from January 8 and 9, 1979; see also *Indian Express*, February 7, 1979.

95. Interview with the Hingorani family (Aman, Shweta, and Priya Hingorani, children of Kapila and Nirmal Hingorani), New Delhi, August 2017.

96. Zizi Papacharissi, *Affective Publics: Sentiment, Technology, Politics* (New York: Oxford University Press, 2015).

97. Cited in Ahuja, "Public Interest Litigation in India," 287. The *Hussainara Khatoon* case led to a "flood" of public interest petitions that were similarly based on media reports that "energiz[ed] social activists, journalists, and a handful of lawyers and legal academicians." These included newspaper articles about the terrible condition of children in jail and remand homes, the employment of children in the carpet industry in flagrant violation of child labor laws, the flourishing practice of bonded labor, the ill health of workers in the slate-pencil manufacturing industry, the sexual exploitation of tribal girls working in public sector units, the bleak conditions of mental asylums, 25 million people suffering from fluorosis after drinking contaminated water. See Hingorani, "Indian Public Interest Litigation," 167–68.

98. Portions of this section are drawn from Roy, "The Death of the Third World Revisited."

99. See chapter 2.

100. See chapter 2.

101. Multiple interviewees of the Long Emergency project, an open-access digital archive of oral histories of Indian journalism and the emergency that I have curated, describe such life histories. See https://longemergency.demx.in/. The generational shift

in journalistic culture has been described by journalist Inderjit Badhwar as a shift from the era of "pontificators and thoughters" to that of "reporters and diggers." As Badhwar and the historian Gyan Prakash have noted, the Bombay-based tabloid *Blitz* was a notable exception in the pre-emergency media field. Since the early years of independence, *Blitz* published many investigative scoops and took on the government in bold and often angry terms. See Inderjit Badhwar, "That Eighties Scoop Show: Indian Journalism Needs a Shot of the Past," *Outlook*, November 12, 2018, and Gyan Prakash, *Mumbai Fables: A History of an Enchanted City* (Princeton, NJ: Princeton University Press, 2010).

102. Other repressive measures directed at the media included three laws that censored and banned media content: the Prevention of Publication of Objectionable Matter Act, 1976; the Parliamentary Proceedings (Protection of Publication) Repeal Act, 1976; and the Press Council (Repeal) Act, 1976. Media were also targeted by financially punitive measures, such as the calculated withdrawal of government advertisements from publications that were perceived to be "hostile" to the regime (and their placement in "friendly" publications). This amounted to a significant financial loss, since government ads were the major revenue source for all publications.

103. While financial and punitive concerns drove some of these closures, professional ethics and values of journalistic freedom were also at stake, as the cases of *Seminar* and *Himmat* magazines show. See Kalpana Sharma, "Himmat During the Emergency: When the Press Crawled, Some Refused to Even Bend," *Scroll*, June 23, 2015, https://scroll.in/article/735844/himmat-during-the-emergency-when-the-press-crawled-some-refused-to-even-bend.

104. There were, of course, several exceptions. Indian journalism histories highlight the few who carried out acts of media resistance in all kinds of inventive ways. These included the publication of blank pages and blank columns to show that censorship was being practiced, the use of humor and satire, and metonymic or indirect reportage that dissimulated critical coverage of the Indian emergency in stories that focused on other subjects and even on other countries. For an important dissenting account, see the comprehensive history of the emergency recently published by Jaffrelot and Anil, in which they critically interrogate the dominant narrative of media resistance during the emergency and argue instead that only a "minority of the fourth estate resisted dictatorship." Media, along with other institutions of Indian democracy, actively contributed to the paradoxical and politically troubling phenomenon of "dictatorship by consent" that constituted the Indian emergency. See Jaffrelot and Anil, *India's First Dictatorship*, chapter 5, 356.

105. The genre of investigative journalism was actively encouraged by a wide range of print media organizations. Even niche magazines like *Debonair*, the men's magazine that was popularly known as the Indian *Playboy*, commissioned and published investigative exposés of political leaders in the 1970s and 1980s, as former *Debonair* editor Vinod Mehta recounted in his memoir. See Vinod Mehta, *Lucknow Boy* (Delhi: Penguin Viking, 2011).

106. Interview with Sopan Joshi (Prabhash Joshi's son), Delhi, July 2014.

107. New media forms of this period include magazine journalism, investigative journalism, and lifestyle journalism.

108. For instance, the immediate incident at the heart of the Kamala story of 1981 was the sale of a marginalized tribal woman, Kamala, to Ashwini Sarin, an undercover

journalist, whose intent was to expose the persistence of human trafficking in India. The involvement of the political establishment in this incident was not readily evident. After all, the phenomenon of human trafficking was linked to structural, economic, and social forces that exceeded the ambit of any specific governmental authority. Some versions of the Kamala story did in fact offer such an analysis. For instance, for the *New York Times* the incident illustrated a larger Indian social problem, which exceeded the role and responsibility of elected officials, bureaucracy, or police. In a similar vein, journalist Khushwant Singh observed that the story was about "endemic poverty." In Vijay Tendulkar's play on the subject, the common experience of patriarchy that united Kamala and the journalist's wife was the main focus. Undercutting the heroic narrative of the journalist who exposes the evils of the political classes, Tendulkar's dramaturgy of the Kamala story foregrounded the intersections and complicities between media and politicians, and their joint responsibility for the reproduction of gendered and classed inequalities; there were no clear-cut heroes or villains in Tendulkar's play. See Ashwini Sarin, "Buying Girls from a Circuit House," *Indian Express*, April 27, 1981, 1; Michael Kaufman, "Price of Woman in India: $306 and Much Sorrow," *New York Times*, August 11, 1981, A2; Vijay Tendulkar, *Kamala*, in *Five Plays*, trans. Priya Tendulkar, Kumud Mehta, and Shanta Gokhale (New Delhi: Oxford University Press, 1996).

109. "Crusader for justice" is a term that peppers many of the recollections about post-emergency journalism in the Long Emergency digital archive.

110. My choice of pronoun is intentional. Most of the big investigative stories of the post-emergency years involved male journalists.

111. Arun Shourie, "Why the Honorable Court Must Hear Us," *People's Union for Civil Liberties Bulletin*, July 30, 1981, http://arunshourie.bharatvani.org/articles/19810730.htm. The role of journalists in the Kamala story was not limited to reporting. Following the publication of the story, journalist Ashwini Sarin, who had purchased Kamala for 2,300 rupees ($306) as part of his undercover investigation of trafficking, brought her to Delhi. The adult woman was placed in an orphanage run by the Arya Samaj, a Hindu reformist social service organization. With the help of the People's Union of Civil Liberties (PUCL), an independent civil liberties organization, Sarin and his editor Arun Shourie then petitioned the Indian Supreme Court in the public interest to issue directions to the relevant state governments to take steps to end trafficking, and to find a suitable home for Kamala. The court ordered Kamala to stay in the Arya Samaj orphanage while the case was being heard. Six months later, in November 1981, Kamala escaped. No one ever found her again.

112. See Roy, *Beyond Belief*, chapter 4.

113. We might even say that the main justification of Nehruvian nation-building was the continued nonresolution of social problems. Nation-building was presented as a process of continual and open-ended becoming rather than being. See Partha Chatterjee, *The Nation and Its Fragments: Colonial and Postcolonial Histories* (Princeton, NJ: Princeton University Press, 1993); David Ludden, "India's Development Regime," in *Colonialism and Culture*, ed. Nicholas Dirks (Ann Arbor: University of Michigan Press, 1992), 247–87; Roy, *Beyond Belief.*

114. The constitution guaranteed a set of social and cultural group rights for religious minorities. The historical inequities of caste discrimination were differently addressed,

through the constitutional introduction of affirmative action measures (reservations) that set aside a proportion of seats in educational institutions and government employment for individuals belonging to historically oppressed caste groups.

115. For a comprehensive overview of India's citizenship regimes and their transformations since independence (at both legal-constitutional and normative-political levels), see Niraja Jayal, *Citizenship and Its Discontents* (Cambridge, MA: Harvard University Press, 2013).

116. See Rajagopal, "The Emergency as Prehistory of the New Indian Middle Class," and Roy, "Angry Citizens," for a discussion of how the emergency and its aftermath consolidated the urban middle class as the primary subject of political address.

117. According to Ernesto Laclau, populism draws on and reproduces an "equivalential" logic that connects or "chains" disparate social demands. See Laclau, *On Populist Reason*.

118. It was claimed that the 1982 judgment on pension liberalization benefited 2.5 million pensioners. It became an important legal precedent for deciding on the arbitrariness of a government law. Common Cause went on to file two more writ petitions in the Supreme Court concerning the issue of pensions. The first concerned family pensions, and the organization claimed that the judgment benefited more than 100,000 widows. The second concerned the restoration of commuted pension and supposedly benefited two million pensioners.

119. The seventy-five-year-old "invalid" Thanawalla, "victim of a weak heart, sciatica, and arthritis," had retired as a government official in 1970 after thirty-nine years of service. He had filled out all the paperwork with his bank in order to receive his pension, but to no avail. The story on Thanawalla's case emphasized bureaucratic obstruction and needless delay. It was titled "Bureaucrats Delay Pension Revision." See *Times of India*, August 7, 1985, 9.

120. Pavan Varma, "Crusader for a Common Cause: H. D. Shourie," in *People Like Us* (Delhi: Har Anand, 2007). See also the memorial volume published by Common Cause in 2005, *Great Crusader for People's Causes H. D. Shourie (1912–2005)*.

121. As Pavan Varma has noted, "among the founding members of Common Cause were the noted writer Khushwant Singh; the late S. Ranganathan, the former Auditor General of India and Member of the Rajya Sabha; former Finance Secretary—now no more—K. P. Mathani; leading advocate Fali Nariman; and Major General U. C. Dubey, a former Area Commander of Delhi." Varma, "Crusader for a Common Cause."

122. See also the list of disputes filed before National Consumer Disputes Redressal Commission: compensation for air crash victims; intravenous fluids; iodized salt; electricity supply; telephones; strikes by Air India flight engineers; printing of maximum sale price on packages; printing of sale price on film packages; refund of deposits by scooter suppliers; medical negligence. Common Cause, *Great Crusader for People's Causes*.

123. The remedies that were sought by the PILs also reflected these location biases. For instance, the "slum problem" was to be addressed by opposing their regularization and getting rid of them altogether, and not by providing residents with basic public utilities. Common Cause, *Great Crusader for People's Causes*.

124. Aditya Nigam distinguishes between the early era of PILs concerned with "suffering," which he terms "PIL Mark 1," and "PIL Mark 2" of the 1990s and beyond,

which reflect the concerns of the dominant neoliberal consensus. See Aditya Nigam, "Embedded Judiciary or, the Judicial State of Exception?" in *The Shifting Scales of Justice: The Supreme Court in Neoliberal India*, ed. Mayur Suresh and Siddharth Narrain (Delhi: Orient Blackswan, 2019), 22–38.

125. See Laclau, *On Populist Reason*, and Common Cause, *Great Crusader for People's Causes*.

126. As Table 1 shows, the wide range of issues addressed by Common Cause included corruption (for example, cases involving the filing of annual income tax returns by political parties; the allotment of petrol pumps and the use of the discretionary quota of petroleum minister Satish Sharma; the iodization of salt; unlicensed blood banks), rent law, illegalities of construction, pollution by slaughterhouses, freedom of information/transparency and accountability, and "voluntary exit" (euthanasia).

127. The prominent influence of Shourie *père et fils* in the public interest firmament of the late 1970s and 1980s is a good example of the overlapping circuits of remedial action in the name of the people. H. D. Shourie and his son Arun Shourie were both involved in early PIL actions, the former as a founder-member of Common Cause, the latter as a senior journalist credited with breaking several iconic investigative journalism stories. Both Shouries would appear before the Supreme Court bench in the 1980s as lead petitioners for different kinds of public interest litigations. On the variegated career of Arun Shourie, from the World Bank to journalism to a BJP minister, see the vivid portrait in Martha Nussbaum, *The Clash Within: Democracy, Religious Violence, and India's Future* (Cambridge, MA: Harvard University Press, 2008).

128. Pavan Varma has described some of these ad hoc groups of "upright citizens" from media, legal, and corporate professional backgrounds. Common Cause received financial support from Vikram Lal, the CEO of the Eicher Motors corporation, and legal support from Prashant Bhushan, a well-known public interest lawyer who went on to cofound the Aam Aadmi Party (and subsequently quit the party). See Varma, "Crusader for a Common Cause."

129. "Shouric is ever on the watch for misdemeanours not only when he goes out for his regular stroll, but also while he is at home reading newspapers. Recently, full-page advertisements in newspapers, released by the government, caught his eye. On the face of it, the advertisements appeared to be informing the public about new projects and policies. But, in effect, what they all seemed to be doing was projecting the image of politicians and political parties. The ads cost millions of rupees—money which, Shourie felt, could be put to better use. So he filed a petition in the Supreme Court. The case is on." Nilima Pathak, "For Other's Sake," *Gulf News*, October 10, 2003, https://gulfnews.com/uae/for-others-sake-1.371846.

Conclusion

1. A prominent recent example is Anastasia Piliavsky, *Nobody's People: Hierarchy as Hope in a Society of Thieves* (Stanford, CA: Stanford University Press, 2020).

2. See the Introduction and chapter 1 for a discussion of Ambedkar and Arendt respectively.

3. Vijay Prashad, ed., *Strongmen: Trump, Modi, Erdogan, Duterte, Putin* (Delhi: LeftWord, 2019).

4. Debasish Roychowdhury and John Keane, *To Kill a Democracy: India's Passage to Despotism* (New York and Oxford: Oxford University Press, 2019).

5. John Keane, *The New Despotism* (Cambridge, MA: Harvard University Press, 2020).

6. See Esra Özyurek, "Miniaturizing Atatürk: Privatization of State Imagery and Ideology in Turkey," *American Ethnologist* 31, no. 3 (2004): 374–91, and Ruth Ben-Ghiat, *Strongmen: Mussolini to the Present* (New York: Norton, 2020).

7. On "Christianism," an ideological-identitarian formation melding race, religion, and nationalism that has been popularized by right-wing European and American movements and is distinct from the religion of Christianity, see Rogers Brubaker, "A New 'Christianist' Secularism in Europe," The Immanent Frame, October 11, 2016, and Philip Gorski, "Revisited: Why Do American Evangelicals Vote for Trump?" The Immanent Frame, December 15, 2020, http://tif.ssrc.org/category/exchanges/religion-world-affairs/the-politics-of-national-identity/.

8. On the left-wing "inclusionary" populism identified with "Chavismo," see Yannis Stavrakakis et al., "Contemporary Left-Wing Populism in Latin America: Leadership, Horizontalism, and Postdemocracy in Chávez's Venezuela," *Latin American Politics and Society* 58, no. 3 (2016): 51–76; and Cas Mudde and Cristobál Rovira Kaltwasser, "Exclusionary vs. Inclusionary Populism: Comparing Contemporary Europe and Latin America," *Government and Opposition* 48, no. 2 (2013): 147–74.

9. See Ben-Ghiat, *Strongmen*, for a detailed discussion of the "virility politics" of contemporary strongmen.

10. See Kalyan, "Eventocracy," also discussed in the Introduction.

11. See Johan Farkas and Jannick Schou, *Post-Truth, Fake News, and Democracy: Mapping the Politics of Falsehood* (London and New York: Routledge, 2020); Steve Fuller, *Post-Truth: Knowledge as a Power Game* (London: Anthem Press, 2018); Lee McIntyre, *Post-truth* (Cambridge, MA: MIT Press, 2017); Peter Pomerantsev, "Why We're Post-fact," *Granta* 20 (2016), https://granta.com/why-were-post-fact/; Jason Stanley, *How Propaganda Works* (Princeton, NJ: Princeton University Press, 2016).

12. Modi's public declarations frequently stray from factual truth and evidentiary conventions. Examples include his 2014 campaign declaration that he will repatriate illegally transferred "black money" to India and deposit 1.5 million rupees (Rs. 15 lakh) in each Indian's bank account; various unverified scientific claims, for example, attributing the genesis of plastic surgery to Vedic India; unprovable claims about a military attack launched by Pakistan in 2019; and inaccurate claims about the death toll of the second wave of the Covid-19 pandemic in 2020.

13. For details of the various actions that consolidated "governmental Hindutva" after the BJP formed a majority government under Narendra Modi in 2014, see Angana Chatterji et al., eds., *Majoritarian State*; Hansen and Roy, eds., *Saffron Republic*; and Aakar Patel, *Price of the Modi Years* (Delhi: Westland, 2021).

14. Nancy Bermeo, "On Democratic Backsliding," *Journal of Democracy* 27, no. 1(2016): 5–19.

15. On the comparative political implications of "populists in power" see Müller, *What Is Populism*, and Kim Lane Scheppele, "Autocratic Legalism," *University of Chicago Law Review* 85, no. 2 (2018): 545–84.

16. See Dilip Bobb, "Me, Myself, and Modi," *Financial Express*, May 11, 2014, https://www.financialexpress.com/archive/me-myself-and-modi/1249462/.

17. The 2019 "Howdy Modi" rally in Houston, Texas, featured Donald Trump and showcased Modi's closeness and "bromance" with the US president. See https://www.usatoday.com/story/news/politics/elections/2019/09/22/trump-bromance-narendra-modi-howdy-modi-rally/2354099001/.

18. Steve Coll, "The Strongman Problem: From Modi to Trump," *New Yorker*, January 18, 2017, https://www.newyorker.com/news/daily-comment/the-strongman-problem-from-modi-to-trump.

19. For example, Modi's claims about his education and his college degrees are alleged to be inconsistent and even untrue. For a summary of the controversy, see "Two Degrees of Separation: The Controversy Over Modi's Educational Qualifications Explained," The Wire, April 30, 2016, https://thewire.in/politics/controversy-over-modis-educational-qualifications-an-explainer.

20. A performing art form in South Asia where performers take on multiple styles and identities to play a range of characters (from the Sanskrit for "many forms," *bahu + rup*).

21. Keane, *The New Despotism*, 124.

22. Keane, *The New Despotism*: 121.

23. The sudden announcement of a nationwide lockdown in March 2020, and the immediate closure of all workplaces and transport, stranded millions of migrant workers in urban centers far from their homes, with no means of livelihood and no way to return. Thousands took the only option available to them, of walking thousands of kilometers to reach home, carrying their possessions, with little to no sustenance along the way, and the state providing scarce assistance. Images of the "migrant exodus" are among the most searing and unforgettable representations of the pandemic in India. See Ritajyoti Bandyopadhyay et al., eds., *India's Migrant Workers and the Pandemic* (London and New York: Routledge, 2021).

24. Amy Kazmin, "Narendra Modi the Style King Puts on the Guru Look," *Financial Times*, July 1, 2021.

25. "While Modi may look as though he is renouncing worldly concerns, his aura is unlikely to fade in the eyes of his devoted Hindu supporters. In India's ancient myths, and in historic Hindu kingdoms, the rulers' spiritual advisers wielded as much clout as kings themselves. Modi's approval ratings are currently at 64 percent, among the highest of major global leaders. 'By looking like a guru, he doesn't necessarily appear as nonpowerful,' said Jaffrelot. 'In Hindu tradition, the most powerful man is the man who gives advice.'" Kazmin, "Narendra Modi the Style King."

26. As we have noted in other work, the paradigms of "movement Hindutva" and "communal politics" that framed discussions of Hindu nationalism in the 1980s–2000s do not apprehend the dynamics of governmental Hindutva and its politics of rule. See Hansen and Roy, eds., *Saffron Republic*.

27. I refer here to Jacques Rancière's evocative idea of politics (and aesthetics) as the "redistribution of the sensible" that undoes the existing "partition" of social and political worlds and brings new, hitherto invisible and unsayable ideas and subjects into presence. See Jacques Rancière, *Dissensus: On Politics and Aesthetics* (New York: Continuum, 2010).

28. See Charles Tilly, "Major Forms of Collective Action in Western Europe, 1500–1975," *Theory and Society* 3, no. 3 (1976): 365–75, and Charles Tilly, *The Contentious French* (Cambridge, MA: Harvard University Press, 1986). For a useful overview of social movement theory's use of the concept of "repertoires," see Eitan Alimi, "Repertoires of Contention," in *The Oxford Handbook of Social Movements*, ed. Donatella Della Porta and Mario Diani (New York: Oxford University Press, 2015), 410–22.

29. Robert Jansen, "Situated Political Innovation: Explaining the Historical Emergence of New Modes of Political Practice," *Theory and Society* 45, no. 4 (2016): 319–60, 321.

30. Ann Swidler, "Culture in Action: Symbols and Strategies," *American Sociological Review* 51, no. 2 (1986): 277.

31. Colin Crouch, *Post-democracy: A Sociological Introduction* (Cambridge: Polity Press, 2004).

32. Crouch, *Post-democracy*, 5.

33. Crouch, *Post-democracy*, 5.

34. This has been discussed in the introduction and chapters 3–4. On the application of the Gramscian concept of passive revolution to the Indian transition, see Sudipta Kaviraj, "A Critique of the Passive Revolution," *Economic and Political Weekly* 23, no. 45/47 (1988): 2429–44.

35. Susanne and Lloyd Rudolph described the evolution of Indian democracy in relation to the distinctive formations of the statist/dirigiste "command polity" in the 1950s and the 1960s, and the "demand polity" characterized by the proliferating pressure of societal claims on the political system in subsequent decades. The thesis of a disjuncture between formal institutional capacity and social mobilization reflects the influence of midcentury modernization theory about the challenges of democratic consolidation in the "new nations" of the developing world. See Rudolph and Rudolph, *In Pursuit of Lakshmi*.

36. See chapter 3 for a brief discussion on Bhave's influence on political leadership in the Long 1970s and his role in the political rehabilitation of Indira Gandhi in the post-emergency period.

37. Gyan Prakash's recent book has a rich and fascinating account of Sanjay Gandhi's role and influence on Indian politics. See Prakash, *Emergency Chronicles*, and Jaffrelot and Anil, *India's First Dictatorship*. For further accounts of the Sanjay Gandhi era, see Sagarika Ghose, *Indira: India's Most Powerful Prime Minister* (Delhi: Juggernaut Books, 2017); Coomi Kapoor, *The Emergency: A Personal History* (Delhi: Penguin Viking, 2015); Vinod Mehta, *The Sanjay Story: From Anand Bhavan to Amethi* (Delhi: HarperCollins, 2012).

38. On the regionalization of Indian politics, see Francine Frankel and M. S. A. Rao, eds., *Dominance and State Power in Modern India: Decline of a Social Order*, vols. 1 and 2 (Delhi: Oxford University Press, 1990); Christophe Jaffrelot, *India's Silent Revolution: The Rise of the Low Castes in North Indian Politics* (New York: Columbia University Press, 2003); Rob Jenkins, *Regional Reflections: Comparing Politics Across India's States* (Delhi: Oxford University Press, 2004); Aditya Nigam and Yogendra Yadav, "Electoral Politics in Indian States: 1989–1999," *Economic and Political Weekly*, August 21–28, 1999, 2391–92; Sudha Pai, *State Politics: New Dimensions* (New Delhi: Shipra, 2000); T. V. Sathyamurthy, ed., *Region, Religion, Caste, and Culture in Contemporary India* (Delhi:

Oxford University Press, 2000); Yogendra Yadav and Suhas Palshikar, "Ten Theses on State Politics," *Seminar* 591 (2018): 14–22; John Wood, ed., *State Politics in Contemporary India: Crisis or Continuity* (Boulder, CO: Westview, 1984).

39. Jenkins, *Democratic Politics and Economic Reforms in India*.

40. Jenkins, *Democratic Politics and Economic Reforms in India*.

41. Kaur, *Brand New Nation*.

42. Raka Ray and Amita Baviskar, eds., *Elite and Everyman: The Cultural Politics of the Indian Middle Classes* (Delhi: Routledge, 2011).

43. Max Weber, "Politics as a Vocation," in *From Max Weber: Essays in Sociology*, ed. and trans. H. H. Gerth and C. Wright Mills (New York and Oxford: Oxford University Press, 1946), 77–128.

44. Paula Chakravartty, "Telecom, National Development, and the Indian State: A Postcolonial Critique," *Media, Culture & Society* 26, no. 2 (2004): 227–49.

45. Erica Bornstein and Aradhana Sharma, "The Righteous and the Rightful: The Technomoral Politics of NGOs, Social Movements, and the State in India," *American Ethnologist* 43, no.1 (2016): 76–90.

46. On "CEO Naidu," see Lloyd Rudolph and Susanne Rudolph, "Iconization of Chandrababu: Sharing Sovereignty in India's Federal Market Economy," *Economic and Political Weekly* 36, no. 18 (2001): 1541–52. On Chief Election Commissioner T. N. Seshan's distinctive political persona, see David Gilmartin, "One Day's Sultan: T. N. Seshan and Indian Democracy," *Contributions to Indian Sociology* 43, no. 2 (2009): 247–84.

47. There have been numerous instances of popular culture icons and celebrities (for example, cricketers, Bollywood stars, actors from regional film industries such as Kolkata's Tollywood) entering politics. However, as the checkered political career of Bollywood superstar Amitabh Bachchan suggests, there is no connection or correlation between celebrity status and electoral success.

48. On the political phenomenon of the superstar politician in South India, see M. S. S. Pandian, *The Image Trap: M. G. Ramachandran in Film and Politics* (Delhi: Sage, 2015); M. Madhava Prasad, *Cine-Politics: Film Stars and Political Existence in South India* (Delhi: Orient Blackswan, 2014); S. V. Srinivas, *Politics as Performance: A Social History of the Telugu Cinema* (Delhi: Permanent Black, 2013).

49. For a classic comparative reference, see Michael Rogin, *Ronald Reagan, The Movie and Other Episodes in Political Demonology* (Berkeley: University of California Press, 1988).

50. As *Pappu* (kid), the derisive nickname that the BJP has bestowed on Congress leader Rahul Gandhi, indicates, the lack of political experience can also be condemned as a negative attribute of political leaders. Of all the outsider archetypes, the Innocent is figured as a representation of popular political agency rather than of political leadership.

51. In December 2012, national and international media circuits were ablaze with news about a horrific gang rape of a young woman in Delhi. Massive crowds mobilized in Delhi and other cities to protest the lack of security for women in the capital city, demanding immediate justice for the perpetrators (the demand was for more punitive rape legislation, and, in many quarters, also for capital punishment). The story of "India's Daughter," or Nirbhaya, the fearless one, as she came to be known, came to symbolize

the fate of every "ordinary" citizen in India, and generated a classic populist storm where the victimized people rose up to confront the indifferent "system," the protests amplified by digital and broadcast media circuits.

52. Several political biographies have tracked the "subaltern" rise of political figures like Mayawati in Uttar Pradesh, Laloo Prasad Yadav in Bihar, and Mamata Banerjee in Bengal. See, for instance, Ajoy Bose, *Behenji: A Political Biography of Mayawati* (Delhi: Penguin, 2009); Monobina Gupta, *Didi: A Political Biography* (Delhi: HarperCollins, 2012); Sankarshan Thakur, *Subaltern Saheb: The Making of Laloo Yadav* (Delhi: Picador, 2006).

53. Modi used this phrase at an election rally in Ghaziabad in April 2014 to refer to an alleged increase in the practice of cow slaughter (and trade in cow meat/carcasses).

54. See Hansen and Roy, *Saffron Republic*.

55. See Hansen and Roy, "What Is New About New Hindutva?" in *Saffron Republic* for an elaboration of this argument.

56. This is the title of Sunil Khilnani's book celebrating the Nehruvian vision of Indian secular democracy. See Sunil Khilnani, *The Idea of India* (New York: Farrar Straus & Giroux, 1999).

57. Christophe Jaffrelot, *Modi's India: Hindu Nationalism and the Rise of Ethnic Democracy* (Princeton, NJ: Princeton University Press, 2021).

58. See, for instance, Laclau, *On Populist Reason*; Mouffe, *For a Left Populism*; and the recent collection of essays in the *Boston Review*'s "Forum" on "Reclaiming Populism" (April 27, 2020), with statements and responses by Adom Getachew, Jason Frank, Thea Riofrancos, Laura Grattan, Ted Fertik and Maurice Mitchell, Eric Pineda, and Nikhil Pal Singh. https://bostonreview.net/forum/adom-getachew-reclaiming-populism/.

59. I refer here to the idea of democracy as "nobody's rule," where the place of power is not occupied by any particular social constituency, and is open to any and all. For a detailed articulation, see Rancière, *Hatred of Democracy*, and John Keane, *The Life and Death of Democracy* (New York: Simon & Schuster, 2009).

60. There is a rich archive of contemporary witnessing/documentation of the Shaheen Bagh protests, especially in media and social media outlets. More retrospective/reflective writing is now being published, and useful reference material includes works by Kiran Bhatia and Radhika Gajjala, "Examining Anti-CAA Protests at Shaheen Bagh: Muslim Women and Politics of the Hindu India," *International Journal of Communication* 14 (2020): 6286–6303; Seema Mustafa, ed., *Shaheen Bagh and the Idea of India* (Delhi: Speaking Tiger, 2020); Shireen Rai, "Feminist Dissent: Shaheen Bagh, Citizens, and Citizenship," *Feminist Dissent* 5 (2020): 265–74; Zia Us Salam and Uzma Ausaf, *Shaheen Bagh: From a Protest to a Movement* (Delhi: Bloomsbury, 2020).

61. Insightful analyses of the farmers' movement are available in a special issue of *Journal of Peasant Studies* edited by Amita Baviskar and Michael Levien. See "JPS Forum on Farmers' Protests in India," *Journal of Peasant Studies* 48, no. 7 (2021): 1341–1418, https://www.tandfonline.com/doi/abs/10.1080/03066150.2021.1998002.

BIBLIOGRAPHY

Abedi, Amir. *Anti-Political Establishment Parties*. London: Psychology Press, 2004.

Ahuja, Monika. *People, Law, and Justice: Casebook on Public Interest Litigation* Vols. 1 and 2. Delhi: Orient Blackswan, 1997.

———. "Public Interest Litigation in India: A Socio-Legal Study." Diss., London School of Economics, University of London, 1996.

Ali, Tariq. "The Fall of the Congress in India." *New Left Review* 1, no. 103 (1977): 43–58.

Alimi, Eitan. "Repertoires of Contention." In *The Oxford Handbook of Social Movements*, edited by Donatella Della Porta and Mario Diani, 401–22. New York: Oxford University Press, 2015.

Alonso, Sonia, et al., eds. *The Future of Representative Democracy*. Cambridge: Cambridge University Press, 2012.

Alvares, Claudia, and Peter Dahlgren. "Populism, Extremism and Media: Mapping an Uncertain Terrain." *European Journal of Communication* 31, no. 1 (2016): 46–57.

Arendt, Hannah. *The Human Condition*. 2nd ed. Chicago: University of Chicago Press, 1998.

Ashraf, Ajaz. "A Capital Test for Muslim Candidate Defying Votebank Politics." *The Hindu*, October 5, 2013. https://www.thehindu.com/opinion/op-ed/a-capital-test-for-muslim-candidate-defying-vote-bank-politics/article5201866.ece.

Athique, Adrian, et al., eds. *Indian Media Economy*. Vols. 1 and 2. New Delhi: Oxford University Press, 2018.

Austin, Granville. *The Indian Constitution: Cornerstone of a New Nation*. Oxford: Clarendon Press, 1966.

———. *Working a Democratic Constitution: A History of the Indian Experience*. Oxford: Oxford University Press, 2003.

Azari, Julia. "How the News Media Helped to Nominate Trump." *Political Communication* 33, no. 4 (2016): 677–80.

Baar, Carl. "Social Action Litigation in India: The Operation and Limitations of the World's Most Active Judiciary." *Policy Studies Journal* 19, no. 1 (1990): 140–50.

Bahal, Aniruddha. "Tale of the Sting." *Open Magazine*, September 2, 2010. https://openthemagazine.com/sports/tale-of-the-sting/.

Bandyopadhyay, Ritajyoti, et al., eds. *India's Migrant Workers and the Pandemic*. London and New York: Routledge, 2021.

Banerjee, Mukulika. *Why India Votes*. London and New York: Routledge, 2014.

Banerjee, Prathama. *Elementary Aspects of the Political: Histories from the Global South*. Durham, NC: Duke University Press, 2020.

Bardhan, Pranab. *The Political Economy of Development in India*. Oxford: Basil Blackwell, 1984.

Basu, Amrita. *Violent Conjunctures in Democratic India*. Cambridge: Cambridge University Press, 2015.

Batabyal, Somnath. *Making News in India: Star News and Star Ananda*. London and New York: Routledge, 2012.

Baviskar, Amita. *Uncivil City: Ecology, Equity, and the Commons in Delhi*. Delhi: Sage, 2020.

———. "Winning the Right to Information in India: Is Knowledge Power?" In *Citizen Action and National Policy Reform*, edited by John Gaventa and Rosemary McGee, 130–46. London: Zed Books, 2010.

Baviskar, Amita, and Michael Levien, eds. "JPS Forum on Farmers' Protests in India." *Journal of Peasant Studies* 48, no. 7 (2021): 1341–1418. https://www.tandfonline.com/doi/abs/10.1080/03066150.2021.1998002.

Baxi, Upendra. "From Takrar to Karar: The Lok Adalat at Rangpur—a Preliminary Study." *Journal of Constitutional and Parliamentary Studies* 10 (1976): 53–64.

———. "Taking Suffering Seriously: Social Action Litigation in the Supreme Court of India." *Third World Legal Studies* 4, no. 6 (1985): 107–32.

———. "The Avatars of Judicial Activism: Explorations in the Geography of (In) Justice." In *Fifty Years of the Supreme Court of India: Its Grasp and Reach*, edited by S. K. Verma and Kusum Kumar. Delhi: Oxford University Press, 2000.

Ben-Ghiat, Ruth. *Strongmen: Mussolini to the Present*. New York: Norton, 2020.

Benkler, Yochai, et al. "Study: Breitbart-Led Right-wing Media Ecosystem Altered Broader Media Agenda." *Columbia Journalism Review* 4, no. 1 (2017). https://www.cjr.org/analysis/breitbart-media-trump-harvard-study.php.

Berger, Suzanne. "Politics and Antipolitics in Western Europe in the Seventies." *Daedalus* 108, no. 1 (1979): 27–50.

Berlant, Lauren. *Cruel Optimism*. Durham, NC: Duke University Press, 2011.

Betz, Hans-Georg Betz. *Radical Right-Wing Populism in Western Europe*. New York: Palgrave Macmillan, 1994.

Bhardwaj, Amit. "Zee-Jindal and Sudhir Chaudhary Tapes: The Battle That Never Was." Newslaundry, July 19, 2018. https://www.newslaundry.com/2018/07/19/zee-naveen-jindal-sudhir-chaudhary-tapes-subhash-chandra.

Bhatia, Kiran, and Radhika Gajjala. "Examining Anti-CAA Protests at Shaheen Bagh: Muslim Women and Politics of the Hindu India." *International Journal of Communication* 14 (2020): 6286–6303.

Bhatnagar, Gaurav. "Kejriwal Government Expands Religious Outreach in Election Year." The Wire, July 31, 2019. https://thewire.in/politics/kejriwal-government-expands-religious-outreach-in-election-year.

Bhushan, Prashant. "Supreme Court and PIL." *Economic and Political Weekly* 39, no. 18 (2004): 1770–74.

Bhuwania, Anuj. *Courting the People: Public Interest Litigation in Post-Emergency India*. Cambridge: Cambridge University Press, 2017.

Bidwai, Praful. *The Phoenix Moment: Challenges Confronting the Indian Left*. Delhi: HarperCollins, 2005.

Björkman, Lisa. "You Can't Buy a Vote: Meanings of Money in a Mumbai Election." *American Ethnologist* 41, no. 4 (2014): 617–34.

Bobb, Dilip. "Me, Myself, and Modi." *Financial Express*, May 11, 2014. https://www.financialexpress.com/archive/me-myself-and-modi/1249462/.

Boltanski, Luc, and Eve Chiapello. *The New Spirit of Capitalism*. London: Verso, 2007.

Bornstein, Erica, and Aradhana Sharma. "The Righteous and the Rightful: The Technomoral Politics of NGOs, Social Movements, and the State in India." *American Ethnologist* 43, no. 1 (2016): 76–90.

Bose, Ajoy. *Behenji: A Political Biography of Mayawati*. Delhi: Penguin, 2009.

Brown, Wendy. *In the Ruins of Neoliberalism: The Rise of Antidemocratic Politics in the West*. New York: Columbia University Press, 2019.

Brubaker, Rogers. "A New 'Christianist' Secularism in Europe." The Immanent Frame, October 11, 2016. http://tif.ssrc.org/category/exchanges/religion-world-affairs/the-politics-of-national-identity/.

———. "Populism and Nationalism." *Nations and Nationalism* 26, no. 1 (2020): 44–66.

Burnham, Peter. "New Labour and the Politics of Depoliticisation." *British Journal of Politics and International Relations* 3, no. 2 (2001): 127–49.

Butler, Judith. *Notes Towards a Performative Theory of Assembly*. Cambridge, MA: Harvard University Press, 2018.

Canovan, Margaret. *Populism*. New York: Harcourt Brace Jovanovich, 1981.

———. "Trust the People! Populism and the Two Faces of Democracy." *Political Studies* 47 (1999): 2–16.

Cassels, Jamie. "Judicial Activism and Public Interest Litigation in India: Attempting the Impossible?" *American Journal of Comparative Law* 37 (1989): 495–519.

CG, Manoj. "At Centre of Stirs Against Graft, a Body with RSS Links, Ex-Babus." *Indian Express*, August 20, 2012. http://archive.indianexpress.com/news/at-centre-of-stirs-against-graft-a-body-with-rss-links-exbabus/990502/.

Chakravartty, Paula. "Telecom, National Development, and the Indian State: A Postcolonial Critique." *Media, Culture & Society* 26, no. 2 (2004): 227–49.

Chakravartty, Paula, and Srirupa Roy. "Media Pluralism Redux: New Frameworks of Comparative Media Studies 'Beyond the West.'" *Political Communication* 30 (2013): 349–70.

———. "Mediated Populisms: InterAsian Lineages—Introduction." *International Journal of Communication* 11 (2017). https://ijoc.org/index.php/ijoc/article/view/6703.

Chakravartty, Paula, and Dan Schiller. "Neoliberal Newspeak and Digital Capitalism in Crisis." *International Journal of Communication* 4 (2010). https://ijoc.org/index.php/ijoc/article/view/798.

Chamaria, Anil, et al. *Survey of the Social Profile of the Key Decision Makers in the National Media*. New Delhi: Media Study Group, 2006.

Chandra, Nandini. "Young Protest: The Idea of Merit in Commercial Hindi Cinema." *Comparative Studies of South Asia, Africa and the Middle East* 30, no. 1 (2010): 119–32.

Chatterjee, Partha. *The Nation and Its Fragments: Colonial and Postcolonial Histories*. Princeton, NJ: Princeton University Press, 1993.

———. "Against Corruption=Against Politics." Kafila, 2011. https://kafilaonline/2011/08/28/against-corruption-against-politics-partha-chatterjee/.

———. *I Am the People: Reflections on Popular Sovereignty Today*. New York: Columbia University Press, 2019.

Chatterji, Angana, et al., eds. *Majoritarian State: How Hindu Nationalism is Changing India*. New York: Oxford University Press, 2019.

Chauhan, Aastha. "Somnath Bharti and the Terrible, Everyday Racism of a South Delhi Mohalla." *Kafila*, 2014. https://kafila.online/2014/01/21/somnath-bharti-and-the-terrible-everyday-racism-of-a-south-delhi-mohalla-aastha-chauhan/.

Chopra, Mannika. "Year of the Fake Sting." The Hoot, December 30, 2007. http://asu.thehoot.org/media-watch/media-practice/year-of-the-fake-sting-2867.

Chopra, Rohit. *The Virtual Hindu Rashtra: Saffron Nationalism and New Media*. Delhi: HarperCollins, 2019.

Chowdhury, Aheli. "Social Movements Post 1990s in India: A Sociological Analysis of Changing Modes of Political Mobilisation." PhD diss., Delhi School of Economics, University of Delhi, 2017.

Chowdhury, Nusrat. *Paradoxes of the Popular: Crowd Politics in Bangladesh*. Stanford, CA: Stanford University Press, 2019.

Clibbens, Patrick. "Mrs. Gandhi's Buried Treasure: 'Economic Offenders' in Emergency India." Paper presented at the CeMIS Colloquium, University of Göttingen, 2015.

Cody, Francis. "Print Capitalism and Crowd Violence Beyond Liberal Frameworks." *Comparative Studies of South Asia, Africa, and the Middle East* 35, no. 1(2015): 50–65.

Coll, Steve. "The Strongman Problem: From Modi to Trump." *New Yorker*, January 18, 2017. https://www.newyorker.com/news/daily-comment/the-strongman-problem-from-modi-to-trump.

Common Cause. *Great Crusader for People's Causes H.D. Shourie (1912–2005)*. Delhi: Common Cause, 2005.

Cottrell, Jill. "Courts and Accountability: Public Interest Litigation in the Indian High Courts." *Third World Legal Studies* 11 (1992): 199–213.

Crouch, Colin. *Post-democracy: A Sociological Introduction*. Cambridge: Polity Press, 2014.

Cunningham, Clark. "Public Interest Litigation in Indian Supreme Court: A Study in the Light of American Experience." *Journal of the Indian Law Institute* 29 (1995): 494–523.

Dandurand, Guillaume. "The Techno-Politics of Food Security in New Delhi: The Re-Materialization of the Ration Card." PhD diss., York University, 2018.

DasGupta, Jyotirindra. "The Janata Phase: Reorganization and Redirection in Indian Politics." *Asian Survey* 19, no. 4 (1979): 390–403.

Dattatreyan, Gabriel. *The Globally Familiar: Digital Hip Hop, Masculinity, and Urban Culture in Delhi*. Durham, NC: Duke University Press, 2020.

Dayal, John, and Ajoy Bose. *The Shah Commission Begins*. Delhi: Orient Longman, 1978.

De, Rohit. "Beyond the Social Contract." *Seminar Magazine* 615 (2010): 43–47. https://www.india-seminar.com/2010/615/615_rohit_de.htm.

———. "Commodities Must Be Controlled: Economic Crimes and Market Discipline in India (1939–1955)." *International Journal of Law in Context* 10, no. 3 (2014): 277–94.

———. *A People's Constitution: The Everyday Life of Law in the Indian Republic*. Princeton, NJ: Princeton University Press, 2018.

Dean, Jodi. "Communicative Capitalism: Circulation and the Foreclosure of Politics." *Cultural Politics* 1, no. 1 (2005): 51–74.

Dean, Jonathan. "Tales of the Apolitical." *Political Studies* 62 (2014): 452–67.

Deshpande, Satish. "Caste and Castelessness: Towards a Biography of the 'General Category.'" *Economic and Political Weekly* 48, no. 15 (2013): 32–39.

———. "Imagined Economies: Styles of Nation-Building in Twentieth Century India." *Journal of Arts and Ideas* 24, no. 5 (1993): 5–35.

Deshpande, Satish, and Usha Zacharias, eds. *Beyond Inclusion: The Practice of Equal Access in Indian Higher Education*. New Delhi: Routledge, 2013.

Dhavan, Rajeev. "Law as Struggle: Public Interest Law in India." *Journal of the Indian Law Institute* 36, no. 3 (1994): 302–38.

———. *The Supreme Court of India: A Socio-Legal Critique of Its Juristic Techniques*. Delhi: N. M. Tripathi, 1977.

Eckert, Julia. "Introduction: Subjects of Citizenship." *Citizenship Studies* 15, nos. 3–4 (2011): 309–17.

Erlingsson, Gissur, and Mikael Persson. "The Swedish Pirate Party and the 2009 European Parliament Elections." *Politics* 31, no. 3 (2011): 121–28.

Esser, Frank, and Jesper Strömbäck, eds. *Mediatization of Politics: Understanding the Transformation of Western Democracies*. New York: Palgrave Macmillan, 2014.

Eyal, Gil. "Anti-politics and the Spirit of Capitalism: Dissidents, Monetarists and the Czech Transition to Capitalism." *Theory and Society* 29, no. 1 (2000): 49–92.

Farkas, Johan, and Jannick Schou. *Post-Truth, Fake News, and Democracy: Mapping the Politics of Falsehood*. London and New York: Routledge, 2020.

Ferguson, James. *The Anti-Politics Machine: Development, Depoliticization, and Bureaucratic Power in Lesotho*. Minneapolis: University of Minnesota Press, 1994.

Flinders, Matthew, and Jim Buller. "Depoliticisation: Principles, Tactics, and Tools." *British Politics* 1 (2006): 293–318.

Fording, Richard, and Sanford Schram. "The Cognitive and Emotional Sources of Trump Support: The Case of Low-Information Voters." *New Political Science* 39, no. 4 (2017): 670–86.

Foucault, Michel. "Nietzsche, Genealogy, History." In *The Foucault Reader*, edited by Paul Rabinow, 76–100. New York: Pantheon, 1984.

Franda, Marcus. *Small Is Politics: Organizational Alternatives in India's Rural Development*. Delhi: Wiley Eastern, 1979.

Frank, Jason. "Populism Isn't the Problem." *Boston Review*, August 15, 2018. https://bostonreview.net/articles/jason-frank-populism-not-the-problem/.

Frankel, Francine. *India's Political Economy: The Gradual Revolution*. 2nd ed. New York: Oxford University Press, 2006.

Frankel, Francine, and M. S. A. Rao, eds. *Dominance and State Power in Modern India: Decline of a Social Order*. Vols. 1 and 2. Delhi: Oxford University Press, 1990.

Fuller, Steve. *Post-Truth: Knowledge as a Power Game*. London: Anthem Press, 2018.

Galanter, Marc. "The Aborted Restoration of 'Indigenous Law' in India." *Comparative Studies in Society and History* 14, no. 1 (1972): 53–70.

———. *Law and Society in Modern India*. Delhi: Oxford University Press, 1989.

———. "Snakes and Ladders: Suo Moto Intervention and the Indian Judiciary." *FIU Law Review* 10, no. 1 (2014): 69–83, 74.

Galanter, Marc, and Jayanth Krishnan. "Bread for the Poor: Access to Justice and the Rights of the Needy in India." *Hastings Law Journal* 55 (2004): 791–97.

Ganti, Tejaswini. *Producing Bollywood: Inside the Hindi Film Industry*. Durham, NC: Duke University Press, 2012.

Gerbaudo, Paolo. "Social Media and Populism: An Elective Affinity?" *Media, Culture & Society* 40, no. 5 (2018): 745–53.

Ghose, Sadhan. "Probe Commissions." *Opinion*, March 7, 1978, 5–8.

Ghose, Sagarika. *Indira: India's Most Powerful Prime Minister*. Delhi: Juggernaut Books, 2017.

Gill, Bani. "In the Shadow of Illegality: The Everyday Lives of African Migrants in Delhi." PhD diss., University of Copenhagen, 2019.

Gilmartin, David. "One Day's Sultan: T. N. Seshan and Indian Democracy." *Contributions to Indian Sociology* 43, no. 2 (2009): 247–84.

———. "Towards a Global History of Voting: Sovereignty, the Diffusion of Ideas, and the Enchanted Individual." *Religions* 3, no. 2 (2012): 407–23.

Girihardas, Anand. *Winners Take All: The Elite Charade of Changing the World*. New York: Knopf, 2018.

Gorski, Philip. "Revisited: Why Do American Evangelicals Vote for Trump?" The Immanent Frame, December 15, 2020. https://tif.ssrc.org/2020/12/15/revisited-why-do-evangelicals-vote-for-trump/

Goswami, Manu. *Producing India: From Colonial Economy to National Space*. Chicago: University of Chicago Press, 2004.

Green, Jeffrey. *The Eyes of the People: Democracy in an Age of Spectatorship*. New York: Oxford University Press, 2009.

Groshek, Jacob. "Helping Populism Win? Social Media Use, Filter Bubbles, and Support for Populist Presidential Candidates in the 2016 US Election Campaign." *Information, Communication & Society* 20, no. 9 (2017): 1389–1407.

Guha Thakurta, Paranjoy. "Media Ownership in India—An Overview." 2012. https://paranjoy.in/article/media-ownership-in-india-an-overview.

Gupta, Monobina. *Didi: A Political Biography*. Delhi: HarperCollins, 2012.

Gupta-Nigam, Anirban. "How Systems Cohere: Niira Radia in 2017." *Bioscope: South Asian Screen Studies* 8, no. 2 (2017): 244–67.

Guru, Gopal. "Two Conceptions of Morality: A Political Reading." *Economic and Political Weekly* 49, no. 17 (2014): 112–17.

Hansen, Thomas Blom. *The Saffron Wave: Democracy and Hindu Nationalism in Modern India*. Princeton, NJ: Princeton University Press, 1999.

———. "Governance and State Mythologies in Mumbai." In *States of Imagination: Ethnographic Explorations of the Postcolonial State*, edited by Thomas Blom Hansen and Finn Stepputat, 221–56. Durham, NC: Duke University Press, 2001.

———. "Babri Masjid and Its Aftermath Changed India Forever." The Wire, December 7, 2017. https://thewire.in/communalism/babri-masjid-aftermath-changed-india-forever

———. *The Law of Force: The Violent Heart of Indian Politics*. Delhi: Aleph Books, 2021.

Hansen, Thomas Blom, and Srirupa Roy, eds. *Saffron Republic: Hindu Nationalism and State Power in India*. Cambridge: Cambridge University Press, 2022.

Havel, Václav. *The Power of the Powerless*. New York: Vintage Classics, 2018.

Hay, Colin. *Why We Hate Politics*. Cambridge: Polity Press, 2007.

Hingorani, Aman. "Indian Public Interest Litigation: Locating Justice in State Law." *Delhi Law Review* 17 (1995): 159–203.

———. "Public Interest Litigation." *Annual Survey of Indian Law* (2013): 969–1000.

Hirschman, Albert. *Exit, Voice, and Loyalty: Responses to Decline in Firms, Organisations, and States*. Cambridge, MA: Harvard University Press, 1970.

Hochschild, Arlie. *Strangers in Their Own Land: Anger and Mourning on the American Right*. New York: New Press, 2016.

Immerwahr, Daniel. *Thinking Small: The United States and the Lure of Community Development*. Cambridge, MA: Harvard University Press, 2015.

Ionescu, Ghita, and Ernest Gellner, eds. *Populism: Its Meaning and National Characteristics*. New York: Macmillan, 1969.

Jaffrelot, Christophe. *India's Silent Revolution: The Rise of the Low Castes in North Indian Politics*. New York: Columbia University Press, 2003.

———. *Modi's India: Hindu Nationalism and the Rise of Ethnic Democracy*. Princeton, NJ: Princeton University Press, 2021.

Jaffrelot, Christophe, and Pratinav Anil. *India's First Dictatorship: The Emergency, 1975–77*. New Delhi: Oxford University Press, 2021.

Jaffrelot, Christophe, and Sanjay Kumar, eds. *Rise of the Plebeians? The Changing Face of the Indian Legislative Assemblies*. New York and New Delhi: Routledge, 2009.

Jaffrelot, Christophe, and Ingrid Therwath. "The Sangh Parivar and the Hindu Diaspora in the West: What Kind of Long-Distance Nationalism?" *International Political Sociology* 1, no. 3 (2007): 278–95.

Jaffrelot, Christophe, and Gilles Verniers. "The Reconfiguration of India's Political Elite: Profiling the 17th Lok Sabha." *Contemporary South Asia* 28, no. 2 (2020): 1–13.

Jansen, Robert. "Situated Political Innovation: Explaining the Historical Emergence of New Modes of Political Practice." *Theory and Society* 45, no. 4 (2016): 319–60.

Jayal, Niraja. *Citizenship and Its Discontents*. Cambridge, MA: Harvard University Press, 2013.

———, ed. *Re-forming India: The Nation Today*. Delhi: Penguin Random House, 2019.

Jeffrey, Roger. *India's Newspaper Revolution: Capitalism, Politics and the Indian Language Press, 1977–99*. Delhi: Oxford University Press, 2000.

Jenkins, Rob. *Democratic Politics and Economic Reform in India*. Cambridge: Cambridge University Press, 1999.

———. *Regional Reflections: Comparing Politics Across India's States*. Delhi: Oxford University Press, 2004.

Jenkins, Rob, and Anne-Marie Goetz. "Accounts and Accountability: Theoretical Implications of the Right-to-Information Movement in India." *Third World Quarterly* 20, no. 3 (1999): 603–22.

Jones, Dawn, and Rodney Jones. "Urban Upheaval in India: The 1974 Nav Nirman Riots in Gujarat." *Asian Survey* 16, no. 11 (1976): 1012–33.

Jyoti, Dhrubo. "December 16 Gangrape: The Real Reason Why Bilkis Bano and Khairlanji Don't Trigger a 'Tsunami of Shock.'" *Hindustan Times*, May 6, 2017. https://tinyurl.com/4bdh2tff

Kalyan, Rohan. "Eventocracy: Media and Politics in Times of Aspirational Fascism." *Theory & Event* 23, no. 1 (2020): 4–28.

Kapoor, Coomi. *The Emergency: A Personal History*. Delhi: Penguin Viking, 2015.

Kaufman, Michael. "Price of Woman in India: $306 and Much Sorrow." *New York Times*, August 11, 1981, A2.

Kaur, Ravinder. "The Innovative Indian: Common Man and the Politics of Jugaad Culture." *Contemporary South Asia* 24, no. 3 (2006): 313–27.

———. *Brand New Nation: Capitalist Dreams and Nationalist Designs in Twenty-First Century India*. Stanford, CA: Stanford University Press, 2020.

Kaviraj, Sudipta. "Indira Gandhi and Indian Politics." *Economic and Political Weekly* 21, nos. 38–39 (1986): 1697–1708.

———. "The Empire of Democracy." In *Anxieties of Democracy: Tocquevillean Reflections on India and the United States*, edited by Partha Chatterjee and Ira Katznelson, 20–49. New York: Oxford University Press, 2012.

Kazin, Michael. *The Populist Persuasion: An American History*. Rev ed. Ithaca, NY: Cornell University Press, 1998.

Kazmin, Amy. "Narendra Modi the Style King Puts on the Guru Look." *Financial Times*, July 1, 2021.

Keane, John. *The Life and Death of Democracy*. New York: Simon & Schuster, 2009.

———. *Democracy and Media Decadence*. Cambridge: Cambridge University Press, 2014.

———. *Power and Humility: The Future of Monitory Democracy*. Cambridge: Cambridge University Press, 2018.

———. *The New Despotism*. Cambridge, MA: Harvard University Press, 2020.

Kent-Carrasco, Daniel. "A Battle Over Meanings: Jayaprakash Narayan, Rammanohar Lohia and the Trajectories of Socialism in Early Independent India." *Global Intellectual History* 2, no.3 (2017): 370–88.

Khilnani, Sunil. *The Idea of India*. New York: Farrar Straus & Giroux, 1999.

Khosla, Madhav. "Making Social Rights Conditional—Lessons from India." *International Journal of Constitutional Law* 8, no. 4 (2010): 739–65.

Kochanek, Stanley. *Business and Politics in India*. Berkeley: University of California Press, 1974.

———. "Review of L. N. Sharma, The Indian Prime Minister: Office and Powers." *Journal of Asian Studies* 37, no. 4 (1978): 785–86.

Kohli, Atul. *India's Democracy: An Analysis of Changing State-Society Relations*. Rev. ed. Princeton, NJ: Princeton University Press, 1990.

———. *Democracy and Discontent: India's Growing Crisis of Governability*. Cambridge: Cambridge University Press, 1991.

———. "Politics of Economic Growth in India, 1980–2005: Part II, The 1990s and Beyond." *Economic and Political Weekly* 41, no. 14 (April 8–14, 2006): 1361–70.

Konrád, György. *Antipolitics: An Essay*. New York: Harcourt, 1984.

Kothari, Rajni. *Memoirs: Uneasy Is the Life of the Mind*. Delhi: Rupa, 2002.

———. "The Non Party Political Process." *Economic and Political Weekly* 19, no. 5 (1984): 216–24.

Krishnan, Anjana. "India." In *The Reuters Institute Digital News Report 2021*, edited by Nic Newman et al., 134–36. Oxford: Reuters Institute for the Study of Journalism, 2021.

Krishnan, Jayanth. "Social Policy Advocacy and the Role of the Courts in India." *American Asian Review* 21, no. 2 (2003): 91–124.

———. "Professor Kingsfield Goes to Delhi: American Academics, the Ford Foundation, and the Development of Legal Education in India." *American Journal of Legal History* 46 (2004): 447–99.

Kurup, Pran. *Arvind Kejriwal and the Aam Aadmi Party: An Inside Look*. Delhi: Bloomsbury India, 2016.

Laclau, Ernesto. *On Populist Reason*. London: Verso, 2005.

Lama, Prawesh. "I'm Deeply Sorry for Pain I've Caused to Jessica Lal's Family, Says Manu Sharma." *Hindustan Times*, June 5, 2020. https://tinyurl.com/3jnpjuu6

Lama-Rewal, Stéphanie. "Metropolitan Democracy from Below: Participation and Rescaling in Delhi." *Territory, Politics, Governance* 11, no. 2 (2023): 338–53.

Lapowski, Issie. "Donald Trump Supporters Are More Susceptible to Clickbait." *Wired*, October 31, 2015. https://www.wired.com/2015/10/donald-trump-supporters-are-more-susceptible-to-clickbait/.

Lieten, Georges. "Janata as a Continuity of the System." *Social Scientist*, 9, no. 5/6 (1980–81): 14–35.

Lokaneeta, Jinee. *The Truth Machines: Policing, Violence, and Scientific Interrogations in India*. Ann Arbor: University of Michigan Press, 2020.

Ludden, David. "India's Development Regime." In *Colonialism and Culture*, edited by Nicholas Dirks, 247–87. Ann Arbor: University of Michigan Press, 1992.

Lunt, Peter, and Sonia Livingstone. "Is 'Mediatization' the New Paradigm for Our Field? A Commentary on Deacon and Stanyer (2014, 2015) and Hepp, Hjarvard and Lundby." *Media, Culture & Society* 38, no. 3 (2016): 462–70.

Maiorano, Diego. "India's Institutions in the Early 1980s: The Pre-history of the Great Transformation." *Modern Asian Studies* 48, no. 5 (2014): 1389–1434.

Malik, Amita. "Dressing Up for Shah." *Times of India*, December 2, 1977.

Marcus, David. "Memory as Homeland." *Dissent* 230 (2008): 120–24.

Mazumdar, Ranjani. *Bombay Cinema: An Archive of the City*. Minneapolis: University of Minnesota Press, 2007.

Mazzarella, William. "Internet X-Ray: E-Governance, Transparency, and the Politics of Immediation in India." *Public Culture* 18, no. 3 (2016): 473–505.

———. "The Anthropology of Populism: Beyond the Liberal Settlement." *Annual Review of Anthropology* 48 (2019): 45–60.

Mazzoleni, Gianpetro. "Towards a 'Videocracy'? Italian Political Communication at a Turning Point." *European Journal of Communication* 10 (1995): 291–319.

McIntyre, Lee. *Post-truth*. Cambridge, MA: MIT Press, 2017.

Mehring, Frank. "All for the Sake of Freedom: Hannah Arendt's Democratic Dissent, Trauma, and American Citizenship." *Journal of Transnational American* Studies 3, no. 2 (2011): 1–32. http://escholarship.org/uc/item/7j88q162.

Mehta, Nalin. *India on Television: How Satellite News Channels Have Changed the Way We Think and Act*. Delhi: HarperCollins, 2008.

Mehta, Uday. "Constitutionalism." In *The Oxford Companion to Politics in India*, edited by Niraja Gopal Jayal and Pratap Bhanu Mehta. Delhi: Oxford University Press, 2010.

———. "The Social Question and the Absolutism of Politics." *Seminar Magazine* 615 (2010): 23–27.

Mehta, Vinod. *Lucknow Boy*. Delhi: Penguin Viking, 2011.

———. *The Sanjay Story: From Anand Bhavan to Amethi*. Delhi: HarperCollins, 2012.

Menon, Nivedita, and Aditya Nigam. "If Only There Were No People Democracy Would Be Fine." *Kafila*, 2011. https://kafila.online/2011/08/22/if-only-there-were-no-people-democracy-would-be-fine/.

Mishra, Pankaj. *Age of Anger: A History of the Present*. New York: Macmillan, 2017.

Moffitt, Benjamin. *The Global Rise of Populism: Performance, Political Style, and Representation*. Stanford, CA: Stanford University Press, 2016.

Morris Jones, W. H. *The Government and Politics of India*. 2nd ed. London: Hutchinson University Library, 1967.

Mouffe, Chantal, ed. *The Challenge of Carl Schmitt*. London: Verso, 1999.

———. *For a Left Populism*. London: Verso, 2018.

Moyn, Samuel. *The Last Utopia: Human Rights in History*. Cambridge, MA: Harvard University Press, 2012.

Mudde, Cas. "The Populist Zeitgeist." *Government and Opposition* 39, no. 4 (2014): 541–63.

Mudde, Cas, and Cristobál Rovira Kaltwasser. "Exclusionary vs. Inclusionary Populism: Comparing Contemporary Europe and Latin America." *Government and Opposition* 48, no. 2 (2013): 147–74.

———. *Populism: A Very Short Introduction*. New York: Oxford University Press, 2017.

———. "Studying Populism in Comparative Perspective: Reflections on the Contemporary and Future Research Agenda." *Comparative Political Studies* 51, no. 13 (2018): 1667–93.

Muehlebach, Andrea. *The Moral Neoliberal: Welfare and Citizenship in Italy*. Chicago: University of Chicago Press, 2012.

Mukherjee, Pranab. *Indira Gandhi Centennial Lecture*. Delhi: Press Information Bureau, 2016.

Müller, Jan-Werner. *What Is Populism?* Philadelphia: University of Pennsylvania Press, 2016

Mustafa, Seema, ed. *Shaheen Bagh and the Idea of India*. Delhi: Speaking Tiger, 2020.

Narain, Iqbal. "India 1977: From Promise to Disenchantment?" *Asian Survey* 18, no. 2 (1978): 103–16.

Narrain, Arvind, and Arun Thiruvengadam. "Social Justice Lawyering and the Meaning of Indian Constitutionalism: A Case Study of the Alternative Law Forum." *Wisconsin International Law Journal* 31, no. 3 (2014): 525–65.

Neyazi, Taberez. *Political Communication and Mobilisation: The Hindi Media in India*. Cambridge: Cambridge University Press, 2018.

Nigam, Aditya. "Embedded Judiciary or, the Judicial State of Exception?" In *The Shifting Scales of Justice: The Supreme Court in Neoliberal India*, edited by Mayur Suresh and Siddharth Narrain, 22–38. Delhi: Orient Blackswan, 2019.

———. "The Non-Party Domain in Contemporary India." Unpublished paper prepared for the State of Democracy in South Asia Report, Lokniti.

Nigam, Aditya, and Yogendra Yadav. "Electoral Politics in Indian States: 1989–1999." *Economic and Political Weekly* 34, nos. 34–35 (August 21–28, 1999): 2391–92.

Ninan, Sevanti. *Headlines from the Heartland: Reinventing the Hindi Public Sphere*. Delhi: Sage, 2007.

Noorani, A. G. "Commissions of Inquiry: Skeletons in the Cupboard." *India Today*, June 15, 1977.

Norris, Pippa. "Why Populism Is a Threat to Electoral Integrity." *LSE European Politics and Policy (EUROPP) Blog*, 2017. http://blogs.lse.ac.uk/europpblog/2017/05/16/why-populism-is-a-threat-to-electoral-integrity/

Nussbaum, Martha. *The Clash Within: Democracy, Religious Violence, and India's Future*. Cambridge, MA: Harvard University Press, 2008.

Oldenburg, Philip. "The Emergency: An Immunization Shot Against Autocracy." Mint, June 22, 2015. https://tinyurl.com/ms8bm2u3

Omvedt, Gail. *Reinventing Revolution: New Social Movements and the Socialist Tradition in India*. London and New York: Routledge, 1994.

Ott, Brian. "The Age of Twitter: Donald J. Trump and the Politics of Debasement." *Critical Studies in Media Communication* 34, no. 1 (2017): 59–68.

Özyurek, Esra. "Miniaturizing Atatürk: Privatization of State Imagery and Ideology in Turkey." *American Ethnologist* 31, no. 3 (2004): 374–91.

Pai, Sudha. *State Politics: New Dimensions*. New Delhi: Shipra, 2000.

Palshikar, Suhas. "Of Radical Democracy and Anti-Partyism." *Economic and Political Weekly* 48, no. 10 (2013): 10–13.

Pandian, M. S. S. *The Image Trap: M. G. Ramachandran in Film and Politics*. Delhi: Sage, 2015.

Panizza, Francisco, ed. *Populism and the Mirror of Democracy*. London: Verso, 2006.

Papacharissi, Zizi. *Affective Publics: Sentiment, Technology, Politics*. New York: Oxford University Press, 2015.

Parthasarathi, Vibodh, and Adrian Athique. "Market Matters: Interdependencies in the Indian Media Economy." *Media Culture & Society* 42, no. 3 (2020): 431–48.

Patel, Aakar. *Price of the Modi Years*. Chennai: Westland, 2021.

Peiris, G. L. "Public Interest Litigation in the Indian Subcontinent: Current Dimensions." *International and Comparative Law Quarterly* 40, no. 1 (1991): 66–90.

Piliavsky, Anastasia. *Nobody's People: Hierarchy as Hope in a Society of Thieves*. Stanford, CA: Stanford University Press, 2020.

Pitkin, Hanna. *The Attack of the Blob: Hannah Arendt's Concept of the Social*. Chicago: University of Chicago Press, 1998.

Poguntke, Thomas, and Susan Scarrow. "The Politics of Anti-Party Sentiment." *European Journal of Political Research* 29, no. 3 (1996): 257–62.

Pomerantsev, Peter. "Why We're Post-fact." *Granta* 20 (2016). https://granta.com/why-were-post-fact/.

Prakash, Gyan. *Mumbai Fables: A History of an Enchanted City*. Princeton, NJ: Princeton University Press, 2010.

———. *Emergency Chronicles: Indira Gandhi and Democracy's Turning Point*. Princeton, NJ: Princeton University Press, 2019.

Prasad, M. Madhava. *Cine-Politics: Film Stars and Political Existence in South India*. Delhi: Orient Blackswan, 2014.

Prashad, Vijay, ed. *Strongmen: Trump, Modi, Erdogan, Duterte, Putin*. Delhi: LeftWord, 2019.

Putnam, Robert. *Bowling Alone: The Collapse and Revival of American Community*. New York: Simon & Schuster, 2000.

Rai, Shireen. "Feminist Dissent: Shaheen Bagh, Citizens, and Citizenship." *Feminist Dissent* 5 (2020): 265–74.

Rajagopal, Arvind. "The Emergency as Prehistory of the New Indian Middle Class." *Modern Asian Studies* 45, no. 5 (2011): 1003–49.

Rancière, Jacques. *Hatred of Democracy* Trans. Steve Corcoran. London: Verso, 2006.

———. *Dissensus: On Politics and Aesthetics*. New York: Continuum, 2010.

Ranganathan, Maya. "Sting Journalism: A Sign of the Times." In *The Indian News Media: From Observer to Participant*, 65–94. Delhi: Sage, 2014.

Rao, Ursula, and Vijayanka Nair, eds. "Special Section: Aadhaar: Governing India with Biometrics." *South Asia* 42, no. 3 (2019): 469–81.

Ray, Raka, and Amita Baviskar, eds. *Elite and Everyman: The Cultural Politics of the Indian Middle Classes*. London and New York: Routledge, 2011.

Ray, Raka, and Seemin Quayum. *Cultures of Servitude: Modernity, Domesticity, and Class in India*. Stanford, CA: Stanford University Press, 2009.

Robin, Corey. *Fear: The History of a Political Idea*. New York: Oxford University Press, 2006.

———. *The Reactionary Mind*. New York: Oxford University Press, 2011.

Rodrigues, Usha, and Maya Ranganathan. *Indian News Media: From Observer to Participant*. Delhi: Sage, 2014.

Rogin, Michael. *Ronald Reagan, The Movie and Other Episodes in Political Demonology*. Berkeley: University of California Press, 1988.

Rosanvallon, Pierre. *Counter-Democracy: Politics in an Age of Distrust*. Cambridge: Cambridge University Press, 2008.

———. *The Populist Century: History, Theory, Critique*. Cambridge: Polity Press, 2021.

Roy, Ananya. *Poverty Capital: Microfinance and the Making of Development*. London: Routledge, 2010.

Roy, Srirupa. *Beyond Belief: India and the Politics of Postcolonial Nationalism*. Durham, NC: Duke University Press, 2007.

———. "Television News and Democratic Change in India." *Media, Culture & Society* 33, no. 5 (2011): 761–77.

———. "Being the Change: The Aam Aadmi Party and the Politics of the Extraordinary in Indian Democracy." *Economic and Political Weekly* 49, no. 15 (2014): 45–54.

———. "Angry Citizens: Civic Anger and the Politics of Curative Democracy in India." *Identities* 23, no. 3 (2016): 362–77.

———. "India 2030 and the Limits of Competitive Futurism." In *Germany and the World 2030*, edited by Stephan Mair et al. Berlin: Economy Press, 2018. https://deutschland-und-die-welt-2030.de/en/article/india-2030-and-the-limits-of-competitive-futurism/.

———. "Target Politics: Digital and Data Technologies and Election Campaigns—A View from India." In *Media and the Constitution of the Political: South Asia and Beyond*, edited by Ravi Vasudevan, 285–310. Delhi: Sage, 2021.

———. "The Political Outsider." In *The People of India: New Indian Politics in the Twenty-First Century*, edited by Ravinder Kaur and Nayanika Mathur, 66–87. Delhi: Penguin Viking, 2022.

———. "The Death of the Third World Revisited: Curative Democracy and World-Making in Late 1970s India." In *Inventing the Third World: In Search of Freedom for the Postwar Global South*, edited by Jeremy Adelman and Gyan Prakash, 239–60. London: Bloomsbury, 2023.

Roychowdhury, Debasish, and John Keane. *To Kill a Democracy: India's Passage to Despotism*. New York and Oxford: Oxford University Press, 2019.

Rudolph, Lloyd, and Susanne Rudolph. "To the Brink and Back: Representation and the State in India." *Asian Survey* 18, no. 4 (1978): 379–400.

———. "Rethinking Secularism: Genesis and Implications of the Textbook Controversy, 1977–1979." *Pacific Affairs* 56, no. 1 (1983): 15–37.

———. "Iconization of Chandrababu: Sharing Sovereignty in India's Federal Market Economy." *Economic and Political Weekly* 36, no. 18 (2001): 1541–52.

Rudolph, Susanne, and Lloyd Rudolph. *In Pursuit of Lakshmi: The Political Economy of the Indian State*. Chicago: University of Chicago Press, 1987.

Ruparelia, Sanjay. "A Progressive Juristocracy? The Unexpected Social Activism of India's Supreme Court." Working Paper 391 (2013), Kellogg Institute, University of Notre Dame.

Sagar. "Caste Away: The Aam Aadmi Party's Perpetuation of Upper Caste Politics." *Caravan Magazine*, 2019. https://caravanmagazine.in/reportage/aam-admi-party-perpetuation-upper-caste-politics.

Sainath, P. "India Shining Meets the Great Depression." India Together, 2016. https://indiatogether.org/depress-op-ed.

Samet, Robert. *Deadline: Populism and the Press in Venezuela*. Chicago: University of Chicago Press, 2019.

Sathe, S. P. "Judicial Activism: The Indian Experience." *Washington University Journal of Law and Policy* 6 (2001): 29–107.

———. *Judicial Activism in India: Transgressing Borders and Enforcing Limits*. New Delhi: Oxford University Press, 2003.

Sathyamurthy, T. V., ed. *Region, Religion, Caste, and Culture in Contemporary India*. Delhi: Oxford University Press, 2000.

Saward, Michael. "The Representative Claim." *Contemporary Political Theory* 5 (2006): 297–318.

Sawyer, Mark. *Racial Politics in Post-revolutionary Cuba*. Cambridge: Cambridge University Press, 2006.

Schaffer, Frederic. *The Hidden Costs of Clean Election Reform*. Ithaca, NY: Cornell University Press, 2008.

Schedler, Andreas. "Anti-Political-Establishment Parties." *Party Politics* 2, no. 3 (1996): 291–312.

Scheppele, Kim Lane. "Autocratic Legalism." *University of Chicago Law Review* 85, no. 2 (2018): 545–84.

Schlesinger, Lee. "The Emergency in an Indian Village." *Asian Survey* 17, no. 7 (1977): 627–47.

Schudson, Michael. *Why Democracies Need an Unlovable Press*. Malden, MA: Polity, 2008.

Sen, Avirook. *Aarushi*. Delhi: Penguin India, 2017.

Sen, Sarbani. *Public Interest Litigation in India: Implications for Law and Development*. Calcutta: Mahanirban Calcutta Research Group, 2002.

Sen, Shaunak. "Decoding the Big Indian Sting." Sarai, 2014. https://sarai.net/decoding-the-big-indian-sting/

———. "Sting Videos: Everydayness as Truth Aesthetic." Marg, September 1, 2018. https://tinyurl.com/2jx7vvh3

Seshu, Geeta. "No, Republic TV–Led News Broadcasters Federation Is Not Fighting 'Lutyens Media.'" Newslaundry, July 31, 2019. https://www.newslaundry.com/2019/07/31/no-republic-tv-led-news-broadcasters-federation-is-not-fighting-lutyens-media.

Sethi, Harsh. "The Immoral 'Other': Debate between Party and Non-Party Groups." *Economic and Political Weekly* 20, no. 9 (1985): 378–80.

Sewell, William. "Historical Events as Transformation of Structures: Inventing Revolution at the Bastille." *Theory and Society* 25, no. 6 (1996): 841–81.

Sezhiyan, Era. *Shah Commission Report: Lost and Regained*. Chennai: Aazhi Press, 2018.

Shah, Ghanshyam. *Protest Movements in Two Indian States*. Delhi: Ajanta, 1977.

Shankar, Shylashri, and Pratap Bhanu Mehta. "Courts and Socioeconomic Rights in India." In *Courting Social Justice: Judicial Enforcement of Social and Economic Rights in the Developing World*, edited by Varun Gauri and Daniel Brinks, 146–82. Cambridge: Cambridge University Press, 2009.

Sharma, Aradhana. "Finding Women Among Common Men." *Kafila*, 2012. https://kafila.online/2012/12/12/finding-women-among-common-men-aradhana-sharma/.

———. "New Brooms and Old: Sweeping Up Corruption in India, One Law at a Time." *Current Anthropology* 59 (2018): S18, S72–S82.

Sharma, Mukul. *Green and Saffron: Hindu Nationalism and Environmental Politics*. Delhi: Orient Blackswan, 2011.

Sharma, Prashant. *Democracy and Transparency in the Indian State: The Making of the Right to Information Act*. London: Routledge, 2015.

Sharma, S. L. "Social Action Groups as Harbingers of Silent Revolution." *Economic and Political Weekly* 27, no. 47 (November 21, 1992): 2557–61.

Shaw, Padmaja. "News Television and Democracy." *Revista de Economia Politica de la Tecnologias de la Informacion y Comunicacion* 11, no. 2 (2019).

Shourie, Arun. "Why the Honorable Court Must Hear Us." *People's Union for Civil Liberties Bulletin*, July 30, 1981. http://arunshourie.bharatvani.org/articles/19810730.htm.

Shrivastava, Rahul. "Populism Mixed with Soft-Hindutva Makes Arvind Kejriwal a Force to Reckon With." *India Today*, February 12, 2020. https://www.indiatoday.in/elections/delhi-assembly-polls-2020/story/populism-mixed-with-soft-hindutva-makes-arvind-kejriwal-1645626-2020-02-12

Sikk, Allan. "Newness as a Winning Formula for New Political Parties." *Party Politics* 18, no. 4 (2012): 465–86.

Sinha, Subir. "Lineages of the Developmentalist State: Transnationality and Village India, 1960–1965." *Comparative Studies in Society and History* 50, no. 1 (2008): 57–90.

Sitapati, Vinay. "What Anna Hazare's Movement and India's New Middle Classes Say About Each Other." *Economic and Political Weekly* 46, no. 3 (2012): 39–44.

Sparks, Colin, and John Tulloch, eds. *Tabloid Tales: Global Debates Over Media Standards*. Lanham, MD: Rowman & Littlefield, 2000.

Srinivas, S. V. *Politics as Performance: A Social History of the Telugu Cinema*. Delhi: Permanent Black, 2013.

Stanley, Jason. *How Propaganda Works*. Princeton, NJ: Princeton University Press, 2016.

Stavrakakis, Yannis, et al. "Contemporary Left-Wing Populism in Latin America: Leadership, Horizontalism, and Postdemocracy in Chávez's Venezuela." *Latin American Politics and Society* 58, no. 3 (2016): 51–76.

———. "Populism, Anti-populism, and Crisis." *Contemporary Political Theory* 17 (2018): 4–27.

Steyerl, Hito. "In Defense of the Poor Image." *e-Flux Journal* 10 (2009). https://www.e-flux.com/journal/10/61362/in-defense-of-the-poor-image/.

Subramanian, Ajantha. *The Caste of Merit: Engineering Education in India*. Cambridge, MA: Harvard University Press, 2019.

Subramanian, Samanth. "The Agitator." *New Yorker*, August 26, 2013.Sundaram, Ravi. "Publicity, Transparency and the Circulation Engine: The Media Sting in India." *Current Anthropology* 56, no. 12 (2015): 297–305.

Susman, Susan. "Distant Voices in the Courts of India: Transformation of Standing in Public Interest Litigation." *Wisconsin International Law Journal* 13, no. 1 (1994): 57–103.

Swidler, Ann. "Culture in Action: Symbols and Strategies." *American Sociological Review* 51, no. 2 (1986): 277.

Swyngedouw, Eric. "Where Is the Political? Insurgent Mobilizations and the Incipient Return of the Political." *Space and Polity* 18, no. 2 (2014): 122–36.

Taggart, Paul. "New Populist Parties in Western Europe." *West European Politics* 18, no. 1 (1995): 34–51.

———. *Populism: Concepts in the Social Sciences*. Philadelphia: Open University Press, 2000.

Tandon, B. N. *PMO Diary II: The Emergency*. Delhi: Konark Press, 2006.

Tarlo, Emma. *Unsettling Memories: Narratives of the Emergency in Delhi*. Berkeley: University of California Press, 2003.

Tejpal, Tarun. "Sleaze, Senseless Greed and Dirty Heroes." *Tehelka*, March 13, 2001. https://archive.tehelka.com/channels/Investigation/tarun.htm.

Tendulkar, Vijay. "Kamala." In *Five Plays*, translated by Priya Tendulkar, Kumud Mehta, and Shanta Gokhale. New Delhi: Oxford University Press, 1996.

Thakur, Sankarshan. *Subaltern Saheb: The Making of Laloo Yadav*. Delhi: Picador, 2006.

Tilly, Charles. *The Contentious French*. Cambridge, MA: Harvard University Press, 1986.

———. "Major Forms of Collective Action in Western Europe, 1500–1975." *Theory and Society* 3, no. 3 (1976): 365–75.

Trehan, Madhu. *Tehelka as Metaphor: Prism Me a Lie, Tell Me a Truth*. Delhi: Roli Books, 2001.

Tripathy, Jyotirmaya. "The Broom, the Muffler and the Wagon R: Aam Aadmi Party and the Politics of De-elitisation." *International Quarterly for Asian Studies* 48, nos. 1–2 (2017): 77–95.

Udupa, Sahana. *Making News in Global India: Media, Publics, Politics*. Cambridge: Cambridge University Press, 2015.

Urbinati, Nadia. "Political Theory of Populism." *Annual Review of Political Science* 22, no. 6 (2019): 111–27.

Us-Salam, Zia, and Uzma Ausaf. *Shaheen Bagh: From a Protest to a Movement*. Delhi: Bloomsbury, 2020.

Varma, Pavan. *People Like Us*. Delhi: Har Anand, 2007.

Viswanath, Rupa. "Commissioning Representation: The Misra Report, Deliberation and the Government of the People in Modern India." *South Asia* 38, no. 3 (2015): 495–511.

Webb, Martin. "Success Stories: Rhetoric, Authenticity, and the Right to Information Movement in India." *Contemporary South* Asia 18, no. 3 (2010): 293–304.

———. "Digital Politics in the Diaspora: U.K. Aam Aadmi Party Supporters Online and Offline." *Television and New Media* 21, no. 4 (2020): 420–33.

Weber, Max. "Politics as a Vocation." In *From Max Weber: Essays in Sociology*, edited and translated by H. H. Gerth and C. Wright Mills, 77–128. New York: Oxford University Press, 1946.

Weiner, Myron. *India at the Polls: The Parliamentary Elections of 1977*. Washington, DC: American Enterprise Institute Press, 1978.

Wilde, Matt. "Populism, Right and Left." Public Books, 2017. https://www.publicbooks.org/populism-right-and-left/.

Wood, John. "Extra-Parliamentary Opposition in India: An Analysis of Populist Agitations in Gujarat and Bihar." *Pacific Affairs* 48, no.3 (1975): 313–34.

———, ed. *State Politics in Contemporary India: Crisis or Continuity*. Boulder, CO: Westview, 1984.

Yadav, Yogendra. "Electoral Politics in the Time of Change: India's Third Electoral System, 1989–99." *Economic and Political Weekly* 34, no. 34/35 (August 21, 1999): 2393–99.

Yadav, Yogendra, and Suhas Palshikar. "Ten Theses on State Politics in India." *Seminar* 591 (2018): 14–22.

Young-Bruehl, Elisabeth. *Hannah Arendt: For Love of the World*. 2nd ed. New Haven, CT: Yale University Press 2004.

Zencirci, Gizem. "Affective Politics of Structural Adjustment: 'Cruel Optimism' and Turhan Selçuk's Cartoons in Turkey, 1983–1986." *Journal of Social History* 53, no. 1 (2019): 53–75.

INDEX

Page numbers in italics denote tables. Endnotes are indicated by "n" followed by the endnote number.